Joint Production of Commodities

The International Library of Critical Writings in Economics

Series Editor: Mark Blaug
Professor Emeritus, University of London
Consultant Professor, University of Buckingham
Visiting Professor, University of Exeter

Joint Production of Commodities

Edited by

Neri Salvadori
Professor of Economics,
Istituto Universitario Navale,
Napoli, Italy

and Ian Steedman
Professor of Economics,
University of Manchester

An Elgar Reference Collection

Published by
Edward Elgar Publishing Limited
Gower House
Croft Road
Aldershot
Hants GU11 3HR
England

Edward Elgar Publishing Company
Old Post Road
Brookfield
Vermont 05036
USA

British Library Cataloguing in Publication Data
is available

ISBN 1 85278 198 X

Printed in Great Britain by Galliard (Printers) Ltd, Great Yarmouth

Contents

Acknowledgements

The editors and publishers wish to thank the following who have kindly given permission for the use of copyright material.

Basil Blackwell for articles: N. Salvadori and I. Steedman (1988), 'Joint Production Analysis in a Sraffian Framework', *Bulletin of Economic Research*, 165–95; I. Steedman (1976), 'Positive Profits with Negative Surplus Value: A Reply to Wolfstetter', *Economic Journal*, **86**, December, 873–6; R. Franke (1986), 'Some Problems Concerning the Notion of Cost-Minimizing Systems in the Framework of Joint Production', *The Manchester School*, **54** (3), September, 298–307.

Editions Economica for excerpts: I. Steedman (1984), 'The Empirical Importance of Joint Production' and Ch. Bidard (1984), 'Choice of Technique in Joint Production' from *La Production Jointe: Nouveaux Débats*, Ch.Bidard.

Gustav Fischer Verlag for article: B. Schefold (1978), 'Fixed Capital as a Joint Product', *Jahrbücher für Nationalökonomie und Statistik*, **192**, 415–39.

Nuova Casa Editrice Cappelli for article: H. D. Kurz (1986), 'Classical and Early Neoclassical Economists on Joint Production', *Metroeconomica*, **38**, 1–37.

Springer-Verlag, Vienna for articles: B. Schefold (1978), 'Multiple Product Techniques with Properties of Single Product Systems', *Zeitschrift für Nationalökonomie*, **38** (1–2) 29–53; B. Schefold (1978), 'On Counting Equations', *Zeitschrift für Nationalökonomie*, **38** (3–4), 253–85; G. Duménil and D. Lévy (1984), 'The Unifying Formalism of Domination: Value, Price, Distribution and Growth in Joint Production', *Zeitschrift für Nationalökonomie*, **44** (4), 349–71; Ch. Bidard (1986), 'Is von Neumann Square?', *Zeitschrift für Nationalökonomie*, **46**, 401–19; N. Salvadori (1988), 'Fixed Capital within the Sraffa Framework', *Zeitschrift für Nationalökonomie*, **48** (1), 1–17.

Every effort has been made to trace all the copyright holders but if any have been inadvertently overlooked the publishers will be pleased to make the necessary arrangement at the first opportunity.

In addition the publishers wish to thank the Library of the London School of Economics and Political Science for their assistance in obtaining these articles.

Introduction

This volume of readings presents 12 contributions to the study of joint production from a standpoint directly inspired by Sraffa's *Production of Commodities by Means of Commodities*. Whilst these essays range widely from historical and empirical matters to highly formal analysis, they all share this common inspiration. All the essays have been previously published but not always in English; (further contributions can be found in Steedman, 1988, vol. 2).

The significance of joint production

Much economic analysis has been based on the assumption that each productive activity produces only a single commodity. Moreover, it has not infrequently been suggested that this is a perfectly adequate basis for economic analysis, the study of joint production systems being, it is implied, the study of a curiosum, or a search for generality for its own sake. There are, on the contrary, several good reasons for rejecting such a view, not only in general but even, more specifically, from a revived 'classical' approach to political economy, deriving from Sraffa's work.

(i)   Much 'mainstream' economic theory takes joint production in its stride: to cite just two famous works, consider Hicks' *Value and Capital* or Debreu's *Theory of Value*. Much theory cast in the activity-analysis mould takes it for granted that joint production must (and can) be allowed for and, of course, the von Neumann model, which is so central to much growth theory, does the same. Nor has the position changed in this respect with the more recent use of 'dual' formulations: cost function, revenue function and profit function formulations of production theory all allow for joint production. Now, if joint production is in fact of empirical importance – as it is; see (iv) below – any revived 'classical' approach which seeks to challenge and even to displace the current 'mainstream' approaches must, necessarily, demonstrate that it can take joint production issues in its stride just as readily as do those 'mainstream' approaches.

(ii) While much 'mainstream' theory permits joint production, as we have just noted, not all of it does and it has been found, indeed, that that can be shown to be a serious weakness. It is known, for example, that (other than in special cases) the presence of joint production prevents a meaningful 'reduction to dated labour terms'; which means immediately that all attempts to construct a 'neo-Austrian' approach to economic theory are open to highly damaging criticism (see H. Hagemann and H. D. Kurz 1976). It has also been shown that, in the presence of joint production, a 'primary-factor-price-frontier' can be *upward* sloping, even when *no* produced inputs are used and *all* the primary inputs are paid *ex post* (so that there are no interest charges of any kind). This, in turn, undermines both various familiar marginalist comparative statics results – concerning shifts in demand or in factor supplies, or the imposition of tariffs – and some of the theory of Hicksian technical progress (see I. Steedman, 1982, 1985). Recognition of joint production, therefore, allows one to extend the 'classical' critique of various marginalist theories.

(iii) Conversely, however, joint production has often been used as the starting point for criticism *of* the 'classical' approach. In Book III, Chapter XVI of his *Principles of Political Economy*, J.S. Mill (1891, p. 387) considered some of the effects of joint production and wrote that, in determining the values of jointly produced commodities, 'we must revert to a law of value anterior to cost of production, and more fundamental, the law of demand and supply. He called that chapter, 'Of Some Peculiar Cases of Value'. Not surprisingly, Jevons seized on this in Chapter V of his *The Theory of Political Economy*.

> On some other occasion I may perhaps more fully point out the fallacy involved in Mill's idea that he is reverting to *an anterior law of value*, the law of supply and demand, the fact being that in introducing the cost of production principle, he had never quitted the laws of supply and demand at all. The cost of production is only one circumstance which governs supply, and thus indirectly influences values. Again, I shall point out that these cases of joint production, far from being 'some peculiar cases', form the general rule, to which it is difficult to point out any clear or important exceptions' (Jevons, 1970, p. 209).

Wicksell too, in the first substantive chapter of his *Lectures on Political Economy* (Volume I), insisted that,

> It happens in many cases, even where a commodity is manufactured under competitive conditions, that its costs of production *cannot be separated* or imputed because its production proceeds simultaneously and in combination with that of other goods.... Such cases, which have been given by Marshall the technical name 'joint supply', are mentioned also by Mill in his chapter, 'Some peculiar cases of value', but, as the chapter heading indicates, Mill regarded them as exceptions to the rule. In reality (as Jevons remarked) they occupy a large, perhaps the largest, part of the field of production (Wicksell 1967, p. 26).

An extensive discussion of the role of joint production in both classical and early neoclassical economics will be found in Chapter 2 by Heinz Kurz.

(iv) Had Jevons and Wicksell been wrong about the empirical importance of joint production, it would perhaps have been possible to maintain that a single-products theory was perfectly adequate to deal with most genuine and important economic questions – and that generality is not to be pursued too far for its own sake in a subject such as political economy. But the brute *fact* is that Jevons and Wicksell were not wrong: as soon as one begins to consider productive processes at the level of detail *necessary* for a Sraffa-based analysis of prices and distribution, one finds that joint production is, *empirically, extremely widespread*. A large number of real world examples, drawn from a wide range of industries and types of activities, is presented in Chapter 1 by Ian Steedman.

We now turn to a discussion of some more formal aspects of the Sraffian analysis of joint production. But we may note at once that our discussion can be relatively brief, since Chapter 3 is indeed a recent survey of the field by the present authors.

Joint production contrasted with single production

The following results are valid for single production but need not hold in general joint production models:

   (i) all products are separately producible and, as a consequence, a system of production is always square and labour values are always positive;

  (ii) a basic commodity can be defined as a commodity which enters directly or indirectly into the production of all the commodities in the system of production; the distinction between basics and non-basics is important since basics have a number of properties which are not shared with non-basics;

 (iii) the Standard commodity exists and consists of positive amounts of basics only;

 (iv) the profit rate reaches a finite and unique value, R, when the wage rate equals zero and the corresponding prices of basic commodities are positive; R is called the 'maximum rate of profit';

  (v) R is the lowest positive real number such that the price equations are satisfied with a zero wage rate;

 (vi) if the profit rate is between zero and R the prices of basic commodities vary as it varies, in general, but remain positive and finite;

 (vii) the relationship between the wage rate and the profit rate is decreasing irrespective of the numeraire chosen;

(viii) prices in terms of the wage rate are increasing and convex functions of the profit rate for each system of production;

 (ix) a cost-minimizing system of production is proved to be any system which can pay the higher wage rate (profit rate) for a given profit rate (wage rate) and it is determined independently of the requirements for use;

  (x) if there exists a system with prices all positive at the given profit rate (wage rate), then there exists a cost-minimizing system of production and in this system all prices are positive;

 (xi) if two different systems are both cost-minimizing at the given profit rate (wage rate), then they have a common price vector.

The fact that these results do not always hold if joint production is allowed has led a number of authors to investigate the hypotheses and the assumptions stated. As already mentioned, these issues are surveyed in Chapter 3 but we may now draw attention to some of the fuller discussions to be found in other chapters. For example, Bertram Schefold, in Chapter 4, explores the conditions under which a joint production system possesses the same economic properties as a single product system. It is quite natural to assume that a single production system is square. But why should one make this assumption with respect to a joint production system? Should it not be possible, in such a system, to have fewer processes than products? This issue is studied in two quite different ways in Chapter 5, by Ian Steedman, and in Chapter 6, by Christian Bidard. Turning our attention from quantities to prices, we may note that Chapter 7 by Gérard Duménil and Dominique Lévy includes a valuable discussion of the conditions under which all commodity prices within a given system are positive.

A focal point of the contrast between single and joint production systems has become the centre of discussion in more recent years: the question of choice of technique. Both Chapters 4 and 5 deal with some problems connected with choice of technique, but it was only in Chapter 8, by Bertram Schefold, that the problem of choice of technique came to be treated as a problem of great interest *per se*. Not surprisingly in this relatively early discussion of the issue, the simplifying assumptions were made that commodities are consumed in proportion to a given vector and that the economy is growing at a uniform rate equal to the profit rate. By implication, Schefold thereby drew attention to the role of 'requirements for use' referred to in (ix) above. For present purposes, these 'requirements of use' may be interpreted as the pattern of net output, which, as is well known, has no bearing on the choice of technique when there are only single product processes.

The significance of requirements for use for the choice of technique in joint production systems was considered explicitly by Salvadori (1982, 1985, both reprinted in Steedman, 1988, vol. 2), and some outstanding issues are considered further in Chapter 10 by Reiner Franke in the present volume. In Chapter 9, by contrast, Christian Bidard develops an alternative approach, which might be interpreted as specifying a restriction on the nature of technology which renders it unnecessary to take account of requirements for use.

Fixed Capital

The importance of the pattern of net output is also reduced when, rather than considering general joint production systems, we consider only fixed capital systems involving no 'pure' joint products, i.e. the case in which the only joint products are used machines. Bertram Schefold, in Chapter 11, begins by analysing systems in which each process produces one final good (perhaps a new machine) and not more than one old machine. Moreover machines are assumed to be non-transferable, i.e., no old machine produced jointly with a particular final good can be utilized in the production of any other final good. Chapter 12, by Neri Salvadori, allows that more than one used machine may be employed in a given process. Of course, non-transferability of used machines is still assumed, since it is known that to allow transferability of used machines is to reintroduce the problems of general joint production systems.

* * *

Having read the papers in this volume, the reader might well feel that some of these discussions have moved a long way from the treatment of joint production found in Sraffa's *Production of Commodities* and, indeed, in certain respects they have so moved and have even led to the rejection of certain statements made by Sraffa in connection with joint production. It remains the case that Sraffa's great work is the source of all the contributions presented in this volume.

Neri Salvadori and Ian Steedman
March 1990

References

Hagemann, H. and H. D. Kurz (1976), 'The Return of the Same Truncation Period and Reswitching of Techniques in Neo-Austrian and More General Models', *Kyklos*, **29**, 678–708.

Jevons, W. S. (1970), *The Theory of Political Economy* [1871], Penguin Books, Harmondsworth.

Mill, J. S. (1891), *Principles of Political Economy* [1848], Routledge & Sons, London.

Salvadori, N. (1982), 'Existence of Cost-Minimizing Systems within the Sraffa Framework', *Zeitschrift für Nationalökonomie*, **42**, 281–98.

Salvadori, N. (1985), 'Switching in Methods of Production and Joint Production', *The Manchester School*, **53**, 156–78.

Steedman, I. (1982), 'Joint Production and the Wage-Rent Frontier', *Economic Journal*, **92**, 377–85.

Steedman, I. (1985), 'Joint Production and Technical Progress', *Political Economy*, **1**, 41–52.

Steedman, I. (ed.), (1988), *Sraffian Economics*, 2 vols, Edward Elgar, Aldershot.

Wicksell, K. (1967), *Lectures on Political Economy* (Volume I) [1901], Routledge & Kegan Paul, London.

Part I
The Significance of Joint Production

[1]

THE EMPIRICAL IMPORTANCE OF JOINT PRODUCTION[*]

Ian Steedman

University of Manchester

The presence of joint production introduces additional complexities into more than one kind of economic theory. In 'standard' theory, for example, it is one source of the non-validity of the non-substitution theorem; it leads to the breakdown of such familiar single-products theory as the inverse relation of real factor returns, of the Rybczynski theorem and of the Stolper-Samuelson theorem; and it gives rise to the free disposal (of outputs) assumption, which is a most embarrassing assumption. In Marxian theory, joint products force a choice between either accepting additive but negative values, surplus value, etc., or abandoning the traditional additive value accounts. While in Sraffa-inspired theory, joint production can lead to 'complex' Standard Commodities; upward sloping wage-profit frontiers; alternative techniques each of which is the cheaper in terms of its own prices; the dependence of basics prices on the production conditions of non-basics; various difficulties in determining whether a commodity is basic or non-basic; and pressing questions about the determination of output levels and its independence of/dependence on the determination of natural prices. It is well known, nevertheless, that writers as far apart in time as Stanley Jevons (The Theory of Political Economy, 1871) and Frank Hahn (The Economic Record, 1975) have cited joint production as a difficulty for Ricardian and 'neo-Ricardian' theory, respectively.

---

* I am grateful to H.J. Abrams, J. Butlin, D. Colman, I. Dobbs, H-D Kurz, W. Thomas and W. Tyson - and to the participants at a seminar in Bremen University, at the Nanterre Colloque, and at the Trieste International Summer School - for very valuable advice and comments.

2

The purpose of this essay is to urge that theorists of all styles
should always treat joint production as the <u>normal</u> case; that theorists of
all kinds should abandon the common (not ubiquitous) practice of treating
single-products as the norm and mentioning joint production, if at all,
only as a footnote complication. This is urged not on the grounds that
joint products can give rise to interesting theoretical issues - though
they can - but on the grounds that joint production simply <u>is</u>, as a matter
of fact, <u>very common</u>. Since the results of single products theory by no
means always carry over in a straightforward way to joint production
theory, it follows that lack of attention to joint production is a serious
failing of any theory. This emphasis is not a matter of seeking theoretical
generality for the sake of generality but of seeking to make theory
adequate to its tasks.

The empirical importance of joint production will be illustrated in
the next two sections, first by means of specific examples of joint products
processes and, second, by a consideration of various phenomena which
undoubtedly exist but which could not do so in a world of single product
activities. It will be seen that in neither section does the argument
have anything to do with the (no doubt very useful) theoretical device of
treating an 'aged' machine as a joint product, along with the 'obvious'
product. On the other hand, some (not all) of the examples will give rise
to questions about the definitions of 'products' and of 'processes'; these
questions will be taken up briefly in a later section but it may be noted
at once that 'product' does <u>not</u> necessarily mean something saleable. On
the contrary, a <u>non</u>-economic criterion is precisely what is required here,
in order that subsequent economic questions should not be begged. Roughly
speaking, any detectable physical consequence of the operation of a
process will be regarded as a product of that process.

I am not sure that it is possible to present a mere list of empirical

3

examples without running the risk of generating boredom on the reader's

part, but perhaps the reader will bear in mind throughout that, as indicated

above, the list does have quite definite implications for the economic

theorist. It is for this reason, combined with the fact that joint

production is far too often neglected, that I have presumed upon the

reader's patience.

SOME JOINT PRODUCTS PROCESSES

Agriculture and Agriculture-Related Activities

1. Sheep-farming produces fleeces, more sheep (lambs), manure, weed

    control, and carcases. (And, in some Arab countries, milk.)

2. Various other livestock farming activities lead to a similar list of

    outputs but some, such as horses and oxen, will produce power as well,

    while others will produce milk. (Dead animals, incidentally, are

    sometimes fed to hounds and thus have a 'scrap value'.)

3. Milking is itself a joint products activity, producing milk and cream.

    (Or should we say that it is the separation process which has joint

    products?) It may also be noted that cheese-making produces whey as a

    by-product, which is used as pig-feed.

4. Slaughterhouse activity produces carcases and/or various cuts ready

    for the butcher, together with bone meal, blood meal, etc.; some of

    the by-products are used in the production of sera and vaccines in

    the pharmaceutical industry. Slaughterhouses on the Danish island of

    Bornholm also extract gall-stones (and export them to certain Asian

    countries as aphrodisiacs). Retail butchering activity produces

    various small cuts of meat, bones and excess fat. (These latter are

    used in making mince, lard and sausages or go to the butchers' waste

    merchant to be used in making bone-meal, tallow and cosmetics.)

4

5. Poultry-farming produces eggs, manure, further poultry, carcases and
    feathers, feet, beaks, etc., which may be used in producing meal.
    Incidentally, a joint product, woodshavings, can be an input into
    poultry keeping.

6. Grain growing produces grain, chaff, straw and stubble. (The straw
    may be used both in stables and as feed and the stubble can be
    ploughed or disced back into the soil as fertilizer.) Grain milling
    will, of course, produce both flour and bran.

7. Root crops naturally provide both the root and the 'tops'; if these
    latter have not been destroyed to facilitate harvesting, they may be
    ploughed in as fertilizer. Any potato harvest, for example, will
    include potatoes of various different sizes; are they joint products?

8. With peas, beans, onions, lettuce, cucumber, etc., any vegetation
    not taken from the field will be ploughed in to enhance soil fertility.

9. Grass crops may provide immediate pasture and will, in any case,
    produce both hay and silage.

10. Rotation, of course, constitutes a textbook example of joint
    production over time.

11. Apiculture produces honey, more bees, beeswax (used in many different
    ways) and, most important, flower pollination.

12. Oil-seed processing produces oil, cake and meal - and, in the case
    of coconuts, coir (fibre for ropes, matting) as well.

13. Pineapple leaves and stems are used in Thailand both for landfilling
    and as cattlefeed.

14. Sugar cane processing produces, in addition to sugars, molasses,
    bagasse (crushed cane, with many uses including as fuel in sugar
    refining itself), filter mud, and large quantities of 'waste' heat.
    Moreover, cane 'tops' left in the fields can be used as animal feed.
    Beet sugar processing produces both sugar and animal feed.

5

15. The processing of hides and skins produces not only leather but also
    flesh, hair and great quantities of effluent.

16. Agricultural 'wastes' are an important source of fuel in some
    countries, e.g. Indonesia, whether through the production of methane
    'Biogas' or in other ways, such as the burning of dung. Needless to
    say, this is only possible because some agricultural processes produce
    joint products. It may be noted, in similar vein, that such 'wastes'
    are an important input to some forms of paper and board production,
    especially in tropical countries without coniferous woods.

Fishing

   It will be clear that many forms of fishing activity will produce
joint products; I give just a few examples.

1. Prawn fishermen fishing off the coast of Northern Ireland will also
   catch codling, haddock, plaice, ray, saithe, solé, turbot and whiting.

2. Herring fishermen fishing off the Isle of Man will also (sometimes)
   take cod and mackerel. Even the herring will, of course, be of
   variable size; this affects the 'average quality' which influences
   the price received per unit of weight.

3. Lobster fishermen find lobsters of varying sizes in their pots -
   and these may be graded and sold at different prices.

4. Pearl fishing.

5. When fish are processed on a freezer ship, the heads, etc., will be
   turned into fish meal.

6. Fish farming will always produce fish of various different sizes
   (probably of a log-normal distribution).

Forestry, Sawmills, Pulp and Paper

1. Forestry activity produces many 'products'. Apart from the creation

6

of (dis-) amenity values, the prevention of water erosion and the
related reduction of water run off to reservoirs, there are many
'wood products'. Thinning, which may take place up to three times,
produces small round wood, for poles, fences, etc. (which can be
important for forestry finance). When the timber is eventually
taken out, some or all of the branches may be left in situ (except
for soft woods located near to the pulp mill); this by-product has
both good effects (conserving water for the new trees) and bad
ones (causing timber disease - fomes - which inhibits successful
replanting). With hardwoods, larger branches, as well as the
central pillar, will be used for building, and the smaller ones for
pulping. It has been estimated that, in 1968, one third of the
timber volume harvested took the form of unused residues (i.e.,
joint products).

2. A sawmill produces many products: logs, sawn timber, offcuts, bark
and sawdust, with many varieties of each. The preparation of logs
for plying produces also the plylog cores which, like offcuts, bark
and sawdust, are used in making particle board. In the processing
of hardwood for sawn wood, veneers or plywood, 40-60% by weight would
be wasted if it were not for the particle board and pulping uses of
the 'residues'. (Sawdust is also used, of course, in cattle pens,
in poultry farms, in butchers' shops and in engineering shops for
cleaning up oil and grease.) Sawmill by-products are sometimes burnt
to drive the mill.

3. Integrated pulp and paper mills will often produce a very wide range
of papers, tissues and paperboards. They produce, too, vast
quantities of effluent. It may also be noted that 'waste' paper
and board is now a major input into paper and board production
(perhaps 50% of the furnish for paper in the UK); there would be

no such waste if all production processes were of the single
product kind.

Mining

1.   All mining activity produces not only ore (coal, etc.) - and ore
     (coal, etc.) of varying grades - but also spoil, tailings, under-
     ground waste, etc. It may also produce changes in water levels,
     nearby or further afield, acid drainage (from coal mines), and
     miners with 'black lung', etc! (I shall not refer again to harmed,
     tired, or more experienced workers as joint products of a
     productive process - but not because I take the point to be
     insignificant.) The 'hole in the ground' produced by mining
     operations may also serve subsequently for waste disposal - or for
     sailing!

2.   As noted above, the immediate product of mining activity will often
     be heterogeneous and will require cleaning and/or grading and/or
     refining; either the mining activity proper or the cleaning/grading/
     refining activities must therefore be regarded as joint products
     processes. To give a simple example, the percentages, by weight, of
     metal in the ore mined may be of the order of 50-60% for iron, 50%
     for lead and zinc, 25% for copper and 20% for aluminium.

3.   Some of the joint products from the processing of coal - coke, gas,
     tar, dyes, etc. - were, of course, amongst those noticed by Mill,
     Marx and Jevons.

4.   It may be noted here that mine tailings, like the slag and ash joint
     products of various other processes, are commonly used in construction,
     landfilling and road building. For example, slag can sometimes be
     used to make blocks for building purposes.

8

Oil

1. The production of crude often involves the joint production of
    natural gas.

2. The processing of crude, is, of course, a joint products process of
    the most striking kind, generating fuel oil, heating oil, diesel
    oil, petrol, jet fuel and petrochemical feedstocks such as naphtha,
    benzene, ethylene and propylene.

Chemicals

    Nearly all - but not quite all - chemical engineering processes,
whether based on synthesis, cracking or substitution, are joint products
processes. A few specific examples follow.

1. The ammonium sulphate fertilizer industry produces as a by-product
    vast quantities of ammonia (which is a major input to acrylic fibre
    production).

2. In many processes, water has to be removed by the use of olium
    (SO_3), so that sulphuric acid is produced as a by-product. (It
    may be sold as it is, or concentrated, or boiled to recover the
    water.)

3. A common 'waste' gas from chemical processes is HCℓ, which is
    dissolved in water and sold (in competition with hydrochloric acid
    producers - though the by-product from some, not all, processes will
    be less pure).

4. Heat is often a major by-product and may, for example, be used in
    electricity generation. (The British CEGB buys in some 5% of its
    electricity from such sources.)

5. Electrolysis of brine produces chlorine, hydrogen and sodium
    hydroxide. (It is interesting to note that, in the U.K. at least,
    sodium hydroxide was the principal product pre 1939 but now it is

9

only a by-product - sometimes, indeed, causing disposal problems -
with the principal product now being the chlorine, used in plastics
production.)

6. Some of the chemical industry's joint products are, of course,
noxious ones, requiring careful (and expensive) disposal - for
example, halogen, various dangerous oily/watery mixtures, slag (used
in road building and in some building materials), ash.

7. The chemicals industry also provides many examples of joint production in the sense of jointness over time, in batch production, semi-
continuous production and even in continuous production. Batch
production, in which the inputs to and outputs from a given plant
are varied over time clearly involves joint costs. (N.b., although
fixed capital is involved, the element of jointness considered here
does not arise from the device of treating 'aged' plant as a joint
product, relevant as that device may still be in the analysis of
batch production.) Pharmaceuticals production will often be of the
batch form; another example is the production of alcohol from
agricultural 'wastes', in which the batch method is important for
its flexibility with respect to inputs (the output will also vary).
It may be noted that batch and continuous production may be combined
as, for example, in the paper industry, already referred to. There,
the early stages of the process, turning wood pulp into viscose,
may be continuous, whilst the viscose is used as the input to a
batch production process, which produces a batch of fine paper, then
a batch of thick, rough paper, then a batch of cellophane, etc.
Flexibility, in the face of uncertain fluctuations in demand, is one
aspect of the batch production contribution to minimizing joint costs
over time.

Semi-continuous production processes (e.g., for plate glass of

varying thickness, strength, transparency, etc.) involve similar
joint costs over time to batch processes; in both cases, of course,
adjustment costs between products are important. Even continuous
processes can involve joint costs over time (as well as simultaneous
joint products), in that there may be alternative final stages to
the continuous process, yielding different outputs.

8.　The question is sometimes raised whether joint production involves
rigidly fixed product proportions. It may therefore be noted briefly
that electrolysis processes may produce the products in fixed
proportions but that, on the other hand, the relative outputs from
cracking processes can definitely be varied by variation of the
residence time, temperature, pressure, catalyst use, etc. The
degree of chlorination of benzene varies rapidly with the amount
of chlorine and even with a fixed input ratio the conversation ratio
is variable. (This leads, in turn, to a problem of recycling the
unconverted inputs. How exactly is a process to be defined when
outputs are cycled back as inputs?)

Metals Production

1.　Any metal production process which involves the refining of ore
will, by definition, produce joint products.

2.　Zinc and copper smelters, for example, produce, amongst other
things, sulphuric acid.

Engineering

1.　It will be clear that, by their very nature, all drilling, planing,
grinding, turning, cutting, punching, nibbling, tapping, shot-
blasting, etc. processes are joint products processes. It would be
a mistake to regard this as a 'trivial' example of joint production;

the handling of swarf in workshops is highly important, both for safety reasons and for the efficient working of the machines and tools involved. That it is far from trivial may be illustrated by a Financial Times report: 'A new range of swarf and oil separating plant designed for the recovery of cutting oils....will recover an average of 17 gallons of oil for every 1,000 lb of steel swarf processed and promises a saving of about £35 per 1,000 lb swarf processed....A typical system capable of handling 2,000 lb of steel swarf an hour would cost around £15,000....Oil recovery a year.... would be in the order of £140,000, says the company.' Another Financial Times report suggested that a different new swarf handling system could deal with 20 tons of swarf per hour.

2.   Joint production over time is commonplace in engineering. The proportion of machine tools which are so designed that only one product can be produced must be extremely small.· (Is it zero?) Tools and machine tools are almost always multi-purpose in terms of which products they can be used to produce.

3.   Workshops, repair shops, forges, foundries, shipyards, tool rooms.... will almost (?) always produce different products over time. Specialist producers of machine tools, will, like shipyards, often produce to order and to customer specification, so that their products will vary over time, even when their own equipment does not.

Electricity

1.   Power stations produce not only electricity, ash, slag, etc. (in great quantities) but also huge amounts of 'waste' heat. (Needless to say, considerable attention is now being paid to the utilization of this heat in combined heat and power (CHP) systems for so-called District Heating.)

2. Oil refineries, chemical works, iron and steel plants, paper mills, etc. often generate (at least part of) their own electricity input as a joint product.

Textiles

1. Keeping dust, 'fly', etc. out of textile machinery is important to the efficient operation of that machinery in various processes; as with swarf (above), 'fly' etc. are not trivial joint products and costs are incurred to keep them out of the machinery (and out of the principal products).

2. Garment producers will always produce 'offcut' joint products and nearly always joint products over time as they change their range of products. (Is there a garment producer who always produces, say, shirts of one size, one colour, one design, one quality, one....?) Seasonal variation of the products is often important.

Transport

Transport systems provide many examples of joint products, both simultaneous joint products and those over time.

1. Buses. Even a single bus, which starts from Stop Zero and proceeds to Stops 1, 2,....,n, produces $[n(n+1)/2]$ different possible passenger journeys; if it then makes the return trip, a total of $n(n+1)$ 'products' will have been produced. The daily output of different 'products', differentiated by starting point, starting time, and finishing point, in a large bus network is thus extremely hetero-geneous; the number of products each day will be very large indeed. The 'peak' problem is, of course, one aspect of this. Other important elements of jointness in costs are that any bus can be switched between routes and that there are large overhead costs in garages, maintenance staff (fitters and cleaners), scheduling staff

and offices.

2. Railways. Everything just said about a bus network applies also to
    a rail network. In addition, track and signalling systems are
    necessarily subject to a great deal of joint use by different
    services (products). Locomotives can readily be switched between
    routes and between hauling of freight and passenger trains.
    Passenger trains will often carry newspapers, letters and parcels
    (in West Germany and the U.K. at least). Some types of freight
    wagon will be used for different kinds of freight on different
    trips (although this is now less common than it used to be).

3. Shipping, airlines, and road haulage systems exhibit, with only minor
    variations, the various types of product jointness exemplified above
    for bus and rail systems.

4. Although it is not strictly relevant to the present section, it may
    be remarked that British Rail carries out its accounting on the
    basis of 'profit centres' and that the apparent importance of joint
    versus non-joint costs naturally depends on both the size of the
    designated 'profit centres' and on the precise composition of the
    activities attributed to them.

Communications

Telephone and postal systems produce joint products in ways closely
analogous to those set out above for transport systems.

Electricity and Gas Distribution

Even if one does not treat electricity (gas), made available at
different places, as different 'products', the 'peak' problem is, of
course, an important source of joint costs; electricity (gas) available
at different times needs to be treated as a set of different 'products'
with, obviously, a significant degree of arbitrariness in the definitions

14

of the 'different products' involved. It will be clear that this is a
different kind of joint production over time from that referred to in
connection with machine tools, repair shops, etc.

Publishing

1.   Most newspapers and magazines combine two joint products - text and
      advertising; the point could, of course, be pressed more finely.
2.   Analogous points can be made with respect to commercial radio and
      television.

Retailing

      Almost by definition, retailing activities produce a range of joint
products. (Examples would be superfluous.) Most wholesaling activities
will do the same. These examples combine joint products with the presence
of large overhead costs.

Medical

      All hospitals, doctors' practices and dental surgeries will produce
joint products over time. (The same will be true of many other service
activities.)

Buildings

      All multi-storey buildings, and very many single-storey ones, provide
joint products both at a moment of time and over time. The same is true
of hotels, restaurants, cinemas, theatres, etc.

      Even if the reader has found the above list rather tedious, a) it
could be made far longer and b) it suffices as it stands to show that
joint products are, as a matter of fact, very, very common. It is quite
wrong to say either that joint production is exceptional or that it is
common but only in the sense that 'aged' fixed capital is a joint product.

15

INDIRECT EVIDENCE OF JOINT PRODUCTION

Rather than presenting specific examples of joint products processes, this section will consider, very briefly, rather more indirect, general evidence of the importance of joint products. In summary form, the argument is that if there were no joint products then there would be no such phenomena as pollution, waste disposal, recycling or quality control; there are such phenomena; therefore there are joint products. It is, of course, true that many pollution and many waste disposal activities arise from the 'joint products of consumption processes', rather than from those of production processes but a) that does not make them irrelevant to the main point being urged in this note and b) production processes also contribute to pollution and to the existence of waste disposal activities. It will be clear that there are important connections between the four types of phenomenon.

Pollution

It will not be necessary here to develop a long catalogue of the various kinds of pollution involving gases, liquids, solids, radioactivity, heat energy, noise energy, vibration, etc., etc. A few specific examples will suffice to render the point vivid.

1.   Motor vehicles exhaust vast quantities of carbon monoxide. And it
      has been estimated that in the U.K. some 7,000 tonnes of lead reach
      the air each year in the same way.

2.   Power stations release millions of tons of sulpher oxides each year
      into the atmosphere. (This leads to the creation of 'acid rain' -
      sulphuric acid - and to certain international disputes!) There is,
      however, the possibility, at a cost, of collecting sulphur dioxide
      from power station effluent and converting it to industrial
      sulphuric acid. Power stations also produce great quantities of

16

'waste' heat, of course, this being even more true of nuclear powered
stations than of conventional ones.

3. According to a <u>Financial Times</u> report on a new vacuum system for
    dealing with the problem of oil pollution, 'Since 1970 at least
    1,400,000 tons of oil have been spilled at sea in various parts of
    the world'. (The reported system can dispose of 40 square metres
    of oil per hour.)

4. The burning of coal and oil is causing a gradual increase in the
    level of carbon dioxide in the atmosphere, which causes the earth
    to radiate less heat back into space - the so-called 'greenhouse
    effect'. (It is a matter of dispute <u>how much</u> the earth's temperature
    varies in relation to the amount of carbon dioxide emitted but the
    existence of the phenomenon is agreed on.)

5. The existence of solid, liquid and heat pollution of rivers requires
    little comment.

    All pollution phenomena constitute evidence of the existence of
    joint products.

Waste Disposal

1. It has been estimated that Greater Manchester alone produces some
    3,000 to 4,000 tonnes of refuse daily (of which two-thirds is
    cellulosic); that in the U.K. as a whole, some 20 million tons of
    household and minor commercial garbage, some 5 million tons of
    'hazardous' waste, some 20-25 million tons of other industrial waste -
    and, of course, unknown quantities of construction waste - are
    produced each year; and that the annual U.K. cost of waste disposal
    is now some £500,000,000. Common disposal methods are, of course,
    landfill and incineration; incineration naturally produces its own
    joint products, which can include electricity, as at the Greater

17

London Council's Edmonton incinerator, where electricity revenue
covers 45% of the incineration costs. Other 'disposal' processes
include 'pyrolysis', to produce oil (20,000 tons), solid fuel
(17,000 tons) and scrap steel (7,000 tons) from 50,000 tons of used
tyres; fermentation of cellulosic material to produce alcohol, as
in Brazil; processes to convert cellulosic refuse into oil (with
water and carbon dioxide by-products) - a recent version is claimed
to obtain 3.5 tonnes of oil from every 10 tonnes of rubbish. It is
hoped that new biotechnological techniques will also be useful in
waste disposal (and in utilizing agricultural by-products).

2. Sewage disposal is, needless to say, a large waste disposal industry;
    it is disputed, I believe, whether more 'fertilizer use' should be
    made of sewage. It has been estimated that the U.K.'s annual sewage
    contains some 2 million tons of protein.

3. Scrapped vehicles and other durables constitute a major joint products
    disposable problem.

4. Disposal of 'hazardous wastes' - including inflammable, corrosive and
    chemically reactive materials, poisons and carcinogens - is a
    particularly important aspect of the existence of joint products,
    whether it involves treatment of the waste, landfill techniques, use
    of boreholes for liquid waste, or incineration. The site which will
    become Britain's largest hazardous waste dump has a licence to dump
    up to 1,300 tonnes of hazardous solids and sludges per day. Disposal
    can, of course, produce its own joint products, such as dangerous
    'leachate' from dumps.

5. Another difficult set of disposal problems involves nuclear wastes,
    from hospitals, laboratories, power stations, reprocessing plants and
    spent fuel - not least because of the length of time required for
    such wastes to become reasonably safe. (Though the toxicity of some

18

dangerous chemicals, by contrast, has an infinite life!) Sea dumping, storage, borehole and solidification techniques are being developed. (A French process can turn nuclear waste into ingots of glass; some West German nuclear waste is being buried in old salt mines, at Asse.) Low-level radioactive waste, as from hospitals, can be incinerated.

It has been estimated that, over the next twenty years, the U.K.'s average annual volume of nuclear waste produced will be $20,000m^3$ of low level waste; $2,000m^3$ of medium level waste; and $50m^3$ of high level waste.

Recycling

1. A large waste processing plant at Wijster, The Netherlands, takes in some 800,000 tons of rubbish per year and extracts re-usable ferrous metals, organic residues, heavy papers and light papers. Other systems extract re-usable metals and then use the remaining waste as fuel.

2. Plastics are a difficult waste in that they will not rot in landfill and can create noxious gases if incinerated – but there are scrap plastic recycling processes which return plastic to the plastics industry in either pellet or sheet form.

3. Waste glass, or 'cullet', is a useful input in glass making; by speeding up the melting of the raw materials, it cuts fuel costs. Nearly 50% of the starting material in Swiss glass-making is cullet.

4. It has been estimated that non-ferrous metal recovery in the U.K. amounts to some 30%, by weight, of non-ferrous metal consumption. Much metal processing scrap is 'prompt' scrap and is immediately fed back into the process; metal stampings, by contrast, are returned to the metal producer. Tinplate from refuse can be re-

cycled as scrap tin and good quality steel; aero engine alloys can
be recycled at a quality suitable for re-use in engines. Silver,
gold, copper and cadmium can be recovered from the drag (rinse)
bath effluent in electroplating processes. Large volumes of
aluminium can be recovered through the recycling of aluminium
beverage cans; in the U.S.A., the volume of recycled cans is said
to be equivalent to the output of two average-sized smelters.

5. There are 'multi-fuel' boilers that can run on certain 'wastes', as
well as on conventional fuels, and steam-generating incinerators
exist which run on toxic acid tar wastes.

6. Solvents can be recycled - e.g. cellulose thinners from motor
manufacturers paintshops - industrial effluent can produce animal
feed protein via the mass cultivation of algae (South Africa), and
food industry effluent can produce methane gas, via bacterial
fermentation. Up to 80% of the caustic soda can be recovered from
aluminium etch solutions.

7. Much paper and board is recycled into paper and board mills. Shredded
paper has proved successful as animal bedding - and used recycled-
paper bedding for poultry is then _itself_ recycled as a soil
conditioner and fertilizer!

8. A Japanese process compresses waste into material for road foundations,
land fill and the production of building materials.

Recycling only occurs because there are joint products.

Quality Control

If every production process consistently produced a single, physically
homogeneous product, there would be no such activity as quality control;
in fact, quality control is a major feature of many production processes.
Such control may separate out, for example, items (batches, etc.) for
sale, items for sale as 'seconds', items requiring further processing,

items to be recycled as raw material, and items to be destroyed. In many
cases, no doubt, quality varies continuously, while quality control is
carried out in terms of set 'benchmark' standards, or gradings, so that
the number of 'different products' involved is, in part, a matter of
convention. (There may be good reasons underlying the conventions, of
course.) That element of convention notwithstanding, the widespread use
of quality control procedures shows that joint products are very common.

MACHINES AS 'PURE' JOINT PRODUCTS

When 'aged' machines <u>are transferable</u> between production processes
they constitute, from the standpoint of theory, <u>pure</u> joint products; one
is not using here the mere <u>device</u> of treating a non-transferable machine
'as if' it were a joint product. Now, as a matter of fact, many types of
'non-specific' capital goods are transferable – and transferred. Many,
perhaps most, buildings fall into this category. There are well-
developed second-hand markets in aircraft, ships, cars and other motor
vehicles. (Most U.K. road haulage companies, i.e. the smaller ones,
purchase second-hand power units and trailers.) There are big markets in
used agricultural machinery. Used plant, machine tools and office equipment are extensively traded, both within and between countries; indeed
there are specialized second-hand machiner valuers and auctioneers and
firms which recondition and then sell used machine tools. (One source of
supply is, of course, closed down factories – e.g. in the U.K. motor
industry in recent years – but usually individual items of equipment
rather than complete plants will be purchased.)

Even equipment which cannot be sold as such may, of course, have
significant scrap value – it is thus still a 'pure' joint product. In
the first four months of 1982, for example, some 10 million deadweight
tons of tanker vessels were sold for scrap.

21

PERIODS, PROCESSES AND PRODUCTS

No amount of (perfectly proper) stress on the idea that statements of fact are dependent on the conceptual categories employed will, I think, suffice to dispose of 'the fact' that joint products are very common. Yet it is true, at the same time, that in presenting our various examples of the fact of joint production, we have encountered at various points a number of necessary distinctions and the need for careful definitions. It has been seen, for example, that there are both 'technical' joint products, produced at the same time, and joint products over time - where a distinction is again needed between cases in which time constitutes the only difference between the joint products and those in which there are other differences as well. The question then arises as to what period of time is regarded as sufficiently short to imply 'technical' joint production as opposed to that over time; closely related, of course, is the question how a process is to be conceived. How far is it useful, for example, to break 'a process' down into a sequence of (sub-) processes and to what extent can such a sub-division make each sub-process a single product one (fixed capital aside)? How is a process to be viewed when output proportions are variable (even if within close limits)? To what extent would it be useful simply to subsume joint production under the wider concept of joint costs? Or even under that of externalities generally? It will be clear that such questions do not necessarily have clear-cut answers; the most appropriate answer may well vary from one context to another. But that is, of course, no reason for losing sight of the questions themselves.

Rather different - but immediately relevant - questions also arise from the above list of examples. One is the extent to which joint production has become more or less important over the last two centuries,

22

say. Of course, one cannot expect a simple answer to this question and
historical investigation is likely to reveal a complex interweaving of
patterns of increasing jointness in some fields and decreasing jointness
in others, resulting perhaps from the increased specialization of
productive activities. (Although activity specialization could occur
without any activity becoming a single product one.) A second, and quite
different, type of question might be posed as follows: 'Yes, there is
indeed a great deal of joint production - but it does not immediately
follow that the results of single-products theory become false. The
patterns of positive outputs within the output matrix might just happen
to be such that the system behaves 'as if' it consisted of single product
processes'. This is, of course, a logical possibility and the matter is
worth pursuing; it is only necessary to insist here that the question
should be pursued rather than begged.

The above, and many other related, questions are all worthy of
detailed consideration and the purely empirical orientation of the present
essay is certainly not intended to suggest otherwise. On the contrary, it
has been designed to emphasise that theoretical discussion of general
joint production systems is entirely necessary and is very far from being
an exercise in economically irrelevant 'abstraction-mongering that can
have no correspondence in reality'. Indeed, one might well ask, and
even insist on, the question 'Which productive activities are single
product ones?'.

CONCLUSION

Phenomena which involve, from the standpoint of the economic
theorist, 'pure' joint production are very common indeed. Economic theory,
within whatever framework it is carried out, should therefore treat
general joint production as the normal case for analysis; single products

theory is far too special, even when it allows for non-transferable

fixed capital.

[2]

METROECONOMICA

Vol. XXXVIII   February 1986   N. 1

CLASSICAL AND EARLY NEOCLASSICAL ECONOMISTS ON JOINT PRODUCTION (*)

Heinz D. Kurz

University of Bremen

I. INTRODUCTION

1. Traditional economic analysis has concentrated on single-product processes of production and single-product firms, giving only passing reference to the more general case ([1]). This preoccupation with single production seems to be based on either or both of the following premises: first, single production is empirically far more important than joint production; secondly, the results derived within a single-products framework essentially carry over to the joint-products case.

While empirical investigations have undermined the first premise, theoretical analysis has raised doubts about the correctness of the second. The view « that these cases of joint production, far from being "some

---

(*) This paper developed from some notes presented on the occasion of the preparatory round table to the foundation of the International Summer School held in Udine in 1980. An earlier version of the present paper (cf. Kurz, 1984) was prepared during a most useful stay at the Faculty of Economics and Commerce, University of Rome, in Winter 1982-83. The support by the University of Rome is gratefully acknowledged. I am indebted to P. Garegnani, S. Parrinello, Ian Steedman and particularly U. Krause for helpful discussion and advice. Moreover, I would like to acknowledge the benefit I derived from comments on the 1984 version by many people and in particular by C. Bidard, M. Blaug, L.L. Pasinetti, L.F. Punzo, P.A. Samuelson and B. Schefold. The responsibility for any errors and misconceptions is of course mine.

([1]) There exist of course notable exceptions to this. Modern general equilibrium theory, for example, generally allows for joint production proper (see, e.g. Arrow and Hahn, 1971). Moreover, the revival of the « classical standpoint » in the theory of value and distribution (Sraffa, 1960) brought with it, as a by-product, a remarkable concern with the problem of joint production (see, e.g., Pasinetti, 1980). Recent contributions to the analysis of the multiproduct firm are summarized by Bailey and Friedlaender (1982).

— 2 —

peculiar cases", form the general rule, to which it is difficult to point out any clear or important exception », has been advocated already one century ago by W.S. Jevons (1965, p. 198); a similar view has been expressed recently by Steedman (1984) on the basis of an account of numerous practical examples of multiple-product processes of production (²). However, from the point of view of economic theory whether or not joint production is predominant in the « real world » does not appear to be that important, since it has been shown that the presence of even one multiple-product process of production in an otherwise single-product system can alter qualitatively some of the characteristic features of the system as a whole (³). Hence the simple fact that joint production exists at all, and is very common indeed, should suffice to make economists take it into account from the very beginning of their analyses.

2. The purpose of the present paper will be to examine the contributions of earlier economists to an analysis of joint production. Unfortunately, consulting works on the history of economic thought does not yield much insight. In fact, in many studies the issue is not even dealt with, as if it had never been a matter of investigation and dispute (⁴). The paper contributes to fill this lacuna in the history of our subject. Emphasis is on the role of joint production in the development of economic theory and the rise and decline of schools of economic thought. It will be argued that the problem of joint production played a significant role in the gradual abandonment of the classical approach to the theory of value and distribution. As is well known, this development culminated in the so-called « marginalist revolution » in the final quarter of the last century. A major concern will be with some of the marginalist econ-

---

(²) Apparently, business economists were generally much better aware of the importance of joint production than most other economists; see, for example, Riebel (1955).

(³) With regard to the theory of international trade see. e.g., the hints in Jones (1979); for the theory of value, distribution and technical progress, see, e.g., Steedman (1982, 1985).

(⁴) In Schumpeter's *History of Economic Analysis* (1954) the problem of joint production is given hardly any attention; it plays no role at all in the works of Dobb (1973) and Walsh and Gram (1980), who counterpose the classical and neoclassical tradition in economic analysis. In treatises which contain some discussion of the problem under consideration the opinion prevails that the first economist ever to deal with joint production was J.S. Mill; see, for example, Stigler (1965, p. 8), Rima (1967, p. 143), Blaug (1968, p. 198), O'Brien (1975, pp. 45 and 95-96), Deane (1978, p. 69) and Ekelund and Hebert (1983, p. 154). Spiegel (1971, p. 355) gives the credit to M. Longfield. We shall see below that the fact of joint production was recognised much earlier in the literature and that some authors endeavoured to come to grips with the analytical difficulties involved.

— 3 —

omists' claim that the classical theory did not and in principle could not deal with joint production in a satisfactory way and that therefore and because of its other deficiencies it had to be jettisoned and a new theoretical approach explored. Moreover, the investigation will throw some light on the role of « demand » in the marginalist treatment of joint production.

The structure of the paper is as follows. In Section II a simple analytical framework will be elaborated by means of which the essentials of alternative approaches to the theory of value in the case of joint production proper can be investigated. This schema is then used to discuss major contributions of late eighteenth and nineteenth century authors. Section III is devoted to an investigation of the classical approach, in particular the analyses of Adam Smith and Marx. Early attempts to explain relative prices in terms of supply and demand are dealt with in Section IV. The contributions of authors such as von Thünen, Longfield, J.S. Mill and von Mangoldt foreshadow the marginalist approach; the main novel element consists in the introduction of the concept of substitutability in consumption. In Section V the treatment of joint production by major representatives of what may be called « mature » marginalism, in particular Jevons and Marshall, will be discussed. It is shown that Marshall generalizes the concept of substitutability to the sphere of production. Section VI draws some conclusions.

II. A SIMPLE FRAMEWORK OF THE ANALYSIS

3. In this Section a simple framework of the analysis will be developed in order to facilitate the comparison of alternative approaches to the theory of value in the case of pure joint production. As we shall see below, early contributions were essentially concerned with the two-products case and the analytical challenge it poses. Unless otherwise stated, the argument in this section will accordingly be developed in terms of the following simplifying assumptions. There are only two products; there are constant returns to scale throughout the economy; there is a single primary factor of production, i.e. homogeneous labour; there is no fixed capital. These simplifications allow us to make extensive use of the familiar two-dimensional graphical analysis of the relations between inputs, outputs and prices (cf. Goodwin, 1970, and Mainwaring, 1984).

— 4 ---

4. First consider a system in which the two products are jointly produced in fixed proportion by a single process of production. Moreover, with view to Adam Smith's fictitious « early and rude state of society » let us assume that the amounts of means of production needed are negligible. In fig. 1 the (net) output vector per unit of « unassisted labour »,

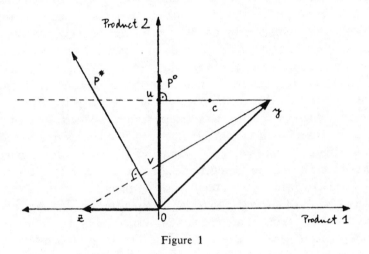

Figure 1

to use Ricardo's term, is given by $y = (y_1, y_2)$. Clearly, the proportion in which the two products are produced need not coincide with those in which they are « required for use » (cf. Sraffa, 1960, p. 43 fn. 2). Let $c = (c_1, c_2)$ be the vector of requirements of the two products. Hence, if the process is activated at the unit level product 1 is overproduced to an amount $y_1 - c_1$. According to the « rule of free goods » of general equilibrium theory all items of a product that is in excess supply assume zero prices. This rule in fact implies that in addition to process y there exists a *disposal* process by means of which product 1 can be costlessly « destroyed » by magic [5]. This activity is given by the negative branch of the horizontal axis. The required amounts of the two products c, can then be attained by a suitable combination of the productive and the disposal activities. Since the price vector may be represented as a

---

[5] See Arrow (1983, p. 31). It is worth mentioning that in general equilibrium theory the assumption of free disposal, according to which « something » can be transformed into « nothing », is coupled with the assumption of the « impossibility of the land of cockaigne» (Nikaido), according to which « nothing » cannot be transformed into « something ».

— 5 —

line drawn normal to the net output-frontier yu, in the present case the price vector is given by $p^0 = (p_1^0, p_2^0)$, where $p_1^0 = 0$.

5. If the bizarre assumption of free disposal is replaced by that of *costly* disposal, and if z_1 units of product 1 can be « destroyed » by one unit of unassisted labour, the unit net output-frontier is represented by yv and the price vector by p^*. The required quantities of the two products are then exactly obtained by an appropriate combination of processes y and z, i.e. by activating the production process at the unit level and the disposal process at the level of $(y_1 - c_1)/z_1$ units of labour. The location of the price vector p^* indicates that in this case the price of the second product is positive, whereas the price of the first is negative [6].

So far we have implicitly assumed that both products are useful, i.e. « goods ». However, it cannot be precluded that one of them could be a « bad », i.e. a thing that is not wanted at all and has to be removed. Under the conditions of production described the bad of necessity has to be produced in order to obtain positive quantities of the good. Let product 1 be a bad and u the vector of requirements for use. Again, u can be produced by means of a combination of processes y and z. (The analysis of the more general case in which the disposal process exhibits some « jointness of destruction » is left to the reader.)

6. The discussion so far can be summarized as follows. Whereas in the case of single production the problem of the underdeterminacy of the price system could not arise because there would always be as many productive processes, and therefore equations, as there are commodities the prices of which are to be ascertained, in the case of joint production the number of productive processes activated may fall short of the number of products produced. Thus in the case depicted only one process may be available to provide both products. Hence the question arises of whether, and in what circumstances, a determinate solution to the system of relative prices will be obtained. As we shall see below, earlier authors were essentially concerned with this problem.

The preceding discussion has shown that determinacy may be procured through the introduction of additional processes, i.e. processes of

---

[6] In case the reader finds it difficult to come to grips with the notion of « negative » prices, it should be remembered that the negativity of the price of a product that has to be removed corresponds with the positivity of the price of the respective disposal service.

— 6 —

free or costly disposal. These serve the purpose of adjusting the proportions in which the products are made available to the (exogenously given)
proportions in which they are needed. By this token the *total* number
of processes used is made equal to the number of products produced,
i.e. a « square » system of production and disposal obtains. However,
there are other routes that lead to a determinate system of relative prices
and that played an important role in the history of economic analysis.
Unless otherwise stated, the argument will be developed in terms of the
assumption that both products are useful, i.e. goods.

7. The first approach, which may be called « classical », calls in question that a situation in which there are « too few » processes of production can prevail for a long period of time. It is argued that the overproduction of certain products triggers off the search for alternative ways
to use or to produce the products, which will eventually result in a *system
of production*, in which the number of commodities is equal to the number
of processes of production in use. Figure 2 illustrates the basic idea in
the case where in addition to process y^1 a second process y^2 becomes
available. It is assumed that the proportions in which the two commodities are produced are sufficiently different so as to render possible
the matching of « supply » and « demand ». In the case depicted a stricly
positive price vector p^{12} obtains [7].

The exploration of new uses of known products and by-products tends

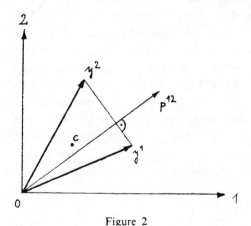

Figure 2

---

[7] The reader may easily check that the substitution of a process of production
for a disposal process does not of necessity entail strictly positive prices.

— 7 —

to increase both the number of commodities and that of the methods of production in existence. The search for new outlets is not restricted to goods in excess supply but applies also to bads for which no useful application has been found hitherto, the more so the higher are the costs of removing the potentially harmful substances. The search for methods of production that allow to turn former bads into goods, thereby increasing the profitability of business, was considered an important source of product and process innovations by Marx and Marshall.

Although some of the considerations of the classical economists on the subject seem to point in the direction of a tendency that brings the number of processes used into equality with the number of products produced, it cannot be claimed that this tendency is clearly expressed in their writings. In fact, there is no presumption that they were fully aware of the problem of underdeterminacy and other complications involved. It was not until Sraffa (1960) that a coherent formulation of the « classical standpoint » was provided. With regard to the case in which two products are jointly produced by a single process he argues: « In these circumstances there will be room for a second, parallel process.... Such a parallel process will not only be possible—it will be necessary if the number of processes is to be brought to equality with the number of commodities so that the prices may be determined » (1960. p. 43) ([8]).

8. According to the classical approach to the problem of joint production the investigation of square systems has a genuine significance. We may now ask what are the implications of variations in the proportion in which the two commodities are required for use. To this end, consider fig. 3 in which it is assumed that three processes are available to produce the two commodities. Obviously, a change in the proportion of net outputs required need not be accompanied by a change in relative prices. If the « new » requirements can be met with the « old » technique, i.e. by an activation of the same processes that were already in use, normal prices remain constant. This is the case, for example, if in fig. 3, starting from c, the amount of commodity 1 is increased without leading to a net product that falls outside the cone defined by the net output vectors y^1

([8]) The emergence of additional methods of production may be regarded as the outcome of competition, which is generally considered a process which enforces the introduction of new, cost reducing methods and new products. For an interpretation of Sraffa's statement along these lines see in particular various contributions by Schefold (most recently 1985).

— 8 —

and y^2 of processes 1 and 2. The required proportion can be obtained through an appropriate change in the levels of operation of the two processes without necessitating any change in prices (and income distribution); in the case depicted the price vector is given by p^{12}.

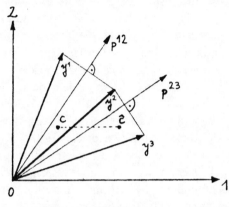

Figure 3

However, as soon as the activity level of process 1 has been reduced to zero and only process 2 is operated at a positive level, this possibility comes to an end. At this point the vector of prices is no longer fully determinate. (What can be said is that the price vector lies in the cone defined by p^{12} and p^{23}.) Without the introduction of a different, additional process, such as process 3, which produces relatively more of commodity 1 than process 2, further variations would result in an excess demand for commodity 1 and lead to a rise in the latter's (market) price. This rise in the relative price of commodity 1 is indeed a prerequisite to the introduction of process 3 which takes the place of process 1 that has just been superseded. In fact, as soon as the price ratio of the two commodities has risen to the level associated with p^{23}, processes 2 and 3 are equiprofitable and can be used side by side in order to meet the « new » requirements for use.

If the idea referred to in paragraph 7 should prove correct that competition sets in motion forces that tend to bring about the equality between the number of methods used and commodities produced, then the role of requirements for use in determining normal prices can make itself felt only through its influence on the choice of technique (or, alternatively, its influence on income distribution).

— 9 —

9. A radically different type of response characteristic of marginalist reasoning prior to the « marginalist revolution » starts from the premise that in the case of joint production the number of processes is generally smaller than the number of commodities. However, the premise of exogenously given proportions in which the commodities are wanted is weakened. To close the system of price determination a fundamentally new explanatory variable is introduced *ad hoc*: the notion of the demand for a commodity elastic with respect to the latter's (relative) price. Hence « demand » is envisaged to adapt to the rigid proportions in which the commodities are produced via flexible relative prices. This is illustrated in fig. 4, where $q = f(p)$ is the (relative) « demand function » of the two commodities that is associated with the unit level of production. The price vector that clears both markets is given by $\tilde{p}$; the slope of the demand curve in E gives the ratio of the two prices: $\operatorname{tg} \alpha = \tilde{p}_1/\tilde{p}_2$. A change in « demand », conceived as a change in the location and shape of the demand function, will entail a change in the price ratio. This kind of approach is to be found in the writings of authors such as Longfield, J.S. Mill, von Mangoldt and Jevons.

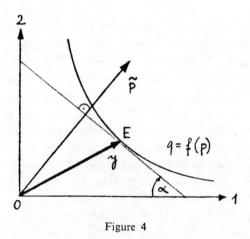

Figure 4

10. Finally, the assumption of rigid output proportions can be removed. It is a characteristic feature of « mature » marginalism that the principle of substitution is generalized to the sphere of production. In Marshall the proportions of (net) outputs are considered to be continuously variable within limits to be ascertained empirically. This combined with the notion of substitution among the various goods consumed as relative

— 10 —

prices vary leads to the generalized marginalist approach to the problem of value in the case of joint production. In fig. 5 it is assumed that there exist infinitely many processes of production which give rise to the net output frontier $\bar{y}y$. The schedule of relative demand then selects that particular process, y^k, which will actually be operated; the associated price vector is p^k. In equilibrium the marginal rate of substitution in consumption is equal to the marginal rate of substitution in production which in turn is equal to the reciprocal ratio of the two prices (tg β).

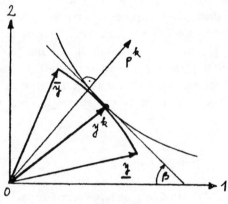

Figure 5

It deserves to be stressed that with continuous substitution the number of processes *operated* will generally fall short of the number of commodities produced. Hence both in the case in which there are « too few » processes (early marginalism) and in the case in which there are « too many » (mature marginalism), demand relationships are assumed to bridge the gap, i.e. to satisfy the condition « that our theory has as many equations as it has unknowns, neither more nor less » (Marshall, 1977, Mathematical Appendix, note XXI, p. 703) ([9]). This is in sharp contrast to the classical approach which supports the idea of a square system of production (and disposal). Demand schedules have no role to play in the determination of relative prices in such a framework ([10]).

Let us now have a closer look at earlier authors' contributions to the problem under consideration. The analytical framework developed in

---

([9]) See also Marshall (1977, note XVIII, p. 702). For a mathematical treatment of joint production with technically variable proportions, see Carlson (1956, chap. V).
([10]) See also Bharadwaj (1978), Arrow (1983, chap. 10) and Garegnani (1983).

— 11 —

the preceding paragraphs may be of some help to organize the material and focus on the main differences within and between different schools of economic analysis.

III. THE CLASSICAL APPROACH

11. Numerous examples of joint production and joint costs are reported in the early literature on husbandry, estate management and farming, in the writings of the mercantilists and physiocrats([11]). This is hardly surprising since the then most important sector of the economy and the major object of the analysis, i.e. agriculture, appears to be characterised by universal joint production. However, it was not until Adam Smith's *Wealth* that an attempt was made to transcend the purely descriptive treatment of the problem and to begin to deal with it in analytical terms. Therefore, Smith's contribution is the starting point of our historical inquiry.

1. *Adam Smith: the rule of « free goods »*

12. It is well known that for one page in Chapter VI of Book I of the *Wealth of Nations* (1776), « Of the Component Parts of the Price of Commodities », Smith appears to hold a pure labour theory of value:

> « In that early and rude state of society which precedes both the accumulation of stock and the appropriation of land, the proportion between the quantities of labour necessary for acquiring different *objects* seems to be the only circumstance which can afford any rule for exchanging them for one another » (Smith, 1976, Vol. I, p. 53; emphasis added).

This passage is immediately followed by the famous deer and beaver example, which describes the specific rule of barter for this hypothetical economy. Smith's argument has generally been interpreted as being concerned with the exchange relationships in a system with single-product

---

([11]) Cases of joint production are mentioned, for example, in Petty (1963, pp. 173-176 and 296; 1964, pp. 392-393 and 594-596), Cantillon (1931, pp. 61-62), Quesnay (1972, p. 11), Turgot (1970, p. 152), and Steuart (1966, pp. 134-135).

— 12 —

processes of production (^{12}). This interpretation is obvious, since Smith nowhere in this chapter mentions joint production. The careful reader will have noticed however that in the passage quoted Smith does not speak of « commodities » as in the chapter's title, but rather refers to « objects ». Although it cannot be excluded that this choice of words is purely accidental, it is perhaps possible to try an interpretation which suggests that it is not, i.e. that Smith used the term « object » on purpose.

To see this, let us ask why in Smith's example beavers and deer may be the objects of desire. In a society of hunters (and in most other societies as well) animals are the « source » of a multitude of use values. In fact, they provide different kinds of meat, furs, hides, bones, tendons, etc., some or all of which can be used either directly or indirectly to satisfy various wants. Each « object » represents thus a *compositum mixtum* of different use values or « goods » (and in addition possibly some bads), which accrue as joint products in the separation process.

Adam Smith was well aware of this. Yet he presupposes a patient reader with a good memory, for it is not until Chapter XI of Book I, « Of the Rent of Land », that the issue is taken up again:

> « The skins of the larger animals were the original materials of cloathing. Among nations of hunters and shepherds, therefore, whose food consists chiefly in the flesh of those animals, every man, *by providing himself with food, provides himself with the materials of more cloathing than he can wear.* If there was no foreign commerce, the greater part of them would be thrown away as *things of no value.* This was probably the case among the hunting nations of North America, before their country was discovered by the Europeans, with whom they now exchange their surplus peltry, for blankets, fire-arms, and brandy, which gives it *some value* » (Smith, 1976, Vol. I, p. 181; emphasis added).

This passage is interesting for several reasons. First, it witnesses of Smith's clear perception of the existence of joint-products processes of production. Secondly, it shows his awareness of the possibility that with joint production the proportions in which the products are produced

---

(^{12}) See, for example, Hollander (1973, chap. 4) and Samuelson (1977). In another paper Samuelson stresses that the case of joint production was well known to the classical writers (Samuelson, 1980, p. 576, fn.).

— 13 —

need not coincide with those in which they are wanted. Third, in it we encounter, possibly for the first time in the history of economic thought, the *rule of « free goods »* ([13]).

13. In the section « Third Sort » of Chapter XI of Book I Smith stresses that whether or not some of the joint products will be in excess supply depends on « the extent of their respective markets », which in turn depends on the level of « improvement » attained by society (Smith, 1976, Vol I, pp. 253-254). To give an example, whereas in Smith's time, i.e. prior to the introduction of freezing and canning techniques, the market for meat was almost everywhere confined to the producing country, the markets for the joint products wool and raw hides were much larger. For, Smith notes, these products « can easily be transported to distant countries, wool without any preparation, and raw hides with very little: and as they are the materials of many manufactures, other countries may occasion a demand for them, though that of the industry of the country which produces them might not occasion any » (p. 254). Therefore, in the « rude beginnings » there will be a tendency to an excess supply of meat due to an insufficient domestic demand and no foreign demand at all, combined with a relatively large foreign demand and a small domestic demand for the joint products wool and hides. In the course of the country's development, however, the domestic demand for meat will rise as a consequence of the growth in population and, other things equal, thus gradually reduce the (relative) superabundance of meat. In fact, it cannot be excluded that at some stage the role of a « free good » is passed on from meat to one (or several) of its joint products.

The discussion of joint production in the *Wealth* is clearly dominated by animal-reaning, yet it is not confined to it. However, the examples given all belong to primary production (agriculture, fishing and mining). Smith illustrates his investigation by means of historical material from Spain, Latin America, England, Ireland and Scotland. He reports some long run trends of relative prices of various joint products and tries to assess the impact of tariffs, export and import restrictions and other regulations concerning a particular product on the prices and quantities traded of its joint products.

([13]) Therefore Varri's contention (1980, pp. 10-11) that the rule of free goods is « completely extraneous » to the theory of value of « classical derivation » cannot be substantiated with reference to Adam Smith.

— 14 —

14. We have seen that apart from some rule of free goods Smith does not feel obliged to introduce essentially new patterns of explanation in the theory of value and distribution in order to cover the case of joint production. In particular, it seems clear that he considers prices determined independently of anything resembling demand schedules. The sort of approach illustrated by means of fig. 4 is not Smith's. He rather takes the required quantities of the different products as historically given, reflecting the current state of needs and wants, which itself is considered the result of a complex process of the formation of consumption habits that is insolubly intertwined with the growth in the division of labour and the change in the technical and social conditions of production. By analogy to the case of single production, Smith argues that the total « natural » price of the joint products has to cover total costs including wages, profits and rents at their normal levels. For example, he writes:

> « Whatever part of this price, therefore, is not paid by the wool and the hide, must be paid by the carcase. The less there is paid for the one, the more must be paid for the other. In what manner *this price* is to be divided upon the different parts of the beast, is indifferent to the landlords and farmers, provided it is all paid to them » (Smith, 1976, Vol. I, p. 259, emphasis added; similarly p. 175).

However, there is a fundamental weakness involved in Smith's whole approach, in that he seems to believe that the cost of production and thus the total price of the composite output can be ascertained independently of and prior to the manner, in which « *this price* is to be divided upon the different parts » of the produce. Whereas this idea holds true in the fictitious state of the « early and rude society », in which all products are assumed to be produced by labour alone, it ceases to hold in a system in which commodities are produced by means of commodities. Since, in general, the proportions in which the various products are produced differ from those in which they are used as means of production, a change in the prices of the products will generally also change the *total* price of the composite product. The result is that the prices of the outputs must be determined through the same mechanism and at the same time as the prices of the inputs and thus the total price of the joint products.

15. Smith's discussion of joint production seems to have left little impression on his contemporaries and successors. To mention but two

of his most important admirers and critics, both Ricardo and Marx in criticizing Smith's rent theory referred to some of the passages in the *Wealth* quoted above, but did not deal with his treatment of joint production (cf. Kurz, 1984). Interestingly, in Ricardo apart from incidental mentioning the entire problem is neglected. This is all the more remarkable, since it appears to be immediately obvious that the presence of joint production poses a serious problem to the labour theory of value. Indeed, it is not clear according to which criterion the labour expended in a process is to be apportioned among the jointly produced products ([14]).

We now turn to Karl Marx (1818-1883), who was a most attentive student of the history of technology and whose work provides us with a multitude of empirical examples of joint production. Since his theory of value and distribution shares the basic elements of the classical surplus approach, it is interesting to see how he tried to reconcile his empirical findings with the essentially single-products framework within which this approach had been formulated.

2. *Karl Marx: « excretions » of production and consumption*

16. During the preparatory phase to the publication of *Das Kapital* (Vol I, 1867), which extended to more than two decades, Marx was at least twice engaged with intensive studies of problems of technology and technical change. This is documented by two of his (altogether more than 180) excerpt-books, which can be dated to the years 1845 and 1851, when Marx was in Brussels and London, respectively (see Marx, 1981 and 1982). Whereas the former book contains essentially excerpts from and critical comments on writings of the English authors A. Ure and C. Babbage, the latter is basically devoted to German authors, such as J. Beckmann, K. Karmasch and in particular J.H.M. Poppe. Since the works referred to by Marx contain a comprehensive account of the knowledge of the time on the history of technology, machinery and industry, Marx was well acquainted with the evolution and the actual state of the

---

([14]) Whereas Smith's contribution is hardly ever mentioned in subsequent works, the example he gives of the development of trade between « new » and « old » countries figures prominently in the literature. It is dealt with, for example, by J.S. Mill, Cairnes and Marshall. Interestingly, Cairnes wants to restrict the economic relevance of joint production to « the industry of newly-settled countries » (Cairnes, 1967, p. 128). D. Stewart refers explicitly to Smith and criticizes that in the context of international trade the prices of the joint products are not regulated « according to what Mr. Smith calls the natural price » (Stewart, 1968, p. 8). See also paragraph 26 below.

— 16 —

techniques of production used in the different industries. Hence he also came across many cases of joint production from almost all branches of production: in the excerpt-books we find examples from agriculture, animal-rearing, mining, forestry, paper manufacturing, the chemical industries, the textile industries, mechanical engineering, etc. In the *Grundrisse* Marx refers to « accessory products » (Marx, 1970, p. 192); in the *Theories of Surplus Value* and *Capital* the problem is dealt with under the entries « waste » and « by-products » ([15]).

17. Even though Marx seems to have been better aware of the existence of multiple-product processes of production than many economists that preceded or succeeded him, in his theory of the general rate of profit and prices of production (cf. *Capital*, Vol. III, Part II) he did not pay attention to the phenomenon under discussion. The reason for this is to be found in Marx's presupposition that the joint products of a process can generally be divided into a main product, whose acquisition is desired and because of which the productive activity is called forth, and one or several by-products that may or may not be useful and that, at any rate, are of secondary economic interest. Marx's position, which consists both in stressing the empirical importance of joint production and in playing down its relevance for the more abstract parts of economic theory is best visible in Volume III of *Capital*. Interestingly, the subject is dealth with in Chapter 5, « Economy in the Employment of Constant Capital », and is introduced in the terms: « The so-called *waste* plays an *important role* in almost every industry » (Marx, 1959, p. 101; emphasis added). The « secondary products » are also dubbed « excretions of production » and are put on the same footing as the so-called « excretions of consumption ».

Marx then goes on to argue that the recycling of the waste is stimulated by the « rising prices of raw materials » and presupposes (*a*) the existence of large amounts of such waste, « such as are available only in large-scale production », (*b*) « improved machinery », and (*c*) « scientific progress, particularly of chemistry, which reveals the useful properties of such waste ».

([15]) For instance, in Vol. I of *Capital*, Marx mentions an example from mining: « Silver is seldom found native; however it occurs in special quartz that is separated from the lode with comparative ease and contains mostly 40-90% silver; or it is contained, in smaller quantities, in copper, lead and other ores which in themselves are worthwhile working » (1954, p. 142, fn.). For further references to examples of joint production in Marx, see Kurz (1984, Section 7).

— 17 —

The fulfilment of the first two conditions is illustrated by historical material from the flax, the cotton and the silk industries (cf. pp. 101-102 and 109); as regards the third condition Marx writes:

« The most striking example of utilising waste is furnished by the chemical industry. It utilises not only its own waste, for which it finds new uses, but also that of many other industries. For instance, it converts the formerly almost useless gas-tar into aniline dyes, alizarin, and more recently, even into drugs » (p. 102) ([16]).

However, as Marx emphasizes, in the present context economy in the employment of constant capital is not only effectuated through the recycling of waste-products but also through the prevention of their occurrence, « that is to say, the reduction of excretions of production *to a minimum*, and the immediate utilisation *to a maximum* of all raw and auxiliary materials required in production » (p. 103; emphasis added). On the premise that the employment of the constant capital could be *perfectly* economized, in the sense of Marx, the phenomenon of joint production would disappear and we would comfortably be back in the framework of a single-product system of production. Marx appears to see strong tendencies at work that point in this direction. Indeed, he speaks of « the capitalist's fanatical insistence on economy in means of production », enforced by competition, « [t]hat nothing is lost or wasted and the means of production are consumed only in the manner required by production itself » (op. cit., p. 83).

18. In order to throw some additional light on Marx's position it is perhaps possible to draw an analogy between his discussion and Sraffa's argument concerning the residual scrap of a durable instrument of production that results as a by-product of the process using this instrument in its last year. Sraffa writes:

« If the scrap (metal, timber, etc.) is interchangeable in use with some other material already accounted for, it simply assumes the

---

([16]) In the *Grundrisse* Marx stresses that one of the characteristic features of modern society consists in its drive « to explore nature in order to discover new useful properties of things » (1970, p. 312; my translation). A similar view was expressed already by Babbage (1832), whose concern was also with the economic utilisation of by-products.

— 18 —

price of the latter without need of an additional process; if it is not completely interchangeable (e.g. scrap iron as compared with pig iron), then there will be room for two processes, producing the same commodity (e.g. steel), but differing in the proportions in which they use the two types of material » (Sraffa, 1960, p. 64, fn. 1).

Marx, on the other hand, refers « to the reconversion of the excretions of production, the so-called waste, into new elements of production, either of the same, or of some other line of industry » (Marx, 1959, p. 79).

The important point is that both in Sraffa's treatment of scrap in systems with fixed capital and in Marx's treatment of waste the joint products that occur are considered close substitutes of raw or auxiliary materials provided by other processes of production, and that therefore the number of processes operated tends to equality with the number of commodities produced. Hence a *determinate* system of prices of production can always be found and there is no need to have recourse to additional determinants other than the technical conditions of production and the real wage rate (the rate of profits). Yet this conclusion is *not* equivalent to the one *implicitly* drawn by Marx in his theoretical investigation that the system of single-product industries is an appropriate framework of the analysis.

To conclude, an objection could be raised against Marx's distinction between what is the main product of a process and what are the by-products. As we have seen, such a distinction is not possible *a priori*, if at all. Yet Marx apparently starts from a system of production, i.e. sets of commodities and processes, that is *actually* in use and in which the distinction is already decided. He then goes on to discuss, one by one, the introduction of new methods of production or new commodities and delineates the possible consequences for the system as a whole. The presence of « waste-products » is essentially considered an insufficiency of the capitalist's control over the production process that acts as a stimulus to improve the technical conditions of production and the organisation of the labour process and to look for profitable outlets for the remaining waste. Marx's investigation of joint production is thus embedded in an analysis which focusses on the evolution of the system of production and which attempts to lay bare its driving forces. In contrast to present-day joint production theory, whose main concern is with the « static » properties of models with multiple-product processes, Marx stresses the specific « dynamic » features of systems that involve some jointness of production. However, in terms of a theory of the rate of profits and prices of production under conditions of general joint production Marx has little to offer.

We now come to review the development of the supply and demand approach to the theory of value with special emphasis on the problem of joint production. We begin with a discussion of contributions prior to the « marginalist revolution ». The first author to be dealt with is J.H. v. Thünen (1783-1850), whose *Der isolierte Staat*, published in 1826, is particularly interesting because of the practical examples provided and the economic conclusions drawn.

IV. EARLY CONTRIBUTIONS TO THE DEMAND AND SUPPLY APPROACH

1. *Johann Heinrich von Thünen: joint production in the isolated state*

19. A major concern of Thünen in his *magnum opus* was with the optimal allocation of economic activities around a town that serves as the market centre, trading urban goods for the rural products of labour and land. For this purpose he elaborated the famous scheme of rings of specialization. In modern reformulations Thünen's space model has generally been interpreted in terms of single-product processes of production (see, for example, Samuelson, 1983). Though not without interest in themselves, these versions fail to reflect a most important aspect of Thünen's reasoning, which derives precisely from the predominance of joint production in the primary sector of the economy.

Thünen argues that in general more than one productive activity will be located in each zone. This is due to the fact that it frequently proves advantageous to organise production in such a way that one activity's output(s) is (are) some parallel activity's necessary input(s). For example, the ring immediately around the town is specialized, in addition to hard-to-transport and quickly perishable vegetables and fruits, in the production of milk, which requires hay and straw for feed and litter. In this ring « [g]rain will be grown only for the sake of its by-product of straw » (Thünen, 1966, p. 14) ([17]). This example makes it clear that the main product cannot be ascertained *a priori*.

Manure is both a joint effect of the consumption process and a joint

---

([17]) The translations from Thünen's work are mine.

— 20 —

product of animal-breeding. For the inhabitants of the town the manure is a « bad » that has to be disposed of: « The citizens want to get rid of the dung even if they do not receive anything in exchange for it, but have to pay for its removal » (p. 209). For the farmers however it is a « good » that is indispensible to production. In remoter districts manure is essentially made from straw. Thünen provides empirical estimates for the straw output of various types of crops, such as wheat, rye, barley and oats (pp. 58-59 and §§ 15 and 16) and attempts to calculate the amount of manure the respective grain crop returns by way of its straw.

A central issue of *Der isolierte Staat* is the fact that the quality of land may be transformed by productive activity, i.e. land is not a fixed, immutable endowment, unaffected by the production process in which it is used (cf. p. 57). Indeed, land can be regarded as part of the annual intake of a process, and qualitatively different land as part of the annual joint output of the process, of which the more conspicuous part consists of the marketable commodities that are the primary object of the process. Thünen deals at length with devices that are designed to re-establish or improve the original fertility of the soil, such as crop rotation and three-fallowing (see especially §§ 14-15 and 21-23).

Forestry yields timber and firewood (§ 19); Thünen points out that the proportion in which the two are produced depends, among other things, on the age at which the trees are cut (p. 196). Distilling (§ 29), i.e. the processing of grain and its conversion into alcohol, is best located in the sixth ring. Thünen adds: « The waste products from distilling can be most profitably used for stock feed; and as this ring depends on livestock anyway, and grain and firewood have their lowest possible value, everything is in favour of distilling » (pp. 275-276). He discusses sheep farming (§ 30) and points out that there is some variability both among the inputs and the outputs. In particular, different qualities of wool, such as coarse and fine wool, and mutton and different proportions among the jointly produced commodities can be obtained by breeding different kinds of sheep, keeping them differently and using different food.

The next author who deserves mentioning is Mountifort Longfield (1802-1894). In his *Lectures on Political Economy*, published in 1834, new considerations on the problem were presented.

2. *Mountifort Longfield: supply and demand regulate prices*

20. It has been widely acknowledged that the major novelty in Longfield's approach to the problem of value and distribution consists in his

— 21 —

attempt to determine the price of a product (as well as the price of a « factor service ») by the « opposing forces » of demand and supply and by building up the notion of a demand schedule on an argument that can be interpreted as an early statement of marginal utility theory (cf. Schumpeter, 1954, p. 465) ([18]).

Joint production is introduced as « a complexity necessarily produced by the manner in which the business of life is conducted ». However, even though it renders « difficult of comprehension » some questions respecting value, it does not, according to Longfield, affect the truth of the « elementary principles » of value theory, which can be summarized as follows:

> « The demand and supply regulate the price, and the cost of production influences it, by confining the supply to such a quantity as can be sold at a price sufficient to repay the cost of production » (Longfield, 1971, p. 245).

How, then, do these principles operate in that case, « often » to be found in reality, in which « the same land, labour, and capital, are ... employed at the same time in the production of several different commodities » (p. 245)?

Whereas with single production demand and supply regulates the price of each single commodity, with joint production it « regulates the price *both of the whole and of each part* » (p. 245; emphasis added). Accordingly, in contrast to Smith, Longfield allows for the possibility that the *total* price and not just the prices of the component parts may be subject to variations due to changes in the factors determining supply and demand. In the special case, however, in which the price of the whole is taken as given,

> « any circumstance that increases the demand for one part ... will diminish the price of the other parts. For as the cost of production has not increased, the principle of competition will prevent the price of all the parts from being more than the cost of production. And as the demand for some part has increased, its price, and its supply will also increase; but this being *necessarily* attended with an increased supply of the other parts, for which there has

---

([18]) Interestingly, in his appraisal of Longfield's contribution Schumpeter does not mention the latter's analysis of joint production.

— 22 —

been no increased demand, will diminish the price of those parts »
(pp. 245-246; emphasis added).

21. The key to an understanding of Longfield's argument is to be
found in the assumption that an increased supply of one part is « *necessarily* attended with an increased supply of the other parts ». His argument is thus *implicitly* based on the premise that only one process of
production is available to produce the two (or several) products. He
thus seems to follow a line of reasoning that is similar to the one illustrated
in fig. 4. Since the number of processes is smaller than the number of
commodities, whose prices are to be ascertained, demand relationships
have to step in to close the system.

As we have seen above (cf. paragraph 7), the *economic* rationale of
this assumption is not at all clear. In fact, Longfield himself contributes
to amplify the doubts as to whether this assumption is appropriate by
pointing out that several of the commodities produced in different joint
production processes serve as close substitutes, i.e. essentially represent
the same use values. Hence, the mere existence of joint production in
itself cannot be taken to imply that without demand relationships the
price system is underdetermined. In his discussion of the « business of
farming » Longfield refers to a standard example of the time in which
he wrote, i.e. the introduction of turnip husbandry. Its direct effect consists in a reduction in the cost of production of sheep (and of wheat), its
indirect one in a decline in the prices of wool and mutton, the main
products of sheep-rearing. The price of mutton (wool) will however decline less (more) than proportionately, since mutton, serving as a close
substitute for beef, at a lower relative price will obtain an increased
demand. At constant cost of production of cattle, « beef sustains a slight
fall of price, while ... hides, cheese, and butter, must experience a corresponding rise » (pp. 246-247).

22. Finally it is worth mentioning that Longfield appears to have
been the first author to reckon transport activities among joint production processes. He writes:

> « Thus the freight of goods outwards and homewards ought to
> pay the expense of the voyage in and out, with the wear and tear
> of the ship, usual profits, &c. If, then, any circumstance connected
> with the state of trade, usually creates a greater demand for freight
> homewards, it will have a proportional effect in diminishing the
> freight of a cargo outwards » (p. 246).

— 23 —

It is well known that the notion of the transport system as a multiple-product industry was reintroduced into analytical economics several decades later in the famous controversy about railway rates, contributed to by F.Y. Edgeworth and A.C. Pigou, among others ([19]).

An approach to joint production similar to Longfield's was advocated by John Stuart Mill (1806-1873), to whose analysis we now turn.

3. *John Stuart Mill: an « anterior » law of value*

23. J.S. Mill considered himself a direct lineal descendant of the classical economists, in particular Ricardo, wishing to restate their doctrine in an elaborate form. In is *Principles of Political Economy*, first published in 1848, the theory of value is given a central place in economic analysis. Interestingly, Mill claims: « Happily, there is nothing in the laws of Value which remains for the present or any future writer to clear up; the theory of the subject is complete » (Mill, 1965, p. 465). Precipitate as it may seem at first sight, this bold assertion in Book III, Chapter 1, becomes incomprehensible once it is confronted with Chapter 16, whose very title « On Some Peculiar Cases of Value » suffices to rouse the suspicion that the theory of the subject cannot be « complete » ([20]). Indeed, Mill's own awareness of « anomalies » in the theory of value and, more important, his suggestions how to tackle them prepared the ground for the abandonment of the classical approach and the development of a fundamentally different theory.

24. One of these « peculiar » cases is joint production, which is introduced by Mill as follows: « It sometimes happens that two different commodities have what may be termed a joint cost of production. ... For example, coke and coal-gas are both produced from the same material, and by the same operation » (pp. 582-583). Mill's subsequent discussion makes it clear that he shares the by now familiar premise of a rigid output proportion, i.e. he does not allow for a multiplicity of alternative processes

---

([19]) Steedman (1984. p. 13) points out that a single bus or train, which starts form Stop Zero and proceeds to Stops 1, 2, ..., n produces $[n(n + 1)/2]$ different possible passenger journeys; if it then makes the return trip, a total of $[n(n + 1)]$ « products » will have been produced.

([20]) Interestingly, G.J. Stigler confirmed Mill's contention precisely with respect to the latter's treatment of joint production: « Mill clearly formulated the problem of joint production. ... He gave the complete and correct solution » (1965, p. 8). As will become clear below, this opinion is difficult to sustain.

— 24 —

to produce the same products. As regards price determination Mill's view is very close to Longfield's:

> « Cost of production can have nothing to do with deciding the value of the associated commodities relatively to each other. It only decides their joint value. ... A principle is wanting to apportion the expenses of production between the two. Since cost of production here fails us, *we must revert to a law of value anterior to cost of production, and more fundamental, the law of demand and supply.* The law is, that the demand for a commodity varies with its value, and that the value adjusts itself so that the demand shall be equal to the supply » (p. 583; emphasis added).

The equilibrating mechanism between demand and supply is seen to work exclusively in terms of variations of relative prices, since the route *via* an adaptation of the system of production to society's needs and wants is closed *ex hypothesi*. In Mill's words:

> « Equilibrium will be attained when the demand for each article fits so well with the demand for the other, that the quantity required of each is exactly as much as is generated in producing the quantity required of the other. If there is any surplus or deficiency on either side; if there is a demand for coke, and not a demand for all the gas produced along with it, or *vice versa*; the values and prices of the two things will so readjust themselves that both shall find a market » (p. 584).

Mill appears to be convinced that in general a unique and stable equilibrium with strictly positive prices for all goods exists.

25. Apparently, the criticism leveled at Longfield also applies to Mill. Neither of the two provides any justification of the strong assumption, on which the entire argument rests, that there do not exist (or come into being) technological alternatives to produce or use the joint products. Furtheron, the « division of explanation » of price determination advocated by Mill, between the classical cost of production approach and the demand and supply approach, attaching to the latter the subsidiary role of ascertaining the relative prices of the joint products, given their « joint value » which is decided by cost of production, can be sustained in a fantastically singular case only: the separation of the analysis into two

— 25 —

distinct stages presupposes that all jointly produced products are pure consumption goods that do not enter the means of production of any process.

26. Finally, it is interesting to notice that Mill concludes his investigation in Chapter 16 by drawing an analogy to the case of international trade. He writes that « the mode in which, when cost of production fails to be applicable, *the other principle steps in to supply the vacancy*, is worthy of particular attention, as we shall find in [Chapter 18, "Of International Values"] that something very similar takes place in cases of much greater moment » (p. 584; emphasis added). Indeed, from an analytical point of view a country's foreign trade (which is assumed to be balanced) can be regarded as an infinite set of fictitious joint production processes, by means of which a number of commodity inputs, i.e. *exports*, are turned into a number of commodity outputs, i.e. *imports* (see the hints in Mill, pp. 602 and 608; see also Parrinello, 1970).

An interesting author in the succession of J.S. Mill is Hans von Mangoldt (1824-1868), whose *Grundriss der Volkswirtschaftslehre* was published in 1863.

4. *Hans von Mangoldt: the derived « supply function »*

27. According to T.W. Hutchison, « Mangoldt's *Grundriss* should certainly be ranked with the three celebrated works of 1871 and 1874, and perhaps *above* two of them » (Hutchison, 1973, p. 179, fn. 2) [21]. Mangoldt's analysis of joint production is to be found in § 67, « The Law of Connected Prices », of Chapter 3 of the *Grundriss*. He distinguishes (p. 54) between two cases of connected production, i.e. pure joint production (or joint production in the technical sense) and what may be called « competing », « alternative » or « rival » (Edgeworth) production which derives from the fact that a firm's (given) productive equipment may be used for several purposes.

As regards the first case Mangoldt uses a mathematical-geometrical method to render precise Mill's approach; for a detailed discussion of his method see Schneider (1960) and Kurz (1984). The upshot of Man-

---

[21] If the ranking of the four authors is to be decided according to the criterion of whether they contributed to an analysis of joint production, then Mangoldt and Jevons have to be considered superior to Menger and Walras; see sections V.1 and V.3.

— 26 —

goldt's reasoning consists in the construction of a « supply function » for one of the commodities conditional on the presence of market equilibrium for the other, a concept we shall encounter again in Marshall. The intersection of this function with the demand function of the respective commodity gives the set of equilibrium prices. It is worth mentioning that Mangoldt does not rule out that the equilibrium price of a product may be zero, i.e. the product is a « free good » (p. 51); nor does he fail to point out the possibility of mutiple equilibria (p. 63).

28. Interestingly, Mangoldt shares Mill's view that the approach under consideration represents a continuation of rather than a fundamental break with the classical theory of value. To indicate the price that equilibrates demand and supply Mangoldt also uses Smith and Ricardo's notion of the « natural price » (p. 47); and in the context of the discussion of joint production he refers to the « centre of gravity of price » which settles down « where the supply is equal to the existing demand » (p. 60). However, this interpretation cannot be sustained, since neither in Smith nor in Ricardo did demand schedules play any role in determining « natural » prices.

Whereas the theorists discussed so far wrongly conceived their contributions as elaborating on the classical approach, the latter was openly blamed to be a dead end in the « marginalist revolution ». The next author whom we have to deal with is William Stanley Jevons (1835-1882), whose *Theory of Political Economy*, first published in 1871, contains a frontal assault on the classical doctrine.

V. THE « MARGINALIST REVOLUTION » AND AFTER

1. *William Stanley Jevons: marginal utility determines prices*

29. Among the « mazy and preposterous assumptions » Jevons (1965, p. xiii) blames the classical economists for, the assumption of single-product industries of production ranks high. It is entirely unrealistic, since « cases of joint production ... form the general rule, to which it is difficult to point out any clear or important exceptions » (p. 198), and it is the source of fundamental misconceptions that render the whole classical analysis worthless. Because of their « obsession » with single production the classics failed to distinguish between *commodities* and « *discom-*

modities », i.e. « substances or things which possess the quality of causing inconvenience or harm » (p. 58). This in turn made them overlook the fact that there may be such things as *zero* or *negative* values. The latter however can be properly understood only if utility-disutility considerations are introduced into the analysis and « demand » is taken into account in the determination of relative prices and income distribution. The deficiency of the classical approach to the problem of value and distribution can even be seen in a more direct way. Indeed, its very basis, the labour theory of value, breaks down, since in the case of joint production « [i]t is impossible to divide up the labour and say that so much is expended on producing X, and so much on Y » (p. 200) ([22]).

30. Jevons starts his investigation with an explicit reference to Mill's discussion, which he calls « one of the most interesting chapters of his *Principles of Political Economy* » (p. 197). Yet he accuses Mill of the fallacy involved in his idea that he is reverting to an « anterior law of value », the law of demand and supply, « the fact being that in introducing the cost of production principle, *he had never quitted the laws of supply and demand at all*. The cost of production is only one circumstance which governs supply, and thus indirectly influences values » (p. 198: emphasis added) ([23]).

Jevons expounds his approach in terms of the same simple example already used by most of his predecessors, in which two products, X and Y, are produced in a *fixed* proportion by means of a *single* process, where

---

([22]) Essentially the same point is made by Wicksell with respect to durable capital goods used for different purposes, i.e. intertemporal joint production. He concludes that it is « just as absurd to ask how much labour is invested in either one or the other annual use as it is to try to find out what part of a pasture goes into wool and what part into mutton » (1934, p. 260). As to the determination of the quantities of labour « embodied » in jointly produced commodities in the case of square systems, see Sraffa (1960, Chap. IX).

([23]) Marshall's comment on Jevons's attack on Mill reads: « The criticism seems to contain an important truth; though the wording of the last part is open to objection. If it had been made in Mill's time he would probably have accepted it; and would have withdrawn the word « anterior » as not expressing his real meaning. The « cost of production principle » and the « final utility » principle are undoubtedly component parts of the one all-ruling law of supply and demand; each may be compared to one blade of a pair of scissors. When one blade is held still, and the cutting is effected by moving the other, we may say with careless brevity that the cutting is done by the second; but the statement is not one to be made formally, and defended deliberately » (Marshall, 1977, p. 675). However, in a later publication Marshall himself appears to be subject to the criticism put forward against Jevons. In *Industry and Trade*, referring to the case of fixed net output proportions, he states: « Cost of production would have no part in determining their relative prices: that would lie wholly in the hands of demand » (1970, p. 192).

— 28 —

homogeneous labour is the only input. Yet Jevons seems to take the particular case of fixed proportions for the general one; indeed he writes that « in cases of joint production there is no such freedom [to vary the ratio in which the two products are generated] » (p. 200). He then defines the increment of utility of an increment of the composite product. Let dl be the increment of labour that yields an additional dx units of commodity X and dy units of commodity Y, then what he calls « the aggregate ratio of utility to labour » is given by

$$\frac{du_1}{dx}\frac{dx}{dl} + \frac{du_2}{dy}\frac{dy}{dl},$$

where du_1/dx and du_2/dy are the « degrees of utility » of dx and dy. In the circumstances given relative prices cannot be determined exclusively in terms of the conditions of production:

« It is plain that we have no equation arising out of these conditions of production, so that the ratio of exchange of X and Y will be governed *only* by the degrees of utility. ... Before we can obtain any ratios of exchange we must have the further equation between the degrees of utility of X and Y, namely, $du_1/du_2 = dy/dx$ » (pp. 200-201; emphasis added).

As it stands, Jevons's argument contains several flaws. What he appears to be aiming at is what is known as *Gossen's (second) Law*, according to which in market equilibrium the exchange ratio between any two commodities is equal to the ratio of the marginal utilities of the respective commodities. Hence, what was called the relative demand function in fig. 4 can now be interpreted as an *indifference curve* of some « representative » consumer. Obviously, contrary to what Jevons maintains, the equilibrium price ratio is not only governed by marginal utilities, but also by the « supply side », i.e. the proportion in which the commodities are produced [24].

31. In the remaining part of his discussion Jevons stresses that in order « to solve the subject fully » (p. 202), « negative utilities » associated with

---

[24] In Taussig's terms the apportionment of the total price between the joint products « depends on the relative demand for them, or, ... on their marginal vendibility » (1929, p. 214; emphasis added).

— 29 —

certain joint products have to be admitted, leading to the phenomenon of « negative values ». In the Section on « Negative or Zero Value » he states:

> « [T]here cannot be the least doubt that people often labour, or pay money to other labourers, in order to get rid of things, and they would not do this unless such things were hurtful, that is, had the opposite quality to utility—disutility. ... Reflection soon shows, in short, that no inconsiderable part of the values with which we deal in practical economics must be *negative values* » (p. 127; see also pp. 128-129 and 202).

Yet a proper analysis of the role of disposal activities in the determination of prices (cf. fig. 1) is not provided by him. In particular, there is no discussion of whether the presence of such activities renders the system « square ».

Closely related to the problem of « bads » is that of pollution and externalities, which can be considered a more indirect evidence of joint production. Jevons was well aware of this. For example, he argues that the waste products of chemical firms are often « fouling the rivers and injuring the neighbouring estates » (p. 202) ([25]).

32. We have seen that earlier supply and demand theorists in order to close the price system introduced *ad hoc* the principle of substitution in consumption in terms of demand schedules. Jevons, in contrast, was particularly concerned with giving this principle a choice theoretical foundation centered around the notion of marginal utility. The twin principle of substitution in production however had yet to be elaborated. This led G.J. Stigler to the judgement: Jevons's « entire analysis is rendered superficial and worthless by the assumption that the jointly produced commodities can be produced only in a fixed ratio » (Stigler, 1941, p. 18) ([26]). The next author is not subject to this sort of criticism. The author under discussion is Alfred Marshall, whose *Principles of Economics* were published in 1890.

([25]) It is interesting to notice that Irving Fisher (1965, p. 120) criticized Jevons on the grounds that discommodities are never of great importance and need receive no special attention. Present-day environmental problems contradict sharply Fisher's opinion.

([26]) Recall that Mill with his basically identical approach was given the credit by Stigler for having provided « the complete and correct solution » (cf. footnote ([20])).

— 30 —

2. *Alfred Marshall: the generalized principle of substitution*

33. In Chapter VI of Book V of the *Principles* Marshall defines as joint products « things which cannot *easily* be produced separately » (Marshall, 1977, p. 321, emphasis added; similarly 1970, p. 181). However, to begin with, Marshall gives a geometrical illustration of the price determination in the « classic » two-products-fixed-proportion case. Essentially, his approach is identical with that of Mangoldt's.

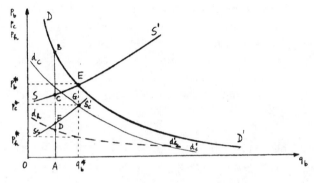

Figure 6

In fig. 6 let SS' be the supply curve for bullocks which yield carcases (meat) and hides (leather); this supply curve is obtained by horizontal summation of all bullock-producing firms' supply curves. Let $d_c d_c'$ be the demand curve for bullocks by carcase users and $d_h d_h'$ the demand curve by hide users, respectively. The total demand curve for bullocks DD' is obtained by vertical summation of these two demand curves. Let DD' cut SS' in E. Then in equilibrium q_b^* bullocks are produced and sold at price p_b^* of which p_c^* goes for the carcase and p_h^* for the hide. Let AB cut SS' in C. From CA, the unit supply price of OA bullocks, cut off CF equal to DA; then F is a point on the *derived supply curve* for carcases. For if it is assumed that the selling price of hides obtained from OA bullocks is always equal to the corresponding demand price DA, it follows that since it costs CA to produce each of OA bullocks there remains a price $CA - CF = CA - DA$, that is FA, to be borne by each of the carcases obtained from OA bullocks. Then $s_c s_c'$, the locus of F, is the (derived) supply curve for carcases; it cuts the respective demand curve $d_c d_c'$ in G, which gives the equilibrium price p_c^* of carcases. Clearly, Marshall's is a partial equilibrium analysis: « Other things must be assumed to be equal (that is, the supply schedule for the whole process of production must be assumed to remain in force and so must the demand schedule for each of the joint products except that to be isolated)» (p. 322) [27].

34. Marshall then goes on to argue: «There are *very few* cases of joint products the cost of production of both of which together is exactly the same as that of one of them alone». Yet if it is possible to modify the proportions of these products,

> «we can ascertain what part of the whole expense of the process of production would be saved, by so modifying these proportions as slightly to diminish the amount of one of the joint products without affecting the amounts of the others. That part of the expense is the expense of production of the marginal element of that product; it is the supply price of which we are in search» (p. 323; similarly Marshall, 1970, p. 193).

The examples Marshall gives to illustrate the flexibility of net output proportions may be grouped in two principal ones: one where the existing technology allows variable proportions, the other where variable proportions are the intended result of innovations (i.e. induced technical progress). Marshall sees strong incentives to render flexible the output proportions. The «stimulus» to innovations is particularly obvious in the case where some of the joint products are discommodities. Since cases of free disposal are considered «exceptional» by Marshall there is an interest on the part of firms to abolish «wasteful» production.

Thus Marshall arrives at the generalized marginalist approach to the theory of value centered around the notions of substitution in consumption and production. This warrants the application of the «general principle», according to which «the relative proportions of the joint products of a business should be so modified that the *marginal expenses of production* of either product should be equal to its *marginal demand price*» (1977, pp. 327-328; emphasis added). Figure 5 illustrates the argument.

35. Some *dynamic* aspects characteristic of new industries that exhibit considerable jointness of production are discussed in greater detail in

---

[27] For a thorough criticism of partial equilibrium analysis and particularly its Marshallian variant see Sraffa (1925).

— 32 —

section 2 of Chapter IV of Book II of *Industry and Trade*. It is argued that the massive treatment of by-products strengthens the tendencies to an increase in the size of the business unit. Moreover, several examples of induced process and product innovations are given:

« Something which was apparently almost valueless is suddenly made the foundation of an important product, either through a new technical discovery or through the rise of a new demand. .... Some of the by-products of petroleum are subtle and costly chemical compounds, for pharmaceutical and other uses; and they demand the thought and care of highly trained professional analysts. The same is true in regard to several by-products of the "heavy" chemical industries. ... In all such industries, new products are frequently coming to the front; and a business, which has abundant capital and is controlled by men with scientific interests and large faculty for high enterprise, may constantly introduce into the world not only *new methods*. but also *new things* ».

With special reference to the colour industry, Marshall continues:

« Nothing is hastily dropped; every intermediate product and every by-product is tried in various combinations, with the hope of getting some new result of value in some industrial process, or of getting at an old result by a shorter or more economical method. Such work as this can be effectively done only by a business that can afford to work long and patiently at each of a vast number of problems » (pp. 238-240; emphasis added).

Apparently, Marshall was particularly aware of the technological and organisational dynamism inherent in modern industry and the·role played by joint production. In this respect he is perhaps closest to Marx, who emphasized the scientific and technological revolutions characteristic of the capitalist mode of production.

However, by far the most important work in the last century on progress made in the economic utilisation of waste and refuse and the accessory products from manufactures was written by a non-economist. P.L. Simmonds' *Waste Products and Undeveloped Substances* (1873) is a fascinating testimony of the technological dynamism characteristic of modern

— 33 —

society ([28]). In some five hundred pages the author provides innumerable empirical examples of joint-products processes and traces sequences of product and process innovations. The *leitmotiv* of the study can be summarized as « dirt is only matter in a wrong place » and it is the task of ingenious people to find out the right place. It is beyond the scope of this paper to discuss in more detail Simmonds' contribution. However, in case the reader is not yet convinced that there is no such thing as single production and that this fact is of the utmost importance for an understanding of technological change he or she is asked to consult the book by Simmonds.

3. *Early contributions to general equilibrium theory and joint production*

36. In contradistinction to Jevons his celebrated contemporaries Menger and Walras paid little attention to the issue under discussion. Apart from incidental references to joint costs the problem is hardly dealt with in Menger's *Grundsätze der Volkswirtschaftslehre*, first published in 1871. Walras in his *Eléments*, first published in 1874, defines productive processes in such a way that little room is left, if any, for joint production (see Walras, 1954. p. 73). Therefore, it is not surprising that the equations of production in Part IV of the *Eléments*, « Theory of Production », are exclusively concerned with single production ([29]). Essentially the same limitation characterizes Pareto's *Manuel d'Economie Politique*, published in 1909, despite the author's remark « that it is not necessary that each good have its own cost of production » (Pareto, 1971, p. 244). G. Cassel, another influential protagonist of general equilibrium theory, in the *Theory of Social Economy*, the German version of which was published in 1918, devotes a few pages to joint production (see Cassel, 1967, Chap. III, § 13). Scrutiny shows that his treatment does not improve on the discussion in Marshall. We may thus conclude that the early developments of general equilibrium theory widely neglected the problem under consideration.

37. Interestingly, K. Wicksell, a most important author in the Austrian tradition, deals with the problem under the heading « Pricing under Imper-

---

([28]) I am grateful to Ian Steedman for drawing my attention to this book; he has pointed out to me that it was owned by Jevons.

([29]) It is worth mentioning that in Appendix II (p. 483, fn. 3) Walras refers to that section in Mangoldt's *Grundriss*, which deals with joint production. Yet Walras abstains from a discussion of the issue. Cases of joint costs are hinted at in several places of the *Eléments* (see, e.g., p. 212); in §§ 378-379 the problem of overhead costs is dealt with.

— 34 —

fect Competition » in section 6 of Chapter II of Volume I of his *Vorle-sungen über Nationalökonomie auf der Grundlage des Marginalprinzips* (1913), an English edition of which was published in 1934. Referring to some German authors, such as F. Neumann, he points out that pheno-mena of joint supply « have been taken by some economists as a pretext for an attack ([30]) on the whole classical theory of exchange » (1934, p. 84). While he does not subscribe to the theory of pricing developed by these authors, which he calls « very peculiar », he supports their critical atti-tude towards the classical approach and insists that in cases of joint production prices are regulated by demand subject to the familiar condi-tion that the sum total of the value of the composite output has to cover all costs of production, including profits at the ordinary rate of interest on the value of capital. He illustrates his argument in terms of an example that was already used by F. Neumann, i.e. the joint supply of town flats. If, before the invention of lifts, town flats commanded a lower rent the higher up they were, then this can be explained as follows: « the rent of the different flats is simply regulated by demand, that is to say, mainly by their respective comfort and suitability for various purposes; or, in the last resort, by their marginal utility » (p. 85). Furthermore, Wicksell stresses that the tendency to build higher and higher buildings and thereby to increase the jointness of supply of housing and offices in the cities is due to the scarcity of land for the buildings to stand on: « The high cost of building sites in towns has led, as is well known, to the erection in recent times of lofty steel and glass structures on the model of the American skyscrapers; otherwise all buildings would presumably be erected only one or at most two storeys high—as in country districts » (p. 85).

VI. CONCLUSION

The problem of joint production played a significant role in the evolu-tion of economic thought since the advent of the classical school. In view of the empirical examples provided it is perhaps possible to confirm Jevons's contention that joint production is the general case. Yet this finding does not warrant the abandonment of the classical approach to the

---

([30]) « Pretext for an attack » is the somewhat misleading translation of the Ger-man term « Angriffswaffe », a literal translation of which would be « weapon of offence ». Wicksell was convinced that the classical authors were justly critized in the case of joint production; he did not accept however the alternative developed by Neumann and others.

— 35 —

problem of value and distribution, as Jevons and his fellow neoclassical economists were inclined to think. Indeed, the basic premise upon which their particular refutation of the classical approach rests proves untenable: it cannot be presumed that with joint production the number of processes operated will necessarily fall short of the number of products produced whose prices have to be ascertained. When all production and disposal processes are properly taken into account the problem of underdeterminacy tends to vanish. Hence it appears to be natural to start from square systems of production and treat the case in which the number of products exceeds the number of processes as a special case rather than the other way round. This implies that there is no need to introduce entirely new explanatory variables in addition to the set of alternative methods of production and disposal available and one of the distribution variables (the real wage or the rate of profit) in order to determine relative prices and the other distribution variable. To be sure, with joint production the requirements for use play a significant role in the theory of value and distribution. However, this role does not appear to consist in rendering an otherwise indeterminate system determinate first, as is the case with the demand schedules in the marginalist approach to joint production. It rather consists in selecting one particular determinate system from a set of feasible alternatives. These considerations make it clear how important is the development of a theory of outputs which will be in harmony with the classical theory of value and distribution.

REFERENCES

Arrow K.J. and Hahn F.H. (1971): *General Competitive Analysis*, San Francisco, Holden-Day.
Arrow K.J. (1983): *Collected Papers of Kenneth J. Arrow*, Vol. 2, *General Equilibrium*, Oxford, Basil Blackwell.
Babbage C. (1971): *On the Economy of Machinery and Manufactures*, first published 1832, reprinted New York, Augustus M. Kelley.
Bailey E.E. and Friedlaender A.F. (1982): « Market Structure and Multiproduct Industries », *Journal of Economic Literature*, Vol. 20, pp. 1024-1048.
Bharadwaj K. (1978): *Classical Political Economy and Rise to Dominance of Supply and Demand Theories*, Calcutta, Orient Longman.
Blaug M. (1968): *Economic Theory in Retrospect*, Homewood, Illinois, Richard D. Irwin.
Cairnes J.E. (1967): *Some Leading Principles of Political Economy Newly Expounded*, first published 1874, reprinted New York, Augustus M. Kelley.
Cantillon R. (1931): *Essai sur la nature du commerce en général*, ed. with an English translation and other material by H. Higgs, London, Macmillan.
Carlson S. (1956): *A Study in the Pure Theory of Production*, New York, Macmillan.
Cassel G. (1967): *The Theory of Social Economy*, New York, Augustus M. Kelley.
Deane P. (1978): *The Evolution of Economic Ideas*, Cambridge, Cambridge University Press.

— 36 —

Dobb M.H. (1973), *Theories of Value and Distribution since Adam Smith*, Cambridge, Cambridge University Press.

Ekelund R.B. and Hebert R.F. (1983): *A History of Economic Theory and Method*, New York, McGraw-Hill.

Fisher I. (1965): *The Nature of Capital and Income*, first published New York 1906, reprinted New York, Augustus M. Kelley.

Garegnani P. (1983): « The Classical Theory of Wages and the Role of Demand Schedules in the Determination of Relative Prices », *American Economic Review, Papers and Proceedings*, Vol. 73, pp. 309-313.

Goodwin R. (1970): *Elementary Economics from the Higher Standpoint*, Cambridge, Cambridge University Press.

Hodgskin T. (1966): *Popular Political Economy. A Lecture on Free Trade in Connection with the Corn Laws*, first published London 1827, reprinted New York, Augustus M. Kelley.

Hollander S. (1973): *The Economics of Adam Smith*, Toronto and Buffalo, University of Toronto Press.

Hutchison T.W. (1973): « The "Marginal Revolution" and the Decline and Fall of English Classical Political Economy », in R.D. Collison Black, A.W. Coats and C.D.W. Goodwin (eds.): *The Marginal Revolution in Economics*, pp. 176-202, Durham, Duke University Press.

Jevons W.S. (1965): *The Theory of Political Economy*, first published 1871, reprinted New York, Augustus M. Kelley.

Jones R.W. (1979): *International Trade: Essays in Theory*, Amsterdam, North-Holland.

Kurz H.D. (1984): « Joint Production in the History of Economic Thought », *Diskussionsbeiträge zur gesamtwirtschaftlichen Theorie und Politik*, Bremen.

Longfield M. (1971): *Lectures on Political Economy*, first published 1834, in R.D. Collison Black (ed.): *The Economic Writings of Mountifort Longfield*, New York, Augustus M. Kelley.

Mainwaring L. (1984): *Value and Distribution in Capitalist Economies*, Cambridge, Cambridge University Press.

Mangoldt H.v. (1863): *Grundriss der Volkswirtschaftslehre*, Stuttgart, Gustav Fischer.

Marshall A. (1970): *Industry and Trade*, first published 1919, reprint of the fourth edition 1923, New York, Augustus M. Kelley.

Marshall A. (1977): *Principles of Economics*, first published 1890, reprint of the eighth edition 1920, London and Basingstoke, Macmillan.

Marx K. (1954): *Capital*, vol. I, Moscow, Progress Publishers.

Marx K. (1956): *Capital*, vol. II, Moscow, Progress Publishers.

Marx K. (1959): *Capital*, vol. III, Moscow, Progress Publishers.

Marx K. (1963): *Theories of Surplus Value*, vol. I, Moscow, Progress Publishers.

Marx K. (1968): *Theories of Surplus Value*, vol. II, Moscow, Progress Publishers.

Marx K. (1970): *Grundrisse der Kritik der politischen Ökonomie, Rohentwurf*, Frankfurt, Europäische Verlagsanstalt.

Marx K. (1981): *Die technologisch-historischen Exzerpte*, ed. by H.-P. Müller, Frankfurt, Ullstein.

Marx K. (1982): *Exzerpte über Arbeitsteilung, Maschinerie und Industrie*, ed. by R. Winkelmann, Frankfurt, Ullstein.

Menger C. (1968): *Grundsätze der Volkswirtschaftslehre*, first published 1871, reprint of the second edition Wien 1923, Aalen, Scientia Verlag.

Mill J.S. (1965): *Principles of Political Economy with Some of Their Applications to Social Philosophy*, first published 1848, ed. by J.M. Robson, Toronto and Buffalo, University of Toronto Press.

O'Brien D.P. (1975): *The Classical Economists*, Oxford, Clarendon Press.

Pareto V. (1971): *Manual of Political Economy*, translation of the French edition of 1927, New York, Augustus M. Kelley.

Parrinello S. (1970): « Introduzione ad una teoria neoricardiana del commercio internazionale », *Studi Economici*, Vol. 25, pp. 267-321.

Pasinetti L.L. (1980): *Essays on the Theory of Joint Production*, London and Basingstoke, Macmillan.

Petty W. (1963): *The Economic Writings of Sir William Petty*, ed. by C.H. Hull, Vol. I. New York, Augustus M. Kelley; (1964) Vol. II.

— 37 —

Quesnay F. (1972): *Quesnay's Tableau Economique*, reprint of the 1759 edition, ed. by M. Kuczynski and R.L. Meek, London, Macmillan.

Ricardo D. (1951 ssq): *The Works and Correspondence of David Ricardo*, ed. by P. Sraffa with the collaboration of M.H. Dobb, Cambridge, Cambridge University Press.

Riebel P. (1955): *Die Kuppelproduktion — Betriebs — und Marktprobleme*, Köln and Opladen, Westdeutscher Verlag.

Rima, I.H. (1967): *Development of Economic Analysis*, Homewood, Illinois, Richard D. Irwin.

Samuelson P.A. (1977): « A Modern Theorist's Vindication of Adam Smith », *American Economic Review*, Papers and Proceedings, Vol. 67, pp. 42-49.

Samuelson P.A. (1980): « Noise and Signal in Debates Among Classical Economists: A Reply », *Journal of Economic Literature*, Vol. 18, pp. 575-578.

Samuelson P.A. (1983): « Thünen at Two Hundred », *Journal of Economic Literature*, Vol. 21, pp. 1468-1488.

Schefold B. (1984): « Sraffa and Applied Economics: Joint Production », *Political Economy*, Vol. 1, pp. 17-40.

Schneider E. (1960): « Hans v. Mangoldt on Price Theory: A Contribution to the History of Mathematical Economics », *Econometrica*, Vol. 28, pp. 380-392.

Schumpeter J.A. (1954): *History of Economic Analysis*, New York, Oxford University Press.

Simmonds P.L. (1873): *Waste Products and Undeveloped Substances: A Synopsis of Progress Made in their Economic Utilisation during the Last Quarter of a Century at Home and Abroad*, London, Robert Hardwicke.

Smith A. (1976): *An Inquiry into the Nature and Causes of the Wealth of Nations*, first published 1776, ed. by E. Cannan, with a new Preface by G.J. Stigler, Chicago, The University of Chicago Press.

Spiegel H.W. (1971): *The Growth of Economic Thought*, Englewood Cliffs, Prentice-Hall.

Sraffa P. (1925): « Sulle relazioni fra costo e quantità prodotta », *Annali di Economia*, Vol. 2, pp. 277-328.

Sraffa P. (1960), *Production of Commodities by Means of Commodities*, Cambridge, Cambridge University Press.

Steedman Ian (1982): « Joint Production and the Wage-Rent Frontier », *Economic Journal*, Vol. 92, pp. 377-385.

Steedman Ian (1984): « L'importance empirique de la production jointe », in C. Bidard (ed.), *La production jointe*, Paris, Economica.

Steedman Ian (1985): « Joint Production and Technical Progress », *Political Economy*, Vol. 1, pp. 41-52.

Steuart J. (1966): *An Inquiry into the Principles of Political Oeconomy*, first published 1767, Vol. II, ed. by A.S. Skinner, Chicago, The University of Chicago Press.

Stewart D. (1968): *Lectures on Political Economy*, first published Edinburgh 1855, Vol. II, reprinted New York, Augustus M. Kelley.

Stigler G.J. (1941): *Production and Distribution Theories*, New York, Macmillan.

Stigler G.J. (1965): *Essays in the History of Economics*, Chicago and London, University of Chicago Press

Taussig F.W. (1929): *Principles of Economics*, first edition 1911, third edition 1929, Vol. I, New York, Macmillan.

Thünen J.H.v. (1966): *Der isolierte Staat in Beziehung auf Landwirtschaft und Nationalökonomie*, first edition 1826, reprint of the second edition 1842, Stuttgart, Gustav Fischer.

Turgot A.R.J. (1970): *Écrits économiques*, ed. by B. Cazes, Paris, Calmann-Lévy.

Varri P. ed. (1982): *I prodotti congiunti*, Milan, Vita e Pensiero.

Walras L. (1954): *Elements of Pure Economics*, translation of the French Edition Définitive of 1926, London, George Allen & Unwin.

Walsh V. and Gram H. (1980): *Classical and Neoclassical Theories of General Equilibrium*, New York and Oxford, Oxford University Press.

Wicksell K. (1934): *Lectures on Political Economy*, vol. I, London, Routledge.

[3]

Bulletin of Economic Research 40:3, 1988, 0307-3378 $2.00

JOINT PRODUCTION ANALYSIS IN A SRAFFIAN FRAMEWORK[1]

Neri Salvadori and Ian Steedman

I. INTRODUCTION

The publication of Piero Sraffa's *Production of Commodities by Means of Commodities* in 1960 was soon to provoke an intense discussion of certain parts of the theories of capital and of value and distribution. Fierce and wide-ranging as that discussion was, it nevertheless almost ignored a substantial portion of Sraffa's book, namely its 'Part II. Multiple-Product Industries and Fixed Capital'. This 'partial' concern with Sraffa's results was understandable and, quite possibly, sensible as a first step. Moreover, it appears to have been consistent with Sraffa's own view of the relative importance of his various findings, for in his preface (1960, p. vi) he wrote:

> 'Whilst the central propositions had taken shape in the late 1920s, particular points, such as the Standard commodity, joint products and fixed capital, were worked out in the thirties and early forties. In the period since 1955, while these pages were being put together out of a mass of old notes, little was added, apart from filling gaps which had become apparent in the process (such as the adapting of the distinction between "basics" and "non-basics" to the case of joint products)'.

Be that as it may, Sraffa's analysis of joint production is a rich source of both insights and theoretical difficulties, a source which has by now inspired a considerable literature of great interest.

There can be little question that in any work, such as Sraffa's book, which is 'designed to serve as the basis for a critique' of the 'marginal theory of value and distribution' (p. vi), joint production must find an important place, simply because joint production is allowed for in many important formulations of that theory. Conversely, in so far as Sraffa's work was intended to suggest the basis for an alternative approach to the theory of value and distribution, it is again necessary that joint production be carefully considered, since major marginalist writers, such as Jevons

[1] We are happy to thank Ch. Bidard, R. Franke, U. Krause, H. Kurz, L. L. Pasinetti, A. Roncaglia, B. Schefold, and two referees for their many helpful comments on a previous draft, even if it has not been possible to incorporate every one of their suggestions in the present version. N. Salvadori thanks the M.P.I. (the Italian Ministry of Public Education) for financial support.

(1970) and Wicksell (1934), have explicitly cited joint products as important phenomena which, they asserted, cannot be analysed within a theory of value of a 'classical' orientation (precisely the tradition to which Sraffa appears to suggest a return). (See Kurz, 1986, for a detailed account of the place of joint products in economic analysis, from Adam Smith onwards.) Moreover, and ultimately more importantly, joint production simply is, as a matter of brute fact, of great empirical importance, quite apart from its fixed capital aspect (Steedman, 1984). Hence a necessary condition for the adequacy of any theory of value and distribution is that it be able to deal with 'pure' joint products *and*, of course, with fixed capital.

The object of this survey article is to show, in a clear and simple way, what has been achieved and which problems remain to be solved. It is hoped that the survey will also show how the work in question, far from being of interest exclusively to 'Sraffa-specialists', is of significance to a wide range of economic theorists.

Sraffa's Part II contains five chapters. Chapter VII, 'Joint Production', provides a general introduction to Sraffa's approach and, more specifically, introduces the concept of 'the proportions in which... commodities... are required for use' (p. 43, n. 2) and establishes the 'assumption that the number of processes should be equal to the number of commodities' (p. 44): requirements for use and 'square' systems will be discussed in Sections 2 and 3. It may already be noted here, however, that Sraffa's first chapter on joint production contains indications that some of his arguments in Part II will be less formal than are those of Part I, dealing with 'Single-Product Industries and Circulating Capital'. Chapter VIII, 'The Standard System with Joint Products', shows how joint products complicate the construction of the Standard commodity and the derivation of the maximum rate of profit for a given technique, and argue that they necessitate a reformulation of Sraffa's concept of 'basic' and 'non-basic' commodities: these matters will be considered in Section 5. Chapter IX, 'Other Effects of Joint Production', deals with the quantities of labour (possibly negative) embodied in a commodity, with 'reduction to dated quantities of labour', and with the possibility that a measure of the real wage may be increased as the uniform rate of profit increases; on these matters, see Sections 6 and 8 below. Chapter X is concerned with 'Fixed Capital'. Sraffa introduces this chapter with the words,

> 'The interest of Joint Products does not lie so much in the familiar examples of wool and mutton, or wheat and straw, as in its being the genus of which Fixed Capital is the leading species. And it is mainly as an introduction to the subject of fixed capital that the preceding chapters devoted to the intricacies of joint products find their place' (p. 63; see also, in similar vein, p. 43, n. 1 — even if land is there put on a par with fixed capital).

Sraffa gives no account of why he regards 'pure' joint products as (relatively) unimportant and the speculation that he emphasized fixed capital because of his implicit concern with capital theory would be just that — a speculation. Section 7 below will be devoted to fixed capital. The final chapter of Part II is Chapter XI, 'Land'. Whilst this chapter is of great interest, it will not be dealt with in the present survey, for the equation system which Sraffa employs in his theory of rent is not, in formal terms, of the joint production kind, even if Sraffa quite properly draws attention to interesting connections between rent theory and joint production theory (pp. 77–8). (It would have been quite natural for Sraffa to work on the theory of rent soon after his famous critical papers of 1925 and 1926; it will thus be of considerable interest for historians of thought to establish at what stage Sraffa did indeed develop the approach presented in this 1960 chapter on 'Land'.) Part III of Sraffa's book consists of the single Chapter XII, 'Switch in Methods of Production', and the closing section of that chapter, and thus of the book, deals with the choice between alternative joint production systems; this issue is considered in Section 4 below.

II. A SYSTEM OF PRODUCTION

Here and throughout this article, rent will be set equal to zero, as explained in Section 1, and labour will be treated as homogeneous. (Or, more exactly, the relative wages of the different kinds of labour will be taken to be fixed, so that labour may be treated as if it were homogeneous.) It may also be noted here that the reader may assume constant returns to scale throughout, for we do not wish to enter into a discussion of the role of constant returns in Sraffa's book (cp., Steedman, 1980).

Let there be a finite number of commodities (say n). A *method of production* (or a *process*) is defined by a triplet $(\mathbf{a}, \mathbf{b}, l)$, where $\mathbf{a}$ is an n-vector whose elements $a_1, a_2, \ldots, a_n$ are the amounts of commodities $1, 2, \ldots, n$ which, jointly with the amount of labour l, produce the amounts of commodities $b_1, b_2, \ldots, b_n$, which are the elements of the n-vector $\mathbf{b}$. Of course, $\mathbf{a} \geqslant \mathbf{0}, \mathbf{b} \geqslant \mathbf{0}, l \geqslant 0$.

In each economy many processes are known, but only a small number of them are operated. Sraffa's analysis of joint production does not begin by analysing the whole technology, i.e. the set of all known processes, but starts by studying a *system of production*, that is a set of processes which may be operated at the same time. In Part I of *Production of Commodities*, Sraffa does not define formally the system of production. However, no difficulty in interpretation arises here: if all methods of production are single product processes and n is the number of commodities involved in production, then at least n processes must be operated; and n processes determine n constraints among the $n-1$ relative prices, the wage rate, and the profit rate. On introducing joint production, Sraffa (1960, Section 50) encounters a difficulty: since at least one process produces more than one commodity, fewer processes than the number of commodities involved could be operated. 'The conditions would no longer be sufficient to deter-mine the prices. There would be more prices to be ascertained than there are processes, and therefore equations, to determine them'. Sraffa suggests meeting this difficulty by an assumption: he assumes that 'the number of processes should be equal to the number of commodities'.

Although Sraffa is very aware (1960, p. 43, n. 2; p. 47) of the fact that, even though the operable processes are equal in number to the com-modities involved, they may not be able to fulfil whatever 'requirements for use'[2] there may be, he does not mention this problem in defining the system of production (cf. Section 51; see also the last paragraph of Section 90, p. 78). Thus a system of production seems to be defined just as a set of *n* processes. But this interpretation is definitely false, since when dealing with single production it is assumed that each process produces a com-modity different from the commodities produced by the other processes of the same system.

Salvadori (1982, 1985) has argued that a system of production can be defined only with respect to given 'requirements for use'.[3] Sraffa would not have emphasized this point because in Part II of his book, where joint production systems are introduced, he was dealing with *one* system (either that actually in use at a single instant of time, as Roncaglia, 1978, suggests, or that which has to prevail in the long run because of competition, as Garegnani, 1976, suggests), so that satisfaction of certain 'requirements for use' was presumably *implicitly* assumed. Furthermore, 'requirements for use' are *explicitly* mentioned by Sraffa in a footnote on the very first page dealing with joint production. Thus we propose:

Definition 1. Let the nonnegative *n*-vector **d** be some requirements for use, and let $(\mathbf{a}_i, \mathbf{b}_i, l_i)$, $i = 1, 2, ..., n$, be *n* methods of production. Then the triplet $(A, B, \mathbf{l})$, where

$$A = \begin{bmatrix} \mathbf{a}_1^T \\ \mathbf{a}_2^T \\ \vdots \\ \mathbf{a}_n^T \end{bmatrix}, B = \begin{bmatrix} \mathbf{b}_1^T \\ \mathbf{b}_2^T \\ \vdots \\ \mathbf{b}_n^T \end{bmatrix}, \mathbf{l} = \begin{bmatrix} l_1 \\ l_2 \\ \vdots \\ l_n \end{bmatrix}$$

will be called a *system of production* (or a technique) *with respect to the requirements for use* **d** if there exists an *n*-vector **x** such that

---

[2] Sraffa's phrase 'requirements for use' is not a standard term in economic analysis and Sraffa provides no explication of this phrase. Thus one is obliged to be cautious in offering an interpretation. Nevertheless it might seem that Sraffa was seeking to de-emphasize the subjective elements in the determination of the pattern of output, without denying them.

[3] Strictly speaking the problem of 'requirements for use' arises also if only single produc-tion holds but some commodities are non-basics (see Section 5 below for the definition of non-basics). In this case, in fact, some non-basics may not be required for use and thus are not produced. This can also affect the maximum rate of profits if some non-basics are self-reproducing (see Sraffa, Appendix B).

JOINT PRODUCTION ANALYSIS IN A SRAFFIAN FRAMEWORK   169

$$\mathbf{x}^T[B-A]=\mathbf{d}^T, \mathbf{x}\geqslant 0 \tag{1}$$

A vector $\mathbf{x}$ satisfying constraints (1) will be said to be an *intensity-vector* of system $(A, B, \mathbf{l})$. If the i-th element of an intensity-vector of a system is positive, we will say that the i-th process of that system is *operated*. Of course, a single product system is just the special case in which B can be made diagonal by numbering processes in the same way as the commodities they produce (and can then be made equal to I by appropriate choice of units), and $\mathbf{x}$ is then positive whenever $\mathbf{d}$ is positive.

It must be stressed that vector $\mathbf{d}$, mentioned in Definition 1, does not need to be a constant; it can be a function of the profit rate, wage rate, price vector, intensity vector, labour vector, input matrix, and output matrix. But there is no need to investigate either the determinants or the complete set of properties of this function.

The prices of production for each system of production are defined by the following equations:

$$B\mathbf{p}=(1+r)A\mathbf{p}+w\mathbf{l} \tag{2.1}$$

$$\mathbf{q}^T\mathbf{p}=1 \tag{2.2}$$

where $\mathbf{p}$ is the price-vector, r is the profit rate, and w is the wage rate. Note that equation (2.2) normalizes prices by setting as numéraire a composite commodity made up of q_1 units of commodity 1, q_2 units of commodity 2, ..., q_n units of commodity n, where $(q_1, q_2, ..., q_n)^T=\mathbf{q}$. Alternatively, if the numéraire consists of one unit of labour, equations (2) are replaced by

$$B\mathbf{p}=(1+r)A\mathbf{p}+\mathbf{l} \tag{3}$$

where $\mathbf{p}$ is now called the labour-commanded price vector.

It will prove helpful to introduce here an alternative representation of equation (2.1). Let vector $\mathbf{y}$ be any semi-positive net output vector and vector $\mathbf{x}$ be the corresponding activity vector. Then

$$\mathbf{x}^TB=\mathbf{x}^TA+\mathbf{y}^T$$

or

$$\mathbf{x}^T=\mathbf{y}^T[B-A]^{-1} \tag{4}$$

if $[B-A]$ is non-singular. Now the vector of capital stocks necessary to support the production of $\mathbf{y}$ is given by $\mathbf{k}$, where $\mathbf{k}^T=\mathbf{x}^TA$ or

$$\mathbf{k}^T=\mathbf{y}^T[B-A]^{-1}A \tag{5}$$

from (4). Hence $[(B-A)^{-1}A]$ is the matrix linking capital stocks, $\mathbf{k}$, to net outputs, $\mathbf{y}$: it will be convenient to follow Pasinetti (1973) in writing (5) as

$$\mathbf{k}^T=\mathbf{y}^TH. \tag{5'}$$

Total labour use will be given by

$$\mathbf{x}^T\mathbf{l}=\mathbf{y}^T[B-A]^{-1}\mathbf{l}$$

170   BULLETIN OF ECONOMIC RESEARCH

hence $\{[B - A]^{-1}l\}$ is the vector of direct and indirect labour requirements per unit of net output for each commodity, call it **v**. The 'vertically integrated' technical coefficients $(H, \mathbf{v})$ are often a useful replacement for the 'direct' coefficients (B, A, l). For example, when $[B - A]$ is non-singular, equation (2.1) may be rewritten as

$$\mathbf{p} = w\mathbf{v} + rH\mathbf{p} \qquad (6)$$

and equation (3) may be re-written as

$$\mathbf{p} = \mathbf{v} + rH\mathbf{p} \qquad (7)$$

Equation (6) shows that the price of each commodity can be expressed as the sum of two terms; the total of direct and indirect wage payments incurred in the production of that commodity plus the profits on the value of the capital stocks required both directly and indirectly.

Sraffa's own assumption asserting that each system contains exactly as many processes as commodities has been considered inappropriate by some economists (see, for instance, Wolfstetter, 1976). On the other hand, Steedman (1976) and Schefold (1978c, 1980a) have shown that, if the economy is assumed to grow steadily at a rate equal to the profit rate and the consumption pattern is independent of prices and incomes, then such an equality can actually be proved if the concept of 'truncation' is introduced into the analysis, i.e. if the assumption of free disposal holds and the term *commodity* is used to refer only to a good which is not overproduced. However, in the general case there is no way to justify the assumption of a number of processes equal to the number of commodities.[4]

Moreover, several authors (Bidard, 1984a; Duménil and Lévy, 1984; Lévy, 1984; Salvadori, 1979a, 1982, 1985) have shown that such an assumption may rule out the existence of 'cost-minimizing systems', if, as above, a 'system' contains, by definition, a number of processes equal to the number of commodities. This has led to the consideration of both *square* and *non-square* systems. A definition of *system of production* generalized to consider non-square systems has been provided by Salvadori (1985, pp. 174-5, see also Craven, 1979, for another definition, not related to Sraffa's analysis). In the following we will assume that the system of production is square, except when explicitly stated otherwise. In doing so, we reflect the general emphasis in the literature which is here being surveyed. It is to be noted, however, that the discussion of square and non-square systems is clearly coming to be a major focus of interest within a broadly Sraffian framework. (See, further, the end of Section 4 below.)

---

[4] Let us consider an economy where there is only one process, $(\mathbf{a}, \mathbf{b}, l)$; $\mathbf{a}' = (1, 1)$, $\mathbf{b}' = (3, 3)$, $l = 1$; the growth rate equals zero, the profit rate equals 1; capitalists consume only commodity 2 and workers consume only commodity 1. Then $p_1 = p_2$, $w = 2p_1$, and no commodity is overproduced. See also Franke (1985, p. 274).

JOINT PRODUCTION ANALYSIS IN A SRAFFIAN FRAMEWORK   171

III. SOME SPECIAL SQUARE SYSTEMS

Since a general analysis of a system of production can provide too few useful results, many authors have considered it more promising to analyse some special cases. This has created a lot of distinctions. A quite rich taxonomy is provided by Giorgi and Magnani (1978); here we will refer only to 'Regular Systems', 'All-Productive Systems', and 'All-Engaging Systems'. All these concepts have been introduced and fully analysed by Schefold (1971, 1976a, 1978b).

A commodity is said to be *separately producible* in system $(A, B, \mathbf{l})$ if it is possible to produce a net output consisting of a unit of that commodity alone with a nonnegative intensity vector. I.e., commodity i is *separately producible* if and only if there exists a nonnegative vector $\mathbf{x}_i$ such that

$$\mathbf{x}_i^T[B-A] = \mathbf{e}_i^T$$

where $\mathbf{e}_i$ is the i-th unit vector. A system of production is called *all-productive* if all commodities are separately producible in it, i.e., if for each semipositive vector $\mathbf{y}$ there exists a nonnegative vector $\mathbf{x}$ such that

$$\mathbf{x}^T[B-A] = \mathbf{y}^T$$

If $(A, B, \mathbf{l})$ is all-productive, then $[B-A]^{-1} \geq 0$. In fact

$$(\mathbf{x}_1, \mathbf{x}_2, \ldots, \mathbf{x}_n)^T[B-A] = (\mathbf{e}_1, \mathbf{e}_2, \ldots, \mathbf{e}_n)^T \equiv I$$

Thus, $[B-A]^{-1} \equiv (\mathbf{x}_1, \mathbf{x}_2, \ldots, \mathbf{x}_n)^T \geq 0$. This is important since equation (2.1) can be written as

$$[B-A]\mathbf{p} = rA\mathbf{p} + w\mathbf{l}$$

i.e.

$$\mathbf{p} = r[B-A]^{-1}A\mathbf{p} + w[B-A]^{-1}\mathbf{l} = rH\mathbf{p} + w\mathbf{v}$$

hence all the properties of single product systems now hold, since the Perron-Frobenius theorem can be applied to the nonnegative matrix H and $\mathbf{v}$ is nonnegative.

A process is *indispensable* within a system of production if it has to be activated whatever net output is to be produced, i.e. process $(\mathbf{e}_i^T A, \mathbf{e}_i^T B, \mathbf{e}_i^T \mathbf{l})$ is *not indispensable* within system $(A, B, \mathbf{l})$ if and only if there is a net output $\mathbf{y} \geq 0$ and nonnegative intensity vector $\mathbf{x}$ such that $\mathbf{x}^T[B-A] = \mathbf{y}^T$ and $\mathbf{e}_i^T \mathbf{x} = 0$. An all-productive system whose processes are all indispensable is *all-engaging*. Obviously, if $(A, B, \mathbf{l})$ is all-engaging, then $[B-A]^{-1} > 0$.

System $(A, B, \mathbf{l})$ is r_0-all-productive (r_0-all-engaging) if the system $((1+r_0)A, B, \mathbf{l})$ is all-productive (all-engaging). Thus, if $(A, B, \mathbf{l})$ is r_0-all-productive then

$$\mathbf{p} = (r-r_0)[B-(1+r_0)A]^{-1}A\mathbf{p} + w[B-(1+r_0)A]^{-1}\mathbf{l}$$

i.e., an r_0-all-productive system has all the simple properties of single production systems for all $r \geqslant r_0$.

Definition 2. If a joint production system $(A, B, 1)$ with det $A \neq 0$, det$[B - A] \neq 0$ has only semi-simple characteristic roots and if none of its eigenvectors is orthogonal to the labour vector 1, it will be called *regular*.

A characteristic root, R_i, of system $(A, B, 1)$ is a root of the equation

$$\det[B - (1 + r)A] = 0.$$

It is said to be semi-simple if

$$\text{rank}[B - (1 + R_i)A] = n - 1,$$

where n is the number of commodities involved in (and, as a consequence, the number of the processes which make up) the system $(A, B, 1)$. The (left) eigenvector $\mathbf{q}_i$ corresponding to the characteristic root R_i is the vector satisfying the equation

$$\mathbf{q}^T[B - (1 + R_i)A] = \mathbf{0}.$$

Schefold (1976a, p. 27) remarks that the set of irregular systems is of measure zero in the set of all possible systems. However, he is very aware that this observation taken by itself does not mean much: what is important is whether or not it is reasonable to assume that all systems are regular and what aspects of reality are lost with this assumption. Schefold maintains that 'there is no economic reason why real systems should not be regular or why irregular systems should exist in reality' (Schefold, 1976a, p. 27). Schefold has derived the following properties of regular systems:

(i) The price-vector of a regular system with n commodities and n processes varies in such a way with the rate of profit that it assumes n linearly independent values at any n different levels of the rate of profit (Schefold, 1976a, pp. 23–25).

(ii) If labour commanded prices of two regular systems with n commodities and n processes, $(A, B, 1)$ and $(F, G, \mathbf{m})$, coincide at $n + 1$ different levels of the rate of profit, then[5] there exists a non-singular matrix M such that $F = MA$, $G = MB$, $\mathbf{m} = M1$ (Schefold, 1976a, pp. 31–32).[6]

---

[5] If the two systems are not regular, then there exist two matrices M and Y such that $F = MA + Y$, $G = MB + Y$, $\mathbf{m} = M1$, $Y\mathbf{p}(r) = 0$ each r, where $\mathbf{p}(r)$ is the price-vector relative to rate of profit r (Schefold, 1976a, p. 31).

[6] This can be easily shown in the following way. Let $\mathbf{p}_1, \mathbf{p}_2, \ldots, \mathbf{p}_{n+1}$ be the labour commanded price vectors relative to the profit rates $r_1, r_2, \ldots, r_{n+1}$. Let $P = [\mathbf{p}_1, \mathbf{p}_2, \ldots, \mathbf{p}_{n+1}]$, $\hat{r}$ be the diagonal matrix having $r_1, r_2, \ldots, r_{n+1}$ on the main diagonal. Then:

$$BP = [A, 1] \begin{bmatrix} P(I + \hat{r}) \\ \mathbf{e}' \end{bmatrix}$$

Since the system is regular the second matrix on the right-hand side is non-singular. Hence,

$$[A, 1] = BP \begin{bmatrix} P(I + \hat{r}) \\ \mathbf{e}' \end{bmatrix}^{-1}$$

JOINT PRODUCTION ANALYSIS IN A SRAFFIAN FRAMEWORK   173

(iii) Each basic[7] and regular system with semipositive left and right eigenvectors corresponding to the smallest positive real R_i is r_0-all-engaging for some r_0 $(r_0 \gtrless 0)$ (Schefold, 1978b).[8]

IV. THE CHOICE OF TECHNIQUE

The study of a single system of production is complemented by the search for the *cost-minimizing system*, i.e the system of production which has to prevail in the long run because of competition. A *cost-minimizing system* is defined as a system of production at whose prices no known process can pay extra-profits.[9] To put the matter in a more formal way, if the *n*-vector *p* and the scalars *r* and *w* are such that

$$[\mathbf{b} - (1 + r)\mathbf{a}]^T \mathbf{p} > wl$$

then the process $(\mathbf{a}, \mathbf{b}, l)$ *pays extra profits* at prices $\mathbf{p}$, rate of profit *r* and wage rate *w*. On the contrary, if

$$[\mathbf{b} - (1 + r)\mathbf{a}]^T \mathbf{p} < wl$$

then the process $(\mathbf{a}, \mathbf{b}, l)$ *incurs extra costs* at prices $\mathbf{p}$, rate of profit *r* and wage rate *w*. Then:

Definition 3. The system of production $(A_k, B_k, \mathbf{l}_k)$ is *cost-minimizing at rate of profit r* if and only if

$$[B_j - (1 + r)A_j]\mathbf{p}_k \leqq w_k \mathbf{l}_j \quad \text{each } (A_j, B_j, \mathbf{l}_j) \quad \in J$$

where *J* is the set of all existing systems of production and $(\mathbf{p}_k, w_k)$ are determined by the following equations:

$$[B_k - (1 + r)A_k]\mathbf{p}_k = w_k \mathbf{l}_k$$

$$\mathbf{q}^T \mathbf{p}_k = 1.$$

The problem of choice of technique was studied first with respect to single production (Levhari, 1965; Garegnani, 1973; Morishima, 1964; Lippi, 1979; Łos and Łos, 1976). In this context the cost-minimizing system for a given rate of profit coincides with the system which is able to pay the highest wage rate. It is to be noted that this coincidence is not

---

[7] A basic system is a system all of whose commodities are basic.

[8] See also the elegant study by Abraham-Frois and Berrebi (1984), which, however, deals only with two by two systems. Bidard (1986a, pp. 411–12) has provided a very simple proof of the following theorem: If the left and right eigenvectors corresponding to

$$R \equiv \text{Inf}\{r; \exists \mathbf{p} \geqslant \mathbf{0}, [B - (1 + r)A]\mathbf{p} \leqq \mathbf{0}\}$$

are unique (up to a scalar) and positive, then the given system is r_0-all-engaging for some $r_0(r_0 \gtrless 0)$.

[9] This definition does not take into account a formal, mathematical complication which may be referred to as a case of degeneracy. A more complex definition is able to take such degeneracy into account (see Salvadori, 1982, p. 285).

174   BULLETIN OF ECONOMIC RESEARCH

ensured in joint production systems and that emphasis then has to be placed on the more fundamental notion of cost-minimizing choice of techniques (cf. Bidard, 1984; Lévy, 1984; Salvadori, 1979a, 1982, 1985; Saucier, 1984). Some special joint production cases were then investigated. Schefold (1978b) is concerned with choice between two systems, one of which is all-engaging. Baldone (1980), Schefold (1976b, 1978a, 1980b), and Varri (1980) analyse the truncation of fixed capital's lifetime as a choice of techniques problem (see Section 7).

A special problem of choice of techniques is also analysed by Schefold (1978c, 1980a; see also Steedman, 1976). The main issue of these two related papers is the relationship between Sraffa's analysis and that of von Neumann. The author proves, in fact, that the Factor Price Frontier analysed by Burmeister and Kuga (1970) and Fujimoto (1975) can be obtained by the analysis of cost-minimizing systems, once free disposal, steady growth at a rate equal to the profit rate, and consumption independent of prices and incomes are introduced into Sraffa's analysis. Thus, Sraffa's analysis and that of von Neumann are shown to yield the same results in this special case.[10]

Schefold (1978c, 1980a) makes it clear, albeit without discussing the point, that the 'requirements for use' matter in determining cost-minimizing systems. This opened the way to the analysis of the problem of choice of techniques among general joint production systems. Bidard (1984a, 1984b, 1986b) and Salvadori, (1979b, 1982, 1984) dealt with this problem. They have provided two different sufficient conditions (neither is more general than the other) for the existence of cost-minimizing systems. They both (i) consider the whole set of square systems of production, (ii) introduce the possibility of comparing two systems in order to determine whether there exists a process in a system which is able to pay extra-profits at the prices of another system, (iii) show that if there exists a process which is able to pay extra-profits at the prices of a system, then there exists another system which is preferable to the previous one. In this way an algorithm is determined which starts from any system and converges to the cost-minimizing system if certain conditions are met.[11] Moreover, if more

---

[10] The case of a uniform growth rate equal to the profit rate is also analysed by Hinrichsen and Krause (1978) and Saucier (1984) without the free disposal assumption. Salvadori (1980) has shown that Schefold's (1978c, 1980a) assumption that the uniform growth rate equals the profit rate can be weakened to allow a uniform growth rate less than or equal to the profit rate for the purpose of proving the existence of an equilibrium in a von Neumann model. But Saucier (1984) and Salvadori (1980) are not concerned with proving that cost-minimizing systems are 'square'.

[11] Two different sets of conditions are considered by the two authors. Bidard first divides the processes into groups called 'sectors'; then each system of production is assumed to be made up of *one* process from *each* sector. An economic interpretation of this hypothesis would be that each sector is defined by the nature of a principal commodity which characterizes the sector. Salvadori assumes the existence of a composite commodity *u* such that the set of systems of production defined by the current requirements for use is contained in the set of processes defined by the assumption that the economy is growing at a rate equal to the

JOINT PRODUCTION ANALYSIS IN A SRAFFIAN FRAMEWORK 175

than one cost-minimizing system exists, they are all compatible[12] with each other. This algorithm is a direct generalization of the procedure adopted by Sraffa for single production in his Chapter XII (Sections 92–95).

It is to be noted that when the conditions specified in Bidard (1984a, 1984b, 1986b) and Salvadori (1979b, 1982, 1984), and referred to in the previous paragraph, are not satisfied, three interesting possibilities arise, none of which can occur in single product systems. The first is that at the prices of each system there exists a process paying extra-profits, so that there exists no cost-minimizing system. The second is that more than one cost-minimizing system can exist and that they are not compatible with each other. The third possibility is that a system with positive prices exists but that the unique cost-minimizing system is associated with a price vector containing a negative price. (See for instance Bidard, 1984a, and Salvadori, 1979b, 1985.)

More recently, authors considering the problem of choice of techniques among joint product systems have preferred to follow more direct procedures without being concerned with the analysis of a single system of production, sometimes (Salvadori, 1988) limiting themselves to proving that there exists a cost-minimizing system of production which is square, or sometimes (Bidard and Franke, 1987; Franke, 1986b) even without being concerned with this latter problem at all. Finally, Salvadori (1985) has provided definitions of 'system of production' and 'cost-minimizing system' which eliminate the difficulties which arise in assuming that all systems are square, but which transform the Sraffa approach in such a way that the result is very close to the von Neumann approach as transformed by Morishima (1960, 1964, 1969).

V. BASICS, NON-BASICS AND THE STANDARD COMMODITY

In the course of discussing single-product, circulating capital systems, Sraffa introduced his important distinction between basic commodities and non-basic commodities. As he put it, 'The criterion is whether a commodity enters (no matter whether directly or indirectly) into the production of *all* commodities. Those that do we shall call *basic*, and those that do not, *non-basic* products' (p. 8). It is then shown that basics have a number of properties which are not shared by non-basics. It is readily seen

---

profit rate and consumption is proportional to u (the assumption is more complex if degeneracy is taken into account). In an unpublished paper Bidard (1986b) has generalized his own procedure and proved, among other things, that if for any system T and any process m which pays extra-profits at prices of T (for a given r) it is possible to find another system T_1 made up by process m and $n-1$ processes in T, such that the process in T which is not in T_1 does not pay extra-profits at prices of T_1, then there exists a cost-minimizing system.

[12] Two systems of production are said to be compatible at rate of profit r if they have the same price vector and the same wage rate at that profit rate. A more complex definition can take into account degeneracy (see Salvadori, 1982, p. 285).

that in a single-product system, as in Definition 1 with $B \equiv I$, if the commodities can be so numbered that matrix A takes the form

$$A \equiv \begin{bmatrix} A_1 & 0 \\ A_3 & A_4 \end{bmatrix},$$

where A_1 and A_4 are both square matrices, then A_4 refers to non-basic commodities. If there exists a group of one or more commodities such that, for every possible A matrix representation, that group always appears in the corresponding A_1, then that group of commodities is the group of *basic* commodities.

However, when Sraffa came to discuss joint products he naturally found that, since a process can produce more than one product, the qualitative distinction between basic and non-basic commodities cannot be represented in terms of the input matrix alone. He was thus led to propose a more abstract definition of basics in terms of linear dependence or independence between the rows of alternative matrices constructed by selecting combinations of corresponding columns from $[B, A]$. But, as he noted, such a definition 'is not nearly so satisfactory from the economic standpoint as the intuitive criterion of "entering, or not entering, the means of production of all commodities"' (Sraffa, 1960, p. 51). It has been noted subsequently, however, that that 'intuitive criterion' can indeed be maintained even in the case of joint production if, rather than considering matrices B and A themselves (which, dimensionally, are process by commodity matrices), one considers instead the matrix H, for example (which is a commodity by commodity matrix). (On matrix H, refer back to Section 2 above.) Thus on the basis of Manara's (1968) fundamental paper, it was pointed out (Steedman, 1977b) that, subject to one caveat (*ibid.*, appendix), Sraffa's formal linear (in-) dependent criterion for basics and non-basics implies that if the matrix H can be written in the form

$$H \equiv \begin{bmatrix} H_1 & 0 \\ H_3 & H_4 \end{bmatrix}, \tag{8}$$

where H_1 and H_4 are square matrices, then H_4 refers to non-basic commodities. If there exists a group of one or more commodities such that, for every possible H matrix representation, that group always appears in the corresponding H_1, then that group of commodities is the group of *basic* commodities. In what follows we suppose the existence of at least one basic and we shall so arrange matrix H that H_1 contains only basics and H_4 contains only non-basics (which implies that H_3 is not null).[13] Since the

---

[13] Steedman (1977b) moved too quickly to the positive identification of the commodities in any H_1 matrix as basics, before considering alternative H matrix representations. For example H_1 itself could have the form attributed to H in the text and in this case, clearly, not all the commodities referred to in H_1 would be basics.

JOINT PRODUCTION ANALYSIS IN A SRAFFIAN FRAMEWORK   177

foregoing applies equally to the single-products case, it transpires that Sraffa's 'intuitive criterion' need not be abandoned in the face of joint products. (See also Schefold, 1971, p. 9.)

In the same line of thought, Pasinetti (1980a) has pointed out that the matrix $B^{-1}A$ can be so ordered as to have a block of zeroes in the top right-hand corner. And Potestio (1980) has noted the analogous point about matrix $[(B-A)^{-1}B]$.[14] It may be added here that the same qualitative property holds good for matrix $[(B-\lambda A)^{-1}A]$, where the real number λ is nonnegative and less than the maximum growth factor. All these results of Steedman (1977b), Pasinetti (1980a), Potestio (1980), and that just given are implicit in the work of Manara (1968) on the distinction between basics and non-basics in square joint production systems. Manara's mathematical argument will not be reported here but the interested reader will wish to consult Section 6 of his paper.

To say that, even with joint production, matrix H can be written as in equation (8), is not yet to say that basics and non-basics retain all their simple, single-products characteristics in the more complex case. For example, in the single-products case the sub-matrix H_1 is completely independent of the conditions of production of non-basics; in the joint production case, by contrast, H_1 depends on these latter production conditions, in general (see Steedman, 1977b, p. 325).

Let us now return to the price equations (6), taking account of the fact that H can be written as in (8). If we partition the vectors $\mathbf{p}$ and $\mathbf{v}$, with $\mathbf{p}_1$ and $\mathbf{v}_1$ referring to basics and $\mathbf{p}_2$ and $\mathbf{v}_2$ to non-basics, we may write equation (6) as

$$\begin{bmatrix} \mathbf{p}_1 \\ \mathbf{p}_2 \end{bmatrix} = w \begin{bmatrix} \mathbf{v}_1 \\ \mathbf{v}_2 \end{bmatrix} + r \begin{bmatrix} H_1 & 0 \\ H_3 & H_4 \end{bmatrix} \begin{bmatrix} \mathbf{p}_1 \\ \mathbf{p}_2 \end{bmatrix}$$

or

$$\mathbf{p}_1 = w(I - rH_1)^{-1}\mathbf{v}_1 \tag{9}$$

$$\mathbf{p}_2 = (I - rH_4)^{-1}(w\mathbf{v}_2 + rH_3\mathbf{p}_1) \tag{10}$$

Whilst one cannot say that equation (9) shows the prices of basics to be independent of the production conditions of non-basics, since H_1 (and $\mathbf{v}_1$) are not thus independent, one can say that the variations of $\mathbf{p}_1$ with r may be examined independently of the variations of $\mathbf{p}_2$ with r; but the converse is not true, from (10). Hence there is still a sense in which basics prices have a logical priority over non-basics prices, even if Sraffa (1960, Section 65) went further than is legitimate in playing down the role of non-basics in a joint production system (Steedman, 1977b, p. 327).

---

[14] Let $\mathbf{q}$ be the vector of gross outputs. With $\mathbf{x}$ and $\mathbf{y}$ defined as above, $\mathbf{q}' = \mathbf{x}'B$ and $\mathbf{y}'(B-A)$. Hence, when $(B-A)$ is non-singular, $\mathbf{q}' = \mathbf{y}'[(B-A)^{-1}B]$; thus the matrix $[(B-A)^{-1}B]$ relates the gross output vector to the net output vector.

In his discussion of single-product, circulating capital systems, Sraffa was able to show straightforwardly that only basic commodities will enter, in positive amounts, into his Standard commodity. The latter is, of course, a composite commodity such that, for the given conditions of production, the vectors of net output, gross output and capital inputs will all be proportional to one another. In vertically-integrated terms, then, the net output y^* will be a Standard commodity if

$$y^{*T} = Ry^{*T}H,$$

where R is the maximum feasible rate of profit for the system in question. If there are non-basics, H may be written as in (8) and thus, in an obvious notation,

$$(y_1^*, y_2^*) = R(y_1^*, y_2^*) \begin{bmatrix} H_1 & 0 \\ H_3 & H_4 \end{bmatrix}$$

or

$$y_1^* = R(y_1^* H_1 + y_2^* H_3) \tag{11}$$

$$y_2^* = R y_2^* H_4 \tag{12}$$

If H_4 has a smaller Perron-Frobenius root than H_1 (as Sraffa, 1960, p. 28, n. 1, assumes) we see from equations (11) and (12) that $y_2^* = 0$ (non-basics do not enter the Standard commodity and the maximum rate of profit depends on H_1, and thus on basic commodities, only). Now, what difference does it make if joint production is introduced? Equations (11) and (12) still hold good — but it is no longer ensured that H is semi-positive. It may be, of course, and, if it is, the single products argument can in effect be repeated. But as soon as H contains one or more negative elements it is, obviously, not possible to appeal to the Perron-Frobenius theorem. Hence y^* may now contain negative elements, as Sraffa (1960, pp. 47–48) recognized; and may contain complex elements (as Sraffa gives no indication of having recognized). Relatedly, R may take complex values and, more generally, the rule which Sraffa (1960, p. 53) gives for choosing the economically significant solution from amongst the alternative mathematical solutions to (11) and (12) is not in fact valid.

It is, of course, still perfectly possible to pre-multiply equation (6) by any y^* and to obtain

$$y^{*T}p = wy^{*T}v + \frac{r}{R} y^{*T}p$$

or

$$\frac{wy^{*T}v}{y^{*T}p} = \frac{R-r}{R}$$

JOINT PRODUCTION ANALYSIS IN A SRAFFIAN FRAMEWORK   179

which says that the real wage, measured as a share of the Standard net product, is a decreasing linear function of the profit rate. But whether this is now a *useful* expression, given what has just been said about y^* and R, is far from clear. (The best discussions of these issues are perhaps Manara, 1968, and Schefold, 1971.)

The conclusion of this section is thus that some of Sraffa's remarks about basics, non-basics, the Standard commodity and the maximum rate of profit, in the joint production context, were less than fully accurate and that some doubt may reasonably be entertained as to the usefulness, in that context, of the concept of Standard commodity and as to the clarity of Sraffa's definition of the maximum rate of profit.

VI. POSITIVE PRICES AND WAGE-PROFIT FRONTIERS

Sraffa (1960, p. 59) has remarked that, if joint production holds, prices with respect to a given system of production may turn negative at some feasible rate of profit, as the rate of profit changes. This problem was first studied with respect to a single system of production (Cogoy, 1977; Duménil and Lévy, 1984; Filippini, 1977; Filippini and Filippini, 1982; Lévy, 1984; Lippi, 1978). By using the Farkas Lemma, or some other Theorem of the Alternative,[15] these authors have proved that some prices are negative if and only if a nonnegative linear combination of some processes yields a greater net net output (i.e., gross output minus $(1 + r)$ times the material inputs) than a nonnegative linear combination of the remaining ones. To put the matter more formally, let us divide the set of processes making up a system of production into two subsets, I and J; if there exist two semipositive vectors $\mathbf{u}$ and $\mathbf{v}$ such that

$$\mathbf{u}^T \mathbf{e}_i = 0 \text{ if the process } (\mathbf{a}_i, \mathbf{b}_i, l_i) \in I$$

$$\mathbf{v}^T \mathbf{e}_j = 0 \text{ if the process } (\mathbf{a}_j, \mathbf{b}_j, l_j) \in J$$

$$\mathbf{u}^T[[B - (1 + r)A], -\mathbf{l}] \geqslant \mathbf{v}^T[[B - (1 + r)A], -\mathbf{l}]$$

then the processes in J are said to *dominate* the processes in I. The authors mentioned have proved that at least one price is negative if and only if some processes are dominated.[16]

The name 'domination' might suggest the idea that the dominated processes could always be eliminated by means of the choice of technique, so that negative prices could not arise in cost-minimizing systems. Moreover, Sraffa himself suggested that 'those among the methods of production that gave rise to such a result [i.e., the possibility of negative prices] would be

---

[15] See, for instance, Gale (1960, pp. 42–9) or Mangasarian (1969, pp. 27–34).

[16] Rampa (1976) and Wolfstetter (1976) refer to a similar property but their arguments are limited to the two by two case.

discarded to make room for others which in the new situation were consistent with positive prices' (Sraffa, 1960, p. 59). Nevertheless, this idea is
not correct in the absence of free disposal, as can be shown by an example
(Salvadori, 1985, pp. 164–165). The concept of dominance is useful,
however, and requires a deeper analysis. The dominated processes, in fact,
can be seen as processes which 'dispose' of some commodities which are
'over-produced' by the dominating processes. This 'disposal' is costly and
negative prices are the payment for the 'service' of disposal.

This leads to the more general question of the treatment of 'disposal'
issues within a Sraffian framework. The introduction of free disposal, of
course, is sufficient to ensure that no price is negative in cost-minimizing
systems (Steedman, 1976; Schefold, 1978c, 1980a; Salvadori, 1985). But
free disposal in general is not a realistic assumption. A better solution is to
introduce free disposal only for some commodities and to allow negative
prices for those commodities which cannot be disposed of costlessly (cf.
Franke 1986a; Hinrichsen and Krause, 1981). For each commodity to be
freely disposed of, one can suppose the existence of a process to which
that commodity is the sole input and from which there is no output. Alternatively, it can be supposed that for each commodity to be disposed of and
for each process producing such a commodity jointly with other commodities, there is another process with the same inputs and the same
outputs but for that particular commodity. This ensures that, in cost-minimizing systems, that commodity cannot have a negative price (Schefold,
1978a, 1980b; Baldone, 1980; Varri, 1980; Salvadori, 1988). (The introduction of these 'fictitious' processes often also helps in proving that cost-
minimizing systems are square.)

Whilst assuming the existence of free disposal only for some products is
clearly superior to assuming free disposal for all products, however, it is
still not acceptable. To assume free disposal for even one product is to
deny the principle of the conservation of mass-energy, one of the most
fundamental principles of Thermodynamics! Every process with some
input must have some product. If that product has a zero value, this may be
related to the complete absence of property rights (e.g., smoke in the air,
radioactive waste at the bottom of the ocean), to complex questions of
externalities in the presence of partially defined property rights (e.g., creation of waste disposal sites), and so on. Difficult, interesting and important
as these issues may be, they are in no way specific to Sraffian economics,
however; no framework of analysis may properly assume free disposal. It
would thus be out of place to pursue these issues here.

We may now turn to more readily resolvable questions. The Farkas
Lemma can be utilized, much as above, to analyse the slope of the wage-
profit relationship. It is well known that such a relationship is decreasing,
whatever the numéraire, if only single product processes exist. On the
contrary, simple examples show that this is not generally true when joint
production is involved. Thus, it is important to study when labour

commanded prices are increasing functions of the rate of profit, because if and only if all of them are so, is the wage rate decreasing whatever the numéraire. It is possible to prove (see, e.g., Filippini and Filippini, 1982, pp. 389–390) that some labour commanded prices are decreasing functions with respect to r if and only if a nonnegative linear combination of some processes yields a greater net net output than a nonnegative linear combination of the remaining ones, even though the former combination has a lower value of capital stock. To put the matter more formally, let us divide the set of processes making up a system of production into two subsets, I and J; if and only if there exist two semipositive vectors $\mathbf{u}$ and $\mathbf{v}$ such that

$$\mathbf{u}^T\mathbf{e}_i = 0 \text{ if the process } (\mathbf{a}_i, \mathbf{b}_i, l_i) \in I$$

$$\mathbf{v}^T\mathbf{e}_j = 0 \text{ if the process } (\mathbf{a}_j, \mathbf{b}_j, l_j) \in J$$

$$\mathbf{u}^T[[B-(1+r)A], -A\,\mathbf{p}] \geqslant \mathbf{v}^T[[B-(1+r)A], -A\mathbf{p}]$$

then some labour commanded prices are decreasing functions with respect to r. Hence it is possible, as asserted above, for a real wage-rate of profit frontier to be upward sloping in a general joint production system. (As will be seen in Section 7, this possibility does not exist in some fixed capital systems.)

We may conclude this section by remarking that even a 'minimal amount' of joint production can lead to negative prices or decreasing labour commanded prices. Consider a joint production system in which the output matrix B is an identity matrix, *except that* the first process also produces an amount $b > 0$ of commodity 2; this is the *only* element of joint production present. On defining $L \equiv [I-(1+r)A]^{-1}$, one can readily show that

$$\mathbf{p} = wL\mathbf{1} - bL\,\mathbf{e}_1\mathbf{e}_2^T\mathbf{p} \tag{13}$$

Then, by multiplying equation (13) by $\mathbf{e}_2^T$

$$\mathbf{e}_2^T\mathbf{p} = w\mathbf{e}_2^TL\mathbf{1} - b\mathbf{e}_2^TL\mathbf{e}_1\mathbf{e}_2^T\mathbf{p}$$

i.e.

$$\mathbf{e}_2^T\mathbf{p} = \frac{w\mathbf{e}_2^TL\mathbf{1}}{1+b\mathbf{e}_2^TL^T\mathbf{e}_1}$$

Thus equation (13) can be re-written as

$$\mathbf{p} = wL\mathbf{1} - \frac{bw\mathbf{e}_2^TL\mathbf{1}}{1+b\mathbf{e}_2^TL\mathbf{e}_1L\,\mathbf{e}_1}$$

Thus, if there exists a commodity i such that

$$\mathbf{e}_i^TL\mathbf{1}\mathbf{e}_2^TL\mathbf{e}_1 < \mathbf{e}_2^TL\mathbf{1}\mathbf{e}_i^TL\mathbf{e}_1 \tag{14}$$

then there exists a real number $b > 0$ such that some price is negative. (Note that **p** is a function of b.) A similar argument applies also to the vector of derivatives of the labour commanded prices; the result is exactly the same as inequality (14) *except that* **l** is replaced by A **p**.

VII. FIXED CAPITAL

As was mentioned in Section 1, Sraffa introduces Fixed Capital, in Chapter X, as the 'leading species' of the 'genus' Joint Production, following the 'old classical idea'[17] of treating old machines left at the end of each period as economically different goods from the machines which entered production at the beginning of the period. Sraffa also presents a model of a system of production with fixed capital based on the assumption that each process utilizes no more than one old machine, the efficiency of each type of machine being constant.

Baldone (1980), Schefold (1971, 1976b, 1978a, 1980b) and Varri (1980) have generalized Sraffa's model to introduce machines whose efficiency is not constant, whilst retaining the assumption that no process employs more than one old machine. When this is done, the economic lifetime of machines is not necessarily equal to the physical life and has to be determined within the model. These authors first consider a system of production and then determine the cost-minimizing system, which is also the system with the optimal lifetime of machines. The procedure most often followed is to discuss first in some detail the case in which fixed capital is used in the production of only one finished good (a consumption good, a circulating capital good, or a new machine): it is then pointed out that the analysis can clearly be extended to the case in which fixed capital is used in the production of any number of finished goods. In the following presentation, however, we shall proceed directly to this more general case.

Let us first divide commodities into two groups, *finished goods* and *old machines* of various ages — call m the number of finished goods and $(n - m)$ the number of old machines. Each process is assumed to produce one and only one finished good (no 'pure' joint production) and, perhaps, one old machine. No old machine can be utilized in the production of a finished good different from that alongside which it is produced (old machines cannot be transferred among sectors; a sector is constituted by all the processes engaged in the production of a given finished good). There is for each finished good one *primary* process which uses exclusively finished goods as inputs, among them (perhaps) the new machine(s).[18]

---

[17] Sraffa (1960, pp. 94–5) refers explicitly to Torrens as the first to use this device to deal with fixed capital, then followed by Ricardo, Malthus, and Marx.

[18] Baldone (1980), Schefold (1971, 1978a, 1980b) and Varri (1980) have suggested that if more than one new machine is utilized in a given process, the single 'old machine' referred to above can be interpreted as a *plant*.

The machine produced by the primary process is utilized by the first *intermediate* process, which (perhaps) produces a machine utilized by the second intermediate process. And so on, until the machine is worn out by the *final* process and has a zero scrap value.

In order to put this matter more formally, let us say that the system $(A, B, \mathbf{l})$ is a *fixed capital system* if matrices A and B can be partitioned in the following way:

$$A = \begin{bmatrix} A_{11} & A_{12} & 0 & 0 & \cdots & 0 \\ A_{21} & 0 & A_{23} & 0 & \cdots & 0 \\ A_{31} & 0 & 0 & A_{34} & \cdots & 0 \\ \cdot & \cdot & \cdot & \cdot & \cdots & \cdot \\ \cdot & \cdot & \cdot & \cdot & \cdots & \cdot \\ A_{t1} & 0 & 0 & 0 & \cdots & 0 \end{bmatrix}$$

$$B = \begin{bmatrix} B_{11} & 0 & 0 & 0 & \cdots & 0 \\ B_{21} & B_{22} & 0 & 0 & \cdots & 0 \\ B_{31} & 0 & B_{33} & 0 & \cdots & 0 \\ \cdot & \cdot & \cdot & \cdot & \cdots & \cdot \\ \cdot & \cdot & \cdot & \cdot & \cdots & \cdot \\ B_{t1} & 0 & 0 & 0 & \cdots & B_{tt} \end{bmatrix}$$

where the dimension of sub-matrix A_{11} (B_{11}) equals m, sub-matrices $A_{i-1,i}$ $(i = 2, 3, \ldots, t)$ are of the form

$$\begin{bmatrix} D \\ 0 \end{bmatrix}$$

where sub-matrix D is diagonal with a strictly positive main diagonal and 0 is a zero sub-matrix (perhaps with no rows), sub-matrices $B_{ii}(i = 1, 2, \ldots, t)$ are diagonal with strictly positive main diagonals, and sub-matrices $B_{i1}(i = 2, 3, \ldots, t)$ are of the form

$$[D\ 0]$$

The interpretation is the following. The first $s_1 = m$ processes produce all the m finished goods, do not produce old machines, and utilize (perhaps) machines arrived at their last year of utilization; then s_2 processes produce s_2 $(\leqslant s_1)$ finished goods jointly with machines arrived at their last year of utilization and utilize one year younger machines, ..., finally the last s_t processes produce s_t $(\leqslant s_{t-1})$ finished goods jointly with one year old machines (which will live t years) without utilizing old machines, t being the maximum number of years any machine can last. Note that commodity 1 is produced jointly with a machine which can last t years and that commodity m is produced either without any machine or, if no commodity is produced without utilizing machines, jointly with a machine which can last the minimum number of years a machine can last.

It can be shown (see Baldone, 1980; Schefold, 1971, 1978a, 1980b; and Varri, 1980) that for a Fixed Capital system as just defined, if the rate of profit is lower than the maximum rate of profit, then the prices of all finished goods are positive. It follows that, if machines can be freely disposed of, then all prices will be nonnegative in the cost-minimizing system. Moreover the determination of the cost-minimizing system is independent of requirements for use (on the assumption that machines are not consumed). All these results are immediate consequences of the fact that if the rate of profit is lower than the maximum rate of growth, then matrix $[B-(1+r)A]$ is invertible and the first m rows of $[B-(1+r)A]^{-1}$ are semipositive. This result can be proved in a way which is very simple but cannot be found in the literature: it is presented in the appendix to the present paper.

Once the prices of used machines are obtained, depreciation can easily be calculated by taking into account that the change in price over one production period is, by definition, the depreciation for that period. Of course the depreciation per period will depend in general on the rate of profit. Even for a given rate of profit, it will depend on the age of the machine and will not be equal to a constant fraction of the value of the machine at the beginning of the period.

Since the vector of derivatives of labour commanded prices with respect to the profit rate is equal to $[B-(1+r)A]^{-1}Ap$, whenever Ap is positive the first m components of that vector of derivatives are positive. In other words the real wage rate in terms of each of the finished goods is inversely related to the rate of profit for the given technique. And since no price is negative in any cost-minimizing system, the real wage rate in terms of each of the finished goods is still inversely related to the rate of profit even when the chosen technique is changing with the rate of profit.

The fixed capital model analysed by Baldone (1980) Schefold (1971, 1978a, 1980b) and Varri (1980), like that presented here and analysed in the appendix, is not able to take into account the joint utilization of used machines.[19] More general models allowing joint utilization of machines

---

[19] The only case of jointly utilized new machines which can be considered is that in which new machines are assembled to constitute a 'plant', so that the 'used machine' is, in fact, constituted by more than one machine (see the preceding footnote). This is, of course, a strong assumption, since cost-minimizing management of fixed capital stock might well involve separating previously jointly utilized machines and reassembling them differently. Of course there may be cases in which the costs of separating and reassembling components of a plant are sufficiently large as to ensure that the cost-minimizing solution will not involve any such dismantling and reassembling; in these cases the concept of 'plant' as proposed by Baldone

JOINT PRODUCTION ANALYSIS IN A SRAFFIAN FRAMEWORK   185

have been introduced more recently[20] by Salvadori (1988). Instead of starting from the analysis of a single system of production to consider the choice of technique at a second stage, Salvadori (1988) follows the procedure of starting from the whole technology, to determine the set of processes which can be operated, in order to prove, finally, the existence of a square cost-minimizing system. Following this procedure it is shown that, even if machines are utilized jointly, the output pattern for consumption goods does not matter in determining the cost-minimizing system, but that for investment goods may do so.[21] The same paper takes into account also the problem of scrapped machines, showing that if the scrap metal etc. is re-utilized directly or indirectly in the production of the same finished goods as were produced by the scrapped machines, the same results can be obtained.

VIII. SOME IMPLICATIONS FOR OTHER ECONOMIC THEORIES

In the final chapter of Part I of his book — Chapter VI, 'Reduction to Dated Quantities of Labour' — Sraffa made one of the few explicit criticisms of marginal theory to be found in that book. After presenting a numerical example, he remarked that it 'seems conclusive in showing the impossibility of aggregating the "periods" belonging to the several quantities of labour into a single magnitude which could be regarded as representing the quantity of capital. The reversals in the direction of the movement of relative prices, in the face of unchanged methods of production, cannot be reconciled with *any* notion of capital as a measurable quantity independent of distribution and prices' (1960, p. 38). The numerical example in question was based on the concept of 'reduction to dated labour', that is, of taking a price system such as equation (3) above, with $B = I$, and rewriting it as follows:

$$\mathbf{p} = \mathbf{l} + (1 + r)A\,\mathbf{p}$$

or

$$\mathbf{p} = \mathbf{l} + (1 + r)A[\mathbf{l} + (1 + r)A\,\mathbf{p}]$$

or

$$\mathbf{p} = \mathbf{l} + (1 + r)A\,\mathbf{l} + (1 + r)^2 A^2[\mathbf{l} + (1 + r)A\,\mathbf{p}],$$

(1980), Schefold (1971, 1978a, 1980b) and Varri (1980) is both acceptable and useful (see Schefold, 1976b, and Salvadori, 1987). Nevertheless, in the most general case the concept of a 'plant' is not acceptable and it is only by carrying out the general analysis that one can determine whether or not one is dealing with such a special case.

[20] Roncaglia (1971) has also considered jointly utilized machines but only for the case of constant efficiency.

[21] Salvadori (1988) assumes steady growth, and therefore the growth rate is a sufficient index of investment; however, the generalization to the case in which there is an individual growth rate for each sector is obvious.

etc. Given that wages are positive (as is already implicit in writing down a vector of labour commanded prices), this process of 'self-substitution' may legitimately be continued without limit, to obtain

$$\mathbf{p} = \mathbf{l} + (1+r)A\,\mathbf{l} + (1+r)^2 A^2\mathbf{l} + \ldots + (1+r)^n A^n\mathbf{l} + \ldots \qquad (17)$$

since the (vector) terms involved tend to zero. Since $(A^n\mathbf{l})$ may be interpreted as a vector of quantities of labour expended n periods before the products are finally available, (17) is said to present a reduction of prices to dated labour terms (compounded by $(1+r)^n$, of course).

How do things stand in the case of joint production? Starting from the price equation (3) we can, if B is non-singular, write

$$\mathbf{p} = (B^{-1}\mathbf{l}) + (1+r)(B^{-1}A)\mathbf{p}$$

or

$$\mathbf{p} = (B^{-1}\mathbf{l}) + (1+r)(B^{-1}A)[(B^{-1}\mathbf{l}) + (1+r)(B^{-1}A)\mathbf{p}]$$

or

$$\mathbf{p} = (B^{-1}\mathbf{l})$$
$$+ (1+r)(B^{-1}A)(B^{-1}\mathbf{l}) + (1+r)^2(B^{-1}A)^2[(B^{-1}\mathbf{l}) + (1+r)(B^{-1}A)\mathbf{p}]$$

etc. But this series may not converge, even at $r = 0$. If we start instead from the vertically-integrated price equations (6), we have

$$\mathbf{p} = \mathbf{v} + rH\mathbf{p}$$

or

$$\mathbf{p} = \mathbf{v} + rH(\mathbf{v} + rH\mathbf{p})$$

or

$$\mathbf{p} = \mathbf{v} + rH\mathbf{v} + r^2 H^2(\mathbf{v} + rH\mathbf{p})$$

or

$$\mathbf{p} = \mathbf{v} + rH\mathbf{v} + r^2 H\mathbf{v} + \ldots + r^n H\mathbf{v} + \ldots \qquad (18)$$

This series will indeed converge for $r = 0$ but, alas, there is no guarantee that it will do so for all the values of r which are compatible with well-defined, positive prices, $\mathbf{p} = (I - rH)^{-1}\mathbf{v}$. In any case, neither H nor $\mathbf{v}$ is certain to be nonnegative, so that the economic interpretation of (18), although possible, may be decidedly artificial, even when (18) may legitimately be expanded indefinitely. (Pasinetti, 1973; Schefold, 1971, 1976, 1980.)

Thus far, then, joint products appear to constitute a serious problem for any attempt — 'Austrian', 'neo-Austrian', or other — to represent production processes and value and distribution relationships in terms of a series of 'dated' labour inputs. The difficulties are somewhat less severe,

JOINT PRODUCTION ANALYSIS IN A SRAFFIAN FRAMEWORK 187

however, if one considers not a general joint production system but a system involving the use of fixed capital in which old machines are not transferable between sectors and there is no other element of joint production present. Following the lead given by Sraffa (1960, pp. 65–6), Schefold (1976, 1980) has shown how the old machine prices may be eliminated from the system of price equations to yield what he calls the 'centre' system:

$$\mathbf{p}^f = \mathbf{l}^c(r) + (1+r)A^c(r)\mathbf{p}^f, \tag{19}$$

where the price vector, $\mathbf{p}^f$, refers only to 'finished commodities' (including new machines but excluding old ones), while $\mathbf{l}^c(r)$ and $A^c(r)$ are a hypothetical labour input vector and a produced hypothetical input matrix whose elements vary with r. The theorem presented in the appendix to the present paper can be used to show the existence and semipositivity of an $(m \times n)$ matrix $Q(r)$ such that

$$Q(r)[B - (1+r)A] = [[I - (1+r)A^c(r)], 0]$$

where $A^c(r)$ is an $(m \times m)$ matrix. Then $\mathbf{l}^c(r) = Q(r)\mathbf{l}$.

Schefold shows that, under reasonable assumptions, (19) may be expanded as

$$\mathbf{p}^f = \mathbf{l}^c(r) + (1+r)A^c(r)\mathbf{l}^c(r) + (1+r)^2[A^c(r)]^2\mathbf{l}^c(r) + \ldots \tag{20}$$

which converges for $0 \leqslant r < R$ and in which $\mathbf{l}^c(r)$ and $A^c(r)$ are semipositive. Yet while (20) might appear to provide a 'reduction to dated labour terms', it will be clear that such an interpretation must be handled with great caution. Unless every machine is of constant efficiency, both $\mathbf{l}^c(r)$ and $A^c(r)$ vary with r, so that it is only in the most hypothetical way that one may interpret $[A^c(r)]^n\mathbf{l}^c(r)$ as a vector of labour inputs n periods in advance. In any case, as Schefold makes clear, (20) cannot be used to justify any notion of a period of production, or any other measure of the quantity of capital, which must fall with r as the methods of production are changed in response to the changing r. One may thus be legitimately sceptical about any attempt to construct a general economic theory in 'neo-Austrian' terms (see also Hagemann and Kurz, 1976).

The Sraffian approach to joint production has also been used to question certain fundamental claims within traditional, 'Anglo-Saxon' Marxian economics. Sraffa pointed out in his Chapter IX that in a joint products system a negative amount of labour might be imputed to the (direct and indirect) production of one or more commodities. In our above notation, that is, $\mathbf{v} = [B - A]^{-1}\mathbf{l}$ need not be a nonnegative vector. (This possibility was also discussed in Gilibert, 1972, and Schefold, 1972.) It was then asked whether it might not follow that a semipositive bundle of commodities, $\mathbf{c}$, acquired by capitalists could exhibit the property $\mathbf{c}^T\mathbf{v} < 0$, even in a system with positive profits, prices and activity levels. That is, in Marxian terminology, whether 'negative surplus value' might not be consistent with positive profits. It was shown by means of a simple numerical example that they are indeed consistent (Steedman, 1975; 1977a, chapter 11), which makes it a little difficult to regard the (traditionally calculated) Marxian surplus value as the 'source' of profit. It has also been shown, within a Sraffian framework, that even in the absence of 'pure' joint products, traditional Marxian value accounting can impute a negative 'labour value depreciation' to a machine when there is falling efficiency (Hodgson and Steedman, 1977; Steedman, 1977a, Chapter X). Thus the Sraffian approach to joint production analysis has a number of awkward implications for traditional Marxian labour value accounting. As some slight recompense, however, Salvadori (1981) has shown that Okishio's well-known theorem (1961) ceases to be valid if, unlike Okishio, one allows for joint production; it is then a logical possibility that, with a given real wage, technical progress will, under competitive pressures, lead to a decline in the rate of profit.

As is now well-known, Samuelson's famous Surrogate Production Function (1962) implicitly involved a very simple labour theory of value: his construction depended in an essential way on the extreme assumption of equal machine/labour ratios in both machine and consumption commodity production. It has also been found, on the basis of Sraffa's approach to correct fixed capital depreciation accounting, that the Surrogate construction was no less dependent on Samuelson's adoption of the (completely implausible) 'radioactive decay' treatment of fixed capital. When depreciation is calculated correctly, capital-reversing (i.e., an increase in the capital-labour ratio as the rate of profit increases) is entirely compatible with 'equal input proportions' in production, machines of constant efficiency, infinitely many alternative techniques and the complete absence of reswitching between techniques (Steedman, 1979). Thus the Surrogate Production Function is even more vulnerable than has often been thought.

We may conclude this section by noting that a careful consideration of joint production reveals the possibility of 'upward sloping' distribution frontiers relating the real returns to primary inputs, e.g., a real wage rate and a real rent rate may be positively related. And this may be so even when 'capital theory' phenomena are entirely absent, there being no produced inputs and all primary inputs being paid *ex post* (Steedman, 1982). The root explanation of this phenomenon is exactly the same as that of the possibility of 'negative surplus value', referred to above: in the presence of joint products, a negative vertically-integrated use of some primary input(s) may be inputed to one or more commodities. Consequently, the coefficient(s) of one or more real primary input returns, in the linear distribution frontier, may be negative, so that some of those returns may be positively related to one another. And once it has been understood that, with joint production, a real wage-real rent frontier (say) may be upward sloping, it can be seen that an import tariff can 'harm' both factors (contrary to the Stolper-Samuelson theorem) and that a factor supply increase can, at constant commodity prices, provoke an increase in the output of both commodities (contrary to the Rybczynski theorem) (*ibid.*). Hence a number of familiar results from 'marginalist' theory are not readily generalizable to the joint production case — i.e., to the empirically relevant case. The same is true of familiar ideas relating to neutral Hicksian technical progress. Such progress can, in the presence of joint production, shift an upward sloping wage-rent frontier inwards towards the origin and can, at both constant relative factor prices and constant relative commodity prices, lead to results quite different from those predicted (correctly) in the single-products case (Steedman, 1985).

A Sraffian approach to joint production analysis has thus already led to a number of significant results concerning 'neo-Austrian', Marxian, Surrogate and '*m* primary factor, *n* final commodity' analyses: there is no reason to think that a Sraffian approach cannot continue to produce results concerning joint production which will have considerable interest for those working within other kinds of economic theory.

IX. CONCLUSION

We have seen that Sraffa's approach to joint production analysis has generated a number of interesting problems and discussions 'internal' to that approach and various implications for different non-Sraffian strands of economic theory. We hope to have shown thereby that both economists working within the Sraffian framework and those working outside it have much to gain from a serious consideration of a Sraffian approach to the important topic of joint production.

Istituto di Studi Economici, I.U.N.
Via Acton, 38
i80133 Napoli, Italy
University of Manchester
Manchester, UK M13 9PL

Invited paper,
revised version
received February 1988

REFERENCES

Abraham-Frois, G. and E. Berrebi (1984). 'Taux de Profit Minimum dans les Modèles de Production' in Bidard, (1984c), pp. 211–29.

Baldone, S. (1980). 'Fixed Capital in Sraffa's Theoretical Scheme', in Pasinetti (1980), pp. 88–137.

Berthomieu, C. and J. and L. Cartelier (1972). eds, *Ricardiens, Keynésiens et Marxistes*, Grenoble, Presses Universitaires.

Bidard, Ch. (1984a). 'Choix Techniques en Production Jointe', in Bidard (1984c), pp. 186–207.

190   BULLETIN OF ECONOMIC RESEARCH

Bidard, Ch. (1984b). 'Jules et Jim' in Bidard (1984c), pp. 208–10.
Bidard, Ch. (1984c). ed., *La Production Jointe, Nouveaux Débats*, Paris, Econo-
mica.
Bidard, Ch. (1986a). 'Is von Neumann Square?', *Zeitschrift für Nationalökonomie*,
Vol. 46, pp. 401–19.
Bidard, Ch. (1986b). *A Combinational Theory of Choice of Techniques*, mimeo,
Université de Paris X-Nanterre.
Bidard, Ch. and Franke, R. (1987). 'On the Existence of Long-Term Equilibria in
the Two-Class Pasinetti-Morishima Model', *Ricerche Economiche*, Vol. 41,
pp. 3–21.
Burmeister, E. and Kuga, K. (1970). 'The Factor-Price Frontier, Duality and Joint
Production', *Review of Economic Studies*, Vol. 37, pp. 11–19.
Cogoy, M. (1977). *Wertstruktur und Preisstruktur*, Frankfurt am Main, Suhrkamp
Verlag.
Craven, J. (1979). 'Efficiency Curves in the Theory of Capital: A Synthesis', in
Patterson and Schott (1979), pp. 76–96.
Duménil, G. and Lévy, D. (1984). 'The Unifying Formalism of Domination: Value,
Price, Distribution and Growth in Joint Production', *Zeitschrift für Nationalö-
konomie*, Vol. 44, pp. 349–71.
Faccarello, G. and Ph. de Lavergne (1977), eds., *Une Nouvelle Approche en
Économie Politique? Essais sur Sraffa*, Paris, Maspero.
Filippini, C. (1977). 'Positività dei Prezzi e Produzione Congiunta', *Giornale degli
Economisti e Annali di Economia*, Vol. 36, pp. 91–9.
Filippini, C. and Filippini, L. (1982). 'Two Theorems on Joint Production', *The
Economic Journal*, Vol. 92, pp. 386–90.
Franke, R. (1985). 'On the Upper- and Lower-Bound of Workers' Propensity to
Save in a Two-Class Pasinetti Economy', *Australian Economic Papers*, Vol. 25,
pp. 271–7.
Franke, R. (1986a). 'Some Problems Concerning the Notion of Cost-Minimizing
Systems in the Framework of Joint Production', *The Manchester School*, Vol.
52, pp. 298–307.
Franke, R. (1986b). *An Extension of the Gale-Nikaido-Debreu Lemma with
Applications to Generalized von Neumann Models*, mimeo, University of
Bremen.
Fujimoto, T. (1975). 'Duality and the Uniqueness of Growth Equilibrium', *Interna-
tional Economic Review*, Vol. 16, pp. 781–91.
Gale, D. (1960). *The Theory of Linear Economic Models*, New York, McGraw-
Hill.
Garegnani, P. (1973). 'Nota Matematica', published as an appendix to the Italian
edition of 'Beni Capitali Eterogenei, la Funzione della Produzione e la Teoria
della Distribuzione' in Sylos Labini, P. (ed.) *Prezzi Relativi e Distribuzione del
Reddito*, Boringhieri, Turin. (This mathematical note was mentioned but not
published in the original English edition of the paper published in the *Review of
Economic Studies*, 1970, Vol. 37, pp. 407–36).
Garegnani, P. (1976). 'On a Change in the Notion of Equilibrium in Recent Work
on Value and Distribution: A Comment on Samuelson' in Brown, M., Sato, K.
and Zarembka, P. (eds.), *Essays in Modern Capital Theory*, Amsterdam, North-
Holland, pp. 25–45.
Gilibert, G. (1972). 'Production Conjointe et Valeurs-Travail Négatives', in

Berthomieu and Cartelier (1972), pp. 229–37.

Giorgi, G. and Magnani, U. (1978). 'Problemi Aperti nella Teoria dei Modelli Multisettoriali di Produzione Congiunta', *Rivista Internazionale di Scienze Sociali*, Vol. 86, pp. 435–68.

Hagemann, H. and Kurz, H. D. (1976). 'The Return of the Same Truncation Period and Reswitching of Techniques in Neo-Austrian and more General Models', *Kyklos*, Vol. 29, pp. 678–708.

Hinrichsen, D. and Krause, U. (1978). 'Choice of Techniques in Joint Production Models', *Operations Research Verfahren*, Vol. 34, pp. 155–71.

Hinrichsen, D. and Krause, U. (1981). 'A Substitution Theorem for Joint Production Models with Disposal Processes', *Operations Research Verfahren*, Vol. 41, pp. 287–91.

Hodgson, G. and Steedman, I. (1977). 'Depreciation of Machines of Changing Efficiency: A Note', *Australian Economic Papers*, Vol. 16, pp. 141–7.

Jevons, W. S. (1970 [1871]). *The Theory of Political Economy*, Harmondsworth, Penguin.

Kurz, H. (1986). 'Joint Production in the History of Economic Thought', *Metroeconomica*, Vol. 38, pp. 1–37.

Levhari, D. (1965). 'A Non Substitution Theorem and Switching of Techniques', *Quarterly Journal of Economics*, Vol. 79, pp. 98–105.

Lévy, D. (1984). 'Le Formalisme Unificateur du Surclassement: Valeur, Prix, Répartition et Croissance en Production Jointe', in Bidard (1984c), pp. 37–51.

Lippi, M. (1979). *I Prezzi di Produzione. Un Saggio sulla Teoria di Sraffa*, Bologna, Il Mulino.

Łos, J. and Łos, M. W. (1976). 'Reswitching of Techniques and Equilibria of Extended von Neumann Models', in Łos, J., Łos, M. W. and Wieczorek, A. (eds.), *Warsaw Fall Seminars in Mathematical Economics 1975*, Berlin, Springer-Verlag, pp. 97–118.

Manara, C. (1968). 'Il Modello di Piero Sraffa per la Produzione Congiunta di Merci a Mezzo di Merci', *L'Industria*, pp. 3–18; English translation in Pasinetti (1980b).

Mangasarian, O. L. (1969). *Nonlinear Programming*, Bombay, Tata McGraw-Hill.

Morishima, M. (1960). 'Economic Expansion and the Interest Rate in Generalized von Neumann Models', *Econometrica*, Vol. 28, pp. 352–63.

Morishima, M. (1964). *Equilibrium, Stability and Growth*, Oxford, Clarendon Press.

Morishima, M. (1969). *Theory of Economic Growth*, Oxford, Clarendon Press.

Neumann, J. von (1945). 'A Model of General Economic Equilibrium', *Review of Economic Studies*, Vol. 13, pp. 1–9.

Okishio, N. (1961). 'Technical Change and the Rate of Profit', *Kobe University Economic Review*, Vol. 7, pp. 86–96.

Pasinetti, L. L. (1973). 'The Notion of Vertical Integration in Economic Analysis', *Metroeconomica*, Vol. 25, pp. 1–29. Reprinted in Pasinetti (1980b).

Pasinetti, L. L. (1980a). 'A Note on Basics, Non-Basics and Joint Production', in Pasinetti (1980b), pp. 51–4.

Pasinetti, L. L. (1980b). ed., *Essays on the Theory of Joint Production*, London, Macmillan.

Patterson, K. D. and Schott, K. (1979). *The Measurement of Capital, Theory and Practice*, London, Macmillan.

192   BULLETIN OF ECONOMIC RESEARCH

Potestio, P. (1980). 'Some Remarks on Vertically Integrated Sectors', *Metroeconomica*, Vol. 32, pp. 63–75.

Rampa, L. (1976). 'Valori Lavoro e Spreco di Lavoro nei Modelli di Produzione Congiunta, *Giornale degli Economisti e Annali di Economia*, Vol. 35, pp. 601–21.

Roncaglia, A. (1971). 'Il Capitale Fisso in uno Schema di Produzione Circolare', *Studi Economici*, Vol. 26, pp. 232–45. English edition in Roncaglia, A. (1978).

Roncaglia, A. (1978). *Sraffa and the Theory of Prices*, New York, John Wiley and Sons.

Salvadori, N. (1979a). 'Mutamento dei Metodi di Produzione e Produzione Congiunta. Un Commento al §96 di *Produzione di Merci a mezzo di Merci'*, *Studi Economici*, Vol. 34, pp. 79–94.

Salvadori, N. (1979b). *Mutamento dei Metodi di Produzione e Produzione Congiunta*, Università degli Studi di Siena, Istituto di Economia, Quaderni dell'Istituto di Economia, N.6, Siena.

Salvadori, N. (1980). 'On a Generalized von Neumann Model', *Metroeconomica*, Vol. 32, pp. 51–62.

Salvadori, N. (1981). 'Falling Rate of Profit with a Constant Real Wage. An Example', *Cambridge Journal of Economics*, Vol. 5, pp. 59–66.

Salvadori, N. (1982). 'Existence of Cost-Minimizing Systems within the Sraffa Framework', *Zeitschrift für Nationalökonomie*, Vol. 42, pp. 281–98.

Salvadori, N. (1984). 'Le Choix de Techniques chez Sraffa: Le cas de la Production Jointe', in Bidard (1984c), pp. 175–85.

Salvadori, N. (1985). 'Switching in Methods of Production and Joint Production', *The Manchester School*, Vol. 53, pp. 156–78.

Salvadori, N. (1987). 'Il Capitale Fisso come "Specie" del "Genere" Produzione Congiunta. Ulteriori Precisazioni ed una Risposta' *Economia Politica*, Vol. 4, pp. 265–75.

Salvadori, N. (1988). 'Fixed Capital within the Sraffa Framework', *Zeitschrift für Nationalökonomie*, Vol. 48, forthcoming.

Samuelson, P. A. (1962). 'Parable and Realism in Capital Theory: The Surrogate Production Function', *Review of Economic Studies*, Vol. 29, pp. 193–206.

Saucier, Ph. (1984). 'La Production Jointe en Situation de Concurrence', in Bidard (1984c), pp. 155–74.,

Schefold, B. (1971). *Mr Sraffa on Joint Production*, Basel, private print. (A revised, published version is forthcoming from Allen and Unwin, London).

Schefold, B. (1972). 'Le Système de Sraffa et la Production Jointe: deux Exemples d'Application', in Berthomieu and Cartelier (1972), pp. 141–56.

Schefold, B. (1976a). 'Relative Prices as a Function of the Rate of Profit: A Mathematical Note', *Zeitschrift für Nationalökonomie*, Vol. 36, pp. 21–48.

Schefold, B. (1976b). 'Reduction to Dated Quantities of Labour, Roundabout Processes, and Switches of Techniques in Fixed Capital Systems', *Metroeconomica*, Vol. 27, pp. 1–15.

Schefold, B. (1978a). 'Fixed Capital as a Joint Product', *Jahrbücher für Nationalökonomie und Statistik*, Vol. 192, pp. 21–48.

Schefold, B. (1978b). 'Multiple Product Techniques with Properties of Single Product Systems', *Zeitschrift für Nationalökonomie*, Vol. 38, pp. 29–53.

Schefold, B. (1978c). 'On Counting Equations', *Zeitschrift für Nationalökonomie*, Vol. 38, pp. 253–85.

JOINT PRODUCTION ANALYSIS IN A SRAFFIAN FRAMEWORK   193

Schefold, B. (1980a). 'Von Neumann and Sraffa: Mathematical Equivalence and Conceptual Difference', *Economic Journal*, Vol. 90, pp. 140–56.

Schefold, B. (1980b). 'Fixed Capital as a Joint Product and the Analysis of Accumulation with Different Forms of Technical Progress', in Pasinetti (1980b), pp. 138–217.

Sraffa, P. (1960). *Production of Commodities by Means of Commodities*, Cambridge University Press, Cambridge.

Steedman, I. (1975). 'Positive Profits wtih Negative Surplus Value', *Economic Journal*, Vol. 85, pp. 114–23.

Steedman, I. (1976). 'Positive Profits with Negative Surplus Value: a Reply to Wolfstetter', *Economic Journal*, Vol. 86, pp. 873–876.

Steedman, I. (1977a). *Marx after Sraffa*, London, New Left Books.

Steedman, I. (1977b). 'Basics, Non-Basics and Joint Production', *Economic Journal*, Vol. 87, pp. 324–28. Reprinted in Pasinetti (1980b).

Steedman, I. (1979). 'Fixed Capital and the Surrogate Production Function', in Patterson and Schott (1979), pp. 65–75.

Steedman, I. (1980). 'Returns to Scale and the Switch in Methods of Production', *Studi Economici*, Vol. 35, pp. 5–13.

Steedman, I. (1982). 'Joint Production and the Wage-Rent Frontier', *Economic Journal*, Vol. 92, pp. 377–85.

Steedman, I. (1984). 'L'importance Empirique de la Production Jointe', in Bidard (1984c), pp. 5–20.

Steedman, I. (1985). 'Joint Production and Technical Progress', *Political Economy*, Vol. 1, pp. 41–52.

Varri, P. (1980). 'Prices, Rate of Profit and Life of Machines in Sraffa's Fixed-Capital Model', in Pasinetti (1980), pp. 55–87.

Wicksell, K. (1934 [1901]). *Lectures on Political Economy, Volume 1*, London, Routledge and Kegan Paul.

Wolfstetter, E. (1976). 'Positive Profits with Negative Surplus Value: a Comment', *Economic Journal*, Vol. 86, pp. 864–72.

APPENDIX

Theorem. Let $(A, B, \mathbf{l})$ be a fixed capital system as defined in Section 7 of the text. If there exists a nonnegative vector $\mathbf{q}$ such that

$$\mathbf{q}^T[B-(1+r)A]=(\mathbf{c}^T, \mathbf{0}^T)$$

where $\mathbf{c}$ is a positive m-vector and $\mathbf{0}$ is a zero $(n-m)$-vector, then matrix $[B-(1+r)A]$ is invertible and the first m rows of $[B-(1+r)A]^{-1}$ are semipositive.

Lemma. $\{\mathbf{u}^T[B-(1+r)A]=(\mathbf{c}^T, \mathbf{0}^T), \mathbf{u} \geq 0\} \Rightarrow \mathbf{u} > \mathbf{0}$.

Proof. It is immediately obtained that

$$\mathbf{u}_t^T B_{tt} = (1+r)\mathbf{u}_{t-1}^T A_{t-1,t} \tag{1.t}$$

$$\mathbf{u}_{t-1}^T B_{t-1,t-1} = (1+r)\mathbf{u}_{t-2}^T A_{t-2,t-1} \tag{1.t-1}$$

$$\vdots$$

$$\mathbf{u}_2^T B_{22} = (1+r)\mathbf{u}_1^T A_{12} \tag{1.2}$$

$$\mathbf{u}_{11}^T B_{11} + \mathbf{u}_2^T B_{21} + \ldots + \mathbf{u}_t^T B_{t1} > 0$$

where $(\mathbf{u}_1^T, \mathbf{u}_2^T, \ldots, \mathbf{u}_t^T) = \mathbf{u}^T$. Hence,

$$\mathbf{u}_1^T [B_{11} + C_{12}B_{21} + C_{12}C_{23}B_{31} + \ldots + C_{12}C_{23} \ldots C_{t-1,t}B_{t1}] > 0, \tag{2}$$

where $C_{i-1,i} = (1+r)A_{i-1,i}B_{ii}^{-1}(i=2, \ldots t)$. Since sub-matrices $C_{i-1,i}(i=2, \ldots t)$ are of the form

$$\begin{bmatrix} D \\ 0 \end{bmatrix}$$

and sub-matrices $B_{i1}(i=2, \ldots t)$ are of the form

$$[D\, 0],$$

the matrix in brackets in inequality (2) is diagonal. As a consequence, $\mathbf{u}_1 > 0$. Then, since sub-matrices $A_{i-1,i}(i=2, \ldots t)$ are of the form

$$\begin{bmatrix} D \\ 0 \end{bmatrix}$$

and sub-matrices $B_{ii}(i=2, \ldots t)$ are diagonal with a strictly positive main diagonal, we obtain from equations (1) that $\mathbf{u}_i > 0 \, (i=2, \ldots t)$.

Proof of the Theorem. Let $\mathbf{a} \geq 0$ be an m-vector, and assume that there exists a vector $\mathbf{v}$ with at least one negative element such that

$$\mathbf{v}^T[B - (1+r)A] = (\mathbf{a}^T, 0).$$

Let j be such that

$$0 > \frac{\mathbf{v}^T \mathbf{e}_j}{\mathbf{q}^T \mathbf{e}_j} \leq \frac{\mathbf{v}^T \mathbf{e}_h}{\mathbf{q}^T \mathbf{e}_h} \qquad \forall h$$

then

$$\left[\mathbf{v} - \frac{\mathbf{v}^T \mathbf{e}_j}{\mathbf{q}^T \mathbf{e}_j}\mathbf{q}\right] \geq 0$$

and

$$\left[\mathbf{v} - \frac{\mathbf{v}^T \mathbf{e}_j}{\mathbf{q}^T \mathbf{e}_j}\mathbf{q}\right]^T [B - (1+r)A] = (\mathbf{a}^T - \frac{\mathbf{v}^T \mathbf{e}_j}{\mathbf{q}^T \mathbf{e}_j}\mathbf{c}^T, 0^T) \equiv (\mathbf{b}^T, 0^T)$$

with $\mathbf{b} > \mathbf{0}$. Then the Lemma applies. Hence we have a contradiction, since the j-th element of vector

$$\left[\mathbf{v} - \frac{\mathbf{v}^T \mathbf{e}_j}{\mathbf{q}^T \mathbf{e}_j} \mathbf{q} \right]$$

cannot be strictly positive. Thus

$$\{ \mathbf{v}^T[B - (1+r)A] = (\mathbf{a}^T, \mathbf{0}^T), \mathbf{a} \geq \mathbf{0} \} \Rightarrow \mathbf{v} \geq \mathbf{0}.$$

Let $\mathbf{y}^T[B - (1+r)A] = \mathbf{0}^T$, then $\mathbf{y} \geq \mathbf{0}$. Moreover, $(-\mathbf{y}^T)[B - (1+r)A] = \mathbf{0}^T$. Then, $\mathbf{y} \leq \mathbf{0}$. Thus $\mathbf{y} = \mathbf{0}$ and $\det([B - (1+r)A]) \neq 0$. As a consequence there exist semipositive vectors $\mathbf{z}_i$ such that $\mathbf{z}_i^T[B - (1+r)A] = \mathbf{e}_i^T (i = 1, 2, \ldots, m)$. Thus the first m rows of the matrix $[B - (1+r)A]^{-1}$ are semipositive.

Part II
System of Production

[4]

Vol. 38 (1978), No. 1-2, pp. 29—53

Zeitschrift für
Nationalökonomie
Journal of Economics
© by Springer-Verlag 1978

Multiple Product Techniques
With Properties of Single Product Systems

By

Bertram Schefold, Frankfurt am Main

(Received September 15, 1977)

In the context of Sraffa systems most economists tend to avoid joint production and prefer to discuss single product systems because of their simple and elegant properties which have often been represented under the familiar headings of activity analysis or linear economic systems outside the circle of the Sraffa school. It is true that joint production raises a number of intricate problems; no straightforward economic assumptions are known which could be made to ensure that prices in joint production systems are positive at a given rate of profit prior to truncation, the distinction between basics and non basics is not easily maintained in the presence of joint production, etc. Sraffa (1960) has hinted at many of the problems involved. I believe, however, that it is possible to characterize those instances of joint production systems which retain some of the simple properties of single product systems, to distinguish them analytically from those with more paradoxical properties and to relate the paradoxes appearing in the theoretical model to obstacles to the competitive formation of prices in the real world.

The present paper which is meant as a preliminary to such a discussion, is concerned firstly with the task of defining a special type of joint production system which exhibits *all* the important properties of single product systems. It will be found that this kind of system is not likely to be found in reality in pure form, but it is nevertheless worthwhile to investigate it, not only because such an investigation helps to clarify the specific properties of single product systems, but mainly because some of the properties concerned are also characteristic for other special joint production systems such

0044-3158/78/0038/0029/$ 05.00

as fixed capital systems and may at least be approximated by real joint production systems[1]. These systems are called all-engaging.

Section 3 discusses switches of technique in all-engaging systems; section 4 shows that nearly all joint production systems will, after truncation, be all-engaging at high rates of profit; the main difficulties with joint production systems occur thus at low rates of profit. Section 5 discusses the most distinguishing feature of joint production systems which are not all-engaging, i. e. paradoxical price changes in reaction to changes of technique.

1. Single Versus Joint Production

We consider the classical model of a capitalist economy in a selfreplacing state. There are n commodities being produced by m processes which can be distinguished by the proportions in which they use each a positive amount of homogeneous labour and some of the produced commodities as inputs and by the proportions in which they produce commodities as outputs. Even if the output of some processes consists of several joint products, conditions of demand will ensure in most cases that, given a wide range of alternative techniques, the number of processes actually employed equals the number of commodities produced; the reason given by Sraffa being that it will otherwise in general not be possible to produce the net output of commodities in the proportions socially required, if the proportions in which techniques are activated can be varied at all (constant returns are not required although we shall assume them in section 4)[2]. On the other hand, prices would be overdeter-

---

[1] Some of the definitions and theorems contained in section 2 of the paper have been discussed in Schefold (1971).

[2] Take the textbook example: Wool and mutton can be produced from sheep in different proportions by slaughtering sheep earlier or later. Farmers in Australia are supposed to slaughter later because wool is easier to transport, farmers in Scotland are supposed to slaughter earlier in order to produce more mutton. The example is meant to show that the proportions in which different outputs are jointly produced are variable even in cases where a natural invariable proportion seems to be given by nature. The number of different (i. e. linearly independent) processes actually in use cannot exceed the number of commodities with positive prices, however, since the price system must not be overdetermined. The proportions in which commodities are to be produced may nevertheless (at least within a certain range) be varied by only varying the activity levels; in our example, an increase in the demand for wool could be satisfied without changing methods and without increasing the production of mutton by diminishing

mined, i. e. in general (except at switchpoints) incompatible with a uniform rate of profit, if the number of processes exceeded the number of commodities. [The argument can be expressed in a mathematically rigourous form for regular systems, as is proved in Schefold (1977 c).]

To begin with it suffices to *assume* that $n=m$ so that with a given rate of profit r, calculated on the basic period of production, relative prices are determined by

$$(1+r)\, Ap + wl = Bp,$$

where A, B are semipositive square matrices whose elements $a_i{}^j$, $b_i{}^j$ ($i, j = 1, \ldots, n$) denote the quantity of good j used (produced) in process i, where the column vectors $l > 0$ and p are the labour vector and the price vector respectively, and where w is the wage-rate. In order to exclude land which requires a special treatment and cases which would be meaningless in the context of our discussions, we shall assume throughout that no row of A and no column of B vanishes and that $\det(B-A) \neq 0$. We measure goods in terms of total output by putting the column sum of each output equal to one (i. e. $eB = e$ where $e = (1, \ldots, 1)$). We normalize $el = 1$.

If B is the identity matrix, we are dealing with single product industries, i. e. with circulating capital. We know then that if the single product system fulfills the sole assumption of being productive, i. e. if it is capable of producing a surplus such that $e(B-A) \geq 0$, the following properties hold:

1. If we assume constant returns to scale, all products are *separately producible*, i. e. it is possible to produce a net output consisting of a unit of anyone commodity with non-negative activity levels.

2. It is possible to define *basic goods* firstly as those goods which enter directly or indirectly the production of all the goods in the system. One assumes that the system contains at least one basic good. The subsystem composed of all the basic goods taken together with the processes producing them is then called the *basic system*. One could also say that all commodities embody positive amounts of all basic, but not of non-basic, commodities. Secondly,

---

the number of farmers in Scotland and increasing that of farmers in Australia. Except for fluke cases where a lower number happens to give the appropriate proportions of outputs the required surplus cannot be produced if the number of processes in use is inferior to the number of commodities produced. The argument does not suppose constant returns.

32   B. Schefold:

it is well known that this part of the system coincides with the part
corresponding to the smallest indecomposable matrix $A_1{}^1$ obtained
after simultaneous permutations of rows and columns of the input
matrix A such that

$$A = \begin{pmatrix} A_1{}^1 & A_1{}^2 \\ A_2{}^1 & A_2{}^2 \end{pmatrix}$$

where $A_1{}^1$ is quadratic and $A_1{}^2$ equals zero. It seems not to have
been remarked before (but it is vital for the understanding of joint
production systems) that the basic single product system coincides
thirdly also with the set of *indispensable processes,* i. e. with the
set of those processes which have to be activated for whatever net
output there is to be produced. (In formulas: Process i is not indispensable if a net output $s = (s_1, \ldots, s_n)$, $s \geq 0$, $s \neq 0$, and non-negative
activity levels $q = (q_1, \ldots, q_n)$ exist such that $q\,(B - A) = s$ and $q_i = 0$).
Fourthly, basic commodities coincide with indispensable commod-
ities in a Sraffa system, i. e. with those which have to be produced
if any nonnegative output is to result ($q\,(B - A) \geq 0$ entails $qb^j > 0$
if j is indispensable). The main economic interest in the distinction
between basics and non-basics derives, however, from two further
properties: If the price of a non-basic is changed because of a tax on
it or because its method of production is changed, only the price of
this and possibly some other non-basics are affected, whereas a
change in the method of production of a basic or a tax on a basic
affects all prices. It follows that the theory of distribution will
mainly be concerned with basics in this latter sense.

3. There is a unique maximum rate of profit which is numerically
equal to the maximum rate of balanced growth of the basic system.
Relative prices of production of basics are defined and positive for
all rates of profit.

3.1. The same can be assumed to be true for the prices of non-
basics, for if it is not the case for some non-basic, its method of
production has to be changed at those rates of profit where its price
is not positive[3].

4. Mr. Sraffa's standard commodity exists and may be used to
express prices and to reveal the known straight line relationship
between the real wage and the rate of profit.

5. If prices are measured instead in terms of the wage rate
(labour commanded $\hat{p} = \frac{p}{w}$), prices will be equal to labour values

---

[3] For this subtle and important point see Bharadwaj (1970).

at $r = 0$, rise monotonically with r, and tend to infinity at the maximum rate of profit R.

6. If an alternative method of production for one of the commodities in a basic single product system is introduced, all prices in terms of the wage rate are simultaneously raised or lowered (or stay the same, if the two methods happen to be introduced at a switchpoint). Supposing that the alternative technique is superior, an invention, say, the real wage (whatever its standard) will be raised by the new technique at a given rate of profit, and the entrepreneurs who are the first to make the transition while the old prices are still ruling, will make surplus profits whereas those who are last and still use the old technique when the new price system has come into use will make losses. The price of the commodity whose method of production is changed will be lower in the new system relative to the price of any other commodity.

None of these properties hold in all joint production systems, but all hold in a modified form for some joint production systems. Take e. g. the first property: If wool and mutton in the example of Note 1 above are pure consumption goods they are, with given methods of production in "Scotland" and "Australia", not separately producible solely by varying activity levels. If a real change in demand requiring that more be produced of a given commodity takes place, methods of production will in general be found to make the change possible; at worst overproduced goods will partly be disposed of[4]. But not many goods have ever to be produced separately in reality, it is therefore not surprising that real systems are not separately producible, although it so happens that only systems where all commodities are separately producible can be easily handled without confronting the problem of truncation.

The production of each commodity with the net product of the economy otherwise remaining the same can be increased and requires always a positive increase of all activity levels *if and only if* all processes are indispensable and all goods are separately producible. In the example above, an increase in the production of wool without an increase of the production of mutton is feasible only if one pro-

---

[4] If the proportion of wool were to be increased relatively to mutton beyond the limit given by the "Australian" method of production where the maximum of wool is obtained, mutton will become overproduced. According to Neoclassical theory its price then drops to zero, it ceases to be a commodity, and only one method, the "Australian" will be used, the number of commodities again being equal to the number of processes and wool being a single product of its method of production.

34   B. Schefold:

cess is expanded and another contracted, because wool and mutton, being pure consumption goods, are not used as inputs. But if the jointly produced goods are used as inputs in different proportions, it may become possible that the increase in demand for one commodity can be met without contracting any of the processes because the increase in the gross production of any joint products in the same process is just absorbed through the increased use of the joint products as inputs.

Joint production systems where all goods are separately producible do therefore not have to be single product systems. Such a system will be called *all-productive*. If it happens that all processes are at the same time indispensable, the system will be called *all-engaging*. Clearly $(B-A)^{-1} \geq 0$ if the system is all-productive, for the activity levels q_i yielding a unit output e_i (e_i is the i-th unit vector) of good e_i will then be non-negative:

$$q_i = e_i (B-A)^{-1} \geq 0.$$

Similarly $(B-A)^{-1} > 0$, if and only if the system is all-engaging[5]. (The definition will be generalised in section 4.)

We shall now first show in a series of steps that all-engaging systems have the same properties as single product systems. Afterwards, some remarks will be made on why general joint production systems which, being unlike single product systems in relation to property 1 above, are also different and uncomfortably complicated in relation to properties 3—6.

Regarding property 2 suffice it to say here that there are *several* possible and meaningful definitions of basics and non-basics in joint production systems. We reserve a full discussion of the various alternatives for another paper and define in accordance with Sraffa: A joint production system A, B is basic if no linear combination of rows of (A, B, l) and no permutation of columns of A, B can be found which transform A and B simultaneously into almost triangular matrices:

$$\begin{pmatrix} A_1^1 & 0 \\ A_2^1 & A_2^2 \end{pmatrix} \begin{pmatrix} B_1^1 & 0 \\ B_2^1 & B_2^2 \end{pmatrix}$$

---

[5] E. g. the following system is all-engaging:

$$A = \begin{pmatrix} 0 & 0 & a_1^3 \\ a_2^1 & 0 & 0 \\ 0 & a_3^2 & 0 \end{pmatrix}, \quad B = \begin{pmatrix} 1 & b_1^2 & 0 \\ 0 & 1 & a_2^3 \\ b_3^1 & 0 & 1 \end{pmatrix}$$

if $(a_1^3, a_2^1, a_3^2) < (1,1,1)$ and

$$a_1^3 a_3^2 > b_1^2, \quad a_1^3 a_2^1 > b_2^3, \quad a_2^1 a_3^2 > b_3^1.$$

Multiple Product Techniques   .   35

where $A_1{}^1$, $B_1{}^1$ are quadratic matrices of the same order. Completely non basic systems with $A_2{}^1 = B_2{}^1 = 0$ should be excluded by assumption. (Linear combinations must be admitted as was stressed by Sraffa (1960) in addition to permutations in order to eliminate land and some peculiar cases which are discussed in Schefold (1971).

Clearly, any price appearing only in the non basic part (A_2, B_2) can be taxed without affecting prices of basics in $(A_1{}^1, B_1{}^1)$, but one cannot say that the commodities produced in the former do not enter indirectly the production of the commodities produced in the latter if the relevant elements of $A_2{}^2$ and $B_2{}^1$ are positive. Each commodity used in A may be said to enter the production of each commodity in B, if $B^T A$ is an indecomposable matrix (B^T is the transposed of B). $B^T A$ can be a positive matrix even if A, B are not only a non-basic but a decomposable system. The definition of basics most appropriate for single product systems therefore seems to have no meaning in joint production systems, but one can show [Schefold (1971)] that a system is basic in the sense of Sraffa if and only if the matrix $(B-A)^{-1} A$ is indecomposable, and this matrix is capable of an interpretation: Since $e_i (B-A)^{-1}$ are the activity levels required to produce one unit of commodity i, $e_i (B-A)^{-1} a^j$ are the amounts of commodity j embodied in commodity i (which may be negative) so that the element (i, j) of $(B-A)^{-1} A$ is zero if and only if j is not embodied in i. The system A, B is thus non basic if the set of commodities can be partitioned into two sets such that the commodities of the first set are embodied in the commodities of the second but not vice versa. Note that the matrix $(B-A)^{-1} A$ of a basic system contains negative elements only if it is not all-productive. The basic part need not be nonnegative after an elimination of non basics involving linear superpositions of rows. The system $[(B-A)^{-1} A, I]$ was interpreted by Pasinetti (1973) by means of the concept of an "integrated industry".

2. Negative Labour Values, Indispensable Processes, and Separately Producible Commodities

In general joint production systems negative prices may appear as formal solutions of the price system indicating that the methods of production are economically not compatible. This can, however, not be the case for the labour values of goods which are separately producible, for if a good i is separately producible, the equation

$$q_i (B - A) = e_i$$

3*

36   B. Schefold:

has a non-negative activity vector as its solution so that u_i, the i-th of the labour values[6]

$$u = (B-A)^{-1} l$$

is positive:

$$u_i = e_i u = e_i (B-A)^{-1} l = q_i l > 0.$$

Moreover, if all values in the system are positive, the price $\hat{p}_i = \dfrac{p_i}{w}$ of commodity i in terms of the wage rate will rise monotonically with r in a neighbourhood of $r = 0$, for by differentiating the price equations we obtain:

$$B \frac{d}{dr} \hat{p} = A\hat{p} + (1+r) \ A \frac{d}{dr} \hat{p}$$

hence

$$\frac{d}{dr} \hat{p}_i (0) = e_i \frac{d}{dr} \hat{p} (0) = e_i (B-A)^{-1} A\hat{p} (0) = q_i Au > 0.$$

But negative labour values can quite easily occur for they may be compatible with positive prices at the ruling rate of profit. They give rise to a curious paradox[7]: If good i is produced by a negative amount of labour $(q_i l < 0)$, and if s is the net output of the economy at the normal activity levels $e = (1, \ldots, 1)$,

$$e (B-A) = s \geq 0,^8$$

the total net output can be *increased* by a small amount δ of commodity i using a *diminished* quantity of labour. For if δ is small, $e + \delta q_i$ are feasible (non-negative) activity levels and

$$(e + \delta q_i) (B-A) = s + \delta e_i \geq s.$$

In the case of fixed capital this paradox is easily resolved: Negative prices, in particular values, can only occur for old machines. An old machine receiving a negative value may still be used, if its price is positive at the ruling rate of profit. But if the process using the

---

[6] That $u = (B-A)^{-1} l$ represent labour values can be shown by means of Mr. Sraffa's subsystems approach which is implicit in the above equations. If e_i is the net output of the system, $q_i l$ is the amount of labour required to produce it directly and indirectly.

[7] See Sraffa (1960), p. 60.

[8] If all elements of a matrix or vector A are greater than those of B, we write $A > B$, if they are greater or equal, we write $A \geqq B$; we write $A \geq B$, if $A \geqq B$ and $A \neq B$.

old machine is truncated, the old machine appears in the net product of the system (which therefore increases) while labour may be saved without reducing output otherwise by raising the level of activity in the process using a younger machine[9]. A similar argument can be constructed in the case of the more general truncations discussed in Schefold (1977 c). It can be seen conversely, on the other hand, that negative labour values are excluded as long as net output cannot be increased by using more labour. Negative labour values occur therefore *if and only if* an output-increasing, labour-reducing change of activity levels is feasible. In this sense they invariably reveal an inefficiency in a stationary system with constant returns to scale, but one which cannot be ruled out as long as prices diverge from values because the rate of profit is positive.

We have found that negative values are excluded for all goods which are separately producible. We now find that, independently of it, negative values can only occur, if some processes are not indispensable.

Theorem 2.1: If some labour values of a joint production system are not positive, some processes are not indispensable.

Proof: If $u_i \leq 0$, $e_i (B-A)^{-1} = q_i \not> 0$. If $q_i^j = 0$, the j-th process is not indispensable. If all q_i^j are either >0 or <0, take $\lambda = \underset{j}{\text{Min}}\, q_i^j$. Then we have

$$|\lambda|\, e\, (B-A) + q_i\, (B-A) = |\lambda|\, s + e_i \geq 0$$

while $|\lambda|\, e + q \geq 0$ with $|\lambda| + q_i^j = 0$ for at least one j. Hence, if all processes are indispensable, values must be positive as they must be, if all commodities are separately producible.

We now prove:

Theorem 2.2: If all products of a joint production system are separately producible and if all processes are indispensable (if the system is all-engaging), the system is basic and possesses the above mentioned qualities (1), (3), (4), and (5) of a basic single product system.

Proof: Since all products are separately producible, $e_i (B-A)^{-1} \geq 0$ for all i, and since all processes are indispensable, $e_i (B-A)^{-1} > 0$ for all i, hence $(B-A)^{-1} > 0$, $q_i = e_i (B-A)^{-1} > 0$, $i = 1, \ldots, n$. If any of the columns of A vanished, say $a^n = 0$, we had $q_i (b^n - a^n) = 0$

---

[9] See Schefold (1977 a).

38   B. Schefold:

for $i < n$ which contradicts $q_i (b^n - a^n) = q_i b^n > 0$ because $q_i > 0$, $b^n \geq 0$. Thus $a^i \geq 0$ for all i and $(B-A)^{-1} A > 0$.

Now, if A, B was a non basic system, $(B-A)^{-1}A$ would be a decomposable matrix contradicting $(B-A)^{-1} A > 0$, therefore A, B is a basic system.

By virtue of the Frobenius theorem there is a unique $R > 0$ and a column vector $p > 0$ so that $R (B-A)^{-1} Ap = p$, hence $(1+R) Ap = Bp$, and there is a unique row vector q with $(1+R)qA = qB$. q must also be positive by virtue of the Frobenius theorem, for $RqA (B-A)^{-1} = q$, and $A (B-A)^{-1} > 0$, since we have assumed that the rows a_i of A are semipositive. q provides the standard commodity.

Now consider prices $\hat{p} = \dfrac{p}{w}$ in terms of the wage rate. That they have the required properties is obvious from the transformation (I is the unit matrix):

$$\hat{p} = [B - (1+r) A]^{-1} i$$
$$= \{(B-A) [I - r (B-A)^{-1} A]\}^{-1} l$$
$$= [I - r (B-A)^{-1} A]^{-1} (B-A)^{-1} l.$$

The relationship between indecomposability, prices, and changes in methods of production will be taken up below.

3. All-Engaging Systems and Switches of Techniques

Theorem 2.2 has made it clear that all-engaging systems are rather like single product systems. They are not only interesting in themselves but also because it can be shown that the finished goods produced by machines in basic fixed capital systems are separately producible while the processes using new machines are indispensable (Schefold 1977 a).

All-engaging systems have similar properties as single product systems also in so far as switches of techniques are concerned.

Theorem 3.1:[10] If we are given an all-engaging system with an alternative method of production for one industry, it follows for any given rate of profit, r, smaller than the maximum rate of profit that all prices $\hat{p}$ (prices in terms of the wage-rate) are lower for one of the two techniques (the "superior") — or else they are all equal.

The theorem clearly implies that wage-rate and real wage are higher for the superior technique at the given rate of profit, if prices

---

[10] The following proof is from Schefold (1971).

are measured in a commodity standard, and it also follows that the inferior technique, if it is at all capable of reaching this highest real wage, reaches it at a lower rate of profit.

We prove the theorem as follows:

(A, B, l) denotes our original system. The question is, whether it is advantageous to replace an industry, say the first (a_1, b_1, l_1) by (a_0, b_0, l_0) (it is assumed, of course, that this replacement is technically feasible). Let $\hat{p}^I$, $\hat{p}^{II}$ denote the two possible price vectors in terms of the wage rate so that

and

$$[b_i - (1+r) a_i] \hat{p}^I = l_i, \ i = 0, 2, \ldots, n$$

$$[b_i - (1+r) a_i] \hat{p}^{II} = l_i, \ i = 1, 2, \ldots, n.$$

Since $b_i - (1+r) a_i$, $i = 2, \ldots, n$ are linearly independent, $\hat{p}^I - \hat{p}^{II}$ is on the straight line through the origin consisting of all vectors x for which

$$[b_i - (1+r) a_i] x = 0, \ i = 2, \ldots, n.$$

The vector y solving

$$Cy = \begin{pmatrix} 1 \\ 0 \\ \vdots \\ \vdots \\ 0 \end{pmatrix} \quad \text{where} \quad C = \begin{pmatrix} b_1 - (1+r) a_1 \\ \ldots \\ b_n - (1+r) a_n \end{pmatrix}$$

is also on this line, $C^{-1} > 0$ (we are in an all-engaging system), hence $\hat{p}^I > \hat{p}^{II}$, $\hat{p}^I < \hat{p}^{II}$ or $\hat{p}^I = \hat{p}^{II}$ [11].

According to theorem 3.1, the superior technique appears to be superior at any point by a criterion which is similar to that of Pareto optimality. The superior technique is superior in theory because it allows a higher real wage at a *given* rate of profit and a higher rate of profit at the given wage in the same way as general equilibrium is Pareto optimal only relative to a given distribution of initial resources. Hence, not distribution but the chosen technique appears to be justified, and the justification is not based on technical efficiency or productivity but on the argument that the superior technique provides a distributional advantage to both classes given the initial distribution. The argument can be matched by the known dual relationship between the rate of profit and the rate of growth.

---

[11] Equality occurs identically in r or at most at n rates of profit: the switchpoints.

40   B. Schefold:

The driving force for the adoption of the new techniques is competition. However, it is difficult to analyse the various possible processes of transition from one technique to the other. Here we shall only be concerned with the proof of the classical proposition that the capitalists who are first to make the transition will reap surplus profits, while those who are last will incur losses. Keynesian arguments about induced changes in incomes and employment, and neoclassical arguments about increases of consumption compensating the sacrifices required for making the transition will not be considered.

Specifically, we have

Theorem 3.2: Let the rate of profit be given. The use of the superior method of production (see theorem 3.1) at prices corresponding to the inferior technique yields surplus profits, the use of the inferior method at prices corresponding to the superior technique implies losses, both relative to "normal profits" corresponding to the given rate of profit. Surplus profits and losses exist irrespective of the standard of prices.

Proof: Using the notation of the proof of theorem 3.1 above and assuming that (a_0, b_0, l_0) represents the new superior technique, losses through using the old technique at new prices would not be made if

$$[b_i - (1+r)\, a_i]\, \hat{p}^I \geqq l_i. \quad i = 1, \ldots, n,$$

which implies, since

$$[B - (1+r)\, A]^{-1} = [I - r\, (B-A)^{-1}\, A]^{-1}\, (B-A)^{-1} > 0$$

for an all-engaging system that

$$\hat{p}^I \geqq [B - (1+r)\, A]^{-1}\, l = \hat{p}^{II}$$

in contradiction to the assumption that $\hat{p}^I < \hat{p}^{II}$, the new technique being superior. The converse case is analogous. If a commodity standard is introduced in place of the standard in terms of the wage rate, i. e. if relative prices are normalised by putting the value of a basket of commodities $d = (d_1, \ldots, d_n)$ equal to one ($dp = 1$, $w = 1/d\hat{p}$), profits or losses will be multiplied by a *positive* factor.

The fact that surplus profit and losses exist irrespective of the standard of prices is of great importance, for it is never true that all prices fall in terms of a commodity standard, if a superior technique is introduced. E. g. if gold is the standard of prices, and the

Multiple Product Techniques   **41**

method of production of gold is improved, the price of gold, being by definition equal to one, does not change. Only if prices are expressed in terms of the wage rate they all fall simultaneously in consequence of technical progress.

For single product systems it is true, nevertheless, that the price of the commodity whose method of production is changed falls relatively to that of any other commodity so that it falls absolutely in terms of any commodity standard, except if the commodity in question serves itself as numéraire. If technical progress takes place in the production of gold, all commodities rise therefore in terms of gold but if technical progress takes place in the production of iron, the gold price of iron will fall while the gold price of other commodities will partly rise and partly fall.

The first entrepreneurs who make the transition to a cheaper method of production in a given industry reap surplus profits in the short run according to theorem 3.2 but a unit of the commodity they produce will purchase a lesser amount of any other commodity when the majority of entrepreneurs have followed suit and competition has lowered the long run price of production to the level determined by the average rate of profit which is assumed to be uniform and constant at the beginning and the end of the transition. (Further dynamic effects on the level of demand, the distribution of income, concentration etc. may in turn affect the rate of profit, but such considerations transcend the formal model.)

Theorem 3.3: If a superior method of production is introduced in a basic single product system in industry i at a given rate of profit r, with new prices in terms of the wage rate $\hat{p}^I$ and old prices $\hat{p}^{II} > \hat{p}^I$, we have

$$\frac{\hat{p}_i^I}{\hat{p}_j^I} < \frac{\hat{p}_i^{II}}{\hat{p}_j^{II}}, j \neq i. \text{ [12]}$$

Proof: Using the notation of theorem 3.1 ($i = 1$) we have

$$C[\hat{p}^{II} - \hat{p}^I] = \begin{pmatrix} c_1 \hat{p}^{II} - c_1 \hat{p}^I \\ 0 \\ \vdots \\ 0 \end{pmatrix}$$

where $C = [I - (1 + r) A]$ and $c_1 \hat{p}^{II} = \hat{p}^{II} - (1 + r) a_1 \hat{p}^{II} = l_1$. Write $C^{-1} = D$, $c_1 \hat{p}^{II} - c_1 \hat{p}^I = \alpha$. We obtain $\hat{p}^{II} - \hat{p}^I = \alpha d^1$, where d^1 is the positive first column of $D > 0$ and where $\alpha > 0$ because of theorem

---

[12] A similar but less general statement is made in **Morishima** (1973), pp. 30—34.

3.1. The assertion is equivalent to

$$(\hat{p}_1^{II} - \hat{p}_1^{I}) \, \hat{p}_j^{II} > (\hat{p}_j^{II} - \hat{p}_j^{I}) \, \hat{p}_1^{II}, \quad j \neq i$$

$$\alpha \, d_1^{1} \, \hat{p}_j^{II} > \alpha \, d_j^{1} \, \hat{p}_1^{II}$$

i. e. to

$$(d_1^{1} \, d_j - d_j^{1} \, d_1) \ \, l > 0$$

where

$$d_i \, l = \sum_{k=1}^{n} d_i^{k} \, l_k = \hat{p}_i^{II}, \quad i = 1, j; \quad l > 0.$$

Our assertion therefore requires us to prove that the principal and almost principal minors of order 2

$$D \begin{pmatrix} 1 & j \\ 1 & k \end{pmatrix} = d_1^{1} \, d_j^{k} - d_1^{k} \, d_j^{1}$$

of the matrix D are nonnegative and that at least one (the principal minor) is positive if k, $2 \leq k \leq n$, varies for each given j, $2 \leq j \leq n$. The minors of D are related to those of the inverse C by the formula[13]

$$D \begin{pmatrix} 1 & j \\ 1 & k \end{pmatrix} = \frac{(-1)^{j+k}}{\det C} \, C \begin{pmatrix} 2, \ldots, k-1, & k+1, \ldots, n \\ 2, \ldots, j-1, & j+1, \ldots, n \end{pmatrix}, j, k = 2, \ldots, n.$$

On the right hand side we have a formula for the elements of the inverse of the matrix $\overline{C} = (c_h^{i}) = (\delta_h^{i} - (1+r) \, a_h^{i})$, $h, i = 2, \ldots, n$. Since $q C \geq 0$ with $q > 0$ entails

$$\sum_{h=1}^{n} q_h \, [\delta_h^{i} - (1+r) \, a_h^{i}] \geq 0, \ i = 2, \ldots, n,$$

the nonnegative matrix $[(1+r) \, a_h^{i}]$, $h, i = 2, \ldots, n$, has a dominant root smaller than one and $(\overline{C})^{-1}$ is nonnegative. The principal minor $d_1^{1} \, d_j^{j} - d_j^{1} \, d_1^{j}$ will be positive since the corresponding minor of $\overline{C}$ is a positive principal minor (Hawkins-Simon condition).

Theorem 3.3 is readily extended to all-engaging systems, although it presupposes an assignment of commodities to industries. Such an assignment is given by passing from the all-engaging joint production system (A, B, l) to the system $[(B-A)^{-1} A, \, I, \, (B-A)^{-1} l]$ which has properties analogous to those of a single product system; we have

$$p = w \, [B - (1+r) \, A]^{-1} \, l = w \, [I - r \, (B-A)^{-1} \, A]^{-1} \, (B-A)^{-1} \, l,$$

$$(B-A)^{-1} > 0, \ (B-A)^{-1} \, A > 0,$$

---

[13] See Gantmacher (1966): chap. I, § 4.

and this system may be interpreted as at the end of section one.

With this we have now shown that all-engaging systems have the same properties as single product systems. In the last section of this paper we shall give some reasons why general joint production systems are that much more difficult. The explanation will be sought by considering changes of input coefficients.

4. General Joint Production Systems

There does not seem to exist a set of simple and yet general assumptions which guarantee that an untruncated joint production system yields positive prices at a given rate of profit comparable to the theorem for single product systems which says that productive indecomposable single product systems yield positive prices between zero and a maximum rate of profit. We must be content to assume that prices are positive at some rate of profit. It is then easy to show that prices will not be positive at all rates of profit but only within one or several bounded intervals in $[0, \infty)$. At the upper boundary of the interval(s) prices in terms of the wage rate need not go to infinity, however, as is the case with single product system; they may also turn negative which indicates that they need not rise monotonically with the rate of profit.

Theorem 4.1: Prices cannot be positive in any joint production system capable of self-reproduction for all rates of profit if the system contains no pure consumption goods, i. e. if all columns of A contain at least one positive element.

Proof: Write $e(B-A) = s$, $s \geq 0$, $s \neq 0$. Therefore

$$eB\hat{p} - (1+r)\, e\, A\hat{p} = s\hat{p} - r\, e\, A\hat{p} = e\, l.$$

Since eA is a positive vector, the expression $(s - reA)$ in $(s - reA)\,\hat{p} = e\, l$ will be a vector with negative components for sufficiently large r while $e\, l$ is constant. Some prices in terms of the wage rate and hence in any other standard must therefore turn negative[14] for sufficiently large r.

---

[14] Prices in terms of the wage rate are not defined at most at n points r_i such that $\det[B - (1+r_i)\, A] = 0$. The lowest of the r_i, $r_i > 0$, if one exists, is the maximum rate of profit of the untruncated system where prices in terms of the wage rate tend to infinity.

All productive basic single product systems have the same simple properties. Mr. Sraffa's method in approaching the diversity of joint production systems had consisted in assuming that all systems considered yielded positive prices at a given rate of profit so that they seemed economically viable; variations of the rate of profit were then examined. The approach exhibited a bewildering number of possible alternative reactions. The systems do not need to have a maximum rate of profit (Manara 1968), prices may fluctuate (without the system, however, being viable at all rates of profit — see theorem 4.1 above), etc. The reason for the "anomalies" must be that the problem of the choice of technique is revealed to be inherent even before any alternative method of production is introduced from outside, i. e. there is the possibility of truncation.

In fact, if we allow for *truncation* to maximize a wage expressed in a standard of *given* composition (the given surplus) at every rate of profit, a monotonically falling wage curve is obtained by choosing the optimum curve among the wage curves of all possible truncations yielding the same real wage (see Burmeister-Kuga 1970). This observation does not solve all problems. The concept of optimum requires clarification and the result depends on the composition of the real wage in a way which is not easy to analyse. Moreover, the truncations need in general not be Sraffa systems in that the number of commodities produced may not be equal to the number of processes used. However, if the system and its truncations are regular in the sense of Schefold (1976 c) one can prove (see Schefold 1977 c) that it suffices to consider only quadratic truncations which are obtained from the original system by deleting an equal number of rows and columns and which are productive Sraffa systems as defined in this article. On any golden rule path the profitable truncation will be found on the envelope of the wage curves of those truncations which are capable of producing the entire basket of consumption goods in the not deleted processes in such a way that the deleted goods (outside the quadratic truncation) are overproduced and receive zero prices while the not deleted commodities (within the truncation) are not overproduced and receive nonnegative and (except in a finite number of points of intersections of wage curves) positive prices. As long as one restricts one's attention to regular systems and to golden rule paths where the rate of growth and the rate of profit coincide, it is thus possible to derive the "optimal" truncation by choosing among alternative Sraffa systems, each being a truncation of the original system. Truncated goods will be overproduced, truncated processes unprofitable, but the point is that the truncation to be chosen will yield the highest real wage, given the rate of profit, and will thus be on the envelope of the wage curves of the truncations fulfilling the quantity requirements. This envelope falls monotonically up to a finite maximum rate of profit so that the choice among alternative truncations appears to be analogous to that among alternative techniques in single product and all-engaging systems as discussed in section 3 above.

But these results depend *crucially* on the assumption that the rate of growth equals the rate of profit, an assumption which is alien to Sraffa's way of thinking. If the rates diverge, e. g. because the system is stationary while the rate of profit is positive, there exists, as I have tried to argue in Schefold (1977 c), no known and universally accepted criterion which would allow to say unambiguously which technique would be chosen through competition, different criteria (e. g. the neoclassical criterion of maximising the value of consumption and the classical criterion of maximising the real wage) could lead to different results and neither represented a true "equilibrium" (in the neoclassical or classical sense).

The difficulties with joint production do therefore not disappear, even if truncation is taken into account, unless the restrictive assumption of an equality of the rate of profit and the rate of growth is made.

A patient analysis of special cases is required in order to analyse the causes of the anomalies, since no satisfactory general theory of joint production seems to exist. A modest proposal for a new approach is discussed in the next section; here I should like to conclude with a theorem which indicates that in spite of the difficulty of the general case, conceptually simple all-engaging systems are, after all, implicit in any regular productive joint production system at *high* rates of profit. More specifically, we call a system all-engaging at rate of profit r if $[B-(1+r) A]^{-1}>0$. Then we have

Theorem 4.2: Let a basic joint production system be given, $A \geq 0$, $B \geq 0$, $\det A \neq 0$, with a maximum rate of profit $R>0$ and with vectors $p \geq 0$, $q \geq 0$ such that $rk\ [B-(1+R)\ A]=n-1$[15], $[B-(1+R)\ A]\ p=0$, $q\ [B-(1+R)A]=0$. There is then $\bar{r}<R$ such that the system is all-engaging for all rates of profit between $\bar{r}$ and R, R is a simple root of $\det [B-(1+r)\ A]=0$ and $p>0$, $q>0$.

Proof: Let Q be the matrix which transforms $A\ (B-A)^{-1}$ into Jordan's normal form T, i. e. $Q\ A\ (B-A)^{-1}=T\ Q$ where T is composed of quadratic matrices ("blocks") on the diagonal and zeroes outside. Since the eigenvalues λ_i of $A\ (B-A)^{-1}$ are roots of

---

[15] This is implied if (A, B) is regular (see Schefold 1976 c, 1977 c).

the equation det $[B-(1+r)\ A]=$det $[I-rA\ (B-A)^{-1}]=$det $[\lambda I-A\ (B-A)^{-1}]=0$, $\lambda=1/r$, and since det $A\neq 0$, we may assume that the first "block" $T_1{}^1$ of Q (on the upper left) is of the form:

$$
T_1{}^1 = \begin{pmatrix}
1/R & & & & \\
1 & 1/R & & & \\
& \cdot & \cdot & & \\
& & \cdot & \cdot & \\
& & & 1 & 1/R
\end{pmatrix}
$$

where the order of $T_1{}^1$ is equal to the multiplicity f of root R of the characteristic equation. One obtains by induction

$$
\hat{T}=(I-r\,T)^{-1} = \begin{pmatrix}
\dfrac{R}{R-r} & & & & & \\
\left(\dfrac{R}{R-r}\right)^2 & \dfrac{R}{R-r} & & & 0 & \\
\cdot & \cdot & & & & \\
\cdot & \cdot & & & & \\
\left(\dfrac{R}{R-r}\right)^f & \left(\dfrac{R}{R-r}\right)^{f-1} \cdot\ \cdot\ \cdot & \dfrac{R}{R-r} & & & \\
0 & \cdot\ \ \cdot\ \ \cdot & 0 & \hat{T}_2{}^2 & & \\
\cdot & & \cdot & & \cdot & \\
\cdot & & \cdot & & \cdot & \\
0 & \cdot\ \ \cdot\ \ \cdot & 0 & & & \hat{T}_{s^s}
\end{pmatrix},
$$

$\hat{T}_2{}^2,\ldots,\hat{T}_{s^s}$ being blocks corresponding to the other roots $R_2,\ldots,R_s$ of det $[B-(1+r)\ A]=0$.

With this, and with $P=Q\ (B-A)$ we get

$$
[B-(1+r)\ A]^{-1} = P^{-1}P\ (B-A)^{-1}\ [I-r\ A\ (B-A)^{-1}]^{-1}\ Q^{-1}Q
$$
$$
= P^{-1}\ [I-r\ Q\ A\ (B-A)^{-1}Q^{-1}]\ Q
$$
$$
= P^{-1}\ \hat{T}\ Q.
$$

From $P\ [B-(1+r)\ A]^{-1}=\hat{T}\ Q$ we obtain $(R-r)\ p_1=Rq_1\ [B-(1+r)\ A]$, $q_1\ [B-(1+R)\ A]=0$ so that the first row q_1 of Q is an eigenvector of $A\ (B-A)^{-1}$, $q_1=\alpha q$, α real. Similarly $[B-(1+r)\ A]^{-1}\ \overline{Q}$

$=\bar{P}\,\hat{T}$, $\bar{Q}=Q^{-1}$, $\bar{P}=P^{-1}$, so that $R\,[B-(1+r)\,A]^{-1}\,\bar{q}^f=(R-r)\,\bar{p}^f$ yields $[B-(1+R)\,A]\,\bar{p}^f=0$, i. e. column f of P^{-1} is proportional to $p\colon \bar{p}^f=\beta\,p$.

It follows that the elements of $[B-(1+r)\,A]^{-1}$ tend to become either all non-negative or all not positive for

$$\lim_{r\to R}\left(\frac{R-r}{R}\right)^f [B-(1+r)\ A]^{-1}=\lim_{r\to R}\left(\frac{R-r}{R}\right)^f \bar{P}\,\hat{T}\,Q=\bar{P}\,E_f^1\,Q$$

$$=\alpha\,\beta\,p\,q$$

where the first element in row f of the quadratic matrix E_f^1 equals one while all others vanish, where $p\,q$ is a nonnegative matrix, and where $\alpha\,\beta>0$ or $\alpha\,\beta<0$. The matrix $\delta\,[B-(1+r)\,A]^{-1}$ will therefore be nonnegative for $\hat{r}=R-\varepsilon$ if we define $\delta=+1$ for $\alpha\,\beta>0$ and $\delta=-1$ for $\alpha\,\beta<0$.

The matrix $\delta\,[B-(1+\hat{r})\,A]^{-1}\,A$ is indecomposable, for otherwise $[B-(1+\hat{r})\,A]^{-1}\,A$ would, after permutations, be almost triangular with all elements in the last m columns on the first $n-m$ rows $(n>m\geq 1)$ being zero. Denoting the last m columns of A, B and unit matrix I by A^2, B^2, I^2 respectively, we should have for the ranks of the $(n, 2\,m)$ matrices

$$m=rk\,\{[B-(1+\hat{r})\,A]^{-1}\,A^2, I^2\}=rk\,[A^2, B^2-(1+\hat{r})\,A^2]$$

$$=rk\,(A^2, B^2)$$

which implied that A, B would be non-basic[16]

$\delta\,[B-(1+\hat{r})\,A]^{-1}$ is thus indecomposable and nonnegative; there is $\lambda>0$, $\tilde{p}>0$ such that $\delta\,[B-(1+\hat{r})\,A]^{-1}\,A\,\tilde{p}=\lambda\,\tilde{p}$. Since $[B-(1+R)\,A]\,p=0$ implies $\delta\,[B-(1+\hat{r})\,A]^{-1}\,A\,p=\delta\,(R-\hat{r})^{-1}\,p$ and since nonnegative eigenvectors are unique and associated only with the dominant root of a nonnegative indecomposable matrix, we have

$$p=\gamma\,\tilde{p},\ \gamma>0,\ \text{and}\ \lambda=\delta\,(R-\hat{r})^{-1}.$$

Above we obtained $\bar{p}^f=\beta\,p$, therefore, with e^f being the f-th unit vector,

$$\bar{p}^f=P^{-1}\,e^f=(B-A)^{-1}\,Q^{-1}\,e^f \text{ or } e^f=Q\,(B-A)\,\bar{p}^f=\beta\,Q\,(B-A)\,p,$$

which yields, if $f\neq 1$ $0=q_1\,(B-A)\,\bar{p}^f=\alpha\,q\,(B-A)\,\beta\,p$

$$=\alpha\,\beta\,\gamma\,R\,q\,A\,\tilde{p}.$$

---

[16] Cf. Schefold (1971), p. 8, p. 10.

48   B. Schefold:

But $q A \tilde{p}$ is positive because $\tilde{p} > 0$ which is a contradiction since $\alpha \beta \gamma R \neq 0$. Thus $f = 1$, R is a simple root and $e^1 = q_1 (B - A) \tilde{p}^1$, therefore $1 = \alpha \beta \gamma R q A \tilde{p}$, implying $\alpha \beta > 0$, $\alpha \beta p q \geq 0$, and $\delta = 1$.

We conclude that $\{I - [B - (1 + \hat{r}) A]^{-1} A\}^{-1}$ is positive in the transformation

$$[B - (1 + \tilde{r}) A]^{-1} = \{I - (\tilde{r} - \hat{r}) [B - (1 + \hat{r}) A]^{-1} A\}^{-1} [B - (1 + \hat{r}) A]^{-1},$$
$$R - \varepsilon = \hat{r} < \tilde{r} < R, \text{ and } [B - (1 + \hat{r}) A]^{-1} \geq 0$$

with no column vanishing so that $[B - (1 + \tilde{r}) A]^{-1}$ and $A [B - (1 + \tilde{r}) A]^{-1}$ is positive, hence there is $\mu > 0$, $\tilde{q} > 0$ such that $\tilde{q} A [B - (1 + \tilde{r}) A]^{-1} = \mu \tilde{q}$. As above one obtains $q = \tilde{q}$, $\mu = R - \tilde{r}$, $\alpha \beta p q > 0$ so that $[B - (1 + r) A]^{-1}$ must be positive for all r in an open intervall, $\tilde{r} < r < R$.

This result is remarkable because the truncation appearing at the maximum rate of profit on the envelope of the wage curves of regular truncations of a regular system fulfills the assumptions of theorem 4.2 which shows that every joint production system (or rather, one of its truncations) will ultimately become allengaging however complex it may be at low rates of profit. In particular, it is clear that the truncation appearing at the highest rates of profit will possess a positive standard commodity. On the other hand we have

Theorem 4.3: A system which is all-engaging at $r = -1$ must (apart from trivial permutations) be a single product system.

Proof: The assertion implies $B \geq 0$, $C = B^{-1} \geq 0$, $\det B \neq 0$. If B is not diagonal, we may assume $b_1^1 > 0$, $b_1^2 > 0$. Since $b_1 c^j = 0$; $j = 2, \ldots, n$; we must have $c_i^j = 0$; $j = 2, \ldots, n$; $i = 1, 2$; contradicting $\det C \neq 0$.

Negative rates of profit do not have a real economic meaning, but the two theorems taken together seem nevertheless to imply that the higher the rate of profit, the more will specific difficulties of joint production disappear and the more will the system approximate the familiar properties of single product systems while negative coefficients of $[B - (1 + r) A]^{-1}$ are characteristic for low rates of profit.

5. A Remark on Technical Progress

Although all-engaging systems are less rare at high rates of profit, the difficulties with joint production in general remain and require a new approach. From the analysis of the reaction of prices to hypothetical variations of the rate of profit I propose to shift the attention to the reaction of prices to hypothetical changes of input coefficients, i. e. I propose to pass from an analysis which is a preliminary to the theory of distribution to an analysis which is a preliminary to the theory of technical progress, and I should like to conclude this paper with an example of this method:

The simplest kind of technical change consists in the saving of the quantity of an input (in particular of a circulating capital good or labour) or in the increases in the quantity of a particular output, all else remaining equal. Here we find the most characteristic difference between single product systems and all-engaging systems on the one hand, and general joint production systems on the other. We formulate the theorem in terms of systems which are all-engaging at $r=0$. The extention for $r>0$ is obvious.

Theorem 5.1: Suppose a coefficient $a_i{}^j$ of the input matrix A or a coefficient l_i of the labour vector l is lowered or a coefficient $b_i{}^j$ of the output matrix is raised a little. All prices in terms of the wage rate will then fall for all rates of profit smaller than the maximum if the system is all-engaging. If the system is not all-engaging at $r=0$ and all labour values are positive, at least one labour value will not fall.

Proof: Consider the general formulas

$$\frac{d\hat{p}}{d a_i{}^j} = (1+r)\,[B-(1+r)\,A]^{-1}\,e^i\,\hat{p}_j$$

$$-\frac{d\hat{p}}{d l_i} = [B-(1+r)\,A]^{-1}\,e^i,$$

$$\frac{d\hat{p}}{d b_i{}^j} = -[B-(1+r)\,A]^{-1}\,e^i\,\hat{p}_j$$

which are obtained from $B\hat{p} = (1+r)\,A\hat{p}+l$ by differentiation (e^i is the i-th unit column vector). The assertions are obvious, since $(B-A)^{-1}>0$, if and only if the system is all engaging at $r=0$, and since $[B-(1+r)\,A]^{-1}>0$ for all-engaging systems, $0 \leq r < R$ (proof of theorem 2.2 above).

We may have $[B-(1+r)\,A]^{-1}>0$ for some $r>0$ even for a system which is not all-engaging at $r=0$, and

$$\frac{d\hat{p}(r)}{dr} > 0$$

even if $[B-(1+r)\,A]^{-1} \not> 0$, but the formula above shows that the element

$$f_k{}^i \text{ of } F = (B-A)^{-1}$$

50   B. Schefold:

is positive, if and only if the labour value $u_k = \hat{p}_k (0)$ of commodity k falls in response to a reduction (increase) of $a_i{}^j$ ($b_i{}^j$), the labour value $u_j = \hat{p}_j (0)$ being positive. Thus we find as the most distinguishing feature of joint production systems which are not all-engaging at $r = 0$ that an increase of physical productivity regarding one input or output will always cause at least one labour value (and in general also one of the prices for $r > 0$) to *rise*. The formula for $\frac{d\hat{p}}{da_i{}^j}$ etc. allows to examine this fact and its origin in the technical structure of the economy in a great variety of cases; here we must be content to consider one extremely simple example:

		commodities			labour		commodities		
		(1)	(2)	(3)	(1)		(1)	(2)	(3)
processes	(1)	80	1	0	70	$\longrightarrow$	150	0	0
	(2)	1	0	0	2	$\longrightarrow$	0	1	1
	(3)	1	0	0	1	$\longrightarrow$	0	0	1

Process (1) could be interpreted as an aggregation of all of the economy except the special processes (2) and (3). In order to honour the heroic days of capital theory we have process (1) produce the versatile commodity (1), leets, which is good both for production and consumption. Processes (2) and (3) are the energy industry; process (2) produces coke (2) (for leets production) and the consumption good gas, process (2) produces gas alone. The inputs to processes (2) and (3) are leets, say coal-leets for (2) and natural-gas-leets for (3)[17].

It is easy to see that $f_1{}^3$ and $f_2{}^3$ are the only negative elements of $F = (B - A)^{-1}$, while all prices are positive[18]. It is thus clear that a small reduction of the amount of labour required to produce commodity (3) in process (3) will, all else remaining equal, increase the labour values of commodities (1) and (2), reduce that of (3), and the same will occur if the amount of commodity (3) produced in process (3) is increased, for

$$dp_k = (-f_k{}^3 \, p_3) \, db_3{}^3 > 0, \quad k = 1, 2, \text{ and}$$

$$dp_3 < 0, \text{ with } db_3{}^3 > 0.$$

---

[17] The system is indecomposable but not basic in the sense of S r a f f a.

[18] More explicitely, one obtains

$$70 F = \begin{pmatrix} 1 & 1 & -1 \\ 0 & 70 & -70 \\ 1 & 1 & 69 \end{pmatrix}$$

Multiple Product Techniques 51

Or, to put it the other way round and in more illustrative terms: If the production of natural gas becomes more difficult (l_3 rises or $b_3{}^3$ falls), the price of gas will, as one should expect, rise, but that of *all* other commodities ("leets" and coke) will *fall*.

The effect looks paradoxical at first sight but it is easily explained in a system where prices just cover costs (here, with zero profits): The rise in "the difficulty of production" (Ricardo) of natural gas renders the latter more expensive and therefore reduces the price which has to be charged for coke, given its cost of production. The cheapening of coke reduces the cost of leets, and the feedback of the reduction in the costs of leets does here not offset the original increase in the difficulty of production of natural gas[19].

It is the main point of this article that such effects will be present whenever a joint production system is not all-productive (r small) or whenever $[B-(1+r)\,A]^{-1} \gneqq 0$. An important conclusion to be drawn for economic theory may be that competition works — if at all — in a fundamentally different way whenever true joint production is present. That commodities as raw materials should be obtainable at cheap prices is in the interest of every entrepreneur in single product systems where each is interested that competition works smoothly in other industries. Here, where the distinction between industries is blurred by joint production, even the producers of leets are interested in an increase of the price of natural gas for that will enable them to obtain cheap coke, while the increase in costs of gas which causes the cheapening of coke *is shifted to consumers*.

It is true that surplus profits regulate the adoption of superior, and losses the rejection of inferior processes in joint production systems on golden rule paths, provided the alternatives are technically feasible (cf. Schefold, 1977 c) Theorem 3.2 above may thus be extended, but theorem 3.3 may not. In single product systems a superior method replaces the one which produces the same commodity. This criterion fails in joint production systems. There must be economic processes corresponding to the analytic procedure of determining which among n methods to produce n commodities will be replaced by the introduction of a superior $(n+1)$-st method, but these processes are necessarily much more complicated on the price side than in the single product case, since the competitive

---

[19] I first thought of similar effects when examining the change in the "true value" of nuclear electricity caused by selling the waste heat from the cooling system to the public via long distance heating pipes instead of dumping it into the environment.

52   B. Schefold:

process can not consist of underselling in the market for only one commodity as in the single product case where the price of the commodity whose method of production is changed falls relatively to all the others.

Not all joint production systems present the same difficulties. E. g. the behaviour of prices in terms of the wage rate is rather normal for small rates of profit in the example above, and a maximum rate of profit exists without truncation. This explains at the same time why economists who learn economic theory by considering single product systems do not go far wrong when discussing real world problems involving *some* joint production and why no pure theory of joint production can exist; for joint production systems exhibiting all intricacies of joint production at the same time are probably economically meaningless. The theorist circumnavigates the difficulties by means of von Neumann's method of inequalities which answers some questions in such an elegant manner that many others tend to get forgotten. And it is shown in Schefold (1977 c) that the method works smoothly only on the Golden Rule path.

In this article it has been tried to prepare a discussion of general joint production systems by examining all-engaging systems which have properties analogous to those of single product systems as regards key technical properties of basic single product systems, and as regards the behaviour of prices in function of the rate of profit. It has also been shown that effects on prices and distribution of changes in methods of production are similar. Finally a relationship between prices and changes in input-output coefficients has been derived which indicated that simple technological changes in all-engaging systems lead to the same kind of change in prices as in single product systems, while prices may behave in a counterintuitive way in general joint production systems, raising questions about the different nature of competition in the general context.

References

K. R. Bharadwaj (1970): On the Maximum Number of Switches Between Two Production Systems; Schweiz. Zeitschrift für Volkswirtschaftslehre und Statistik *CVI*, pp. 409—428.

E. Burmeister and K. Kuga (1970): The Factor Price Frontier, Duality and Joint Production, Review of Economic Studies *37*, pp. 11—19.

F. R. Gantmacher (1966): Matrizenrechnung, Bd. I, II; Berlin.

C. F. Manara (1968): Il modello di Pierro Sraffa per la produzione congiunta di merci a mezzo di merci; L'industria, pp. 3—18.

Multiple Product Techniques 53

M. Morishima (1973): Marx's Economics, Cambridge.

L. L. Pasinetti (1973): The Notion of Vertical Integration in Economic Analysis, Metroeconomica, XXV.

B. Schefold (1971): Theorie der Kuppelproduktion, Basel (private print).

B. Schefold (1976a): Nachworte, in: P. Sraffa: Warenproduktion mittels Waren, Frankfurt, pp. 129—226.

B. Schefold (1976b): Relative Prices as a Function of the Rate of Profit, Zeitschrift für Nationalökonomie 35, pp. 21—48.

B. Schefold (1976c): Different Forms of Technical Progress, Economic Journal 86, pp. 806—819.

B. Schefold (1977a): Fixed Capital as a Joint Product, to appear in: Jahrbücher für Nationalökonomie und Statistik, 192.

B. Schefold (1977b): Reduction to Dated Quantities of Labour, Roundabout Processes and Switches of Technique in Fixed Capital Systems, to appear in: Metroeconomica, XXVIII.

B. Schefold (1977c): Von Neumann and Sraffa: Mathematical Equivalence and Conceptual Difference, to be published.

P. Sraffa (1960): Production of Commodities by Means of Commodities, Cambridge.

Address of author: Prof. Dr. Bertram Schefold, Institut für Markt und Plan, Johann-Wolfgang-Goethe-Universität, Fachbereich Wirtschaftswissenschaften, Schumannstraße 60, D-6000 Frankfurt am Main 1, Federal Republic of Germany.

[5]

The Economic Journal, **86** (*December* 1976), 873–876

Printed in Great Britain

POSITIVE PROFITS WITH
NEGATIVE SURPLUS VALUE: A REPLY
TO WOLFSTETTER*

Since I have already had the opportunity of discussing the purpose of my original argument and its relationship to the work of Marx and of Morishima (Steedman, 1976) and since the principal interest of Wolfstetter's comment might be thought to lie in his remarks concerning Sraffa's analysis of joint production, I shall concentrate here on assessing those remarks, relegating all other points to a footnote.[1]

Wolfstetter (§V) objects to Sraffa's analysis of joint production (Sraffa, 1960, part II) on the grounds that it is formulated in terms of equations rather than inequalities and that the number of production processes used is equal to the number of commodities; he asserts that no criterion of economic choice is invoked to explain the activity levels considered and the pricing of products which are produced in permanent excess. He asserts further (§II) that Sraffa considers only systems with strictly positive prices and activity levels but provides no conditions for the existence of such systems.[2]

In the following remarks I shall not adhere rigidly to Sraffa's approach – I shall, for example, assume constant returns to scale – nor do I intend to attribute any arguments or views to Sraffa. It will be shown, however, that a particular piece of analysis which is very much in the "spirit" of von Neumann (1945–6) yields certain results which are perfectly compatible with those of Sraffa's analysis; the implication for Wolfstetter's remarks will be clear. The analysis referred to is that embodied in Burmeister and Kuga's Minimum Real-Wage Frontier (1970), as modified by Fujimoto (1975) in his discussion of von Neumann equilibria.[3]

Let there be n products and m alternative joint-product methods of production. Let A, B be $m \times n$ semi-positive matrices,[4] the ith rows of which show

---

* I should like to thank R. Hartley, V. Pandit and, in particular, S. A. Moore for helpful discussion.

[1] (i) Contrary to the assertion in Wolfstetter's second sentence, my original argument in no way contradicts the analysis presented by Morishima (1974); on this point and on the issue raised in Wolfstetter's second footnote, see Steedman (1976). (ii) The term "Sraffa-system" in Wolfstetter's section II is perhaps unfortunate since Sraffa does not consider a growing economy. It may be noted that the existence of a "standard commodity" has nothing whatever to do with returns to scale, since no question of the actual production, or even the producibility, of that composite commodity ever arises; cf. Sraffa (1960, §56). (iii) It may clarify Wolfstetter's n. 1, p. 869 to note that in my original example the net output $C^1 = (3, 5)$ cannot be produced *exactly* even with 7 units of labour (or, indeed, with any other number of labour units). (iv) It is not entirely clear how one is to interpret Wolfstetter's statements (§V) that all propositions defining Marx's "labour theory of value" involve a stationary reference system and that it is economically meaningless to formulate such a system in the "spirit" of Sraffa, since Marx himself formulated his theory in terms of equations, not inequalities.

[2] The reader cannot fail to be struck by the speed with which Wolfstetter presents his "critique" and by Wolfstetter's apparent readiness to attribute "mistakes" to Sraffa without adequate discussion.

[3] I shall focus attention on the questions which products have positive prices and which production methods are actually used; for a discussion of activity *levels* in the context of von Neumann equilibria, see Fujimoto (1975). Sraffa, for his purposes, took production levels as given, of course.

[4] There is assumed to be at least one positive entry in each row of A and in each column of B.

respectively the inputs to and the outputs from the ith method when it is operated by a_i units of homogeneous labour: let a be the strictly positive column vector with elements $(a_1, ..., a_m)$, w be a semi-positive row vector showing, at an arbitrary scale, the proportions in which the n products enter the real wage and r be the (non-negative) rate of profit. Consider, for a given value of r, the following (primal) linear programming problem:

$$\text{max. } L = w.p,$$
$$\text{s.t. } B.p \leqslant (1+r) A.p + a,$$
$$p \geqslant 0,$$

where p is an n-dimensional column vector of labour-commanded prices.

In the primal problem L is the labour commanded by the wage-bundle w and is therefore the reciprocal of the real wage rate; the primal problem thus determines the *lowest* real wage rate and the associated prices consistent with the given value of r, under competitive conditions. Let $L^*(r)$ be the optimal value of the programme at any given r; then the graph of $[L^*(r)]^{-1}$ against r is the Minimum Real-Wage Frontier of Burmeister and Kuga, as modified by Fujimoto.

It will be clear that the primal problem always has a feasible solution, namely $p = 0$; the dual will also have a feasible solution provided that the system A, B is capable of producing a positive net output of every product and that r is less than the von Neumann maximal growth rate. Both these conditions will be assumed to be met and thus an optimal solution exists.

Consider first a value of r such that both the primal problem and its dual have unique, non-degenerate optimal solutions. It is easy to show[1] that in such a situation the number of processes actually used in the optimal solution must be exactly equal to the number of products with a positive price.[2] Using the term "commodity" to mean "a product with a positive price" – a reasonable usage in an economic context[3] – it may thus be said that the number of processes actually used, and the number of price relations which are equalities, will be exactly equal to the number of "commodities". It follows that a tableau representing the price relations for those processes which are actually used, and from which products which are not "commodities" disappear because of their

---

[1] Let the vectors, l, s, x be vectors of primal slack variables, dual slack variables and dual non-slack variables, respectively: let $N(z)$ be the *number* of positive z variables in an optimal solution. Considering basic (extreme point) solutions only, we know from the basic theorem that $N(p) + N(l) + k_1 = m$ and that $N(x) + N(s) + k_2 = n$, where $k_1(k_2)$ is non-negative and is positive if and only if the primal (dual) solution is degenerate. From the complementary slackness conditions, we also know that

$$N(p) + N(s) + k_3 = n \quad \text{and that} \quad N(x) + N(l) + k_4 = m,$$

where $k_3(k_4)$ is non-negative and is equal to the number of binding constraints in the dual (primal) solution which are associated with zero non-slack variables in the primal (dual) solution; e.g. k_4 is the number of processes which make no loss, yet are not used. It follows immediately that

$$[N(x) - N(p)] = (k_1 - k_4) = (k_2 - k_3).$$

If both primal and dual solutions are non-degenerate then $k_1 = k_2 = 0$; hence $k_3 = k_4 = 0$ and, as stated in the text, $N(x) = N(p)$.

[2] The basis vectors in an optimal solution are linearly independent; one does not, therefore, need to *assume* that Wolfstetter's F matrix has full rank, contrary to what he appears to imply.

[3] Needless to say, no issue of substance turns on the adoption of this particular usage.

zero prices, will take precisely the form of the *equation* systems discussed by Sraffa. Such a tableau will, that is, involve only equations, and not inequalities, and it will have an equal number of production methods and "commodities".[1]

Consider now the effect on the optimal solutions of, say, increasing r. We may suppose that this change at first leaves the set of basic variables for each optimal solution unchanged, merely altering the particular values of those basic variables; it may be noted, in particular, that the real wage rate, $[L^*(r)]^{-1}$, and the positive prices will change just as is suggested by Sraffa's analysis. Eventually, however, r will, in general, reach a "switch-point" level. Such "switch-points" can, from a formal linear-programming point of view, be of three kinds: (a) the primal can be unique but degenerate, with its dual being non-unique but non-degenerate; (b) as in (a) but with primal and dual interchanged; (c) both primal and dual can be non-unique and degenerate. The economic significance of such "switch-points" is that a switch of type (a) involves a change from one Sraffa-like system to another in which the set of products which are "commodities" is unchanged but the set of methods used is different (a Method Switch); a switch of type (b) involves no change in the set of methods used but does involve a change in the set of products which are "commodities" (a Commodity Switch); at a switch of type (c) both the set of methods and the set of "commodities" change. (Sraffa's two discussions of switches under joint production, (1960, §§ 70, 96) would both seem to relate to what are here called Method Switches.)

The Minimum Real-Wage Frontier can thus be derived as follows by an analysis in the "spirit" of Sraffa. With m available production methods and n products, there is a finite number, N, of "square" systems in which the number of methods actually used is equal to the number of "commodities".

$$(N = \Sigma_{j=1}^k \, (^mC_j) \cdot (^nC_j), \quad \text{where } k = \min \, [m, n].)$$

Taking w as given and following Sraffa's analysis of price movements as r is varied, one can construct for the ith such "square" system a wage-profit frontier, $w_i(r) = [w \cdot p_i(r)]^{-1}$, where $p_i(r)$ is the vector of labour-commanded prices for the products included in system i. Any part (parts) of that frontier for which any element in p_i is negative can then be eliminated, as can any part (parts) for which, at the corresponding r and p_i, any method not included in system i would make a profit over and above the rate r. When this has been done for every possible "square", Sraffa-like system, the lower envelope of the resulting frontiers will be the Minimum Real-Wage Frontier.[2] The latter

---

[1] Wolfstetter's final paragraph would seem to imply that in my article no attention was paid to the *economic* determination of activity levels or to the possibility of zero prices. That any such implication is false may be seen by simple reference to the section of that article entitled "An Implicit Assumption" (Steedman, 1975, pp. 120–1). The interested reader might also care to check that if the appropriate numbers from my numerical example are inserted into the above primal problem (with $w = (3, 5)$ and $r = 20\%$) the unique optimal solution is precisely that $p_1 = \frac{1}{2}, p_2 = 1$ and $L^* = 6$, with both processes being used, as shown in my original argument.

[2] It was pointed out by Sraffa that for a given "square" system the real wage might be *positively* related to r (Sraffa, 1960, § 72). The Minimum Real-Wage Frontier, however, can never slope upwards. (If p^* is optimal for $r = r_1$, then it is feasible for $r = r_2 > r_1$; hence $L^*(r_2) \geqslant L^*(r_1)$.) It follows that any such positive relation between the real wage and r can only occur off the Minimum Real-Wage Frontier.

construct, which is impeccably von Neumann-like in "spirit", taking full account of the choice of production methods and the possible existence of zero-priced products, can thus be obtained by the repeated application of Sraffa's analysis of "square" joint production systems.

I do not, of course, wish to suggest that the above, very brief discussion provides a full account of the relationship between Sraffa-like and von Neumann-like analyses of joint production: it clearly does not.[1] It should, nevertheless, suffice to indicate that that relationship may be closer than might at first appear and that the first task of anyone wishing to make a serious contribution to the comparative evaluation of such analyses is to locate exactly where they differ in substance (and not merely in appearance).

IAN STEEDMAN

University of Manchester

Date of receipt of typescript: June 1976

REFERENCES

Burmeister, E. and Kuga, K. (1970). "The Factor-Price Frontier, Duality and Joint Production." *Review of Economic Studies*, pp. 11–19.
Fujimoto, T. (1975). "Duality and the Uniqueness of Growth Equilibrium." *International Economic Review*, pp. 781–91.
Morishima, M. (1974). "Marx in the Light of Modern Economic Theory." *Econometrica*, pp. 611–32.
von Neumann, J. (1945–6). "A Model of General Economic Equilibrium." *Review of Economic Studies*, pp. 1–9.
Sraffa, P. (1960). *Production of Commodities by Means of Commodities*. Cambridge University Press.
Steedman, I. (1975). "Positive Profits with Negative Surplus Value." ECONOMIC JOURNAL, pp. 114–23.
—— (1976). "Positive Profits with Negative Surplus Value: A Reply." ECONOMIC JOURNAL, pp. 604–7.

[1] Among the many issues which have not been raised here are the determination of output levels, the role of Sraffa's basics and non-basics, the conditions for reswitching with joint production and the relationship between the minimum real wage and competitive equilibrium (cf. Burmeister and Kuga, 1970, §2.2).

[6]

Vol. 46 (1986), No. 4, 407—419

Journal of Economics
Zeitschrift für Nationalökonomie
© by Springer-Verlag 1986

Is von Neumann Square?

By

Christian Bidard, Paris, France*

(Received June 27, 1986; revised version received September 18, 1986)

The most obvious difference between Sraffa's [8] and von Neumann's [4] formalizations of joint production is that Sraffa begins with a square productive system $(A, l) \rightarrow B$ $(A \geq 0, l \geq 0, B \geq 0)$, while the number of processes and that of goods normally differ in von Neumann's approach. The necessary subsistence of the workers is implicitly incorporated in matrix A but, as Sraffa explicitly takes labour and surplus wages into account, he is able to determine the price system p associated with any uniform profit rate r $(0 \leq r < R)$ as the solution to

$$(1+r) Ap + wl = Bp.$$

However, the calculation of $p = (B - (1+r) A)^{-1} l$ (the surplus wage w is chosen as numeraire) does not solve all the difficulties: some of the prices may be negative, or may decrease (the real wage increases) with the rate of profit. These paradoxical behaviours are avoided if we limit our attention to "good" Sraffa systems, i. e. to square systems satisfying the supplementary property $(B - (1+r) A)^{-1} > 0$, at least for high[1] rates of profit $(r \in]r_0, R[)$: in this case, prices are positive and vary in the right direction and, more generally, the main properties of single-product techniques are preserved [1, 5].

The gap between von Neumann systems and well-behaved Sraffa systems thus appears to be considerable. Yet we intend to

---

* With acknowledgements to G. Abraham-Frois, P. A. Samuelson and especially to B. Schefold and I. Steedman.

[1] If the inverse matrix is positive for some $\bar{r}$, its derivative has the same property, hence the inverse matrix increases and remains positive on $[\bar{r}, R[$, R being the first root of det $(B - (1+r) A)$ greater than $\bar{r}$.

408   Ch. Bidard:

prove that, except for flukes, the two approaches are compatible. To establish this result, we will begin with rectangular von Neumann systems and prove that, in almost all cases, the number of efficient methods equals that of commodities (goods not produced in excess) and, moreover, that the square active part $(\bar{A}, \bar{B})$ of (A, B) satisfies the required condition $(\bar{B} - (1 + r)\,\bar{A})^{-1} > 0$ for $r \in \,]r_0, R[$. As a consequence of this single production-like behaviour, a non-substitution theorem is established for multiple-product systems at high profit rates.

The proof itself is based on geometrical considerations set forth in the following paragraph and is left unformalized; applications to von Neumann's and Sraffa's problems are examined later.

I. Moving Polyhedra

Let us begin with two physical experiments:

First experiment: When playing dice, the first part of a die to touch the table is always a corner, never a whole edge or a whole face.

Second experiment: Let K_0 be a convex polyhedron located in R_+^3 at time $t = 0$; its vertices I, II, III ... are moving (deformations are allowed), and, at time $t = T$, K_t leaves R_+^3. The three normal ways of leaving are illustrated below and correspond to a contact between:

— the origin and a 2-face of K_T (Fig. 1)
— an axis and an edge of K_T (Fig. 2)
— a 2-face of R_+^3 and a vertex of K_T (Fig. 3).

The common feature of these cases is that:

(A1) The dimensions of the contact elements add up to 2 $(0 + 2$ or $1 + 1$ or $2 + 0)$; exceptional cases correspond either to a "too low" (point against edge, ...) or to a "too high" (face against edge, ...) contact order;

(A2) The contact elements are "transversal" to each other; this assumption excludes for instance that the line [I, II] (Fig. 2) coincides with the axis e_3.

Unusual cases are practically excluded if the motion of K_t, $t \in [0, T]$ is governed by coefficients chosen at random. A complete justification of the intuitive idea that the Lebesgue measure of the set of abnormal cases is null would require the tools of integral geometry and would highly complicate the argument. The present paper only intends to bring out the inner connections of Sraffa's and von Neumann's approaches to joint production, and formal

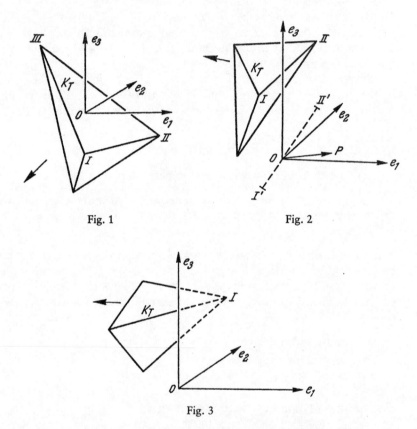

Fig. 1   Fig. 2

Fig. 3

exactness will be sacrificed to this end. Exceptional cases will be briefly discussed to provide mathematical counter-examples, but also because some of them are of economic interest.

An economic interpretation of the second experiment is the following: let a_i and b_i be the input and output vectors of the different von Neumann processes for n goods ($i \in I$, $a_i \in R_+^n$, $b_i \in R_+^n$), and let us consider the convex polyhedron K_t whose vertices are $c_i(t) = b_i - (1+t) a_i$. Then $K_t \cap R_+^n$ represents net products available for consumption when the rate of accumulation is $g = t$. When t increases, the polyhedron "falls" ($c_i(t)$ decreases) and the time T

410   Ch. Bidard:

at which it leaves $\Omega = R_+^n$ coincides with the von Neumann maximal
rate of growth G:

$$G = \sup \{g; \exists \, q \geqslant 0 \quad q \, (B - (1+g) \, A) \geqq 0\},$$

or

$$G = \sup \{g; K_g \cap \Omega \neq \emptyset\}. \tag{1}$$

Figures 1 to 3 are just photo-finishes for $n = 3$, $g = G$.

II. The von Neumann Problem

The von Neumann profit rate R is defined as

$$R = \inf \{r; \exists \, p \geqslant 0 \quad (B - (1+r) \, A) \, p \leqq 0\}.$$

By a separation theorem, it follows that:

$$R = \sup \{r; K_r \cap \dot{\Omega} \neq \emptyset\}. \tag{2}$$

It follows from (1) and (2) that $G \leq R$ but, more precisely R and
G coincide unless K_t "slides" along a face of Ω, a case which corresponds to a reducible system[2].

We define a *generic von Neumann system* (G. N. S.) as a finite
collection of vectors $(a_i, b_i) \in R_+^n \times R_+^n$ such that (A, B) is irreducible
and that, at $r = R$, K_r leaves R_+^n normally, i. e. according to assumptions A1 and A2 supra.

Let us study the three normal cases at the rate $R = G$:

— In Fig. 1, no good is produced in excess, and 0 is obtained by
  operating the three processes I, II and III.
— In Fig. 2, good 3 is overproduced, and I and II are the two
  efficient processes.
— In Fig. 3, goods 1 and 2 are overproduced, and I is the only
  efficient process.

Hence, for G. N. S., the number of efficient methods is that of
non-overproduced goods, and the matrices $(\bar{A}, \bar{B})$, extracted from
the original system (A, B) and corresponding to efficient methods
and to commodities[3], are square (their dimensions are respectively
3×3, 2×2 and 1×1). Moreover, we have the following properties:

---

[2] In this sense, (A, B) is reducible if a proper subset of goods can be
produced using only inputs from the same subset.

[3] By commodity, we mean a positively priced good. Overproduced
goods are not commodities, nor are those goods which, though their own
rate of growth is equal to G, have by exception a null price; such goods
are excluded in G. N. S. by assumption (A2).

Is von Neumann Square?   411

— In Fig. 1, 0 is a strictly positive barycenter of vectors representing the three efficient methods I, II and III, and there exists a
strictly positive vector orthogonal to the plane (I, II, III), the
other methods being under this plane: hence we have, for some
positive activity (row-) vector $q \in R_+^3$ and some positive price
(column-) vector $p \in R_+^3$:

$$\left.\begin{array}{ll} \exists ! \ q > 0 & q\,((1+T)\,\bar{B}-\bar{A}) = 0, \\ \exists ! \ p > 0 & ((1+T)\,\bar{B}-\bar{A})\,p = 0. \end{array}\right\} \tag{3}$$

In Thompson's and Weil's terminology [10], q and p are
generalized eigenvectors; we shall speak of net (row or column-)
vectors of (A, B) associated with $\varLambda = \frac{1}{1+T}$. They are unique up
to a factor (u. f.); these vectors, when completed by zeros, de-
fine the relative activity levels and relative prices of the von
Neumann problem.

— Let us project Fig. 2 onto the commodity space defined by the
first two goods. The origin is then a barycenter of the projec-
tions I' and II' of I and II, and there exists a positive vector
$p \in R_+^2$ orthogonal to [I', II'].

— By projection onto the first axis, we obtain similar conclusions
for Fig. 3.

Hence, in the three normal cases, the efficient part $(\bar{A}, \bar{B})$ is
not only quadratic, but also satisfies relations (3), with dim $q =$
dim p being respectively 3, 2 and 1.

The following lemma derives from Schefold [5] and Bidard [1]:

Lemma: If a quadratic system $(\bar{A}, \bar{B})$, with $\bar{B} \geq 0$ and det $(\bar{B} -
(1+r)\,\bar{A}) \not\equiv 0$, admits a unique (u. f.) positive net column-vector p
and a positive net row-vector q associated with $\varLambda = \frac{1}{1+R} > 0$, then
$(\bar{B} - (1+r)\,\bar{A})^{-1}$ is positive on a non-empty interval $]r_0, R[$.

Proof: For any $l \geq 0$, the unique (u. f.) solution to the homogeneous
equation

$$\exists ? \ (x, w) \qquad (1+r)\,\bar{A}x + wl = \bar{B}x$$

is $(p, 0)$ for $r = R$ and (x, w), with $x = w\,(\bar{B} - (1+r)\,\bar{A})^{-1}\,l$, for
det $(\bar{B} - (1+r)\,\bar{A}) \neq 0$. With a correct normalization of the solution,
and since $p > 0$, x is positive by continuity on a neighbourhood of

412   Ch. Bidard:

R. By premultiplying both terms of the equation by the net row-vector $q > 0$, we obtain

$$w q l = q \bar{B} x - q \bar{B} x \frac{1+r}{1+R} = (R-r) \frac{q \bar{B} x}{1+R}$$

hence $w > 0$ for $r < R$. Therefore $\frac{x}{w} = (\bar{B} - (1+r) \bar{A})^{-1} l$ is positive on some interval $]r_l, R[$ and, by choosing successively all basis vectors for l, we obtain that the inverse matrix is positive on some $]r_0, R[\neq \emptyset$.   Q. E. D.

The assumption

(A3) $\det (\bar{B} - (1+r) \bar{A}) \not\equiv 0$

is added to (A1) and (A2) to define G. N. S. We have thus established:

Theorem 1: From an irreducible generic von Neumann model of production, it is possible to extract one square system $(\bar{A}, \bar{B})$ consisting of operated methods and commodities at the rate $R = G$, and such that:

— Methods, resp. goods, inside the truncation are efficient, resp. not overproduced;

— The net rows and columns of $(\bar{A}, \bar{B})$ associated with $\frac{1}{1+R}$ are positive and unique (u. f.); when completed by zeros, they represent the relative activity levels and prices of the whole system;

— There exists a non-empty interval $]r_0, R[$ on which $(\bar{B} - (1+r) \bar{A})^{-1} > 0$.

Apart from reducibility of (A, B), exceptional cases correspond either to $\det (\bar{B} - (1+r) \bar{A}) \equiv 0$, or to non-transversality, or to a wrong contact order between R_+^n and the convex hull of vectors $b_i - (1+G) a_i$, $i \in I$.

A numerical example illustrating theorem 1 is:

Example 1: three goods X, Y, Z and three processes I, II, III.

(I)	1	1	1	→ 3	4	1
(II)	2	3	2	→ 5	4	5
(III)	3	1	5	→ 1	10	2

The efficient part is framed ($R = G = 100\%$; the von Neumann activity levels $q_I = 1$, $q_{II} = 1$, $q_{III} = 0$ and prices $p_x = 0$, $p_y = 1$, $p_z = 2$ are given by the net row and column of the subsystem).

It is interesting to examine the types of anomaly (other than $R \neq G$) which may occur in exceptional cases: let us distinguish these situations according to the contact order, which is too high (example 2) or too low (example 3).

Example 2: Agricultural production with land.

Let X and Y be two agricultural goods produced on a single type of land L, which enters and leaves, unchanged, each of the two production processes:

$$0.2\,X + 0.3\,Y + 1\,L \rightarrow 1\,X \qquad + 1\,L \qquad \text{(I)}$$

$$0.3\,X + 0.2\,Y + 1\,L \rightarrow \qquad 1\,Y + 1\,L. \qquad \text{(II)}$$

The growth rate of the agricultural goods alone would be 100%, but land restricts the growth rate to $G = 0\%$ (self-reproduction). For this limit rate, the set K_0 is the segment [I, II], where $I = (0.8, -0.3, 0)$ and $II = (-0.3, 0.8, 0)$, whose contact order with R_+^3 is 3 instead of 2 (Fig. 4).

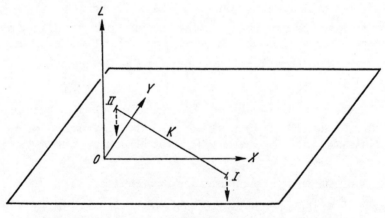

Fig. 4

We have $R = G = 0\%$ and the von Neumann prices are $p_X = p_Y = 0$, $p_L = 1$. It might at first seem possible to extract from (A, B), and even in two different ways, a quadratic system $(\bar{A}, \bar{B})$ consisting

414   Ch. Bidard:

only of the commodity land:

$$0.2\ X + 0.3\ Y + \boxed{1\ L} \rightarrow \quad 1\ X + \qquad \boxed{1\ L}$$

or

$$0.3\ X + 0.2\ Y + \boxed{1\ L} \rightarrow \qquad\quad 1\ Y + \boxed{1\ L}$$

with $\bar{A}=[1]$ and $\bar{B}=[1]$ satisfying the conditions of the previous lemma.

   The problem here is that self-reproduction of each isolated process I or II is impossible. To guarantee self-reproduction, we have to consider both methods simultaneously, which reintroduces a difference between the number of commodities and that of processes (rectangular systems).

Example 3: Two goods X, Y, and three processes I, II, III.

$$1\ X + 1\ Y \rightarrow 2\ X + 2\ Y \qquad\qquad\text{(I)}$$
$$1\ X + 1\ Y \rightarrow 3\ X \qquad\qquad\text{(II)}$$
$$1\ X + 1\ Y \rightarrow \quad\ 3\ Y \qquad\qquad\text{(III)}$$

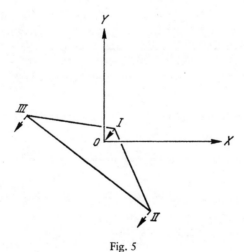

Fig. 5

The maximal growth and profit rates are $G=R=100\%$, obtained by using only method (I). Fig. 5 shows we are in a situation of exceptional contact, of order 0 instead of 1, between K_T and R_+^2.

It is easy to check that one cannot extract from (A, B) a square system such that, for a null price given to the excluded good, the profit rate of the excluded methods would be inferior.

In this case, we have more goods than processes, a symmetrical situation to that of example 2. We interpret this situation as resulting from a "collision of switchings": modifying slightly the coefficients of method I

$$1 \, X + 1 \, Y \rightarrow (2+\alpha) \, X + 2 \, Y \qquad |\alpha| < \varepsilon \qquad (I_\alpha)$$

the optimal technique is composed of:

— processes I_α and III if $\alpha > 0$;
— process I_α if $\alpha = 0$;
— processes I_α and II if $\alpha < 0$.

For infinitesimal variations of coefficients, we have two different switchings which occur at the same point for $\alpha = 0$.

III. The Sraffa Problem

While the existence of positive net vectors at the rate $R = G$ is a feature of a von Neumann model, the equivalent property $(\bar{B} - (1+r) \, \bar{A})^{-1} > 0$ for $r \in]r_0, R[$ cannot be interpreted in this model, as there is no other profit rate than R. But we may suppose[4], with Sraffa, that each process requires labour (the assumption of a strictly positive labour vector is too restrictive, but is used for the sake of simplicity) and we normalize it by choosing $l_i = 1$. Then:

— We can consider profit rates r lower than R and give a meaning to the production prices $p = (\bar{B} - (1+r) \, \bar{A})^{-1} \, l$;
— The vector $c_i(r) = b_i - (1+r) \, a_i$ is the net product associated with $l_i = 1$, if $g = r$.

In geometrical representations, the price vector associated with n production methods at the profit rate r is defined by $p \cdot c_i(r) = l_i = 1$ and is orthogonal to the affine hyperplane generated by $c_i(r)$, $i = 1, \ldots, n$; K_{1+g} is the set of available consumption baskets per worker when the growth rate is g.

---

[4] "The quantity of labour employed in each industry has now to be represented explicitly, taking the place of the corresponding quantities of subsistence" [8, § 10].

The positivity of $(\bar{B}-(1+r)\,\bar{A})^{-1}$ ensures a correct behaviour of the production prices on the range $]r_0, R[$, and most properties of single production prices hold good on this set of high profit rates. One must, however, stress that the range of efficiency of the dominant technique can be smaller than $]r_0, R[$: for instance, if the coefficients of our first numerical example are those associated with $l_I = l_{II} = l_{III} = 1$, the matrix $\left(\text{with } \lambda = \dfrac{1}{1+r}\right)$

$$(\bar{B}-(1+r)\,\bar{A})^{-1} = \frac{\lambda}{(2\lambda-1)\,(8\lambda+1)} \begin{bmatrix} 5\lambda-2 & 1-\lambda \\ 3-4\lambda & 4\lambda-1 \end{bmatrix}$$

is positive for $\varLambda = \dfrac{1}{2} < \lambda < \dfrac{3}{4}$ and prices are positive and increasing for $33\% < r < 100\% = R$ (and even on a larger segment). However for these prices

$$p_1(\lambda) = 0 \qquad p_2(\lambda) = \frac{\lambda\,(4\lambda-1)}{(2\lambda-1)\,(8\lambda+1)} \qquad p_3(\lambda) = \frac{2\lambda}{(2\lambda-1)\,(8\lambda+1)}$$

it is easy to check that method III yields super-normal profits for $r < 50\%$ (considering the prices, the positive rent amounts to $\left(\lambda-\dfrac{2}{3}\right)\dfrac{12\,(2\lambda+1)}{(2\lambda-1)\,(8\lambda+1)}$ and must be included in a new dominant technique).

As for quantities, the positivity of the inverse matrix also ensures that any consumption basket $\bar{d} \geq 0$ can be produced at the positive activity levels $\bar{y}$ given by $\bar{y} = \bar{d}\,[\bar{B}-(1+g)\,\bar{A}]^{-1}$, and this leads to a non-substitution theorem for joint production. Though it is known that such a result is generally false for multiple-product systems, it becomes true in a neighbourhood of $R = G$; this property deserves a closer examination.

IV. A Non-Substitution Theorem for Joint Production

A non-substitution result states that the efficient technique is independent of demand, the reason being that the cost-minimizing technique is able to produce any semi-positive output vector, given a suitable choice of the relative activity levels.

Let us discuss this proposition for high profit rates: in normal cases where theorem 1 applies, there is *one* technique able to produce *some* non-negative basket of commodities at $g = G$, and by continuity one technique able to produce some (semi-)positive basket at $g = G - \varepsilon$ and such that, for the associated prices, methods outside this technique do not yield supernormal profits. The problem is to prove that this technique can produce *any* small semi-positive basket. It appears that complications are linked to "abnormal cases", to the existence of overproduced goods or to the dropping of the Golden Rule assumption:

— Let us begin with the abnormal case represented in Fig. 5. For $r = R - \varepsilon$, the efficient technique to produce a consumption basket with a given direction $d = (d_1, d_2) \geq 0$ is made up of methods I and II if $d_1 > d_2$ and of I and III if $d_1 < d_2$: it clearly depends on the direction of demand.

— The discussion of the case where the contact order is too high, as in Fig. 4, would exhibit some singularities, but, without studying thoroughly all the details, we can say that the causes of substitution refer to the previous or to the following reasons.

— Figure 3 is considered as normal. It appears however that, if the consumption basket d belongs to the plane (e_2, e_3), it will be produced by method I and free disposal of good 3 if d is under 0I, and by method I and free disposal of good 2 if it is above; as free disposal methods deserve well of economic theory and cannot be dismissed, they enter into the definition of the optimal technique, which depends on the direction of d.

The result is generalized to all cases where the vector d belongs to the space of overproduced goods. As was noted by Schefold [6], the real wage then remains positive at the maximal profit rate. The economic interpretation of such cases, which cannot be considered as rare from a mathematical point of view (at least for $d \gneq 0$ given), is that they correspond to situations where the production of consumption goods by means of capital goods is "easier" than the self-reproduction of capital goods, in the sense that the capital goods bound the maximal accumulation rate of the whole system.

— If, in Fig. 3, or more generally for any number of goods but normal cases, the direction d is strictly positive, each component of the real wage tends towards zero when r tends towards R. Goods which are overproduced at $r = R$ thus remain locally in excess supply, while the formula $\bar{y} = w \, \bar{d} \, [\bar{B} - (1+r) \, \bar{A}]^{-1} > 0$ applies to the production of commodities ($\bar{d}$ = components of d corresponding to commodities; $w \cong 0$ number of units of $\bar{d}$ paid to each worker); hence the Neumannian technique is able to produce any (small) positive consumption vector, and we are in a non-substitution situation.

418   Ch. Bidard:

— Up to now, the profit and the accumulation rates have been identified. In joint production, the problem outside the Golden Rule case is that cost-minimizing properties are related to prices, hence to r, while the "requirements for use" [8, § 50, note 2] refer to quantities and, indirectly, to g. Though this double reference often creates difficulties, the situation is quite simple here: if $g \leq r$ is assumed instead of $g = r$, the condition $(\bar{B} - (1+g)\,\bar{A})^{-1} > 0$ is the one to be considered, and it implies $(\bar{B} - (1+r)\,\bar{A})^{-1} > 0$ (see note 1). Hence our previous considerations easily extend to $g = G - \varepsilon \leq r \leq \leq R = G$, whether the consumption baskets of the two classes of society are or are not identical.

Theorem 2: For generic von Neumann systems, the unique dominant technique in a neighbourhood of the maximal accumulation rate is able to produce *any* sufficiently small and strictly positive surplus consumption basket.

The range of validity of this non-substitution result is more restricted than that of the usual theorem for single production, since it requires that the surplus part w of the wage be small and that capitalists accumulate the main part of their profits.

Conclusion

The aim of the above analysis was to reconcile von Neumann's and Sraffa's approaches to joint production, and to prove that joint production has a "good" behaviour in a neighbourhood of the maximal growth rate. The realization of this objective and the resolution of some paradoxes of Sraffian joint production require one to step outside the letter of Sraffa's work; this is clear in at least two respects:

— The rule according to which the range of variation of the profit rate would be $[0, R]$ or $]-1, R]$, R being the first positive root of $\det (B - (1+r)\,A) = 0$ [8, § 64] lacks a strong foundation; it is not even justified for "all-engaging systems" [5, 1], i. e. systems for which the set $\{r; [B - (1+r)\,A]^{-1} > 0\}$ is not empty. The correct rule — which avoids, for instance, Manara's paradox [3] — is that R coincides with von Neumann's profit and growth rate [2].

— The theory of joint production is inherently inseparable from that of the choice of techniques, a point on which Sraffa's statements are loose or dubious [8, § 96]. Apparently quadratic production systems must then be treated as rectangular ones, and we have

Is von Neumann Square?   419

to extract the quadratic sub-system $(\overline{A}, \overline{B})$ corresponding to the active part (cf. example 1 above).

The idea of a connection between Sraffa's and von Neumann's approaches to joint production stems from Schefold's work on choice of techniques [6, 7]. Following Steedman's formalization [9], Schefold studies this question by assuming a given relative net product (a problem that he names a "von Neumann problem", but this terminology is confusing); though he explicitly denies any application of his analysis to the true von Neumann problem, Schefold proves that, at high profit rates, the efficient technique defines a well-behaved Sraffa system. In his analysis, exceptional cases are identified as non-regular systems (A, B, l, d).

References

[1] C. Bidard: The Extended Perron-Frobenius Theorem and Joint Production, Paris X-Nanterre University (1984).

[2] C. Bidard: The Maximum Rate of Profits in Joint Production, Metroeconomica 38, (1985), N. 4.

[3] C. F. Manara: Il modello di Piero Sraffa per la produzione congiunta di merci a mezzo di merci, L'Industria 1 (1968), pp. 3—18.

[4] J. von Neumann: A Model of General Equilibrium, Review of Economic Studies 13 (1945/46), pp. 1—9.

[5] B. Schefold: Multiple Product Techniques with Properties of Single Product Systems, Zeitschrift für Nationalökonomie 38 (1978), pp. 29—53.

[6] B. Schefold: On Counting Equations, Zeitschrift für Nationalökonomie 38 (1978), pp. 253—285.

[7] B. Schefold: Von Neumann and Sraffa: Mathematical Equivalence and Conceptual Difference, Economic Journal 90 (1980), pp. 140—156.

[8] P. Sraffa: Production of Commodities by Means of Commodities, Cambridge, 1960.

[9] I. Steedman: Positive Profits with Negative Surplus Value: A Reply to Mr. Wolfstetter, Economic Journal 86 (1976), pp. 873—876.

[10] G. L. Thompson and R. L. Weil: Von Neumann Model Solutions are Generalized Eigensystems, Zeitschrift für Nationalökonomie, Suppl. 1 (1971), pp. 139—154.

Address of author: Prof. Christian Bidard, Université de Paris X-Nanterre, U. E. R. de Sciences Economiques, 200 Avenue de la République, F-92001 Nanterre-Cedex, France.

Printed in Austria

[7]

Vol. 44 (1984), No. 4, pp. 349—371

Zeitschrift für
Nationalökonomie
Journal of Economics
© by Springer-Verlag 1984

The Unifying Formalism of Domination:
Value, Price, Distribution and Growth in Joint Production*

By

Gérard Duménil and Dominique Lévy, Paris

(Received February 17, 1984; revised version received August 2, 1984)

The properties of the prices of production formalism in the case of simple production are now well-known but the properties of the joint production case introduced in the works of J. Von Neumann (1938) and P. Sraffa (1960) remain unfamiliar to many economists. As a result, two attitudes have arisen. Some scholars classify the case of joint production as an obscure intellectual curiousity; others attempt to exploit its puzzling properties in order to further the analysis of a certain number of concepts and mechanisms. The authors of this article have opted for the latter approach and have already published three comprehensive studies on this topic encompassing the problems of prices, distribution and growth (Duménil-Lévy (1982 a, 1982 b, 1983)). In these three articles, the idea of "domination" arises as a unifying concept. The purpose of the present analysis is to demonstrate the power of this theoretical tool in dealing with a wide variety of problems.

The investigation has six parts, followed by a mathematical appendix:

1. The formal *definition of domination* will be presented.
2. It will then be applied to the problem of the so-called *positivity of values and prices.*
3. It will also be applied to the problem of *distribution*, (i. e. under what circonstances is it impossible to give more to all agents.)

---

* This paper has been translated into English by Serge A. S. Demyanenko with the assistance of D. Foley. It is an extended version of a paper presented at the conference "Production jointe et capital fixe" (Nanterre, 1982).

4. The domination formalism will be applied to the analysis of *balanced growth*.

5. The notion of domination significantly clarifies the *relation between prices and quantities*. On this basis, the alternative theories of a simple relation of symmetry or an actual interdependence of the two will be discussed.

6. Finally, the explanatory power of this concept in studying the *choice of technology* will be considered. The term domination will thus be justified economically[1].

I. The Domination Formalism

The object of the first section is to define the concept of "domination" in a general linear model of production and to investigate its basic properties.

1. Notation

m number of processes of production

n number of products

A, B matrices ($m \times n$) of inputs and outputs

$\vec{V}$ column vector with m components (with $\vec{V} \geq \vec{0}$)

$\bar{W}$ row vector with n components (with $\bar{W} \geq \bar{0}$)

s scalar (positive)

$$M(s) = B - (1+s)\,A. \tag{1}$$

Each row $\bar{M}_i(0) = \bar{B}_i - \bar{A}_i$ of $M(0) = B - A$ represents the net product of each process where its level of activity is equal to one. By extension, we refer to the row of $M(s)$ as an "s-net product".

For all the vectorial inequalities, the following conventions will be used:

$$\vec{V} > \vec{W} \quad \text{if} \quad \forall k \quad V_k > W_k$$

$$\vec{V} \geq \vec{W} \quad \text{if} \quad \forall k \quad V_k \geq W_k \ \text{ and } \ V_k \neq W_k$$

$$\vec{V} \geqq \vec{W} \quad \text{if} \quad \forall k \quad V_k \geq W_k$$

---

[1] The present paper is self consistent and all the proofs are given. However, the three articles mentioned above provide more comprehensive sets of results. The first one is related to sections 2 and 6 of the present study. The second corresponds to section 3; the third to sections 4 and 5.

The Unifying Formalism of Domination   351

2. Definition of Domination

The matrix $M(s)$ can exhibit either row domination $D(\vec{V}, s)$ or column domination $D(\vec{W}, s)$. According to the economic problem considered, $\vec{V}$, $\vec{W}$ and s represent different variables. For instance, $\vec{V}$ can be specified as $\vec{L}$, vector of direct labor inputs, $\vec{W}$ as $\bar{Q}$, purchasing power of the hourly wage. The scalar s can denote the rate of profit or the rate of growth.

Definition 1: *The matrix $M(s)$ is said to exhibit a row domination in relation to a vector $\vec{V}$ if:*

$$\exists \, \bar{\alpha} \geq \bar{0} \text{ and } \bar{\beta} \geq \bar{0} \text{ such that } \begin{cases} \bar{\alpha} \, M(s) \leq \bar{\beta} \, M(s) \\ \bar{\alpha} \, \vec{V} \geq \bar{\beta} \, \vec{V} \end{cases}$$

with $\alpha_i \beta_i = 0 \; \forall i$ and at least one strict inequality among the $n+1$.

In one economic application, a slightly different definition of domination is needed. This condition will be denoted $D'(\vec{V}, s)$:

$$\exists \, \bar{\alpha} \geq \bar{0} \text{ and } \bar{\beta} \geq \bar{0} \text{ such that } \begin{cases} \bar{\alpha} \, M(s) \leq \bar{\beta} \, M(s) \\ \bar{\alpha} \, \vec{V} > \bar{\beta} \, \vec{V} \end{cases}$$

$$\text{with } \alpha_i \beta_i = 0 \; \forall i.$$

This new condition is a particular case of the previous one where the last inequality is necessarily strict.

$\bar{\alpha} \, M(s)$ represents a linear combination of the rows of the matrix $M(s)$:

$$\bar{\alpha} \, M(s) = \sum_{i \in I} \alpha_i \, \bar{M}_i(s).$$

I the set of processes for which $\alpha_i > 0$ is the *dominated* set of processes.

Similarly, $\bar{\beta} \, M(s)$ represents another linear combination of the rows of $M(s)$:

$$\bar{\beta} \, M(s) = \sum_{j \in J} \beta_j \, \bar{M}_j(s).$$

J the set of processes for which $\beta_j > 0$ denotes the *dominating* set of processes.

We define column domination by the same conditions, interchanging rows and columns.

Radical row domination denoted $RD_r(s)$ can be introduced as a particular case of domination where $\bar{\beta} = \bar{0}$ [2]. The definition no longer depends on $\vec{V}$.

Definition 2: *A situation of row radical domination is said to exist if:*

$$\exists \, RD_r(s) \Leftrightarrow \bar{\alpha} \geq \bar{0} \text{ such that } \bar{\alpha} \, M(s) \leqq \bar{0}.$$

Symmetrically, radical column domination will be denoted $RD_c(s)$:

$$\exists \, RD_c(s) \Leftrightarrow \vec{\alpha} \geq \bar{0} \text{ such that } M(s) \, \vec{\alpha} \leqq \vec{0}.$$

A graphical representation of row domination is proposed in appendix B.

3. Two Theorems

The following two theorems state well known results of linear algebra using the concept of domination (see, for instance, Gale (1960) corollary 2 and theorem 2.10, p. 49).

Theorem 1: *Either the matrix $M(s)$ exhibits row domination in relation to $\vec{V} \geq \bar{0}$ ($D(\vec{V}, s)$) or the equation $M(s) \, \vec{X} = \vec{V}$ has a strictly positive solution:*

$$\not\exists \, D(\vec{V}, s) \Leftrightarrow \exists \, \vec{X} > \bar{0} \text{ such that } M(s) \, \vec{X} = \vec{V}.$$

Theorem 2: *Either the matrix $M(s)$ exhibits radical row domination ($RD_r(s)$) or the set of inequalities $M(s) \, \vec{X} > \bar{0}$ have a non-negative solution $\vec{X} \geq 0$ [3]:*

$$\not\exists \, RD_r(s) \Leftrightarrow \exists \, \vec{X} \geq \bar{0} \text{ such that } M(s) \, \vec{X} > \bar{0}.$$

Symmetrical theorems hold for column domination.

A slightly different version of theorem 1 exists for domination D' (see Gale (1960), theorem 2.6, p. 44):

---

[2] $RD_r(s)$ is always a particular case of $D(\vec{V}, s)$ when $\vec{V}$ is strictly positive. If $\vec{V}$ is semi-positive and if $\det M(s) = 0$, M can exhibit a $RD_r(s)$ and no $D(\vec{V}, s)$.

[3] Non-negativity can be replaced by strict positivity:

$$\not\exists \, RD_r(s) \Leftrightarrow \exists \, \vec{X} > \bar{0} \text{ such that } M(s) \, \vec{X} > \bar{0}.$$

The Unifying Formalism of Domination   353

Theorem 1′: *Either M (s) exhibits row domination with respect to $\vec{V}$ (D′ ($\vec{V}$, s)) or the equation M (s) $\vec{X} = \vec{V}$ has a non-negative solution:*

$$\nexists\, D'\, (V, s) \Leftrightarrow \exists\, \vec{X} \geqq \vec{0} \text{ such that } M\,(s)\, \vec{X} = \vec{V}.$$

The concept of domination and its properties ultimately depend on Stiemke's theorem. Various related concepts developed in this article are its modified forms adapted to economics.

II. Existence of a Price System

In this section, we use the concept of domination to study the problem of the existence of prices of production, that is, price systems that imply an equal profit rate for all processes. Labor values are considered here as a particular case of prices of production with a zero rate of profit.

We will consider row dominations, both radical and non radical:

> s is the rate of profit r.
>
> $\vec{V}$ is the vector of direct labor imputs in the production technology $\bar{L}$.

1. Beyond Positivity

In the neoricardian perspective, the problem of the existence of a price system is directly posed in terms of prices of production: does a set of *positive* prices exist (which guarantee an evenly distributed rate of profit)?

If a productive system leads for a given value of r to negative prices, this simply means that such a system of prices cannot exist for that rate of profit. However, other sets of prices which do not guarantee a uniform rate of profit could be defined and allow the system to function. In what follows, the question of the existence of prices will be addressed in a perspective broader than the usual neoricardian problematic, including price systems which do not necessarily result in an evenly distributed rate of profit.

In fact, the problem of prices of production involves two concepts of equalisation of returns, an equal rate of profit on capital, and a uniform wage rate for labor. We will treat these issues separately.

354   G. Duménil and D. Lévy:

2. A Uniform Rate of Profit or a Uniform Rate of Wages

One can demonstrate the following two propositions: (see appendix):

Proposition 1: *The simultaneous existence of a price system guaranteeing a uniform rate of profit, r, and a positive but not neccessarily uniform rate of wages w_i is equivalent to the absence of radical row domination $RD_r(r)$.*

When the m rates of profit r_i of the m processes are not uniform, an average rate of profit $\bar{r}$ can be defined:

$$\bar{r} = \frac{\text{Total profit}}{\text{Total advanced capital}} = \frac{\bar{Z}B\bar{p} - (\bar{Z}A\bar{p} + \bar{Z}\bar{L}w)}{\bar{Z}A\bar{p} + \bar{Z}\bar{L}w}. \tag{2}$$

The average rate of profit depends not only on the wage-prices and the technology, but also on the levels of activity $\bar{Z}$: $\bar{r} = \bar{r}(\bar{Z})$.

Proposition 2: *If there is no radical domination for a given value of the rate of profit (no $RD_r(r)$), then a vector of prices and a rate of wages such that the average rate of profit is r, also exist.*

Proposition 2 implies nothing for the individual rates of profit which can be negative. The reciprocal of proposition 2 is more problematic:

Proposition 2': *We consider a price system, $\bar{p}$, a rate of wages, w, and the resulting average rate of profit, $\bar{r}(\bar{Z})$, which is a function of the levels of activity $\bar{Z}$. We define $\bar{r}_{\min}$ the minimum value of $\bar{r}(\bar{Z})$ when $\bar{Z}$ varies:*

$$\bar{r}_{\min} = \min_{\bar{Z} \in R_+^n - \{0\}} \bar{r}(\bar{Z}).$$

Then, there exists no radical row domination, $RD_r(\bar{r}_{\min})$.

3. The Existence of Prices of Production

The non-radical domination formalism applies to the case of the twofold equi-remuneration of labor and capital, i. e., to the case of prices of production $\frac{\bar{p}}{w}(r)$. This price system is the solution of the set of linear equations:

$$B\bar{p} = (A\bar{p} + \vec{L}w)(1+r) \tag{3}$$

or

$$M(r)\frac{\bar{p}}{w} = (1+r)\vec{L}.$$

The Unifying Formalism of Domination 355

Thus, using theorem 1, one obtains:

Proposition 3: *The existence of prices of production is equivalent to the absence of row domination for the vector* $\vec{L}$ *and the scalar* r:

$$\exists \frac{\vec{p}}{w}(r) > \vec{0} \Leftrightarrow \not\exists D(\vec{L}, r).$$

Proposition 3 does not imply the uniqueness of the vector of prices of production. It is only in the case of $m = n$ and of a non singular matrix $M(r)$ that this uniqueness is guaranteed. In this case the price vector would be:

$$\frac{\vec{p}}{w} = (1 + r) M(r)^{-1} \vec{L}. \tag{4}$$

Labor values $\vec{\Lambda}$ in the traditional sense of the term constitute a particular case of prices of production for $r = 0$ [4]:

Proposition 4: *The existence of values is equivalent to the absence of row domination for the vector* $\vec{L}$ *and the scalar* 0:

$$\exists \vec{\Lambda} > \vec{0} \Leftrightarrow \not\exists D(\vec{L}, 0).$$

4. Variations of Prices of Production with r

In this subsection we only consider the case where the prices of production are given by (4).

Wage-prices $\frac{\vec{p}}{w}$ are increasing functions of r according to certain conditions which can be interpreted in terms of domination as well. It is convenient for this purpose, to consider the column vector of wage-prices of advanced capital, $\vec{K}(r)$:

$$\vec{K}(r) = \frac{1}{w}(A\vec{p} + \vec{L}w) = BM(r)^{-1}\vec{L}. \tag{5}$$

---

[4] Investigating the conditions for the positivity of values or of prices of production, several authors such as Rampa (1976), Wolfstetter (1976), Filippini (1977), Filippini and Filippini (1982), Fujimori (1977) and (1982), or Lippi (1978) refer to properties similar to our domination relation. Rampa considers what he calls the "unquestionable inferior efficiency" of productive processes and Wolfstetter "absolutely inferior" processes. Their approaches are limited to the $n = 2$ model and cannot be regarded as general since they can only be applied to productive systems (viable economies). Filippini's and Fujimori (1977)'s definitions of "dominated" processes are, however, equivalent to our own.

356   G. Duménil and D. Lévy:

Since:

$$\frac{d}{dr}\left(M\,(r)^{-1}\right) = M\,(r)^{-1}\,A\,M\,(r)^{-1},$$

the vector of the derivatives of wage-prices in r is:

$$\frac{d}{dr}\left(\frac{\vec{p}}{w}\,(r)\right) = M\,(r)^{-1}\,\vec{K}\,(r).$$

One thus arrives at the following equivalence:

Proposition 5 [5]: *The strict monotonicity of wage-prices in the profit rate is equivalent to the absence of row domination for the vector $\vec{K}\,(r)$ and the scalar r:*

$$\frac{\vec{p}}{w}\,(r)\ \begin{array}{c}\text{strictly}\\\text{increasing}\end{array}\ \Leftrightarrow\ M\,(r)^{-1}\,\vec{K}\,(r) > \vec{0}\ \Leftrightarrow\ \nexists\,D\,(\vec{K}\,(r),\,r).$$

III. Conditions for Antagonistic Relations of Distribution

In the joint production case, the wage-profit rate relation can display the most surprising behavior, in particuliar, regions in which rate of profit and wages both increase[6]. We model the real wage as the bundle of commodities $\vec{Q}$ corresponding to the hourly purchasing power of labor power.

To study this problem, we will employ the concept of *non-radical domination*:

s	is the rate of profit r.
$\bar{W}$	is the real hourly wage $\bar{Q}$.

---

[5] The three first propositions also hold when the wages are not advanced. Conversely, proposition 5 is not verified if wages are paid post factum. Under such assumptions, prices of production are given by $\frac{\vec{p}}{w} = M\,(r)^{-1}\,\vec{L}$ (instead of (4)). The derivative of $\frac{\vec{p}}{w}$ is then $\frac{d}{dr}\left(\frac{\vec{p}}{w}\right) = M\,(r)^{-1}\,\vec{k}\,(r)$ where $\vec{k}\,(r)$ is the vector of constant capital, $\vec{k}\,(r) = A\frac{\vec{p}}{w}$ (instead of (5)). $\frac{\vec{p}}{w}\,(r)$ is an increasing function of its argument if there is no dominations in $M\,(r)$ in relation to vector $\vec{k}\,(r)$ (no $D\,(\vec{k}\,(r),\,r)$). This result is identical to that of Filippini and Filippini (1982) in their theorem 2.

[6] Cf. E. Burmeister and K. Kuga (1970) or B. Schefold (1978 a).

The Unifying Formalism of Domination   357

1. Antagonism between Wages and Profit Rates

When prices of production prevail (or within the vicinity of such prices) workers are assumed to defend their purchasing power over the wage bundle[7].

We now consider a situation where at the uniform rate of profit r_0 and associated wage-prices $\frac{\vec{p}}{w}(r_0)$, workers can afford the bundle $\bar{Q}$:

$$\bar{Q}\,\frac{\vec{p}}{w}(r_0)=1. \tag{6}$$

It can be said that such a situation is antagonistic if no other set of prices (the rate of profit not being necessarily uniform) exists which proves preferable to every agent (wage-earners considered as a group and capitalists separately for each process of production):

Definition 3: *A situation of distributional antagonism is said to exist if:*

$$ \not\exists\,\frac{\vec{p}}{w} \ such\ that \begin{cases} r_i\left(\frac{\vec{p}}{w}\right) \ge r_0 \ for\ i=1,2,\ldots,m \\[2mm] \bar{Q}\,\frac{\vec{p}}{w} \le 1 \end{cases} \tag{7}$$

with at least one strict inequality.

In the first condition, $r_i\left(\frac{\vec{p}}{w}\right)$ denotes the rate of profit of process i at the price system $\frac{\vec{p}}{w}$. If there exists such a $\frac{\vec{p}}{w}$, these disequilibrium prices benefit every capitalist.

The second condition assures that wage-earners can purchase a commodity bundle equal to or greater than $\bar{Q}$ for each of its components.

Such a definition of antagonism is stronger than the mere requirement of an increasing price of the wage bundle concomitant with an increasing rate of profit[8].

---

[7] This bundle does not necessarily correspond to actual consumption. If a physical numeraire $\bar{N}$, existed, the workers' position could express itself through the demand for a certain nominal wage w. In this case the bundle of commodities $\bar{Q}$ would be $w\bar{N}$.

[8] Our definition is not the same as the one chosen by G. Abraham-Frois and E. Berrebi. For these authors, a distributional antagonism prevails if, whatever the numeraire, wages evolve inversely to the uniform rate of profit (Abraham-Frois, Berrebi, 1982).

2. Conditions for the Distributional Antagonism

In the appendix, we show that the previous definition of antagonism is equivalent to the absence of column domination according to vector $\bar{Q}$. The following logical equivalences hold:

Proposition 6:

$$Distributional\ antagonism \Leftrightarrow \not\exists\, D\,(\bar{Q},\,r) \Leftrightarrow$$
$$\exists\, \bar{y} > \bar{0}\ such\ that\ \bar{y}\, M\,(r) = \bar{Q}.$$

IV. Reproduction and Growth

We now turn to problems related to quantities of goods actually
produced. In what follows, we take:

s	as the rate of growth ϱ.
$\bar{W}$	as the total consumption of the period $\bar{C}$.
$\bar{V}$	as the quantities of labor employed $\bar{L}$.

1. Productivity

The concept of the productivity of the matrix of input coefficients
which governs the viability of a simple production system, i. e. its
capability to reproduce itself, can be extended to the joint production case.

Definition 4: *The system is said to be productive if one can find a
semipositive vector of levels of activity $\bar{Z}$ resulting in a net product positive in all its components:*

Productivity $\Leftrightarrow \exists\, \bar{Z} \geq \bar{0}\ such\ that\ \bar{Z}\, M\,(0) > \bar{0}.$

Theorem 2 shows that the absence of radical domination is equivalent to the productivity of the system.

Proposition 7: *The productivity of a production system is equivalent
to the absence of radical column domination for the scalar $\varrho = 0$:*
Productivity $\Leftrightarrow \not\exists\, RD_c\,(\varrho = 0).$

2. Balanced Growth (BG)

This expression describes a growth path on which each component of the net product increases at the rate ϱ which, assuming

growth of labor at the same rate, satisfies the following two conditions:

a) The output of one period is sufficient to meet the input requirements of the next with some excess permitted.

b) A given consumption bundle $\bar{C}$ is also provided.

Definition 5: *The system is said to have a Balanced Growth Path at a rate ϱ if there exists a non-negative vector $\bar{Z}$ such that*

$$\bar{Z}\,B \geq (1+\varrho)\,\bar{Z}\,A + \bar{C}.$$

It can be shown that (see appendix):

Proposition 8: *The absence of radical column domination for a scalar ϱ is a sufficient condition for the existence of a balanced growth path:*

$$\nexists\,R\,D_c\,(\varrho) \Rightarrow \exists\,B\,G\,(\varrho,\,\bar{C}).$$

In some limit cases, the reciprocal can be false. However one has:

Proposition 8′: *If all the products are useful (that is to say either they are consumption goods and/or they are production goods), the existence of a balanced growth path is a sufficient condition for the absence of radical column domination for the scalars ϱ' less than ϱ:*

$$\exists\,B\,G\,(\varrho,\,\bar{C}) \Rightarrow \nexists\,R\,D_c\,(\varrho')\ \text{for}\ \varrho' < \varrho.$$

It should be pointed out that the condition related to productivity (Proposition 7) is a particular case of this new condition. This suggests an extension of the concept of productivity to the one of ϱ-productivity.

3. Balanced Equilibrium Growth (BEG)

A balanced equilibrium growth path is defined by the same conditions as for balanced non-equilibrium growth except that condition (a) is strengthened to rule out any excess production.

Definition 6: *The system is said to have a Balanced Equilibrium Growth path at a rate ϱ if there exists a non-negative vector $\bar{Z}_h$ such that $\bar{Z}_h\,B = (1+\varrho)\,\bar{Z}_h\,A + \bar{C}$.*

The vector of levels of activities $\bar{Z}_h$, is a solution of the equation:

$$\bar{Z}_h\,M\,(\varrho) = \bar{C}.$$

360   G. Duménil and D. Lévy:

If $M(\varrho)$ is a non singular matrix, $\bar{Z}_h$ is equal to:

$$\bar{Z}_h = \bar{C}\, M(\varrho)^{-1}.$$

As a result of theorem 1', positivity of $\bar{Z}_h$ is equivalent to the absence of domination $D'(\bar{C}, \varrho)$:

Proposition 9: *The existence of BEG $(\varrho, \bar{C})$ is equivalent to the absence of column domination for the vector $\bar{C}$ and the scalar ϱ:*

$$\exists\, BEG\,(\varrho, \bar{C}) \Leftrightarrow \bar{Z}_h = \bar{C}\, M(\varrho)^{-1} \geq \bar{0} \Leftrightarrow \nexists\, D'(\bar{C}, \varrho).$$

4. Efficiency of BEG

Various concepts of the efficiency of growth can be defined. One is presented here as an example in the *BEG* case.

It might be assumed that the equilibrium characteristic of *BEG* provides growth with a certain efficiency since quantities are perfectly produced and utilized with no superfluous production. This is not always the case, however, as desequilibrium may result in a higher rate of growth.

In any event, the concept of efficiency has meaning only if we assume that labor is limited.

Definition 7: *An BEG $(\varrho, \bar{C})$ path is efficient if there exists no BG $(\varrho, \bar{C})$ utilizing no more additional labor allowing for the same consumption but with a higher rate of growth $(\varrho' \geq \varrho)$:*

Efficiency of BEG $(\varrho, \bar{C}) \Leftrightarrow \exists\, \bar{Z}' \geq \bar{0}$ and ϱ' such that:

$$\cdot\ \bar{Z}'B \geq (1+\varrho')\,(\bar{Z}'A + \bar{C})$$

$$\left.\begin{array}{l} \cdot\ \varrho' \geq \varrho \\ \cdot\ \bar{Z}'\bar{L} \leq \bar{Z}_h\,\bar{L} \end{array}\right\} \text{ with at least one strict inequality.}$$

Proposition 10: *The absence of column domination is equivalent to the efficiency of balanced equilibrium growth paths:*

Efficiency of BEG $(\varrho, \bar{C}) \Leftrightarrow \nexists\, D(\bar{L}, \varrho) \Leftrightarrow M(\varrho)^{-1}\bar{L} > \bar{0}.$

V. Price and Quantity Duality: Formal Symmetry or Interdependence?

The conditions thus far defined and interpreted in terms of domination address both problems of prices and distribution, and problems of quantities. All these conditions are similar; they consist

The Unifying Formalism of Domination 361

of the absence of row or column dominations for given vectors and scalars. Thus, the question of the exact nature of this price-quantity relation arises: formal symmetry or interdependence?

Already in the simple production case the existence of prices of production and values are dependent on a property related to quantities: the productivity of the system. With the famous von Neumann model, the assertion of the interdependence of price and quantity relations on balanced growth path is complete.

1. Productivity and Positivity of Prices

In paragraph V (I), productivity is presented as a condition on the matrix $M(0)$; a condition which can be formulated in two different ways:

Productivity $\Leftrightarrow \exists \, \bar{Z} > \bar{0}$ such that $\bar{Z} M(0) > \bar{0} \Leftrightarrow \exists \, \vec{\lambda} \geq \vec{0}$

$$\text{such that } M(0) \, \vec{\lambda} \leq \vec{0}.$$

The positivity of prices of production is a sufficient condition for two properties:

Positivity of prices of production $\Rightarrow \exists \, \vec{\lambda} \geq \vec{0}$ such that $M(0) \, \vec{\lambda} > \vec{0} \Leftrightarrow \exists \, \bar{Z} \geq \bar{0}$

$$\text{such that } \bar{Z} M(0) \leq \bar{0}.$$

One is thus confronted in general with the independence of conditions for productivity and positivity of prices of production, which are related by this formal symmetry. In joint production, one can find non-productive systems where positive prices of production exist.

2. The Price-Quantity Symmetry

The results derived thus far concerning prices of production and BG are summarized in the following table:

— Results concerning prices of production:

Existence of prices of production for r	$\Leftrightarrow$	No row domination in $M(r)$ with respect to $\bar{L}$
Existence of a distributional antagonism between capitalists and wage-earners	$\Leftrightarrow$	No column domination in $M(r)$ with respect to $\bar{Q}$

— Results concerning growth:

Existence of *BEG* for ϱ ⇔ No column domination in $M(\varrho)$ with respect to $\bar{C}$

BEG is efficient   ⇔ No row domination in $M(\varrho)$ with respect to $\bar{L}$

3. From Symmetry to Interdependence

If one identifies ϱ with r and $\bar{Q}$ with $\bar{C}$, these symmetrical relations become completely interdependent:

$$
\left[
\begin{array}{l}
\text{Existence of prices of produc-} \\
\text{tion for } r \\
\\
\text{Existence of a distributional} \\
\text{antagonism between wage-ear-} \\
\text{ners and capitalists whose} \\
\text{processes are used in the } BEG \\
\text{path}^9
\end{array}
\right]
\Leftrightarrow
\left[
\begin{array}{l}
\text{Existence of } BEG \text{ for} \\
\varrho = r \\
\\
BEG \text{ is efficient} \\
\\
\\
\end{array}
\right]
$$

These remarkable results are sometimes summarized by the statement that the law of markets (a price mechanism) leads to the most rapid growth (a statement about quantities). Herein lies the meaning of von Neumann's demonstration (J. von Neumann, 1938).

However, all these results evaporate as soon as one relaxes von Neumann's assumptions by permitting capitalists to consume and by allowing for a growth rate inferior to the rate of profit (J. G. Kemeny, O. Morgenstern, G. L. Thompson, 1956, or M. Morishima, 1960). Under these more general assumptions, the only general result which can be demonstrated and which may have genuine economic significance is the following:

Proposition 11: *If there exists a set of prices of production and a distributional antagonism, the economy is, at a minimum, capable of BG for every $\varrho \leq r$.*

VI. The Choice of Technique

In this last section, we intend to address one aspect of a complex mechanism which cannot be thoroughly investigated within

---

[9] This restriction is the consequence of the difference between the two definitions of domination (*D* and *D'*).

the limits of this article, namely, what occurs if the aforementioned conditions are not met? In other words, what happens if the domination situation prevails?

We will limit ourselves to that first problem addressed in this article, the existence of a price system. Our basic claim is that the existence of relations of domination which obstruct the formation of prices of production induces a feedback mechanism upon the choice of technique.

Also, this investigation will conclude our analysis of domination by introducing an economic justification of the term itself.

1. Incompatibility of a Set of Processes

The domination relation $D(\vec{L}, r)$ expresses a type of incompatibility of production processes. No price system can exist which provides them with an equal rate of profit.

The underlying reason for this could simply be that there are too many processes. If the economy utilizes more processes than products ($m > n$), it is impossible in general for them to yield the same rate of profit. In the simple production case, this corresponds to a situation where the same products are obtained by different processes. Except for mere coincidence or chance, there is no reason for such different processes to be equally profitable. It is therefore possible to demonstrate that if $m > n$, some domination relations will prevail. In the case of $m \leq n$, domination can also occur. An evenly distributed rate of profit is impossible in such instances.

Domination is a sign that only investment in the most advantageous process is appropriate as we will now illustrate in a two goods three-process model.

2. The Choice of One Process

We consider the plane of the row vectors of $M(r)$ divided by labor inputs (cf. Appendix B). Each point (i) corresponds to one process and represents the extremity of vector $\dfrac{\vec{M_i(r)}}{L_i}$.

Fig. 1 exhibits two processes (1) and (2) which have equal rates of profit at the price system corresponding to the slope of the line connecting them. In such a situation, it is possible to identify which types of processes capitalists will reject and adopt.

The straight line passing through (1) and (2) and which divides the space into two regions is the locus of all linear combinations of processes (1) and (2) having weights whose sum is equal to one.

364   G. Duménil and D. Lévy:

Since we have normalized the processes by labor time, region $S\pi$
consists of points representing processes which, for the ruling prices
and wages, yield a higher rate of profit than r. The reverse is true
for region $s\pi$.

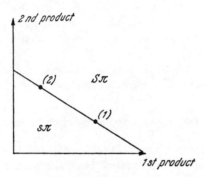

Fig. 1. Super- and Sub-Profitable sets

Fig. 1 therefore summarizes the domination relation and identifies what types of new processes capitalists may be induced to
adopt if the original situation is defined by (1) and (2). This problem is more complex, however, since any modification of the technique defines a new situation of distribution which may undercut
the original choice.

3. Stability of a Modification of Technique

Let us consider three processes in competition as indicated by
Fig. 2 (a).

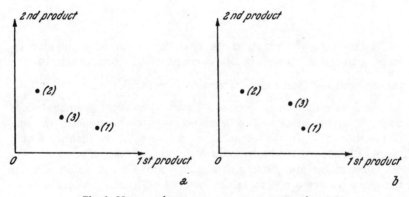

Fig. 2. How to choose two processes among three?

The Unifying Formalism of Domination 365

Process (3) is dominated by a linear combination of process (1) and (2). If (3) is suppressed, thus suppressing the domination, there exists a set of price which provides (1) and (2) with an evenly distributed rate of profit. At those prices, (3) appears sub-profitable and there is no incentive for any one to adopt it.

If process (1), which belongs to the dominating linear combination, is suppressed, the new set of price equally rewards processes (2) and (3). But in such an instance, process (1) appears super-profitable according to the new set of prices, so that capitalist entrepreneurs would be induced to adopt it.

In case 2 (b), process (3) dominates the linear combination of (1) and (2). If (1) (or (2)) is discarded, this choice is confirmed by the new set of prices but there is no mechanism guaranteeing the right choice between (1) and (2). If (3) is suppressed, it necessarily appears super-profitable according to prices corresponding to an equal rate of profit for (1) and (2); and this could initiate its re-appearance.

One thus reaches the following three conclusions:

a) If the abandoned process belongs to a dominated linear combination, in the domination relation, it is sub-profitable according to the new set of prices.

b) If the abandoned process belongs to a dominating linear combination, it proves to be super-profitable according to the new set of prices and should be reintroduced.

c) If there exist several dominated processes (as is the case in (b)), nothing can indicate which process must be abandonned. There exists a perfect symmetry between (1) and (2) in the 2 (b) graph.

Two types of conclusions thus confront us. First, the proposed term "domination" appears to be economically justified. In capitalist competition, processes belonging to dominating linear combinations actually eliminate processes of the dominated linear combination. Second, one can identify new problems involving the possible indeterminancy of the choice of technology in particular situations. The answer which springs to mind in this regard is the possible impact of demand. Such considerations, however, would lead us too far astray from our present project.

Conclusion

A broad range of economic questions, from the existence of a system of prices to the existence of balanced growth paths can be tackled with the same basic concept of domination which has been proposed. This theoretical tool was introduced as an algebraic device to account, within a unified framework, for a numbers of properties of a productive system. In fact, the case of the existence of a price system as related to the question of the choice of technology reveals the fundamental economic significance of the concept. From various points of view, a set of production processes can have a kind of internal inconsistency, which makes it incapable of functioning as an economic system. The domination relation which refers to the domination of one set of processes by another set provides a theoretical account of these inconsistencies in various situations and from various points of view. It thus points to economically significant hierarchic relations, such as the existence of prices of production or of balanced growth paths.

Appendix A: Proofs of Propositions

Proof of Proposition 1

$\bar{p}$ is a set of strictly positive prices, r, a rate of profit and, w_i $(i = 1, 2, \ldots, n)$, a set of strictly positive rates of wages. All these variables are related by n equations:

$$\bar{B}_i\, \bar{p} = (1 + r)\, (\bar{A}_i\, \bar{p} + L_i\, w_i) \qquad (i = 1, \ldots, m).$$

Thus

$$(\bar{B}_i - (1 + r)\, \bar{A}_i)\, \bar{p} = (1 + r)\, L_i\, w_i > 0 \qquad (i = 1, \ldots, m).$$

Using the definition of $M(r)$ (cf. Eq. (1)), these m inequalities become:

$$M(r)\, \bar{p} > \vec{0}.$$

Theorem 2 with $s = r$ and $\vec{X} = \bar{p}$ ensures the absence of radical row domination $RD_r(r)$.

Proof of Proposition 2

If the absence of radical row domination is assumed, theorem 2 guarantees the existence of a strictly positive price vector $\bar{p}$ such that $M(r)\, \bar{p} > \vec{0}$. Thus a strictly positive rate of wages $\tilde{w}$ can be defined by the relation:

$$\tilde{w} = \frac{\vec{Z}\, M(r)\, \bar{p}}{\vec{Z}\, \vec{L}\, (1 + r)} \tag{A.1}$$

where $\vec{Z}$ is any vector of activity levels. The price system does not guarantee an evenly distributed rate of profit. But an average rate of profit $\bar{r}$ can be defined (cf. Eq. (2)). Using the expression (A.1) for $\tilde{w}$, a straightforward computation gives:

$$\bar{r} = r.$$

Proof of Proposition 2'

By definition $\bar{r}(\bar{Z})$ is greater or equal to $\bar{r}_{min}$. Thus for any $\bar{Z}$ the following inequality is verified (cf. Eq. (2)):

$$\frac{\bar{Z}B\bar{p} - (\bar{Z}A\bar{p} + \bar{Z}\bar{L}w)}{\bar{Z}A\bar{p} + \bar{Z}\bar{L}w} \geq \bar{r}_{min}$$

or

$$\bar{Z}(B - (1 + \bar{r}_{min})A)\bar{p} \geq \bar{Z}\bar{L}w(1 + \bar{r}_{min}) > 0.$$

Since this inequality hold for any $\bar{Z}$, it also hold for $(B - (1 + \bar{r}_{min})A)\bar{p}$:

$$M(\bar{r}_{min})\bar{p} = (B - (1 + \bar{r}_{min})A)\bar{p} > \bar{0}.$$

Theorem 2 completes the proof.

Proof of Proposition 6

We consider, r_0, a rate of profit, and, $\frac{\bar{p}}{w}(r_0)$, the associated wage-prices of production:

$$\bar{B}_i \frac{\bar{p}}{w}(r_0) = (1 + r_0)\left(\bar{A}_i \frac{\bar{p}}{w}(r_0) + L_i\right) \qquad i = 1, \ldots, m. \qquad (A.2)$$

When the price system $\frac{\bar{p}}{w}$ is not equal to $\frac{\bar{p}}{w}(r_0)$, it does not lead to a uniform rate of profit. The individual rates of profit $r_i\left(\frac{\bar{p}}{w}\right)$ are given by the equations:

$$\bar{B}_i \frac{\bar{p}}{w} = \left(1 + r_i\left(\frac{\bar{p}}{w}\right)\right)\left(\bar{A}_i \frac{\bar{p}}{w} + L_i\right) \qquad i = 1, 2, \ldots, m. \qquad (A.3)$$

Substracting (A.2) from (A.3) one obtains:

$$\bar{B}_i \Delta \frac{\bar{p}}{w} = (1 + r_0)\bar{A}_i \Delta \frac{\bar{p}}{w} + \left(r_i\left(\frac{\bar{p}}{w}\right) - r_0\right)\left(\bar{A}_i \frac{\bar{p}}{w} + L_i\right)$$

or:

$$r_i \left(\frac{\vec{p}}{w} \right) = r_0 + \frac{\bar{M}_i (r_0) \, \Delta \frac{\vec{p}}{w}}{\bar{A}_i \, \frac{\vec{p}}{w} + L_i} \tag{A.4}$$

with $\Delta \frac{\vec{p}}{w} = \frac{\vec{p}}{w} - \frac{\vec{p}}{w} (r_0)$.

The first condition of (7) is equivalent to the positivity of $\bar{M}_i (r_0) \, \Delta \frac{\vec{p}}{w}$, the second condition associated with Eq. (6) leads to the negativity of $\bar{Q} \Delta \frac{\vec{p}}{w}$, thus:

$$\begin{array}{c} \text{Distributional} \\ \text{antagonism} \end{array} \Leftrightarrow \exists \, \Delta \frac{\vec{p}}{w} \text{ such that } \left\{ \begin{array}{l} M (r) \, \Delta \frac{\vec{p}}{w} \geq \bar{0} \\[2mm] \bar{Q} \, \Delta \frac{\vec{p}}{w} \leq 0 \end{array} \right.$$

with at least, one strict inequality.

The symmetrical of theorem 1 for column domination, with $s = r_0$ and $\bar{X} = \bar{Q}$ gives the end of the proof.

Proof of Proposition 8

Using the theorem 2 and the absence of radical domination, one obtains:

$$\exists \, R D_e (\varrho) \Leftrightarrow \exists \, \bar{Z} > \bar{0} \text{ such that } \bar{Z} \, M (\varrho) > \bar{0}.$$

If one chooses $\bar{Z}' = \lambda \bar{Z}$ with the scalar λ large enough, the vector $\bar{Z}' M (\varrho)$ is larger than $\bar{C}$ and thus there exists a $BG (\varrho, \bar{C})$ path.

Proof of Proposition 8'

By definition, the economic system follows a BG path if:

$$\exists \, \bar{Z} \geq \bar{0} \text{ such that } \bar{Z} \, B \geq (1 + \varrho) \, \bar{Z} \, A + \bar{C}$$

$$\text{or } \bar{Z} \, M (\varrho) \geq \bar{C}.$$

If one chooses a rate of growth ϱ' strictly inferior to ϱ, and if the system follows a BG path, the vector

$$\bar{Z} \, M (\varrho') = \bar{Z} \, M (\varrho) + (\varrho - \varrho') \, \bar{Z} \, A$$

is bigger than $\bar{C}+(\varrho-\varrho')\,\bar{Z}\,A$. As all the products are useful, this last vector is strictly positive:

$$BG\,(\varrho,\bar{C}) \;\Rightarrow\; \exists\,\bar{Z}\geq\bar{0}\ \text{such that}\ \bar{Z}\,M\,(\varrho') >\bar{0}\ \text{for all}\ \varrho'<\varrho.$$

Using theorem 2, one obtains the absence of radical domination.

Proof of Proposition 10

If one defines the rates of growth $\varrho_i^*\,(\bar{Z})$ by the relation

$$\bar{Z}\,\bar{B}^i=(1+\varrho_i^*\,(\bar{Z}))\,(\bar{Z}\,\bar{A}^i+C_i)$$

it can be shown that definition 7 is equivalent to

Definition 7': The $BEG\,(\varrho,\bar{C})$ is efficient if:

$$\exists\,\bar{Z}\geq\bar{0}\ \text{such that}\ \varrho_i^*\,(\bar{Z})\geq\varrho\quad \text{for}\ i=1,2,\ldots,n$$
$$\bar{Z}\,\bar{L}\leq\bar{Z}_h\,\bar{L}$$

with at least one strict inequality.

The equivalence of the two definitions follows from the usefulness (see proposition 8') of all the products.

The rates of growth $\varrho_i^*\,(\bar{Z})$ verify equations which are equivalent to Eqs. (A.4) for the rates of profit $r_i\left(\frac{\bar{p}}{w}\right)$:

$$\varrho_i^*\,(\bar{Z})=\varrho+\frac{\varDelta\,\bar{Z}\,\bar{M}^i\,(\varrho)}{\bar{Z}\,\bar{A}^i+C_i} \tag{A.5}$$

with $\varDelta\,\bar{Z}=\bar{Z}-\bar{Z}_h$.

So the efficiency of BEG is equivalent to the non-existence of a vector $\varDelta\,\bar{Z}$ such that:

$$\left.\begin{array}{l}\varDelta\,\bar{Z}\,M\,(\varrho)\geq\bar{0}\\ \varDelta\,\bar{Z}\,\bar{L}\leq0\end{array}\right\}\ \text{with, at least, one strict inequality.}$$

Theorem 1 completes the proof.

Appendix B: Graphical Representation of Row Domination

If $n=m=2$, the domination can be demonstrated graphically. We also assume $\vec{V}$ to be strictly positive $(\vec{V}>\vec{0})$ and the matrix $M\,(s)$ to be regular $(\det M\,(s)\neq0)$.

370   G. Duménil and D. Lévy:

We assume that the first process is dominated by the second in a non-radical row domination:

$$\bar{\bar{\alpha}} = (\alpha_1, 0), \quad \bar{\bar{\beta}} = (0, \beta_2)$$

with

$$\alpha_1 \neq 0 \quad \text{and} \quad \beta_2 \neq 0.$$

The two conditions of definition 1 become:

$$\alpha_1 \overrightarrow{M^1(s)} \leqq \beta_2 \overrightarrow{M^2(s)}$$

$$\alpha_1 V_1 \geqq \beta_2 V_2.$$

Dividing the first inequality by the second, we obtain:

$$\frac{\overrightarrow{M^1(s)}}{V_1} \leqq \frac{\overrightarrow{M^2(s)}}{V_2}.$$

In order to identify such relations, we represent (Fig. 3) the space of row vectors of matrix $M(s)$.

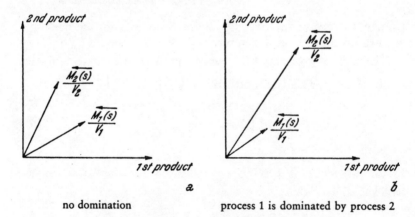

              a   b

no domination   process 1 is dominated by process 2

Fig. 3. Graphical representation of domination

References

G. Abraham-Frois and E. Berrebi (1982): Taux de profit minimum dans les modèles de production; Colloque "Production jointe et capital fixe".

E. Burmeister and K. Kuga (1970): The Factor Price Frontier, Duality and Joint Production, Review of Economic Studies 37, 11—19.

G. Duménil and D. Lévy (1982 a): Valeur et prix de production, le cas des productions jointes. Revue Economique 33, pp. 30—70.

G. Duménil and D. Lévy (1982b): Les avatars de la frontière de la frontière du prix des facteurs, Economie Appliquée *XXXV*, pp. 163—201.

G. Duménil and D. Lévy (1983): Prix et quantités: le cas des productions jointes, Economie Appliquée *XXVI*, pp. 411—445.

C. Filippini (1977): Positivita dei prezzi e produzione congiunta, Giornale degli Economisti et Annali di Economia *XXXVI*, pp. 91—99.

C. Filippini and L. Filippini (1982): Two Theorems on Joint Production, The Economic Journal *92*, pp. 386—390.

Y. Fujimori (1977): Outputs, Values and Prices in Joint Production, Working Paper, University of Josai, Japan.

Y. Fujimori (1982): Modern Analysis of Value Theory, Lecture Notes in Economics and Mathematical Systems 227, Berlin—Heidelberg.

D. Gale (1960): The Theory of Linear Economic Models, London—New York.

J. G. Kemeny, O. Morgenstern and G. L. Thompson (1956): A Generalization of the Von Neumann Model of an Expanding Economy. Econometrica *24*, pp. 115—135.

M. Lippi (1979): I prezzi di produzione — Bologne.

M. Morishima (1960): Economic Expansion and the Interest Rate in Generalised Von Neumann Models, Econometrica *28*, pp. 352—363.

L. Rampa (1976): Valori Lavoro et spreco di lavoro nei modelli di produzione congiunta, Giornale degli Economisti et Annali di Economia *35*, pp. 601—621.

P. Sraffa (1960): Production of Commodities by Means of Commodities, Cambridge.

B. Schefold (1978 a): Multiple Product Techniques with Properties of Single Product Systems, Zeitschrift für Nationalökonomie, Journal of Economics *38*, pp. 29—53.

B. Schefold (1978b): Fixed Capital as a Joint Product, Jahrbücher für Nationalökonomie und Statistik *192*, pp. 415—439.

J. Von Neumann (1938): A Model of General Economic Equilibrium, The Review of Economic Studies *13*, 1945—1946, pp. 1—9.

E. Wolfstetter (1976): Positive Profits with Negative Surplus Value: A Comment, The Economic Journal *86*, pp. 864—872.

Address of authors: Gérard Duménil and Dominique Lévy, Cepremap, 142, rue du Chevaleret, Paris (13e), France.

Part III
Choice of Techniques

[8]

Vol. 38 (1978), No. 3-4, pp. 253—285

Zeitschrift für
Nationalökonomie
Journal of Economics
© by Springer-Verlag 1978

On Counting Equations

By

Bertram Schefold, Frankfurt

(Received September 19, 1978)

1. Introduction

Productive S r a f f a joint production systems are known to possess a number of properties which appear to be counterintuitive, if contrasted with single product systems: prices may fluctuate even if expressed in terms of the wage rate, they may turn negative, the standard commodity may not exist etc. If joint production is, by contrast, approached in terms of inequalities (von Neumann's method), positive prices and a trade-off between real wages and the rate of profit obtain but the solution will in general not allow to activate all processes, some commodities are overproduced and the resulting system of commodities with positive prices in activated processes need not be "quadratic", i. e. the number of positive activity levels need not be equal to the number of positive prices in an optimal solution.

The two approaches to joint production thus appear to be analytically different and to lead to contrasting results but in this article we shall show that they are essentially equivalent from a mathematical point of view as Steedman [1976] has indicated in a short note, and as has already been shown for fixed capital systems in Schefold [1978 a]. An accompanying paper (Schefold [1979]) focuses on the interpretation of the formal similarity of both models, and on their conceptual difference. Here we are mainly concerned with the presentation of the mathematical framework.

In what is loosely termed the "von Neumann approach" the balanced growth path for a capitalist society is thought to be determined in a competitive process summarized by the linear programme

$$\text{Max } dp! \text{ S. T. } (B - (1+r) A) p \leq l, p \geq 0,$$
$$\text{Min } ql! \text{ S. T. } q (B - (1+g) A) \geq d, q \geq 0,$$

where A and B are input and output matrices, l the labour vector and d a vector of consumption goods. These data form the system (A, B, l, d). The optimal prices p in the primal lead, if the rate of profit r equals the rate of growth g, to a choice of technique which maximizes consumption per head by producing the given output for consumption d with the minimum amount of labour.

Sraffa concentrates on the effects of changes of the rate of profit on relative prices in a given quantity system

$$(1+r)\,Ap + wl = Bp,$$

where A and B are *quadratic* input and output matrices. He assumes that the system is in a "self-replacing" state, i. e. that the system is capable of stationary reproduction or of growth but we will introduce the more special assumption of balanced growth at a rate g (mostly taken to be equal to r), with constant returns to scale and with a given basket d as the output of consumption goods. Sraffa introduces prices first in the context of basic single product systems (where prices can be shown to be positive between $r=0$ and a maximum rate of profit), he then simply assumes that prices are positive at some "actual" rate of profit in the joint production case and varies the rate of profit in order to examine the consequent changes of prices, and the effects of those changes on the choice of technique. A change in distribution may either render an alternative process more profitable, to be introduced at a switchpoint where the "new" process replaces a pre-existing process so that both the "old" and the "new" system have the same number of commodities and processes in use. Or a price (e. g. of an old machine) may turn negative at what we will call a point of truncation where the old machine ceases to have positive value and is eliminated (truncated) from the system together with the process using it so that the number of processes in use and commodities with positive prices is $n-1$ if it was equal to n in the original system. Finally, a new method of production may be introduced at a constant rate of profit if it represents technical progress. We can draw the curve of the real wage expressed in terms of basket d in each case for each of the alternative systems and we find that at any given rate of profit the system with the highest real wage is to be preferred.

The systems considered by Sraffa are all capable of "self-replacement", or, in our context, of producing the required basket of consumption goods. This is obvious in a comparison of single product systems differing by the method of production employed in one industry. All prices and activity levels are then positive in both

On Counting Equations

systems, and I have proposed a similar interpretation for an analogous comparison in the case of fixed capital (Schefold [1978 a]): Only prices of old machines may be negative in fixed capital systems while prices of new machines can be determined directly through discounting in an "integrated system" after an elimination of old machines. Hence the possibility of interpreting the prices of old machines as book values (old machines need not be traded) so that a suboptimal untruncated system can exist economically if the book values are not ascertained. But it turns out that prices of new machines in terms of the wage rate are lowest for the optimal truncation and that competition in respect to the prices of new machines and other finished goods will choose a truncation for which all book values (if they are ascertained) are positive.

Both cases (single product and fixed capital systems) have thus in common that the alternative systems being compared are capable of fulfilling the quantity conditions (assuming constant returns) but (at $r = g$) only the system to be chosen will minimize the amount of labour employed, given d. Prices are positive in each single product system being compared, although prices of a suboptimal system lead to surplus profits if applied to an optimal system. Prices of old machines are not all positive in all suboptimal truncations, but models can be conceived where prices of old machines are not ascertained so that suboptimal truncations have an economic meaning in fixed capital systems.

In this article we shall confront Sraffa's approach with von Neumann's by singling out all the different quadratic systems $(\bar{A}, \bar{B}, \bar{l}, \bar{d})$ implicit in (A, B, l, d) and among those quadratic sub-systems which allow the production of d we shall look for the most profitable. Similarly, if (A, B, l, d) is already a quadratic Sraffa system with positive prices, the *truncation* of the system or the elimination of processes which may be necessary because some prices (e. g. of machines) turn negative as r is varied, is also analysed by comparing the corresponding truncated quadratic Sraffa systems. In any given joint production system for which we do not have $(B - A)^{-1} \geq 0$ the choice of technique is an inherent problem since not all processes are indispensable to the production of a net output (cf. Schefold, 1978 b). To assume that all conceivable alternative "systems" or "truncations" can thus be compared "in the air", before a system is installed, amounts admittedly to a bold hypothesis but later we shall see that the truncations will come up "one by one" as one moves on the envelope of wage curves so that we are enabled to return eventually to Sraffa's method in its pure form.

256   B. Schefold:

Among the Sraffa systems to be formed from the elements of
(A, B, l, d) we have thus only to compare all systems fulfilling the
quantity conditions. Each of them is then in itself meaningful at
least in that an ideal planner may compare all systems fulfilling
quantity conditions in order to choose the optimum among them,
but some systems compared may have positive Sraffa prices so
that they can be compared as capitalist economies. Competition is
shown to lead to the same result anyway; the optimum system at
each $r = g$ is that yielding the *highest real wage,* and it will be shown
to imply positive Sraffa prices. The real wage is highest, since the
maximization of consumption per head is equivalent to the maximization of the real wage on a golden rule path where only capitalists
save. The chosen system is the most profitable in that it is the one
yielding the highest rate of profit if the real wage is given. Finally,
and in the present case most importantly, the solution to the linear
programming problem will, at each $r = g$, in general be given by one
and only one of the implicit systems so compared. This will surprise many because other linear programming problems do not, in
general, produce quadratic solutions. But we show that apart from
certain exceptions the goods "outside" the optimal system will be
overproduced (hence they are not part of the commodity producing
system), and that the processes outside the truncation are unprofitable and not used while conversely the processes inside are used and
the prices inside are positive, with strict equality of the number of
activities used and commodities with positive prices. Hence "counting of equations" works. It further turns out that surplus profits
will induce the adoption of superior methods if they happen not to
be used, and losses will penalize the mistaken use of inferior processes. In this sense, the Sraffa approach with explicit "equalities"
within the system both for prices and for quantities, and with implicit inequalities without, is equivalent to the von Neumann
approach where equalities and inequalities are both shown explicitly
but where it is usually not recognized that the equalities define in
general a quadratic Sraffa system as optimal solution.

Steedman [1976] obtains a *minimum* wage curve (not really in
the spirit of Sraffa) because he seeks the minimum of the wage
curves with non-negative prices at a given rate of profit while we
seek the maximum wage curve among those capable of producing
the required real wage. The not optimal wage curves in Steedman's
approach violate the quantity conditions, the not optimal curves in
our approach violate the price conditions but both come to the
same result. We prefer to base our considerations on a comparison
of the systems for which the quantity conditions can be fulfilled for

On Counting Equations   257

reasons of economic interpretation. This implies a focus on the dual
of the linear programme which minimizes the amount of labour
used directly and indirectly to produce the surplus for consumption
at a given rate of growth whereas Steedman focuses on the primal
although the economic interpretation of the primal is problematic
(see Schefold [1979]). Note that "Max *dp*!" means that the real
wage is to be minimized, since the prices of the linear programme
are expressed in terms of labour commanded.

2. Comparing Wage Curves and Optimal Solutions: General Case

The *original set of processes* (A, B, l, d), $A = (a_i{}^j)$, $B = (b_i{}^j)$, $l = (l_i)$,
$d = (d_j)$, $i = 1, \ldots, m$; $j = 1, \ldots, n$ contains a finite number of qua-
dratic *systems* or *truncations* $(\bar{A}, \bar{B}, \bar{l}, \bar{d})$, of order s, $1 \leq s \leq \text{Min } (m, n)$,
$\bar{A} = (a_\mu{}^\nu)$, $\bar{B} = (b_\mu{}^\nu)$, $\bar{l} = (l_\mu)$, $\bar{d} = (d_\nu)$, $\mu = i_1, \ldots, i_s$; $\nu = j_1, \ldots, j_s$; $1 \leq i_1 <$
$\ldots < i_s \leq m$; $1 \leq j_1 < \ldots < j_s \leq n$; which consist of the elements of an
equal number of corresponding rows and columns of A, B, l and d
(l is a column vector, d a row vector). We will mainly use the term
truncation when we want to emphasize that we are talking about
a subsystem of a larger system. The components of vector d will,
in general, be positive in so far as they denote consumption goods
and zero in so far as they denote machines (old and new ones)
and other pure means of production; we shall say that commodity j
is a consumption good if $d_j > 0$ and a mean of production if $d_j = 0$.
We assume $l > 0$. We write $\bar{a}^j$, $\bar{b}^j$ for the truncated columns of
A, B, etc.

The truncated vector $\bar{d}$ is produced by activity levels $\bar{q}$ at rate
of growth g if $\bar{q} (\bar{B} - (1 + g) \bar{A}) = \bar{d}$. A truncation $(\bar{A}, \bar{B}, \bar{l}, \bar{d})$ is *productive* of (at least) d at rate of growth g if there is $\bar{q} \geq 0$ such
that $\bar{q} (\bar{B} - (1 + g) \bar{A}) \geq \bar{d}$ and if $q (B - (1 + g) A) \geq d$ where q is the
augmented vector of $\bar{q}$, i. e. the vector the elements of which are
equal to the corresponding elements of $\bar{q}$ for processes used in the
truncation and zero otherwise: $\bar{q}_\mu = q_i$ for $\mu = i = i_1, \ldots, i_s$; $q_i = 0$ for
all other i. A truncation is productive of at least d at rate of
growth g, in short, if d can be produced and possibly partly overproduced by activating processes used in the truncation only, and
if this concerns both commodities in the truncation and commodities
outside. A truncation which is productive of d at $\bar{g}$ is productive
of d at all $g < \bar{g}$, $g \geq 0$.

A truncation is *q-feasible* at rate of growth g, if $\bar{q} (\bar{B} - (1 + g) \bar{A})$
$= \bar{d}$, $\bar{q} \geq 0$, and if $q (B - (1 + g) A) \geq d$ where q is the augmented

258   B. Schefold:

vector of $\bar{q}$. A truncation which is q-feasible at g is productive of d at g, but it is very important to realize that the converse is not necessarily true in general joint production systems. A truncation is *strictly q-feasible* at rate of growth g if there is $\bar{q} > 0$ such that $\bar{q}\,(\bar{B} - (1+g)\,\bar{A}) = \bar{d}$ and $q\,(b^j - (1+g)\,a^j) > d_j$ for all $j \neq j_1, \ldots, j_s$, with $d_j > 0$ and/or $\bar{a}^j + \bar{b}^j \neq 0$, and $q\,(b^j - (1+g)\,a^j) = 0$ for $j \neq j_1, \ldots, j_s$ with $d_j = 0$, $\bar{a}^j = \bar{b}^j = 0$, i. e. if the truncated vector of consumption demand is produced without overproduction at positive (not only semipositive) activity levels within the truncation and if *all* consumption goods and all those means of production outside the truncation are overproduced which are at all used and produced in the processes activated in the truncation. Means of production which are neither used nor produced in the processes activated for the truncation are called *phantom goods*; they can obviously not be overproduced.

The vector q provides in each of these three cases a feasible vector in the dual of the linear programme. The analogous definition on the price side is simpler: a truncation is *q-feasible (strictly q-feasible)* if there is $\bar{p} \geq 0$ $(\bar{p} > 0)$ such that $(\bar{B} - (1+r)\,\bar{A})\,\bar{p} = \bar{l}$ and if the augmented vector p fulfills $(B - (1+r)\,A)\,p \leq l$ (with $(b_i - (1+r)\,a_i)\,p < l_i$ for all $i \neq i_1, \ldots, i_s$). Truncations which are q-feasible and which have non-negative prices are called "viable". They may be regarded as proper S r a f f a systems fit for a comparison not only from the point of view of planning but also of pricing. Note that a viable truncation will either be a solution to the linear programme or it is not p-feasible because it allows extra profits. For if a truncation is both q-feasible and p-feasible, the corresponding augmented vectors provide optimal solutions to the linear programme, since q and p will each be feasible in the programme and since

$$ql = \bar{q}\bar{l} = \bar{q}\,(\bar{B} - (1+r)\,\bar{A})\,\bar{p} = \bar{d}\bar{p} = dp.$$

A truncation which is both p-feasible and q-feasible will be called almost perfect; if it is both strictly q-feasible and strictly p-feasible, it is called perfect.

Conversely, among the optimal solutions at $r = g$ there is always one given by the augmented vectors of an almost perfect system or truncation. The programme can thus be solved by looking at the wage curves of alternative truncations. They are now to be analysed:

If a system $(\bar{A}, \bar{B}, \bar{l}, \bar{d})$ is given, and if $\det (\bar{B} - (1+r)\,\bar{A})$ does not vanish identically in r, the "wage curve" is where it does not

On Counting Equations

diverge to infinity defined by

$$w\,(r) = \frac{1}{\bar{d}\,[\bar{B} - (1+r)\,\bar{A}]^{-1}\,\bar{l}}$$

except in a finite number of points with $\det(\bar{B} - (1+r)\,\bar{A}) = 0$. An analysis as in 3.7 below shows that values for $w\,(r)$ can nevertheless be defined so that the curve exists for all r with $\bar{d}\,(\bar{B} - (1+r)\,\bar{A})^{-1}\bar{l}$ $\neq 0$ and is continuous even in isolated points where $\det(\bar{B} - (1+r)\,\bar{A})$ $= 0$. Obviously $w\,(R) = 0$ if R is a characteristic root of a "regular" system (see Schefold [1976 a], and section 3 below), but $w\,(R) \neq 0$ is possible in the "irregular" case. The equations

$$\bar{q}^{\mathrm{I}}\,(\bar{B} - (1+r)\,\bar{A}) = \bar{d}, \quad (\bar{B} - (1+r)\,\bar{A})\,\bar{p}^{\mathrm{I}} = \bar{l}$$

can be solved uniquely if $\det(\bar{B} - (1+r)\,\bar{A}) \neq 0$, but if $\det(\bar{B} - (1+r)\,\bar{A})$ $= 0$, the equations will admit of no solution in the regular case (see 3.7 below) and may admit of several solutions $\bar{q}^{\mathrm{I}}, \bar{q}^{\mathrm{II}}, \bar{p}^{\mathrm{I}}, \bar{p}^{\mathrm{II}}$ etc. in the irregular case. The wage curve can, if solutions to both equations exist, then be defined by $w\,(r) = 1/\bar{q}^{\mathrm{I}}\,\bar{l}$ and we can prove that the wage curve even of a truncation with $\det(\bar{B} - (1+r)\,\bar{A}) = 0$ will

1. be uniquely determined, where such solutions exist, i. e. $w\,(r) = 1/\bar{d}\bar{p}^{\mathrm{I}} = 1/\bar{d}\bar{p}^{\mathrm{II}} = 1/\bar{q}^{\mathrm{I}}\,\bar{l} = 1/\bar{q}^{\mathrm{II}}\,\bar{l}$ etc.

2. be given by the wage curve of a "subtruncation" $(\bar{\bar{A}}, \bar{\bar{B}}, \bar{\bar{l}}, \bar{\bar{d}})$ contained in $(\bar{A}, \bar{B}, \bar{l}, \bar{d})$ with $\det[\bar{\bar{B}} - (1+r)\,\bar{\bar{A}}]$ not vanishing identically,

3. if the augmented vectors p, q to any one of the multiple solutions $\bar{p}^{\mathrm{I}}, \bar{q}^{\mathrm{I}}$ are non-negative and solve the linear programme, the other augmented vectors to all the other solutions $\bar{q}^{\mathrm{II}}, \bar{p}^{\mathrm{II}}$ etc. also solve the linear programme, if they are q-feasible and p-feasible respectively.

4. If multiple solutions $\bar{q}^{\mathrm{I}}, \bar{q}^{\mathrm{II}}, \bar{p}^{\mathrm{I}}, \bar{p}^{\mathrm{II}}$ to a truncation exist locally (globally), wage curves of several different subtruncations cross locally (coincide globally).

To prove this, note that if for a truncation of order n (omitting bars and putting $1 + r = \varrho$)

$$q\,(B - \varrho A) = d, \quad (B - \varrho A)\,p = l$$

can be solved, not all minors of $B - \varrho A$ vanish (for otherwise $B - \varrho A = 0$ while we assume $l > 0$) and there is a greatest not vanishing minor, $B_1{}^1 - \varrho A_1{}^1$, of order $m < n$, consisting of the first m rows and columns, say, with det $(B_1{}^1 - \varrho A_1{}^1) \neq 0$ and

$$(B_2 - \varrho A_2) = M\,(\varrho)\,(B_1 - \varrho A_1); \quad (B^2 - \varrho A^2) = (B^1 - \varrho A^1)\,N\,(\varrho),$$

where $M\,(\varrho)$ and $N^T\,(\varrho)$ are matrices of order $(n - m, m)$. The equations can be solved if and only if (locally or globally)

$$l_2 = M\,(\varrho)\,l_1, \quad d_2 = d_1\,N\,(\varrho).$$

All solutions are then given by

$$p = \begin{bmatrix} B_1{}^1 - \varrho\,A_1{}^1 & B_1{}^2 - \varrho\,A_1{}^2 \\ 0 & I \end{bmatrix}^{-1} \begin{bmatrix} l_1 \\ \tilde{l} \end{bmatrix}$$

where the vector $\tilde{l}$ consists of $n - m$ free parameters. One obtains, using

$$N\,(\varrho) = (B_1{}^1 - \varrho\,A_1{}^1)^{-1}\,(B_1{}^2 - \varrho\,A_1{}^2):$$
$$dp = d_1\,(B_1{}^1 - \varrho\,A_1{}^1)^{-1}\,l_1 - d_1\,(B_1{}^1 - \varrho\,A_1{}^1)^{-1}\,(B_1{}^2 - \varrho\,A_1{}^2)\,\tilde{l} + d_2\,\tilde{l}$$
$$= d_1\,(B_1{}^1 - \varrho\,A_1{}^1)^{-1}\,l_1 - d_1\,N\,(\varrho)\,\tilde{l} + d_2\,\tilde{l} = d_1\,(B_1{}^1 - \varrho\,A_1{}^1)\,l_1,$$

the transformation of ql being analogous. (1) and (2) follow at once. (3) follows from $\bar{q}^1\,\bar{l} = \bar{d}\bar{p}^1 = \bar{q}^{11}\,\bar{l} = \bar{d}\bar{p}^{11}$. (4): If multiple solutions for p and q exist, the equations involving $M\,(\varrho)$, $N\,(\varrho)$ must hold, either locally or — $M\,(\varrho)$, $N\,(\varrho)$ being polynomial matrices — globally. But wherever they hold, at least one row of $(B_2 - \varrho A_2)$ may be exchanged against one of $(B_1 - \varrho A_1)$ to obtain a different not vanishing minor of order m if $B_2{}^1 - \varrho A_2{}^1 \neq 0$. After exchanging the corresponding element of l, this minor is found to belong to a wage curve with the same value for the wage at r. Similarly for columns. If $B_2 - \varrho A_2 = 0$, $B^2 - \varrho A^2 = 0$, the wage curve is at the same time the wage curve of $B_1{}^1 - \varrho A_1{}^1$ and of $B - \varrho A$. ($B_2{}^1 - \varrho A_2{}^1 = 0$, $B_1{}^2 - \varrho A_1{}^2 = 0$ while $B_2{}^2 - \varrho A_2{}^2 \neq 0$ contradicts the assumption that $B_1{}^1 - \varrho A_1{}^1$ is a not vanishing minor of maximal order.)

(1)—(4) imply that we may restrict our attention to truncations with not identically vanishing determinants in our attempt to find the solution to the Sraffa or the von Neumann approach on the basis of a construction of the system of wage curves. Of course, only wage curves with non-negative activity levels (prices) need be

On Counting Equations

drawn (except for the purpose of some more sophisticated comparisons). Intersecting or coinciding wage curves point to multiple solutions.

We now imagine the wage curves of q-feasible truncations for $-1 \leq r < \infty$ where they exist to be drawn in bold lines. The envelope of these wage curves is denoted by E or $w_E(r)$. All other wage curves are then drawn as dotted lines where they are defined.

Theorem 2.1: Suppose (A, B, l, d) is a set of m processes and n commodities with $a_i \geq 0$ (each process uses at least one input), $b^j \geq 0$ (each commodity is produced), $l > 0$ (each process uses labour), $d \geq 0$ (there exists at least one consumption good). The envelope E of wage curves of q-feasible truncations is then continuous and monotonically falling from a finite value at $r = -1$ to a non-negative value at the maximum rate of profit R, $-1 < R < \infty$. At each r, $-1 \leq r < R$ there are almost perfect truncations on E the augmented vectors of which are solutions to the linear programme (of section 1 above) which can be solved for $-1 \leq r < R$ but not for $r > R$, and no q-feasible truncation extends beyond R.

Remark: E falls strictly monotonically if and only if $q A p > 0$, and $w_E(R) > 0$ if and only if the linear programme can be solved at R, only if d is not positive and only if there is, apart from the price vector solving the programme at R, another vector $\tilde{p} \geq 0$ with $(b_i - (1+R) a_i) \tilde{p} = 0$ for those processes i which are activated at R. In other words, E falls strictly monotonically if and only if the aggregate value of inputs is positive, and the wage may not tend to zero if there are "limiting means of production" and if there are prices at R giving zero value to net output in each industry used at R.

Theorem 2.1 requires us to prove the simple

Lemma 1: If C is a matrix and $\bar{q} > 0$ a vector such that $\bar{q} C \geq 0$, there exists either a semipositive vector $\tilde{p} \geq 0$ such that $C \tilde{p} = 0$ or there is a positive vector $q > 0$ such that $q C > 0$.

Proof: The alternatives are obviously incompatible. The halfspace $H = \{x | \bar{q} x \geq 0\}$ is bounded by $\partial H = \{x | \bar{q} x = 0\}$, $\underline{H} = H - \partial H$. If $C \tilde{p} \neq 0$ for all $\tilde{p} \geq 0$, the convex hull L of those columns c^j of C which are in ∂H does not contain the origin and is therefore separated from it by a $(n-2)$-dimensional hyperplane J. J defines in conjunction with $\bar{q}$ the $(n-1)$-dimensional hyperplane ∂K which borders the halfspace K containing L. If q is a vector in the interior of $K \cap R^+$ we have $q c^j > 0$ for c^j in L. All other c^j are in $\underline{H}$, therefore $q C > 0$ if q is chosen sufficiently close to $\bar{q}$ and $q > 0$.

262   B. Schefold:

Proof of Theorem 2.1: We start from the linear programme. Consider any $g=r$ where optimal solutions p, q exist. They can, after permutations, be arranged in the following tableau (c^j are the columns, c_i the rows of the matrix $C=B-(1+r)\,A$) where k is the number of positive activity levels, h of positive prices, s of zero activity levels in processes not making losses (degeneracy) and t of zero prices for not overproduced goods (degeneracy). The corresponding blocks $C_i{}^k$ of matrix C are also shown:

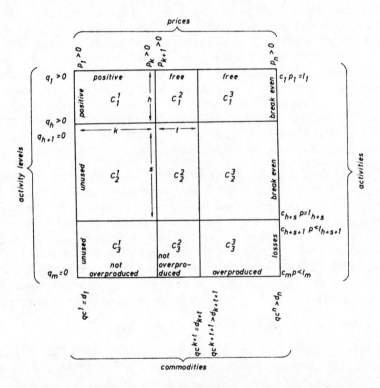

We can show that if optimal solutions exist at $r=g$, there are always some which can be interpreted as the augmented vectors of prices and activity levels of a truncation which is almost perfect at $r=g$. To find them we note first (see S t e e d m a n [1976]) that according to the basis theorem the solution can be chosen such that the number of positive prices and non zero slack variables v (unprofitable activities) in the canonical form of the primal

$$\text{Max } dp \ \text{ S. T. } (C, I) \binom{p}{v} = l, \ \binom{p}{v} \geq 0$$

On Counting Equations   263

does not exceed the rank m of (C, I), hence $k + [m - (h + s)] \leq m$ or $k \leq h + s$. Similarly for the dual $h \leq k + t$. Such a choice of the optimal solutions p, q can be assumed to have been made; we call it the canonical solution.

Suppose first that $k \leq h$. The almost perfect truncation we are looking for is then given by the first h rows and columns of A, B, to be denoted by $\bar{A}$, $\bar{B}$, the vectors of the corresponding components of p, q, d, l by $\bar{p}$, $\bar{q}$, $\bar{d}$, $\bar{l}$. Clearly, since $h \leq k + t$, $\bar{q}\,(\bar{B} - (1 + g)\,\bar{A}) = \bar{d}$, and $(\bar{B} - (1 + r)\,\bar{A})\,\bar{p} = \bar{l}$ since trivially $h \leq h + s$, while p, q are the augmented vectors of $\bar{p}$, $\bar{q}$. The truncation is almost perfect, we have $1/w = ql = \bar{q}\bar{l} = \bar{d}\bar{p} > 0$ since $\bar{q} > 0$, $\bar{l} > 0$. An analogous reasoning applies if $h \leq k$, one then has $1/w > 0$ since $\bar{q} \geq 0$, $\bar{l} > 0$. This is the canonical truncation $\bar{C} = (\bar{B} - (1 + r)\,\bar{A})$. At each r where the linear programme admits of solutions, one is given by the augmented vectors of the canonical truncation. This is on the envelope of q-feasible truncations because Min ql implies the maximisation of $1/\bar{q}\bar{l}$.

The primal has feasible solutions for all r because $l > 0$, the dual in a neighbourhood of $r = -1$ because $b^j \geq 0$, all j, hence $\lambda e B > d$ for sufficiently large $\lambda > 0$ where $e = (1, 1, \ldots, 1)$. If the programme can be solved for $\bar{r} > -1$, it can also be solved for all r with $\bar{r} \geq r \geq -1$, for if q is feasible in the dual at $\bar{r}$, it is feasible for $r - 1 \leq r \leq \bar{r}$. There is on the other hand $R > -1$ such that no solution exists for $r > R$, for if $q \geq 0$ with $q[B - (1 + r)A] \geq d$ existed for all r, we should have $q\,[B - (1 + r)\,A]\,p \geq dp > 0$ if p is a fixed positive vector, but this contradicts $[B - (1 + r)\,A]\,p < 0$ for large r because $a_i \geq 0$, all i. E thus extends over a connected interval $-1 \leq r < R$ and falls monotonically from $r = -1$ to R, for if $-1 \leq r_1 < r_2 < R$ we have, with $q\,(r_2)$ feasible in the dual at r_2 and $p\,(r_1)$ in the primal at r_1:

$$1/w_E\,(r_1) = dp\,(r_1) \leq q\,(r_2)\,(B - (1 + r_2)\,A)\,p\,(r_1)$$

$$= q\,(r_2)\,[(B - (1 + r_1)\,A) - (r_2 - r_1)\,A]\,p\,(r_1)$$

$$\leq q\,(r_2)\,l - (r_2 - r_1)\,q\,(r_2)\,Ap\,(r_1)$$

$$= 1/w_E\,(r_2) - (r_2 - r_1)\,q\,(r_2)\,Ap\,(r_1).$$

Strictly monotonous falling is thus implied at r_1 for $r_2 \to r_1$ if

264   B. Schefold:

$qAp>0$ at r_1. E is continuous, on the other hand, because

$$1/w_E\,(r_2) = dp\,(r_2) \leqq q\,(r_1)\,(B-(1+r_1)\,A)\,p\,(r_2)$$
$$= q\,(r_1)\,[(B-(1+r_2)\,A+(r_2-r_1)\,A)]\,p\,(r_2)$$
$$\leqq q\,(r_1)\,l+(r_2-r_1)\,q\,(r_1)\,Ap\,(r_2)$$
$$= 1/w_E\,(r_1)+(r_2-r_1)\,\alpha\,(r_2),$$

$$w_E\,(r_2) \geqq w_E\,(r_1)\,\frac{1}{1+\beta\,(r_2)}$$

where $\alpha\,(r_2)\geqq 0$, $\beta\,(r_2)\geqq 0$ and $\lim_{r_2\to r_1}\beta\,(r_2)=0$; the wage curves form-
ing E must therefore be connected without "steps". $w_E(r)$ is constant
in those intervals where $qAp=0$. If and only if $w_E(R)>0$, the linear
programme can be solved at R. Suppose the processes which are
activated at R are denoted by A_1, B_1 so that there is $\bar{q}>0$ with
$\bar{q}\,[B_1-(1+R)\,A_1]\geqq d$. If there was no $\bar{p}\geqq 0$ with $[B_1-(1+R)\,A_1]\,\bar{p}$
$=0$, there would be $\tilde{q}>0$ such that $\tilde{q}\,[B_1-(1+R)\,A_1]>0$ by virtue
of the Lemma, implying $\lambda\tilde{q}\,[B_1-(1+R+\varepsilon)\,A_1]>d$ for large $\lambda>0$
and small $\varepsilon>0$ contradicting the assumption that R is the maximum
rate at which the programme can be solved.

Corollaries to Theorem 2.1: Corollaries 1 and 6 assume that (A, B, l, d) is itself a quadratic Sraffa system.

1. Suppose truncation I is at $r=g$ on E and system II is a
q-feasible truncation below. We then have:

a) If I is the original system, the application of the augmented
price vector p^{II} of II in system I implies extra profits if $p^{II}\geqq 0$.

b) If II is the original system, the application of the augmented
price vector p^I in II implies losses, and p^{II} has at least one negative
component.

These statements can be reversed if II is of order $n-1$.

2. Denote the $n+1$ systems which can be formed to produce
n commodities d_j by means of n out of $n+1$ methods of production
(a_i,b_i,l_i); $i=0, 1,\ldots,n$; $j=1,\ldots,n$ by $(A^{(i)}, B^{(i)}, l^{(i)})$; $i=0,1,\ldots,n$;
their price vectors (in terms of labour commanded) by $p^{(i)}$, their
wage curves in terms of $d=(d_1,\ldots, d_n)$ by $w^{(i)}\,(r)$; $i=0,\ldots, n$;
where i is the method *omitted*. Suppose that the systems $0, 1,\ldots,s\leq n$
are viable (q-feasible and $p^{(i)}>0$) at $r=g$, $\det\,(B^{(i)}-(1+r)\,A^{(i)})\neq 0$,
while no other truncation to be formed from (a_i,b_i,l_i); $i=0,1,\ldots,n$;
is q-feasible. If and only if $w^{(0)}\,(r)>w^{(i)}\,(r)$; $i=1,\ldots, s$; we have
$(b_i-(1+r)\,a_i)\,p^{(i)}>l_i$ and $(b_0-(1+r)\,a_0)\,p^{(0)}<l_0$, $i=1,\ldots, s$.

On Counting Equations 265

3. Suppose a truncation is productive of d for some g, $0 \leq g \leq R$, and suppose that the augmented price vector is strictly p-feasible, with $1/d\bar{p} > w_E$ at $r = g$. The truncation will then not be q-feasible for $g = r$ and overproduction of components of $\bar{d}$ with positive prices cannot be avoided, using non-negative activity levels. The maximum of consumption per head (baskets of d) which can be obtained by activating all the processes used in the truncation and no others will be lower than on E at $g = r$, while the real wage $1/\bar{d}\bar{p} = 1/\bar{q}\bar{l}$ expressed in terms of $\bar{d}$ is by assumption higher. In formulas: $1/\bar{d}\bar{p} > w_E(r) > \bar{c}(g)$ where $\bar{c}(g) = \text{Max } 1/\bar{h}\bar{l}$ S.T. $\bar{h} \geq 0$ and $\bar{h}(B_1 - (1+g) A_1) \geq d$, A_1, B_1 being the processes used in the truncation $\bar{A}$, $\bar{B}$.

4. No truncation is productive of d at any $g > R$.

5. If all truncations are q-feasible in all intervals in which they are productive, there is no wage curve of a productive truncation above E and in each productive truncation with positive prices at r the real wage in terms of d will be equal to consumption per head at $g = r$.

6. If the original system is q-feasible with positive prices at $r = g$, it is on E $\left(\text{hence } \dfrac{dw}{dr} < 0\right)$ and it will remain on E for those (and only those) variations of d for which it remains q-feasible (limits to "non-substitution"). The same holds for truncations on E which are p-feasible.

Proof of Corollaries:

1. Since II is q-feasible, with — for simplicity here and below 5, 6 — not vanishing determinants:

$$q^{II}l = \bar{q}^{II}\bar{l}^{II} = \bar{d}^{II}(\bar{B}^{II} - (1+r) \bar{A}^{II})^{-1} \bar{l}^{II} = \bar{d}^{II}\bar{p}^{II} = dp^{II}$$

where $\bar{p}^{II} = [\bar{B}^{II} - (1+r) \bar{A}^{II}]^{-1} \bar{l}^{II}$, p^{II} augmented vector of $\bar{p}^{II}$. Since q^{II} is feasible in the dual, p^{II} cannot be feasible in the primal, for otherwise II would be on E because $q^{II}l = dp^{II}$. If $p^{II} \geq 0$, p^{II} can only not be feasible if it implies extra profits outside system II (case a), but if II is itself the original system, $p^{II} = [B - (1+r) A]^{-1} l$ and p^{II} can only not be feasible by having at least one negative component. On the other hand p^I is feasible, $[B - (1+r) A] p^I \leq l$, and if p^I did not imply some losses in II (the original system), we should have $[B - (1+r) A] p^I = l$, hence $p^I = p^{II} \geq 0$ which is a contradiction (case b). The converse is proved as under 2 for a and is trivial for b.

2. Here we prove only the converse. With $b_i - (1+r)\ a_i = c_i$; $i = 0, \ldots, n$; and with $q_1^{(0)}\ c_1 + \ldots + q_n^{(0)}\ c_n = q_0^{(1)}\ c_0 + q_2^{(1)}\ c_2 + \ldots + q_n^{(1)}\ c_n = d$ we have

$$0 < q_0^{(1)}\ (l_0 - c_0\, p^{(0)}) = q_0^{(1)}\ l_0 - d p^{(0)} + q_2^{(1)}\ c_2\, p^{(0)} + \ldots + q_n^{(1)}\ c_n\, p^{(0)}$$
$$= q_0^{(1)}\ l_0 + q_2^{(1)}\ l_2 + \ldots + q_n^{(1)}\ l_n - d p^{(0)} = [1/w^{(1)}] - [1/w^{(0)}]$$
$$= q_1^{(0)}\ (c_1\, p^{(1)} - l_1).$$

Similarly for $i = 2, \ldots, n$.

3. If a truncation $\overline{A}, \overline{B}, \overline{l}$ above E was q-feasible, we should have $\overline{q}\ [\overline{B} - (1+r)\ \overline{A}] = \overline{d}, \ \overline{q} \geq 0$. The augmented vector q of $\overline{q}$ with $q\ [B - (1+g)\ A] \geq d$ would be feasible in the dual with $1/ql = 1/\overline{q}l$ greater than on E which contradicts the optimality of E. But the truncation is productive at g so that there is $\overline{h} \geq 0$ with $\overline{h}\ [\overline{B} - (1+g)\ \overline{A}] \geq \overline{d}$ and $\overline{h}\ [B - (1+g)\ A] \geq d$. Since the system is not q-feasible, $\overline{h} \neq \overline{q}$, and $\overline{q}$ is not non-negative, while $\overline{p}$ is positive.

4. Since the primal has feasible solutions for all r, it is the dual which ceases to have feasible solutions at R.

5. The first part follows from the definition of E, the second from $\overline{q} = \overline{d}\ [\overline{B} - (1+g)\ \overline{A}]^{-1} \geq 0, \ \overline{p} = [\overline{B} - (1+r)\ \overline{A}]^{-1}\ \overline{l} \geq 0, \ ql = \overline{q}\overline{l} = \overline{d}\overline{p} = dp.$

6. As long as $q = d\ [B - (1+g)\ A]^{-1} \geq 0, \ p = [B - (1+r)\ A]^{-1}\ l \geq 0,$ p and q must be optimal because the optimum is characterised by $ql = dp$ for feasible q and p.

The main point to be retained for the comparison of systems is this: a viable truncation (q-feasible with positive prices within the truncation) is either on E (optimal) and its augmented price vector is p-feasible or its augmented price vector causes surplus profits if applied to some process outside the truncation, indicating that a transition to some other truncation (presumably containing this process) should be made. In particular, if we face a given system with one alternative method of production, total labour employed will, according to the proof of corollary 2, diminish (or increase) by an amount exactly equal to the labour commanded by the extra profits (or losses) caused if the alternative method is fully used to produce the same amount of consumption goods, but if prices are those of the given system. If the system is the "world", the losses (or extraprofits) of a country, accepting world prices, world wage rate and the world rate of profit but using one "backward" (or "advanced") method under golden rule conditions, must be covered by a monetary and real subsidy (will generate a favourable balance) exactly equal to the wage cost of the hours of work wasted (saved).

3. Properties of Regular Systems

Theorem 2.1 has shown that at least one optimal solution to the linear programme is given by a quadratic truncation, and the corollaries confirm that a comparison of optimal and suboptimal truncations in terms of systems is meaningful in that surplus profits and losses guide the adoption and rejection of processes in transitions from suboptimal to optimal truncations and systems. It is, however, still possible that wage curves of different truncations coincide in entire intervals, so that the solution can globally be multiple and not unique. This possibility is unwellcome from the economic point of view (especially on the price side) and leaves room for solutions which are not quadratic (although superpositions of quadratic truncations). Economic intuition says that such anomalies must be flukes. In order to show (in section 4) that this is in fact the case we turn to a discussion of regular systems in this section (which is a self-contained piece of analysis).

Since a joint production system $p = [\bar{B} - (1+r)\,\bar{A}]^{-1}\,\bar{l}$ can be transformed into a single product system $p = [I - r\,A]^{-1}\,l$ with $A = (\bar{B} - \bar{A})^{-1}\,\bar{A}$ (indecomposable if $\bar{A}, \bar{B}$ is basic, and not necessarily non-negative) and with $l = (\bar{B} - \bar{A})^{-1}\,\bar{l}$ (Schefold [1971] and Schefold [1978 b]), we start with single product systems (A, l) without assuming $A \geq 0$, $l \geq 0$.

Generalising Schefold [1976 a], a system (A, l, d) [A (n, n)-input output matrix, l column vector of labour inputs, d row vector of surplus] is called regular, if

1. det $A \neq 0$,

2. one and only one eigenvector is associated with each eigenvalue of the characteristic equation of A, written in the form det $[I - (1+r)\,A] = 0$, i. e. det $[I - (1+R)\,A] = 0$ implies $rk\,[I - (1+R)\,A] = n - 1$ where R is any (possibly complex) eigenvalue,

3. for any complex eigenvector q, $(1+R)\,q\,A = q$, we have $q\,l \neq 0$,

4. for any complex eigenvector x, $(1+R)\,A\,x = x$, we have $d\,x \neq 0$.

Matrix A may be given Jordan's normal form: one knows that there is a non singular matrix Q such that $Q\,A\,Q^{-1}=T$, $T=$ diag $\{T_1^1,\ldots,T_g^g\}$, with

$$T_i^i = \begin{pmatrix} (1+R_i)^{-1} & & & \\ 1 & (1+R_i)^{-1} & & 0 \\ & \cdot & \cdot & \\ & & \cdot & \cdot \\ 0 & & 1 & (1+R_i)^{-1} \end{pmatrix}$$

The symbol diag $\{T_1^1,\ldots,T_g^g\}$ denotes a matrix with the quadratic blocks T_i^i on the diagonal and zeros outside. If the system is regular, the R_i, $i=1,\ldots,g$, are all different. Matrix T_i^i is of order f_i where f_i is the multiplicity of root R_i, $f_1+\ldots+f_g=n$, and where n is the order of matrix A, hence

$$\det[I-(1+r)\,A]=\gamma\,(R_1-r)^{f_1},\ldots,(R_g-r)^{f_g}, \ \gamma \text{ constant.}$$

The roots R_i may be multiple, but, by assumption, only one eigenvector is associated with R_i; we call such roots semi-simple. If all characteristic roots are simple $(f_i=1)$, they are all different, $g=n$, $T_i^i=(1+R_i)^{-1}$; $i=1,\ldots,n$; and T is a diagonal matrix. The identity matrix is an example of a matrix with one multiple root which is not semi-simple but of multiplicity n with n linearly independent eigenvectors.

It is convenient to label vectors and components by a double index: $(1,\ldots,n)$ is replaced by $[(1,1),\ldots,(1,f_1),(2,1),\ldots,(2,f_2),\ldots,(g,f_g)]$. Assumption 3 about regular systems can then be expressed as $v_{i,1}\neq 0$, $i=1,\ldots,g$; where $Ql=v$, and assumption 4 as $c_{i,f_i}\neq 0$, $i=1,\ldots,g$, where $d\,Q^{-1}=c$.

The only irregular systems which are of any economic interest appear to be the following (Schefold [1976 a]):

a) systems with pure consumption goods, i. e. systems where one column vanishes, and systems incorporating land,

b) systems with labour value prices (l eigenvector of A),

c) systems where the surplus is in standard proportions (d eigenvector of A).

Case b and c are of considerable analytic interest but have to be considered apart. Case a is ruled out if we focus on the basic part of each system. However, special allowance for pure consumption goods could be made in section 4 below at the cost of some additional complications in the proof of theorem 4.1.

In order to show that irregular systems are exceptional from the mathematical point of view we consider the n^2 variables a_1^1,

$a_2{}^1$, $a_1{}^2$,..., $a_n{}^n$ as independent and the complex variable r as dependent in the equation

$$\varphi\,(r,\,A) = \det\,[I - (1+r)\,A] = \sum_{\nu=0}^{n} b_\nu\,(1+r)^\nu = 0.$$

The equation then defines implicitly a multivalued function $\mathbf{R}^{n^2}\to\mathbf{C}$. The coefficients b_ν ($b_n = \det A$;...; $b_1 = a_1{}^1 + \ldots + a_n{}^n$; $b_0 = 1$) are polynomials in $a_i{}^j$; $i, j = 1,\ldots, n$. A system will, as far as matrix A is concerned, certainly be regular if the n eigenvalues are different, i. e. if the n values implicitly defined by $\varphi\,(r,\,A) = 0$ are different. Exceptions will occur for given A if and only if $\det A = 0$ (degree of polynomial reduced) or if the discriminant D which is a polynomial in $b_0,\ldots, b_n$ vanishes. Discriminant D and $\det A$ may now be regarded as polynomials in n^2 real variables $a_i{}^j$; $i, j = 1,\ldots, n$ which do not vanish identically, and $D = 0$ and $\det A = 0$ define algebraic manifolds of dimension $n^2 - 1$ in $\mathbf{R}^{n^2}$. Their graphs in $\mathbf{R}^{n^2}$ are of measure zero. Multiple roots are thus exceptional, and multiple roots which are not semi-simple even more so. The set of vectors l in $\mathbf{R}^n$ which do not fulfill assumption 3 for given A, is composed of at most n hyperplanes in $\mathbf{R}^n$ and hence of n-dimensional measure zero, for if l is orthogonal to a complex eigenvector q, $(1+R)\,qA = q$, it is also orthogonal to the complex conjugate vector $\bar{q}$, $\overline{(1+R)\,\bar{q}A} = \bar{q}$ $= (1+\bar{R})\,\bar{q}A$, hence l is orthogonal to the real vector $q + \bar{q}$. Similarly for assumption 4.

Irregular systems are thus exceptional but may be of interest insofar as they permit simplifications which may be regarded as useful approximations to the more general case, but generalisations from this simplification should be made with care.

Theorem 3.1: Let two regular systems $(A,\,l,\,d^{\mathrm{I}})$, $(F,\,m,\,d^{\mathrm{II}})$ be given. Their wage curves will be identical, i. e. $d^{\mathrm{I}}p^{\mathrm{I}} \equiv d^{\mathrm{II}}p^{\mathrm{II}}$ if and only if both systems are of the same order and if A and F are similar matrices with

$$\sum_{\varphi=\gamma}^{f_i} (c^{\mathrm{I}}{}_{i,\,\varphi}\,v^{\mathrm{I}}{}_{i,\,\varphi-\gamma+1} - c^{\mathrm{II}}{}_{i,\,\varphi}\,v^{\mathrm{II}}{}_{i,\,\varphi-\gamma+1}) = 0,$$

$$\gamma = 1,\ldots, f_i;\ i = 1,\ldots, g;$$

where

$$QAQ^{-1} = T = SFS^{-1},$$

$$d^{\mathrm{I}}\,Q^{-1} = c^{\mathrm{I}},\ d^{\mathrm{II}}\,S^{-1} = c^{\mathrm{II}},\ Ql = v^{\mathrm{I}},\ Sm = v^{\mathrm{II}}.$$

(For simpler conditions see 3.8, for joint production see 3.9 below.)

Proof: Using the notation explained above, we have for any regular system (A, l, d)

$$dp = d\,Q^{-1}Q\,[I-(1+r)\,A]^{-1}Q^{-1}Ql = d\,Q^{-1}[I-(1+r)\,QAQ^{-1}]^{-1}Ql$$
$$= c\,\hat{T}v,$$

where $\hat{T} = [I-(1+r)\,T]^{-1}$,

$\hat{T} = \mathrm{diag}\{\hat{T}_1{}^1, \ldots, \hat{T}_g{}^g\}$,

$$
\hat{T}_i{}^i =
\begin{pmatrix}
\left(1-\dfrac{1+r}{1+R_i}\right) & & & \\
1 & \left(1-\dfrac{1+r}{1+R_i}\right) & & 0 \\
& \cdot & \cdot & \\
& & \cdot & \cdot \\
0 & 1 & & \left(1-\dfrac{1+r}{1+R_i}\right)
\end{pmatrix}^{-1},
$$

$\hat{T}_i{}^i$ being a quadratic matrix of order f_i. One obtains by induction

$$
\hat{T}_i{}^i =
\begin{pmatrix}
\dfrac{1+R_i}{R_i-r} & & & 0 \\
\left(\dfrac{1+R_i}{R_i-r}\right)^2 & \dfrac{1+R_i}{R_i-r} & & \\
\cdot & \cdot & \cdot & \\
\left(\dfrac{1+R_i}{R_i-r}\right)^{f_i} & \cdots & & \dfrac{1+R_i}{R_i-r}
\end{pmatrix}.
$$

With
$$\hat{T}v = Z\,u\,(r),$$

where $Z = \mathrm{diag}\{Z_1{}^1, \ldots, Z_g{}^g\}$,

$$
Z_i{}^i =
\begin{pmatrix}
v_{i,1} & & & 0 \\
v_{i,2} & v_{i,1} & & \\
\cdot & & \cdot & \\
\cdot & & & \\
v_{i,f_i} & \cdots & & v_{i,1}
\end{pmatrix}
$$

and $u\,(r)$ is the transposed vector of vector

$$u^T\,(r) = \left[\frac{1+R_1}{R_1-r}, \ldots, \left(\frac{1+R_1}{R_1-r}\right)^{f_1}, \frac{1+R_2}{R_2-r}, \ldots, \left(\frac{1+R_g}{R_g-r}\right)^{f_g}\right],$$

we can write
$$dp = c\,Z\,u\,(r).$$

If two regular systems are given, $d^I p^I$ and $d^{II} p^{II}$ may both be expressed in this form. Consider $d^I p^I$, $d^{II} p^{II}$ as meromorphic functions of r in C. Since the relevant components of c^I, c^{II}, v^I, v^{II} are positive, the singularities (poles) of dp^I and dp^{II} must be the same and of the same order, if $d^I p^I = d^{II} p^{II}$; hence A and F must have the same characteristic equation; they are similar matrices with (after permutations) the same diagonal form T and the same vector $u(r)$ so that

$$0 = d^I p^I - d^{II} p^{II} = (c^I Z^I - c^{II} Z^{II}) u(r).$$

The columns of the matrix $U = [u(r_1), \ldots, u(r_n)]$ are given by the vector $u(r)$, taken in n different points $r_1, \ldots, r_n$ (none of which equals one of the poles $R_1, \ldots, R_g$). If U was singular, there would be a not vanishing row vector a such that $aU = 0$. The polynomial of at most degree $n - 1$ $\chi = \varphi \psi$ where $\varphi(r) = (R_1 - r)^{f_1} \ldots (R_g - r)^{f_g}$, $\psi = au(r)$ would therefore vanish in n points, therefore identically, which is impossible since it is easy to see that neither φ nor ψ vanishes in more than n points. Hence $\det U \neq 0$, implying

$$c^I Z^I = c^{II} Z^{II},$$

which is the condition more explicitly stated in the theorem. The converse is proved by following the argument backwards.

We list a number of corollaries of this theorem most of which are used in the main part of the paper.

3.2: Modified assumption: Theorem 3.1 still holds if it is assumed that (A, l, d^I) is regular and that (F, m, d^{II}) is of the same order as (A, l, d^I). If $d^I p^I \equiv d^{II} p^{II}$, (F, m, d^{II}) will then also be regular. (The proof is analogous to that of 3.1.)

It follows from 3.1 that two regular systems of different order, i. e. involving a different number of commodities and processes, can never have the same wage curve.

It follows from the above that the regularity of (A, l, d) entails the regularity of the transposed system (A^T, d^T, l^T) since

$$d [I - (1 + r) A]^{-1} l = l^T [I - (1 + r) A^T]^{-1} d^T.$$

3.3: If the systems (A, l, d^I) and (F, m, d^{II}) are of order n and m respectively, their wage curves intersect in at most $n + m - 1$ points or everywhere, for $dp^I = dp^{II}$ entails $\varphi \psi d^I p^I = \varphi \psi d^{II} p^{II}$ where φ, ψ are the characteristic polynomials of A and F respectively. On both sides of $\varphi \psi d^I p^I = \varphi \psi d^{II} p^{II}$ there are polynomials of at most degree $n + m - 1$.

An exception may highlight the importance of the various regularity assumptions: If (A, l, d) is any regular basic single product system with maximum rate of profit $R > 0$, the system $[A, l, q\,(I-A)]$ where $q\,(I-A)$ is the standard commodity will not be regular. In fact, the latter system will have the wage curve $w = 1 - (r/R)$ which is the same wage curve as that of the one commodity system (A, l, d) with $A = a = (1+R)^{-1}$, $l = 1$ and $d = \dfrac{R}{1+R}$, for $(1+r)\,ap + wl = p$ yields $w = 1 - (r/R)$ if we normalize $(1+R) = Rp$.

3.4: Behaviour of price vector: The price vector of a regular system of order n, $p\,(r)$, (in terms of labour commanded) assumes n independent values at n different rates of profit, for otherwise there would be a vector a with $ap\,(r) = 0$ for $r = r_1, \ldots, r_n$. This implied $a\,Q^{-1}\,Z u\,(r) = b u\,(r) = 0$, $r = r_1, \ldots, r_n$; where $b = a\,Q^{-1}\,Z$ $\neq 0$; in the notation used above which is impossible by virtue of the argument used in the proof of theorem 3.1 (cf. Schefold, [1976 a]).

3.5: Behaviour of vector of activity levels: The activity levels $q = d\,(I - (1+g)\,A)^{-1}$ of the regular system (A, l, d) may be interpreted as prices of the transposed system (A^T, d^T, l^T) which is regular according to 3.2. The vector of activity levels therefore assumes n linearly independent values at n different rates of growth.

3.6: Vanishing points: Each component of the vectors p and q vanishes in at most $n-1$ points if the system is regular, for the adjoint $[I - (1+r)\,A]_{\mathrm{Ad}}$ consists of polynomials of at most degree $n-1$; if any component vanished at n or more points, it vanished identically. But if a component of p or q vanished identically in a regular system, this implied that p or q would be contained in a hyperplane of $\mathbf{R}^n$ which is impossible because of 3.4 and 3.5.

3.7: Maximum rate of profit and limits in approaching it: The equations

$$[I - (1 + R_i)\,A]\,p = l$$
$$q\,[I - (1 + R_i)\,A] = d$$

have no solution for a regular system (A, l, d), since e. g. the first, with $i = 1$, say, can be transformed to obtain

$$Q\,[I - (1 + R_1)\,A]\,Q^{-1}\,Qp = [I - (1 + R_1)\,T]\,Qp = Ql$$

which has no solution since the first row of $[I - (1 + R_1)\,T]$ vanishes while $q_1\,l \neq 0$.

On Counting Equations 273

On the other hand, we obviously have

$$\lim_{r \to R_i} w\,(r) = \lim_{r \to R_i} \frac{1}{d\,(I - (1+r)\,A)^{-1}\,l} = \lim_{r \to R_i} (c\,\hat{T}\,v)^{-1} = 0$$

and the limits

$$\lim_{r \to R_i} (R_i - r)^{f_i}\,q = \lim_{r \to R_i} (R_i - r)^{f_i}\,d\,[I - (1+r)\,A]^{-1},$$

$$\lim_{r \to R_i} (R_i - r)^{f_i}\,p = \lim_{r \to R_i} (R_i - r)^{f_i}\,[I - (1+r)\,A]^{-1}\,l$$

exist and are proportional to the unique eigenvectors of the regular system (A, l, d) associated with R_i, for

$$\lim_{r \to R_i} (R_i - r)^{f_i}\,d\,[I - (1+r)\,A]^{-1} = \lim_{r \to R_i} (R_i - r)^{f_i}\,d\,Q^{-1}\,\hat{T}\,Q.$$

All elements of $(R_i - r)^{f_i}\,\hat{T}$ tend to zero for $r \to R_i$ except the first element in the last row of $\hat{T}_i^{f_i}$ which tends to $(1 + R_i)^{f_i}$. The vector will therefore in the limit be proportional to the unique q_i given by $(1 + R_i)\,q_i\,A = q_i$. Similarly for p.

Economically, the behaviour of q in the limit means that activity levels on a balanced growth path will get proportional to "standard proportions" or to the "von Neumann" vector as the rate of growth tends to its maximum (supposing $R_i > 0$, $q_i > 0$).

The maximum rate of profit R of basic single product systems $(A \geq 0)$ is known to be a simple root of the characteristic equation of A (theorem of Frobenius). Thus $f_1 = 1$ if, without loss of generality, $R_1 = R$. Prices $p\,(r)$ in terms of the standard commodity $q\,(I - A)$ with $q\,(I - A)\,p\,(r) = 1$, $p = w\,[I - (1+r)\,A]^{-1}\,l$, $w = 1 - (r/R)$ therefore fulfill

$$\lim_{r \to R} p\,(r) = \lim_{r \to R} w\,\hat{p}\,(r) = \lim_{r \to R} \frac{R - r}{R}\,[I - (1+r)\,A]^{-1}\,l = p\,(R)$$

where $\hat{p}\,(r)$ are again prices in terms of the wage rate, w the standard wage rate and $p\,(R)$ prices at the maximum rate of profit

$$(1 + R)\,A\,p\,(R) = p\,(R)$$

normalized so that $q\,(I - A)\,p\,(R) = 1$.

The remarkable fact is that the limit for q is independent of d (the need to approach the maximum rate of growth becomes as it were more important than the task to produce a specific output), and the limit for p is independent of l (wages become insignificant).

3.8: Simple roots: If and only if A and F are similar, there is a matrix N, $\det N \neq 0$, with $F = NAN^{-1}$, for $QAQ^{-1} = T = SFS^{-1}$ implies $F = NAN^{-1}$, $N = S^{-1}Q$. Using matrix N, the conditions of theorem 3.1 may be expressed thus, if all roots are simple:

The wage curves of the regular systems (A, l, d^{I}), (F, m, d^{II}) will be identical if and only if A and F are of the same order and there is a non singular matrix N with $F = N\,A\,N^{-1}$, $Nl = m$, $d^{\mathrm{II}}N = d^{\mathrm{I}}$.

These conditions are sufficient for the identity of the wage curves since

$$d^{\mathrm{II}}\,p^{\mathrm{II}} = d^{\mathrm{II}}\,[I - (1+r)\,F]^{-1}\,m = d^{\mathrm{II}}\,[I - (1+r)\,NAN^{-1}]^{-1}\,m$$
$$= d^{\mathrm{II}}\,N\,[I - (1+r)\,A]^{-1}\,N^{-1}\,m = d^{\mathrm{I}}\,p^{\mathrm{I}}.$$

The conditions are necessary. No coefficient v_i^{I}, v_i^{II}, c_i^{I}, c_i^{II} vanishes if all roots are simple and the system is regular, hence we may define

$$\Delta = \mathrm{diag}\,\{v_1^{\mathrm{II}}/v_1^{\mathrm{I}}, v_2^{\mathrm{II}}/v_2^{\mathrm{I}}, \ldots, v_n^{\mathrm{II}}/v_n^{\mathrm{I}}\}, \det \Delta \neq 0, \text{ and } N = S^{-1}\,\Delta\,Q.$$

With this we have, since T is diagonal, $NAN^{-1} = S^{-1}\Delta QAQ^{-1}\Delta^{-1}S$ $= S^{-1}\Delta T\Delta^{-1}S = S^{-1}TS = F$, and $\Delta Ql = \Delta\,v^{\mathrm{I}} = v^{\mathrm{II}} = Sm$, hence $Nl = m$. Analogously $\bar{\Delta} = \mathrm{diag}\,\{c_1^{\mathrm{I}}/c_1^{\mathrm{II}}, c_2^{\mathrm{I}}/c_2^{\mathrm{II}}, \ldots, c_n^{\mathrm{I}}/c_n^{\mathrm{II}}\}$, $\bar{N} = S^{-1}\bar{\Delta}\,Q$, $\bar{N}AN^{-1} = F$, $d^{\mathrm{II}}\bar{N} = d^{\mathrm{II}}\,S^{-1}\bar{\Delta}\,Q = c^{\mathrm{II}}\bar{\Delta}\,Q = c^{\mathrm{I}}Q = d^{\mathrm{I}}$. But the conditions of theorem 5.2 yields $c_i^{\mathrm{I}}\,v_i^{\mathrm{I}} = c_i^{\mathrm{II}}\,v_i^{\mathrm{II}}$ if all roots are simple, hence $\bar{\Delta} = \Delta$, $\bar{N} = N$.

3.9: Joint production systems: Since prices of a joint production system (A, B, l, d), $Bp = (1+r)\,Ap + l$, can be expressed as $p = [I - (1+r)\,(B-A)^{-1}\,A]^{-1}\,(B-A)^{-1}\,l$ and since an analogous transformation is possible for activity levels, yielding $q = d\,[B - (1+r)\,A]^{-1}$ $= d\,(B-A)^{-1}\,[I - (1+r)\,A\,(B-A)^{-1}]^{-1}$, the results obtained in 3.1—3.8 are valid for joint production systems. In particular, the joint production system (A, B, l, d) can be said to be regular, if $[(B-A)^{-1}\,A, (B-A)^{-1}\,l, d]$ is regular, and since $dp = d\,[B - (1+r)\,A]^{-1}\,l = ql$ for all r, $[A\,(B-A)^{-1}, l, d\,(B-A)^{-1}]$ will then also be regular (see 3.2); $(B-A)^{-1}\,A$ and $A\,(B-A)^{-1}$ are similar. In the formulas $1+r$ and $1+R_i$ have to be replaced by r and R_i. Theorem 3.1 may be restated as follows:

If two joint production systems $(A, B, l, d^{\mathrm{I}})$ $(F, G, m, d^{\mathrm{II}})$ are regular, their wage curves are identical if and only if $[(B-A)^{-1}\,A, (B-A)^{-1}\,l, d^{\mathrm{I}}]$ and $[(G-F)^{-1}\,F, (G-F)^{-1}\,m, d^{\mathrm{II}}]$ fulfill the conditions of theorem 3.1. If all roots are simple, these conditions may be restated as $MAP = F$, $MBP = G$, $Ml = m$, $d^{\mathrm{I}}P = d^{\mathrm{II}}$.

On Counting Equations

These conditions are sufficient for the identity of the wage curves since d^{II} $p^{II} = d^{II}$ $[G-(1+r) F]^{-1}$ $m = d^{I} P [G-(1+r) F]^{-1} Ml = d^{I}$ $\{M^{-1} [G-(1+r) F] P^{-1}\}^{-1} l = d^{I} p^{I}$.

They are necessary since according to 3.8 we must have $N (B-A)^{-1} AN^{-1} = (G-F)^{-1} F$, $Nl = m$, $d^{II}N = d^{I}$ which implies the conditions above if we define $M = (G-F) N (B-A)^{-1}$ and $P = N^{-1}$.

3.10: Equal prices in two systems: If a price in terms of labour commanded, say p_i, is the same for all rates of profit in two systems (A, l) and (F, m) such that (A, l, e_i) and (F, m, e_i) are regular, with all roots being simple, we have $F = NAN^{-1}$ and $Nl = m$ with the n-th row of N $n_i = e_i$, for we must have $e_i N = n_i = e_i$. More generally: if m prices, the first m, say, are equal in both systems, regularity conditions being fulfilled, we must have $F = NAN^{-1}$, $Nl = m$ with

$$N = \begin{bmatrix} I & 0 \\ & N_2 \end{bmatrix} \begin{matrix} \} \, n \\ \} \, n-m \end{matrix} .$$

This leads to the theorem proved in S c h e f o l d [1976 a]: If all prices of two regular systems are equal, the systems are identical, if they are single product systems, and they are related by $F = MA$, $G = MB$, $m = Ml$, if they are joint production systems. It follows as in S c h e f o l d [1976 a] that prices of two different regular joint production systems may coincide in at most n points or else they are related by $F = MA$, $G = MB$, $m = Ml$, for the equation

$$[G-(1+r) F] [B-(1+r) A]^{-1} l = m$$

is equivalent to

$$[G-(1+r) F] [B-(1+r) A]_{Ad} l = m \det [B-(1+r) A],$$

which is an equation of polynomials of degree n.

3.11: Switchpoints and truncations: *Points of truncation* are either points where one activity level vanishes so that $n-1$ processes involving n commodities coexist with non-negative prices (case A). Or they are points where one price vanishes so that n processes involving $n-1$ commodities coexist (case B). For any given price or activity level this may happen in at most $n-1$ points as we saw in 3.6, but the same can now be shown from a different point of view. We discuss case B: We have, with $C = B-(1+r) A$, $c_i p = l_i$; $i = 1, \ldots, n$; $p \geq 0$, with $p_n = 0$, say, $q c^j = d^j$; $j = 1, \ldots, n$; $q \geq 0$. We then can find non-negative activity levels such that d^n is overproduced, for $C^{-1} l = p$, $p_n = 0$, $l > 0$, implies that the last row $\hat{c}_n$ of $\hat{C} = C^{-1}$ is not positive.

18*

Therefore $(q + \varepsilon \, \hat{c}_n) \, C = d + \varepsilon \, e_n$ (e_n n-th unit vector), and $\varepsilon > 0$ can be increased until at least one component of q vanishes. The corresponding row and the n-th column are to be taken away to obtain the truncation which has a switchpoint with C regarding commodities $1, \ldots, n-1$, but different activity levels. The extent of overproduction of commodity n may be varied, as may be illustrated by noting that case B (*normal* truncation) is the one encountered in fixed capital systems: an old machine of age T has to be truncated when its price is negative. We are here considering the borderline case where its price is zero at a point where all other prices are the same for the truncated and the untruncated system while activity levels are undetermined in that a greater or lesser overproduction of the old machine is permissible at price zero. Activity levels are therefore at this point free to vary continuously between the activity levels of the untruncated system which are uniquely determined such that the machine of age T is still used and not overproduced and the activity levels of the truncated system where the machine of age T is still produced (overproduced) although it does not belong to the truncation because it is not used. Case A (*dual* truncation) seems economically less relevant.

In either case the real wage is the same for the original system and its truncation, since ql or dp is the same for both. In fact, the real wage is the same for all truncations $\overline{C}$ which can be formed with det $\overline{C} \neq 0$ by deleting one of n rows where a price or one of n columns where an activity level of the original system vanishes. The wage curve of the original system is therefore crossed by up to n wage curves of truncations at such a point. Supposing that all these truncations are regular, we have, if each of the n prices and n activity levels vanishes in $n-1$ points, up to $2\,n\,(n-1)$ points where the wage curve of the original system is crossed by a bushel of n wage curves of truncations of order $n-1$. According to 3.3 the wage curve of the original system is crossed at most $n + (n-1) - 1 = 2n-2$ times by each of its n^2 truncations, yielding also $2\,n\,(n-1)$ crossing points taking account of the fact that n truncations may be involved in each (cf. also Corollary 1).

Switchpoints as they are known from the literature are points where $n+1$ methods for the production of n commodities coexist at the same prices, and where activity levels are up to a point indeterminate ("method switches"). If there are non-negative activity levels to produce d with $n+1$ methods, the same is also possible with only n methods according to the basis theorem; and the method to be omitted may or may not be uniquely determined.

Formally, there could also be switches of commodities: if $n+1$ commodities are produced with n methods, activity levels could at one rate of growth happen to be such that no commodity was overproduced while prices were indeterminate, but no economically meaningful example of this seems to be known. "Slightly overproduced" consumption goods would not receive zero prices in reality because a minor excess of production could be disposed of if competition is not absolutely perfect; the consumption good would at any rate be charged a positive price. Means of production, on the other hand, are typically machines and rather objects of truncations than of "commodity switches" (cf. also Corollary 2).

3.12: International trade: an instructive caricature. Suppose capital movements equalise the rate of profit in Britain and France and suppose that this rate of profit varies greatly and frequently. Suppose that the workers estimate their real wage by the amount of time they need to earn the money for their favorite drink, called beer in Britain and wine in France. If they succeed in equalising the wage in this sense in both countries whenever the rate of profit varies, the economies of Britain and France must be essentially the same (3.1) and beer is wine (3.10) if we know that both economies are regular systems.

The following observation is equally far removed from reality but a little more serious in so far as it is related to a famous theorem in international trade theory: if relative prices are imposed from outside on a regular economy, there is at most one rate of profit compatible with them. For if relative prices, expressed e. g. in terms of the first commodity, were the same at two rates of profit, i. e. if

$$p_i(r_1)/p_1(r_1) = p_i(r_2)/p_1(r_2), \quad i = 2, \ldots, n;$$

the vector $p(r_1)$ would be proportional to $p(r_2)$ contradicting 3.4.

4. Counting of Equations

If all relevant truncations are regular and different, multiple solutions to the linear programme occur only at points where different wage curves cross, and the solution is always quadratic outside these points. Sraffa's "counting of equations" is then vindicated: there are at least as many processes as commodities to be produced (for otherwise the consumption basket could not be produced in the required proportions), but prices leave on the other hand no room for more processes than there are commodities.

One is therefore tempted to assume that *all* truncations are regular because irregular systems are of measure zero in the space of all systems of given order, but there is a little snag: regularity conditions require that det $(\bar{B} - (1+r)\,\bar{A})$ does not vanish identically (where $\bar{A}, \bar{B}$ is a truncation) but many truncations may contain entire columns of zeros for both $\bar{A}$ and $\bar{B}$ belonging to truncated machines. The statement that non-negative systems are regular with probability one is misleading in so far as non-negative systems are with probability one positive! Zeros contain a very specific information. There is little difference between 1 and 1.0001, but a model may behave in a qualitatively different way economically and mathe- may behave in a qualitative different way economically and mathematically according as to whether an element equals 0.0001 or whether it is strictly equal to zero. The question therefore arises whether systems with a given pattern of zeros are likely to be regular. The answer is easy in the case of single product systems; it suffices to assume det $A \neq 0$. (Cf. the remark about pure consumption goods at the beginning of section 3 above.) Similarly one may postulate det $(B - A) \neq 0$ for any independent joint production system as in Schefold [1971]. Truncations are more difficult; but there is no harm, as far as I can see (after examining fixed capital and other cases) in the restricted assumption that at least those truncations are regular which are q-feasible for some g, $0 \leq g < R$, and which fulfill det $(\bar{B} - (1+g)\,\bar{A}) \neq 0$. They will then contain at least one consumption good $(\bar{d} \neq 0)$ and they will not contain columns with all outputs and inputs vanishing $(\bar{a}^j = \bar{b}^j = 0)$. The assumption leaves ample room for complicated given patterns of zeros in A, B and d. We shall assume, moreover, that all regular truncations are different in that they have different characteristic equations or, which is a slightly lesser requirement, applicable if all characteristic roots are distinct: two different regular truncations of the same order $(\bar{A}, \bar{B}, \bar{l}, \bar{d})$ and $(\bar{\bar{A}}, \bar{\bar{B}}, \bar{\bar{l}}, \bar{\bar{d}})$ are assumed never to be related by linear equations of the form $\bar{A}N = M\bar{\bar{A}}$, $\bar{B}N = M\bar{\bar{B}}$, $\bar{l} = M\bar{\bar{l}}$, $\bar{d}N = \bar{\bar{d}}$ with M, N being non singular quadratic matrices (see 3.9 above)*.

---

   * For the main statements of 4.1 it would also be sufficient to assume that all truncations $(\bar{A}, \bar{B}, \bar{l}, \bar{d})$ with det $(\bar{B} - (1+r)\,\bar{A}) \neq 0$ and $\bar{d} \neq 0$ have different wage curves. Explicit reference to regularity could thus be avoided at the cost of loosing some mathematical and economic insights as to the causes of coinciding wage curves.

On Counting Equations 279

Adding these two assumptions to those made for theorem 2.1 and assuming that the original set of processes is in the stationary state capable of producing a surplus of both final and intermediate goods in that there is $q \geq 0$ such that $q(B - A) > 0$, we obtain a statement which is considerably stronger than theorem 2.1 and which confirms that a quadratic solution consisting of equalities emerges at the same time as a result of a comparison of systems (where the counting of equations is the point of departure) and as a solution to or the outcome of the von Neumann approach which starts from inequalities (4.1). 4.2 shows that normally $w(R) = 0$; the "last" truncation appearing on E behaves rather like a single product system.

Theorem 4.1: The envelope E of q-feasible wage curves is continuous and falls strictly monotonically from a positive finite value at $r = 0$ to $w_E(R) \geq 0$ at a maximum rate of profit $R > 0$. The solution to the linear programme is unique, and given by the augmented vectors of prices and activity levels of a uniquely determined perfect truncation except at a finite number of "critical" points and except in so far as prices of phantom goods (although they can be put equal to zero) are (within limits) indeterminate in entire intervals*. E is intersected by not coinciding wage curves of different truncations in each critical point. Critical points with multiple solutions (if they occur) can always be regarded as superpositions of points of truncation and switchpoints (see 3.11) and conversely.

4.2: We cannot have $w_E(R) > 0$ with all q-feasible truncations at R without columns of simultaneously vanishing inputs and outputs (i. e. with $\bar{a}^j + \bar{b}^j \neq 0$ for all j in $\bar{A}$, $\bar{B}$) being regular. If $w_E(R) = 0$,

---

* Consider e. g. the case of a lorry which could be used for up to twenty years but which is only used for ten years in the optimal truncation of a pure fixed capital system. The eleven year old lorry will be produced but not used, hence it is overproduced and has price zero, but lorries of ages between twelve and twenty years are neither used nor produced; they are imaginary or 'phantom goods'. Positive shadow prices could be ascribed to them in a von Neumann world if they were small enough not to cause unused processes to turn profitable but such a positive price would not make sense from the point of view of Sraffa. General von Neumann systems as discussed in section 2 above can even lead to solutions with "phantom commodities"; i. e. phantom goods with prices which cannot be put equal to zero but which are indeterminate within a positive range. By proving that the optimal solution is given by a perfect truncation we prove the corollary that such phantom commodities cannot exist under the assumptions of theorem 4.1 except at critical points.

if $(\bar{A}, \bar{B})$ is the "last" truncation appearing on E (for $r - \varepsilon < r \le R$), and if $(\bar{A}, \bar{B})$ is basic, we have $(\bar{B} - (1+r)\bar{A})^{-1} > 0$ for $R - \delta < r < R$, and some $\delta > 0$. R is a simple root of $\det(\bar{B} - (1+r)\bar{A}) = 0$ and there is a positive standard commodity associated with R for $\bar{A}, \bar{B}$.

Proof of Theorem 4.1: Using the notation of the proof of theorem 2.1 above (the tableau) we can state independently of the special assumptions for theorem 4.1:

Lemma 2: If the solutions to the linear programme at $r = g < R$ are chosen such that the numbers $h + s - k$ in the primal and $k + t - h$ in the dual are maximized, the solutions are canonical and the matrices

$$C^* = \begin{bmatrix} C_1{}^1 \\ C_2{}^1 \end{bmatrix}, \quad C^{**} = [C_1{}^1, C_1{}^2]$$

have maximal rank k and h respectively.

For otherwise we should e. g. have $rk\, C^{**} < h$ so that there would be an open convex set Q of vectors $\bar{q} > 0$ with $\bar{q}\, C^{**} = (d_1, \ldots, d_{k+t}) = d^{**}$ which, augmented with zeros, solved the dual. The boundary points of Q would also solve the dual but with less than h positive components or with one of the inequalities turned into an equality contrary to the assumption that $k + t - h$ is maximal. This ensures also that the solutions are canonical.

It follows (still independently of special assumptions) that the linear programme can have multiple solutions only if at least one canonical tableau is degenerate. Suppose, no tableau was degenerate while there were several solutions to the primal and/or the dual. If a tableau corresponding to a pair of optimal solutions p, q is not canonic, its corresponding canonical tableau is degenerate and the assertion is proved. If each tableau is canonical, and not degenerate, each involves a quadratic truncation for $s = t = 0$ implies $h = k$ since $k \le h + s$, $h \le k + t$. The positive prices and activity levels are the same for both, since the j-th component of p must vanish for all solutions of the primal if commodity j is overproduced for one solution of the dual, and similarly the i-th component of all solutions of the dual must vanish if process i turns out to be unprofitable for one solution of the primal, while other elements of p or q do not vanish if $s = t = 0$. There is therefore one and only one quadratic truncation corresponding to all solutions of the primal and dual. This truncation $C_1{}^1$ has not vanishing determinant (Lemma 2) so that $\bar{p}, \bar{q}$ and the augmented vectors p, q are uniquely determined contradicting the assumption and showing that both the solution to the linear programme is unique and the truncation yielding this solution.

Consider a point $r=g$ where the solution is chosen according to the assumption of Lemma 2. The quadratic matrix of order (k, k) consisting of k linearly independent rows of C^* is denoted by $\hat{C}^*$, the quadratic matrix of order (h, h) consisting of h linearly independent columns of C^{**} is denoted by $\hat{C}^{**}$. $\hat{C}^*$ is a p-feasible truncation, $\hat{C}^{**}$ is a q-feasible truncation with no vanishing column and with $\bar{q}\,\hat{C}^{**}=\hat{d}^{**}\neq0$; it is regular. $\hat{C}^*$ and $\hat{C}^{**}$ define wage curves w^* and w^{**} (cf. section 2) with $w^*(r)=w^{**}(r)$ because $d^*p^*=dp=ql=q^{**}l^{**}$. We distinguish four cases of degeneracy:

a) If $h>k$, the wage curves w^* and w^{**} can only intersect, not coincide, because the sum of the order of the poles of w^{**} as a complex function equals h whereas the sum of the order of the poles of w^* is k if $\hat{C}^*$ is regular, and less otherwise (cf. 3.1, 3.3 above).

b) If $h=k$, $s>0$, and if $\hat{C}^*=\hat{C}^{**}$, there are s rows in C^* which are not in $\hat{C}^*$ and which do not vanish because $l>0$, $p^*>0$. One of them may be exchanged against a row of $\hat{C}^*$ so that the resulting matrix $\tilde{C}$ has a not vanishing determinant at r and hence a wage curve $\tilde{w}$. If $\tilde{w}$ and w^* coincided in an interval, $\tilde{C}$ would be regular according to 3.2 because $\hat{C}^*=\hat{C}^{**}$ is regular, but wage curves of different regular truncations of the same order have been assumed not to coincide. The same argument applies to w^* and w^{**}, if $\hat{C}^*\neq\hat{C}^{**}$.

c) If $h<k$, and if we are not at a critical point, all columns $\hat{c}^j=\hat{b}^j-(1+r)\,\hat{a}^j$ of C^{**} which are not in $\hat{C}^{**}$ fulfill $\hat{a}^j=\hat{b}^j=0$, hence $d_j=0$, for if $\hat{a}^j+\hat{b}^j\neq0$, column j could be exchanged against a column of $\hat{C}^{**}$ in such a way that the resulting truncation $\hat{C}^{***}$ would fulfill $\det\hat{C}^{***}\neq0$; $\hat{C}^{***}$ would be q-feasible, hence regular, and would engender a wage curve different from w^{**}, hence r would be critical, contrary to the assumption. Let, without loss of generality, $\hat{a}^j=\hat{b}^j=0$ for $1\leq j\leq K$ and for $K+h+1\leq j\leq k+t$. We can assume $K\geq k-h>0$ but we must have $K<k$ because $d^{**}p^{**}>0$, $\hat{C}^{**}=[\hat{c}^{K+1},\ldots,\hat{c}^{K+h}]$. There are K rows $i_1<\ldots<i_K$ in C^* with $i_K\leq h+s$ and with $i_1\geq h+1$ such that we obtain a not singular matrix $\tilde{C}=(c_\sigma^j)$; $\sigma=i_1,\ldots,i_K$; $j=1,\ldots,K$; because $\det\hat{C}^*\neq0$ and because $c_i^j=0$; $i=1,\ldots,h$; $j=1,\ldots,K$. The matrix $\bar{C}=(c_\sigma^j)$;

282   B. Schefold:

$\sigma = 1, \ldots, h, \; i_1, \ldots, i_K; \; j = 1, \ldots, K+h$; is q-feasible and $\det \overline{C} =$ $(\det \tilde{C}) \, (\det \hat{C}^{**}) \neq 0, \, \bar{d} \neq 0$, hence $\overline{C}$ is a regular truncation, its wage curve crosses w^{**} at r and does not coincide with w^{**} because the order of $\overline{C}$ is not equal to that of $\hat{C}^{**}$ since $K > 0$. Point r is therefore critical*.

  d) $h = k, \, t > 0$. We may now assume that $s = 0$, hence $C_1^1 = \hat{C}^*$. If the point is not to be critical, we have $\hat{C}^* = \hat{C}^{**}$ and — for the same reason as at the beginning of case c $(h < k)$ above — vanishing columns in C^{**} which are not in $\hat{C}^{**}$, hence $C_1^2 = 0, \, B_1^2 = 0, \, A_1^2 = 0,$ $d_j = 0, \; j = k+1, \ldots, k+t$. Now it is clear that this constellation $(h = k, \, t > 0)$ can be found in entire intervals without critical points. For if there exist unique vectors $\bar{p}, \bar{q}$ such that $C_1^1 \, \bar{p} = \bar{l}, \, \bar{q} \, C_1^1 = \bar{d}$ and such that the augmented vectors of $\bar{p}, \bar{q}$ are optimal solutions at each r, prices $p_{k+1}, \ldots, p_{k+t}$ can be equal to zero in this interval although the corresponding goods are neither used nor produced (hence not overproduced). These prices are indeterminate within the limits given by the inequalities $h+1, \ldots, n$ (*in*equalities because $s = 0$ outside critical points).

  It follows from a, b, c, d that critical points, i. e. points where not coinciding wage curves cross or touch the envelope, are finite in number and that they are isolated points. There is no degeneracy at other points and $h = k, \, s = 0$, except in so far as $t > 0$ is possible for means of production which are neither used nor produced in the optimal truncation (case d).

———————

  * Case $h < k$ gives rise to phantom commodities in intervals if the wage curves of $\overline{C}$ and $\hat{C}^{**}$ happen to coincide because $\overline{C}$ is not regular. Suppose e. g. that

$$A = \begin{bmatrix} A_1^1 & 0 \\ A_2^1 & A_2^2 \end{bmatrix}, \quad B = \begin{bmatrix} B_1^1 & 0 \\ B_2^1 & B_2^2 \end{bmatrix}, \quad l = \begin{bmatrix} l_1 \\ l_2 \end{bmatrix}, \quad d = (d_1, d_2)$$

is a decomposable Sraffa system with (A_1^1, B_1^1), (A_2^2, B_2^2) being pairs of quadratic matrices. If all prices of basics p_1 and of non basics p_2 are positive in a neighbourhood of $r = 0$, say, if $d_2 = 0$ and if only the basic processes are activated, there will be no feasible solution to the primal of the form $(p_1, 0)$, i. e. with prices of non basics $p_2 = 0$, if $(B_2^1 - (1+r) \, A_2^1) \, p_1$ is not $\leqslant l_2$. Some non basics are then "phantom commodities" because at least one non basic process would become profitable if one did not ascribe positive prices to non basic goods. The wage curve of the system and of its basic part coincide since $d_2 = 0$, and herein lies the irregularity of (A, B, l, d), but it is absurd first to introduce non basics and then to exclude them from basket d.

Points of truncation and switches in the sense of 3.11 are clearly points where the tableau is degenerate. Conversely, if the tableau is degenerate with $h = k+1$, $t=1$, $s=0$, we have a point of truncation (case B in 3.11), and if it is degenerate with $h = k$, $t=0$, $s=1$, we have a switchpoint (method switch in 3.11). All other cases are superpositions of these, with possibly reversed roles of activity levels and prices.

The envelope of the q-feasible wage curves is strictly monotonically falling because wage curves of regular systems cannot be constant in any interval. The productivity assumption ensures $R > 0$.

Proof 4.2: If we had $w_E(R) > 0$, the linear programme could be solved at R, the solution being represented as in the tableau of Lemma 2, and $\bar{q} \, C_1 \geqq d$, $\bar{q} > 0$. Let $\bar{c}^1, \ldots, \bar{c}^{k+t}$ denote the columns of C^{**}, and suppose that (without loss of generality since the difference between $C_1{}^1$ and $C_1{}^2$ does not matter in what follows) $\bar{c}^j \neq 0$; $j = 1, \ldots, J$ and $\bar{c}^j = 0$, $j = J+1, \ldots, k+t$. If $\bar{c}^j = 0$, we must have $\bar{a}^j = \bar{b}^j = 0$, $d_j = 0$, for otherwise $\bar{c}^j$ could be exchanged against a column of $\hat{C}^{**}$ to form a truncation $\bar{C}$ with $\bar{q} \, \bar{C} = \bar{d}$ so that $\bar{C}$ would be regular, but then det $\bar{C} = 0$ because $\bar{c}^j = 0$. This is impossible according to 3.7 above since $w_E(R) = \bar{q} \bar{l} > 0$. Suppose there was no $\tilde{p} \geqq 0$ such that $\bar{c}^1 \tilde{p}_1 + \ldots + \bar{c}^J \tilde{p}_J = 0$. There would then be $\tilde{q} > 0$ according to Lemma 1 with $\tilde{q} \, (\bar{c}^1, \ldots, \bar{c}^J) > 0$ and since $\tilde{q} \, \bar{c}^j = d_j = 0$, $j = J+1, \ldots, k+t$, $\tilde{q} \, [B_1 - (1+r) \, A_1] \geqq d$ for some $r > R$ contradicting the assumption. There must therefore be $\tilde{p} \geqq 0$ with (without loss of generality) $(\tilde{p}_1, \ldots, \tilde{p}_K) > 0$, with $\tilde{p}_{K+1} = \ldots = \tilde{p}_J = 0$, and with

$$-\bar{c}^K = \bar{c}^1 \, (\tilde{p}_1/\tilde{p}_K) + \ldots + \bar{c}^{K-1} \, (\tilde{p}_{K-1}/\tilde{p}_K)$$

therefore

$$-\bar{q}\bar{c}^K = \bar{q}\bar{c}^1 \, (\tilde{p}_1/\tilde{p}_K) + \ldots + \bar{q}\bar{c}^{K-1} \, (\tilde{p}_{K-1}/\tilde{p}_K).$$

Since the left hand side is not positive, the right hand side not negative, equality can only hold if $\bar{q} \, \bar{c}^K = 0$, and since the same argument can be applied to $\bar{c}^1, \ldots, \bar{c}^{K-1}$ we have $\bar{q} \, \bar{c}^1 = \ldots = \bar{q} \, \bar{c}^K = 0$. This implies that the quadratic truncation $\bar{C} = (\bar{c}^1, \ldots, \bar{c}^h)$ has vanishing determinant if $K \geqq h$, and if $K \leqq h$, det $\bar{C} = 0$ because $\bar{c}^K$ is a linear combination of $\bar{c}^1, \ldots, \bar{c}^{K-1}$. But $J \geqq h$ since $rk \, C^{**} = h$, and $\bar{C}$ (which is q-feasible) is regular, hence det $\bar{C} = 0$ is imcompatible with $\bar{q}\bar{C} = \bar{d}$ according to 3.7, therefore $w_E(R) = 0$. The remainder of 4.2 follows from Schefold [1978 b], theorem 4.2.

5. Example

We conclude with the example

$$A = \begin{bmatrix} 1/12 & 1/6 \\ 1/4 & 1/6 \end{bmatrix}, \ B = \begin{bmatrix} 3/4 & 1/3 \\ 1/4 & 2/3 \end{bmatrix}, \ l = \begin{bmatrix} 1/6 \\ 5/6 \end{bmatrix}, \ d = \left(\frac{79}{144}, \ \frac{1}{36} \right)$$

with the wage curve

$$w \ (r) = \frac{(24/13) \ (2-r) \ (r+6)}{4 \, r - 1}.$$

The wage curve is negative for $r < 1/4$, it diverges at $r = 1/4$ and falls monotonically from $+\infty$ to zero between $r = 1/4$ and $R = 2$. One finds $q > 0$ for $9/11 < r < R$ and $p > 0$ for $1/2 < r < R$ so that the system as a whole will be superior for $9/11 < r < R$, and it will in fact be superior independently of d for $1 < r < R$ since $[B - (1 + r) \ A]^{-1} > 0$ for $1 < r < R$ (cf. theorem 4.2).

Truncation is inevitable for $0 < r < 9/11$. The four truncations to be considered are given by

$$w_i{}^j \ (r) = \frac{1}{\bar{q} \, \bar{l}} = \frac{b_i{}^j - (1+r) \ a_i{}^j}{d_j \, l_i}, \ i, j = 1, \ 2.$$

The truncations $w_2{}^1$ and $w_2{}^2$ are not productive of d, let alone q-feasible for $g \geq 0$; one finds that $w_1{}^1 \ (g)$ is q-feasible for $0 \leq g \leq 9/11$ and $w_1{}^2 \ (g)$ is q-feasible for $9/11 \leq g \leq 1$, while $w \ (r)$ is only productive of d, but not q-feasible for $0 \leq g \leq 9/11$ so that the envelope $w_E \ (r)$ consists of $w_1{}^1 \ (r)$ for $0 \leq r \leq 9/11$ and $w \ (r)$ for $9/11 \leq r \leq R$. A dual truncation occurs at $r = 9/11$.

The four truncations are shown in the diagram:

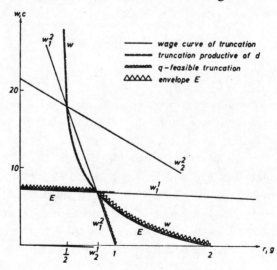

On Counting Equations 285

The *Diagram* showing wage curves of two sector model and of its four truncations. Note that disequilibrium is possible, if $g < r$, e. g. if $r = 9/10$, $g = 1/4$.

Equations:

$$w_1{}^1(r) = \frac{576}{79} - \frac{72}{79}\, r, \; w_1{}^2(r) = 36 - 36\, r,$$

$$w_2{}^1(r) = -\frac{216}{395}\, r, \; w_2{}^2(r) = 21\frac{3}{5} - 7\frac{1}{5}\, r.$$

References

E. Burmeister und K. Kuga [1970]: The Factor Price Frontier, Duality and Joint Production, Review of Economic Studies *37*, pp. 11—19.

M. Morishima [1973]: Marx's Economics, Cambridge.

B. Schefold [1971]: Theorie der Kuppelproduktion, Basel (private print; second edition in preparation).

B. Schefold [1976 a]: Relative Prices as a Function of the Rate of Profit, Zeitschrift für Nationalökonomie *36*, pp. 21—48.

B. Schefold [1976 b]: Different Forms of Technical Progress, Economic Journal *86*, pp. 806—819.

B. Schefold [1977]: Reduction to Dated Quantities of Labour, Roundabout Processes and Switches of Technique in Fixed Capital Systems, to appear in: Metroeconomica *28*.

B. Schefold [1978 a]: Fixed Capital as a Joint Product, Jahrbücher für Nationalökonomie und Statistik *192*, pp. 415—439.

B. Schefold [1978 b]: Multiple Product Techniques With Properties of Single Product Systems, Zeitschrift für Nationalökonomie *38*, pp. 29—53.

B. Schefold [1979]: Von Neumann and Sraffa: Mathematical Equivalence and Conceptual Difference; submitted for Economic Journal.

P. Sraffa [1960]: Production of Commodities by Means of Commodities, Cambridge.

I. Steedman [1976]: Positive Profits With Negative Surplus Value: A Reply, Economic Journal *86*, pp. 873—876.

Address of author: Prof. Dr. Bertram Schefold, Institut für Markt und Plan, Universität Frankfurt, Schumannstraße 60, D-6000 Frankfurt am Main, Federal Republic of Germany.

[9]

1

CHOICE OF TECHNIQUES IN JOINT PRODUCTION

by **Christian BIDARD**
University of Paris X Nanterre

The number of available processes being equal to that of goods, a productive system is written

$$(A,l) \rightarrow I \qquad \text{in single production}$$
$$(A,l) \rightarrow B \qquad \text{in joint production}$$

A and B being square matrices, I the identity matrix and l the column-vector of labour. For a uniform rate of profit, r, the price-and-wage vector (p,w) is the solution to

$$(1+r)(Ap+wl) = Bp$$

i.e. it is defined up to a factor of proportionality by the formula

$$p = w(\lambda B-A)^{-1}l \qquad \text{where} \quad \lambda = 1/(1+r)$$

It is assumed that $\det(\lambda B-A) \neq 0$.

When several methods are available in each industry (or, in joint production, in each sector) the working of the market can be simulated by an algorithm which determines the technical combination of methods actually operated according to the following procedure. The rate of profit r being given, a method is arbitrarily selected in each industry; a price vector (p_1,w) is associated with this set of n methods, on the basis of which the profitability of non-operated processes can be calculated by means of the ratio between the value of the outputs and that of the inputs. If all these ratios are less than $1+r$, the procedure is finished. If one of them exceeds $1+r$, let us replace the initial method in <u>one</u> industry by a new one which is potentially more profitable : a new set is thus defined, which is associated with a new price-and-wage vector (p_2,w) at the rate of profit r; and so forth until a combination of methods and a price system are reached, such that the profitability of non-operated methods is not greater than that of operated methods.

The aim of the paper is to study the existence, the uniqueness and the properties of this dominant technique, as well as the convergence of the algorithm : the question is to determine the conditions under which prices constitute a coherent and efficient guide for the choice of techniques. Sraffa [8] has proved that in viable single production and for any allowed rate of profit every step from one technical combination to the next one induces a rise of the real wage, whatever the unit wage basket may be, and that the final stable technique maximizes the real wage (or, equivalently, minimizes all labour-commanded prices). In joint production the problem is more complex and even the coherence of the choice between two methods is unclear, as is shown by the following example of twin paradoxes.

I - PARADOXES IN JOINT PRODUCTION

We know, at least since Sraffa ([8], Part 2) that, in contradistinction to single production, the price system is not necessarily positive in viable joint production. Another difference is that every process is in competition with any other, whereas in single production competition only works inside subsets of processes characterized by the nature of the output.

Our starting point is to show that there exist situations where, independently of any consideration on the global rationality resulting from individual decisions, the very coherence of the local choice made by each capitalist is questionable. This is illustrated by two paradoxes which arise even with a restricted choice and when the other just-mentioned sources of difficulty are eliminated.

Example 1 : In a first economy with two goods and labour, let two methods named (1.1) and (1.2) be in competition in sector 1 :

$$(1.1) \quad : \quad a_{11} = 3/8 \qquad a_{12} = 1 \qquad l_1 = 1 \quad \rightarrow \quad b_{11} = 9/8 \qquad b_{12} = 6$$

$$(1.2) \quad : \quad a'_{11} = 1 \qquad a'_{12} = 0 \qquad l'_1 = 2 \quad \rightarrow \quad b'_{11} = 9/2 \qquad b'_{12} = 3$$

sector 2 being defined by :

$$(2) \quad : \quad a_{21} = 0 \qquad a_{22} = 1 \qquad l_2 = 1 \quad \rightarrow \quad b_{21} = 3/2 \qquad b_{22} = 3$$

It is assumed that methods (1.1) and (1.2) are not in competition with method 2, so that the possible choices at the global level are (1.1,2) and (1.2,2); for a general rate of profit equal to $r=0$ ($\lambda=1$) the two systems are viable. Until Section 7, devoted to the question of the numeraire, prices are expressed in terms of the wage (w = 1).

If the initial choice is (1.1,2), the corresponding price system is ($p_1 = 1/2$, $p_2 = 1/8$, w = 1). But method 1.2, which is available, yields on the basis of this price system a profit rate r' satisfying

$$(a'_{11}p_1 + a'_{12}p_2 + wl'_1)(1+r') = b'_{11}p_1 + b'_{12}p_2$$

which amounts to r' = 5 %, greater than the general profit rate. Hence we switch from system (1.1,2) to system (1.2,2). Once these methods are operated, the price vector is modified and becomes ($p'_1 = 2/5$, $p'_2 = 1/5$, w' = 1). The profitability of process (1.1), which is still available, is given by r" satisfying

$$(a_{11}p'_1 + a_{12}p'_2 + w'l_1)(1+r") = b_{11}p'_1 + b_{12}p'_2$$

i.e. r" = 22 % :unexpectedly, method (1.1) now appears as more profitable than (1.2). So the economy perpetually oscillates from one combination to the other, and capitalists are always unsatisfied.

Example 2 : The twin numerical example is :

(1.1) $a_{11} = 3/8$ $a_{21} = 1$ $l_1 = 2$ → $b_{11} = 9/8$ $b_{12} = 6$
(1.2) and (2) as in the previous example .
It only differs from Example 1 by the quantity of labour in method (1.1).

If now the initial choice is (1.1,2) we have ($p_1 = 1/6$, $p_2 = 3/8$, w = 1) and the profitability of method 1.2 for these prices is r' = -13 %, which is less than the general rate of profit, so that capitalists will not change their choice. But if the initial choice is (1.2,2), then ($p'_1 = 2/5$, $p'_2 = 1/5$, w = 1) and the profitability of method 1.1 is r" = -31 %, a result which again corroborates the existing choice.

Whatever its position -(1.1,2) or (1.2,2)-, the economic system is stable and capitalists think they have made the right choice. From one example to the other, quietude has replaced qualm but the situation is no more satisfying intellectually. A first target is therefore to delimit these situations and to determine conditions under which the price system is a coherent guide for capitalists'decisions.

4

II - THE COHERENCE OF BINARY CHOICES

Let two processes be in competition in the first sector

(1.1) $(a_{11},...,a_{1n},l_1)$ $\longrightarrow$ $(b_{11},...,b_{1n})$

(1.2) $(a'_{11},...,a'_{1n},l'_1)$ $\longrightarrow$ $(b'_{11},...,b'_{1n})$

the other methods being given in the other $(n-1)$ sectors. As will soon be made clear, the technical coefficients only matter in the form of the row-vectors $(\lambda b_{11} - a_{11},..., \lambda b_{1n} - a_{1n}) = \lambda b - a$, resp. $\lambda b' - a'$, which we denote by 1.1 and 1.2 and call "net product" of method (1.1), resp. (1.2), by a slight misuse. Let $p = (\lambda B - A)^{-1} l$, resp. $p' = (\lambda B' - A')^{-1} l'$, the price vector attached to the use of method (1.1), resp. (1.2) : the binary choice between (1.1) and (1.2) is coherent if one process is more profitable than the other on the basis of prices p as well as on the basis of prices p'.

For the price system p, the gain or loss of profit for each method (1.2), (2),...,(n) with respect to the normal profit rate r amounts to $12.p - l'_1$, $2.p - l'_2,...,n.p - l'_n$, i.e., it corresponds to the successive components of $e = (\lambda B' - A')p - l' = (\lambda B' - A')(\lambda B - A)^{-1} l - l'$. Similarly, for the price vector p', the vector of gains and losses of methods (1.1), (2),...,(n) is $d = (\lambda B - A)(\lambda B' - A')^{-1} l' - l$, i.e. $d = -Me$ with $M = (\lambda B - A)(\lambda B' - A')^{-1}$.

But components 2 to n of vectors d and e are null, because processes (2),...,(n) yield exactly the profit rate r for p and p'. According to the above formula, the relationship between their first components is $d_1 = -m_{11}e_1$, m_{11} being the "north-west" coefficient of matrix M. And since $\lambda B - A$ and $\lambda B' - A'$ only differ by their first rows, M only differs from the identity matrix by its first row, hence

$$m_{11} = \det M = \frac{\det(\lambda B - A)}{\det(\lambda B' - A')}$$

To sum up : if $\det(\lambda B - A)$ and $\det(\lambda B' - A')$ have the same sign, d_1 and e_1 have opposite signs and the choice between (1.1) and (1.2) is coherent; if not, we are in the case of the first (if $d_1 > 0, e_1 > 0$) or the second (if $d_1 < 0$, $e_1 < 0$) paradox. Note that only the produced input coefficients matter in the statement of the coherence condition, and that the quantity of labour influences the type of the paradox, not the paradoxical nature itself.

It can be checked that the data of the previous numerical examples are such that the determinants have opposite signs.

III - GEOMETRICAL AND ECONOMIC INTERPRETATIONS

Let us give a geometrical interpretation of the algebraic condition of coherence. We represent the net vectors λb-a associated with each method for one unit of labour(strictly speaking,it is assumed that each method requires labour , but the restriction is unimportant). For two goods and two methods (1.1) and (2), any vector which is a net product of the technique made of these two processes is written α1.1 + β2 ($\alpha > 0$, $\beta > 0$) and belongs to the convex cone spanned by 1.1 and 2, its exact position depending on the respective activity levels α and β.

It is intuitively clear for n=2 and n=3 (Figure 1) that the determinants (1.1, 2, (3)) and (1.2, 2, (3)) have the same sign if and only if the convex cones they generate have a non-null intersection.

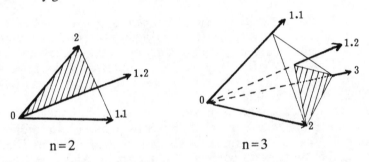

$$n = 2 \qquad\qquad\qquad n = 3$$

FIGURE 1

This result can be rigorously justified in the general case of two systems of n vectors in R^n which have (n-1) vectors in common (corollary of Theorem 3 below). Hence

Theorem 1 : The binary choice between two techniques which have n-1 methods in common and which differ by one process is coherent if and only if the two corresponding determinants have the same signs or, equivalently, if the convex cones spanned by the net vectors have a non-empty interior intersection.

An economic interpretation of the coherence condition can be given. Assume that capitalists save all their income and accumulate at the rate g=r. The physical product available for workers' consumption is y[B-(1+g)A], y being the row-vector of activity levels. It then appears that two production systems which differ by one method are comparable if they can produce some common wage basket V. If this is the case, the geometrical representation also shows which system is preferred to the other : any net product α1.1 + β2 represented on Figure 1 by a vector whose extremity belongs to segment [1.1,2] is produced by one unit of total labour ($\alpha > 0$, $\beta > 0$, $\alpha + \beta = 1$), and technique (1.2,2) associated with a higher real wage is

6

preferred to (1.1,2). This general property can be enunciated in the space of quantities as well as in the space of prices :

Preference criterion between techniques(quantity space).

Let two production systems differ by one process and let V be a common net product. The preferred method is the one which produces a higher quantity of V per unit of labour.

Preference criterion between techniques (price space) .

Under the same conditions, the preferred process is the one which minimizes the price of V in terms of the wage rate.

These criteria only work for baskets which belong to the common intersection, not for every net basket. When the intersection is empty, one may check that the initial paradoxes correspond to the two following configurations

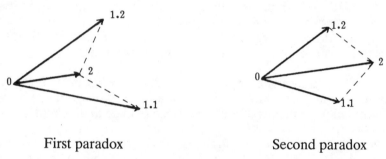

First paradox   Second paradox

FIGURE 2

IV - THE COHERENCE OF SECTORAL CHOICES.

We may now consider more complex situations.

First, the choice between several production methods belonging to the same sector is clear under the assumption of coherent binary choices : all determinants $(\lambda B-A)$, $(\lambda B'-A')$, $(\lambda B''-A'')$, ... have the same sign, there exists a vector V common to the convex cones of these techniques, and the optimal technique is the one which maximizes the number of units of V per head and which minimizes the price of V in terms of the wage; and the algorithm converges towards the optimal combination, since the price of V decreases at each step.

A further stage considers general choices. For instance N. Salvadori [6] studies the set of techniques made of n methods out of a given collection which are able to produce a net product V. In this paper, we stick to the notion of a sector : the production methods are shared among n "competition groups". The notations are simplified by assuming n=3, though our proofs will be general: methods denoted as 1i, 2j, 3k are the ith, j th and k th in groups 1, 2 and 3; if I,J,K are the numbers of methods within these groups, there exist IxJxK techniques made of one method out of each group. An economic justification of this idea is that each group is characterized by the nature of its main product which defines the sector, even if joint products appear in the physical production and contribute to the sector's   financial profitability.

We say that the sectoral choices are coherent if, whatever the operated methods in (n-1) sectors , the last sector can select one and only one (up to indifference) optimal method.

Theorem 2 : Sectoral choices are coherent if and only if all determinants det (1i, 2j, 3k) have the same sign.

Indeed, the identity of sign of all determinants is equivalent to the fact that any two determinants which differ by one method have the same sign. Hence the case is reduced to the previous one, and the identity of sign leads to the choice of one technique (up to indifference).

The statement of the coherence condition is mathematically satisfactory but its economic interpretation will be clearer if we transform its formulation by means of a theorem due to Gale and Nikaido.

Theorem 3 : Sectoral choices are coherent if and only if any two techniques (1i, 2j, 3k) and (1i', 2j', 3k') can obtain some common r-net product by strictly positive combinations of activity levels.

Proof : If two cones which differ by one process have a common interior intersection V

$$V = \alpha 1i + \beta 2j + \gamma 3k = \alpha' 1i' + \beta' 2j' + \gamma' 3k \qquad (\alpha, \beta, \gamma, \alpha, \beta, \gamma' > 0)$$

then det (V, 2j, 3k) = α det(1i, 2j, 3k) = α'det (1i', 2j, 3k).
Hence any two determinants which differ by one process have the same sign. By three successive changes, it appears that all determinants have the same sign (sectoral coherence of choices).

Conversely, let us assume all determinants have the same sign and, for given methods 1i, 2j, 3k, 1i',2j',3k' consider matrix A defined by A(1i) = 1i', A(2j) = 2j', A(3k) = 3k'. The determinant of A is positive, as well as its principal minors :after being completed by values 1 on its diagonal and 0 elsewhere, a minor rxr becomes a determinant nxn, so that all these minors appear as mixed combinations det (1i", 2j", 3k")/det (1i, 2j, 3k) with i"=i or i', j=j' on j', k"=k or k', hence are all positive.

8

The Gale-Nikaido theorem [3] asserts that a matrix A for which all principal minors are positive admits a solution to $x > 0$, $y = Ax > 0$. With $x = \alpha 1i + \beta 2j + \gamma 3k$, y is both written as $y = \alpha'1i + \beta'2j + \gamma'3k$,$(\alpha',\beta', \gamma') > 0$, and as $y = \alpha 1i' + \beta 2j' + \gamma 3k'$, $(\alpha, \beta, \gamma) > 0$, i.e. y is a strictly positive combination of both sets of techniques.

Q.E.D.

When applied to the special case of binary choices (card J = card K = 1), Theorem 3 leads to Theorem 1, the formal proof of which had been temporarily postponed.

To sum up, the sectoral coherence of choices is characterized by four criteria :
- when a method is modified in one sector, the sign of the determinant of the net products is unchanged;
- when a method is modified in one sector, the new and the old open convex cones spanned by the net products have a non-null intersection;
- when several methods are modified in several sectors, the sign of the determinant is unchanged;
- when several methods are modified in several sectors, the two corresponding convex cones have a non -null intersection.

The equivalence of the second and fourth criteria is unexpected, the formal proof being given by the consideration of the determinants. Example 4 below will show that the fourth criterion does not imply that all convex cones have a common intersection.

V - THE GLOBAL COHERENCE OF CHOICES

The notion of sectoral coherence helps one to understand individual decisions but is not rich enough to take into account the effects of the decisions in one sector on those of another sector and the effects of the feedbacks. The notion of global coherence considers the system as a whole : we no longer assume that the operated processes are given in (n-1) sectors. Sectoral coherence remains however a necessary condition for global coherence.

We examine the existence and uniqueness of a dominant technique and study the convergence of the algorithm towards it. It is to be noted that sectoral coherence is indeed a sufficient condition for global coherence.

Theorem 4. Let the collection $\mathcal{C}$ of techniques $T_{ij} = (1i, 2j, 3k)$, $i \in I$, $j \in J$, $k \in K$, satisfy the condition stated in Theorem 2. There exists one and, up to indifference, only one dominant technique in $\mathcal{C}$.

Proof of existence :Let C_1 (resp. C_2 and C_3) be the convex compact cones spanned by convex combinations of vectors 1i, $i \in I$ (resp. 2j, $j \in J$ and 3k, $k \in K$), and let $C = C_1 x C_2 x C_3 \subset R^9$. The function $f : (u_1, u_2, u_3) \in C \rightarrow V \in R^3$ such that $u_1.V = u_2.V = u_3.V = 1$ is well- defined (because the endomorphism $V \rightarrow (u_1.V, u_2.V, u_3.V)$ of R^3 into itself is surjective, as $\det(u_1,u_2,u_3) \neq 0$) and continuous with values in a convex compact subset D of R^3.

With each $V \in D$ let us associate the convex compact subset $g(V) = g_1(V) x g_2(V) x g_3(V)$ of C defined by

$$g_i(V) = \{u_i \in C_i; \ u_i.V = \inf_{u \in C_i} u.V\}$$

Then the product set-valued mapping fxg: $CxD \rightarrow DxC$ is upper hemi-continuous with convex values and, according to the Kakutani theorem, admits a fixed point u^*_1, u^*_2, u^*_3, V^* for which :

$$u^*_1.V^* = u^*_2.V^* = u^*_3.V^* = 1 = \inf_{u_1 \in C_1} u.V^* = \inf_{u_2 \in C_2} u.V^* = \inf_{u_3 \in C_3} u.V^*$$

These relationships mean that $(p=V^*,w=1)$ is the system of production prices associated with the use of (u_1^*, u_2^*, u_3^*) and that no other combination yields extra-profits at these prices. Moreover, though u_1^* has been defined as a convex combination of vectors 1i, we can assume that u_1^* is indeed equal to some vector 1i, corresponding to a vertex of C_1 where the linear form $u_1 \rightarrow u_1.V^*$ is minimal; and similarly for u^*_2 and u^*_3.

Proof of uniqueness : Two techniques are called indifferent when they are associated with the same price vector. We intend to show the uniqueness of the price vector associated with dominant techniques.

Let p_1 and p_2 be two different price vectors associated with two dominant techniques denoted as (1.1, 2.1, 3.1) and (1.2, 2.2, 3.2) - some methods may be common, however - .By definition

$$11.p_1 = 21.p_1 = 31.p_1 = 1$$

and by definition of a dominant technique

$$12.p_1 \leq 1, \ 22.p_1 \leq 1, \ 32.p_1 \leq 1 \qquad \text{with at least one strict inequality.}$$

Hence for any vector $V = \alpha 1.1 + \beta 2.1 + \gamma 3.1 =$ $\alpha'1.2 + \beta'2.2 + \gamma'3.2$ $(\alpha,\beta, \gamma ,\alpha', \beta', \gamma'>0)$ - such a vector exists by Theorem 3 - we have

$$\alpha + \beta + \gamma = V.p_1 = (\alpha'1.2 + \beta'2.2 + \gamma'3.2).p_1 < \alpha' + \beta' + \gamma'$$

while the reversed inequality $\alpha'+\beta'+ \gamma'<\alpha+\beta+\gamma$ is proved using the fact

that the second technique is also dominant:we must have $p_1 = p_2$.
Q.E.D.

Geometrically speaking, the dominant technique (1.1, 2.1, 3.1) is characterized by the fact that all r-net products 1i, 2j and 3k are located under the hyperplane spanned by the extremities of 1.1, 2.1, 3.1. If V is a net product common to the dominant technique and to another, the price of V in terms of the wage is minimized by the dominant technique.

VI - CONVERGENCE OF THE ALGORITHM AND CYCLES

We now study the working of the algorithm defined in the introduction. In fact, the procedure is not completely defined : for a non-dominant technique, there often exist several methods which yield extra-profits at the corresponding prices and a complete definition of the procedure should specify which sector has priority and which method of this sector will be inserted at the next step of the algorithm. Whatever these complementary rules may be, the algorithm stops if a dominant technique is reached and goes on if not. As there are finitely many techniques, the only way not to reach a dominant technique is to cycle. An example is :

Example 3 : There are three goods and three sectors in the economy, and two methods in each sector. Each of these methods is defined by the r-net product $b-(1+r)a$ obtained by a unit a labour :

First sector	Second sector	Third sector
$1.1 = (10,-1,8)$	$2.1 = (8,10,-1)$	$3.1 = (-1,8,10)$
$1.2 = (20,3,-3)$	$2.2 = (-3,20,3)$	$3.3 = (3,-3,20)$

The condition of sectoral coherence is satisfied, as the determinants of the eight techniques : $T_1 = (11,21,31)$, $T_2 = (12,21,31)$, $T_3 = (12,22,31)$, $T_4 = (11,22,31)$, $T_5 = (11,22,32)$, $T_6 = (11,21,32)$, $T_7 = (12,21,32)$, $T_8 = (12,22,32)$ are positive, because each diagonal element is greater than the sum of the absolute values of the elements of the same row (the idea of a main product). The preferences between these techniques are represented on the diagram

$$T_1 \qquad T_1 \qquad T_1$$
$$\downarrow \qquad \downarrow 1 \qquad \downarrow 1$$
$$T_2 \to T_3 \to T_4 \to T_5 \to T_6 \to T_7 \to T_2$$
$$\downarrow \qquad \downarrow \qquad \downarrow$$
$$T_8 \qquad T_8 \qquad T_8$$

Two techniques which differ by one method are connected by an arrow which points to the preferred one : each technique is compared with three others, according to the method which is changed and, in agreement with Theorem 4, T_8 is the only dominant technique. The interesting

interesting feature of this example is the existence of a cycle $T_2 \to T_3 \to T_4 \to T_5 \to T_6 \to T_7 \to T_2$, so that the algorithm might not converge towards T_8.

In fact, the problem is not a serious one for the working of the procedure itself, since among the complementary rules we mentioned at the beginning of this section, we can adopt : "In the case of a cycle, explore a new path at the next crossing", so that the algorithm is forced to converge towards the dominant technique. But the example shows that the eight techniques have no common net product V, otherwise the price of V in terms of the wage would decrease at each step and no cycle would exist : this simple monotonicity argument, which works for single production and for Salvadori's problem, cannot be used here, which justifies the more complex proof of Theorem 4.

VII - THE NUMERAIRE

It is important to remark that the definition of a dominant technique, the preference relation between two techniques which differ by one method and the working of the algorithm do not normally depend on the choice of numeraire : a change therein does not affect relative prices (p,w), all prices being multiplied by the same coefficient .Hence nominal extra-profits or deficits due to some alternative method are modified by the same factor but the decision to insert or to reject the method depends on the sign and not on the magnitude of this gap.

There is an exception to the above rule, which is connected with the issue of negative prices in joint production : if we consider two numeraires, the price of one in terms of the other being negative, extra-profits become deficits and vice-versa because the multiplicative factor is negative. The previous analysis does not support Sraffa's statement (§ 50) according to which "only those methods of production are practicable which, in the conditions actually prevailing (i.e. at the given wage or at the given rate of profits) do not involve other than positive prices". If we refer to Figure 1, a rotation of the whole figure does not change the dominant technique, though the associated price vector is modified at will and may have negative components : the dominant technique is independent of the sign of the price component and some prices may be negative for the dominant technique, while another dominated technique has positive prices.

12

VIII - NOTES ON THE HISTORY OF THE PROBLEM.

Let us mention briefly some previous works which are directly connected with our topic.

A. von Neumann.

The main difference between von Neumann's problem [4] and ours is :

- The profit rate (or the growth rate) is not given in the von Neumann problem and the aim is to reach an extremal rate.

- There is no explicit labour in von Neumann's problem. However, at the maximal profit rate of a system with labour, the wage is null and it is analytically equivalent to set $w=0$ or $l=0$.

- von Neumann considers inequalities with complementarity conditions while we have equalities. Due to the free disposal assumption, von Neumann's prices are semi-positive, while we may have negative prices.

B. Schefold.

Generalizing a previous study on the economic life-time of machines, B. Schefold establishes results which have similarities with von Neumann's as well as with Sraffa's :starting from an optimization problem,he obtains semi-positive prices and square systems. The analogy between general joint production and single production is noticeable [7].

C. General Equilibrium Theory.

This theory [2] contains a theory of choice of techniques. Under a constant returns assumption, the profit rate is null and for the equilibrium price vector (which is semi-positive under the free disposal assumption) the operated methods are balanced, while the others do not pay extra-profits. The proof of existence in Theorem 4 is very similar to the famous Gale-Nikaido-Debreu lemma which is the key to the existence of a general equilibrium. Some results of uniqueness have been obtained by using the notion of P-matrix [3,5] but the connexion with our result is less obvious here.

D. Sraffa.

The algorithm of choice of techniques and the characterization of the dominant technique by its wage-maximization property are studied in [8, Chapter 12], and the very last section is devoted to joint production. In this case, Sraffa proposes to start from a profit rate r where $(n+1)$ methods are indifferent and, at the profit rate $r+\Delta r$, to select the technique which maximizes the real wage. The maximization rule would therefore be general, at least if the prices in terms of the wage, $p_i/w(r)$, increase with r. A quite similar idea is used in our Appendix. But it is difficult to approve

Sraffa's statement without restriction, as the assumptions are not precisely defined : for instance, when Sraffa refers to the wage, does he mean "for any wage basket V" or "for a fixed given wage basket" ?

Our interpretation of Sraffa's wording is as follows : the study of single-product systems shows that -with <u>any</u> basket as a numeraire- the dominant technique maximizes the real wage. In joint production ,the level of the real wage also allows one to classify the various techniques and the possibility against which Sraffa intends to secure himself is that the ranking depends on the commodity i or j chosen as numeraire : in joint production we may have

$$\frac{w}{p_i}(I) > \frac{w}{p_i}(II) \quad \text{and} \quad \frac{w}{p_j}(I) < \frac{w}{p_j}(II)$$

for two systems (I) and (II). However the condition he considers is not relevant, as shown by Figure 3.

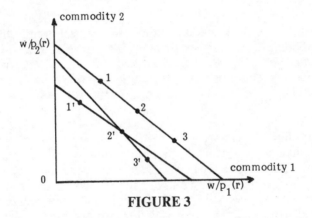

FIGURE 3

Three methods are available to produce two goods :
$$(a_1, l=1) \to b_1 \ , \qquad (a_2, l=1) \to b_2 \ , \qquad (a_3, l=1) \to b_3$$
and their respective net products $b_i - a_1$ are represented on Figure 3 by points 1,2,3 at the profit rate r and by points 1', 2', 3' at the profit rate r'>r.

At the profit rate r, points 1, 2, 3 are on line (D) whose equation is x.p = w and whose intersections with the axes define the real wages $w/p_1(r)$ and $w/p_2(r)$:the three methods are indifferent.At the profit rate r' slightly greater than r, the real wages w/p_1 and w/p_2 are lower and Sraffa's condition is therefore fulfilled. However the real wage maximization rule leads to the choice of (1', 2') or of (2', 3') according as commodity 1 or 2 is the numeraire.Sraffa's rule is therefore imprecise and cannot be general,even if it holds in special cases.

14

E. Salvadori.

In a parallel but independent study [6], Salvadori establishes the existence of a dominant (or cost-minimizing in his terminology) technique when all techniques are able to produce the same given basket. This result has similarities with Theorem 4, though the two notions of technique are quite different : we have classified methods into "competition groups" or sectors (methods 1i, 2j, 3k,...), while Salvadori refers to net products; our "sectoral assumption" and his "given net product assumption" are independent and neither can be reduced to the other. The results are therefore independent. However Salvadori also shows that two neighbouring techniques are comparable if and only if they can produce the same net product (Theorem 1 above).

APPENDIX : Criteria for choice of techniques

For viable single-product systems and a feasible profit rate r, the algorithm for the choice of techniques relies on the calculation of the production prices at each step. The following criterion is based on the sign of a determinant.

Let two methods (a^1_{ij}, l^1_i) and (a^2_{ij}, l^2) be in competition to produce one unit of good i and (p,w) be the price vector corresponding to the use of the first method :

$$(\lambda I - A)p - wL = 0 \qquad\qquad \text{(n equations)}$$

Method (a^2_{ij}, l^2_j) is indifferent to the other method if it yields the same profit rate at prices (p,w), i.e. if

$$\lambda p_i - a^2_{ij}\, p_i - w\, l^2_i = 0 \qquad\qquad \text{(1 equation)}$$

The price vector satisfies (n+1) homogeneous equations, which are not independent. Hence the $(n+1)\times(n+1)$ determinant $\Delta\,(1,2)$

$$\Delta\,(1,2) = \begin{vmatrix} \lambda I - A & -L \\ -\Delta \bar{a}_{ij} & -\Delta l_i \end{vmatrix}$$

with $\Delta a_{ij} = a^2_{ij} - a^1_{ij}$, $\Delta l_i = l^2_i - l^1_i$ is null. Hence:

Indifference criterion : Two production methods (a^1_{ij}, l^1_i) and (a^2_{ij}, l^2_i) are indifferent iff $\Delta(1,2) = 0$.

For given coefficients and a variable profit rate, the roots of the polynomial $\Delta(1,2)$ are the switching points between the two techniques. Since Δ is of degree n in , the number of switching points is at most equal to n [1].We now prove:

Preference criterion.
For a feasible profit rate, method 1 is preferred to method 2 iff $\Delta(1,2) < 0$.

Proof : Let us assume $\Delta(1,2) > 0$ and introduce a fictitious method 3 defined by $a^3_{ij} = a^2_{ij}$ and $l^3 = l^2 + l$, $l > 0$. We compare methods 1 and 3 by means of the previous criterion : since
$$\Delta(1,3) = \Delta(1,2) - l\,\det(\lambda I - A)$$
with $\Delta(1,2) > 0$ and $\det(\lambda I - A) > 0$, there exists a positive value of l such that $\Delta(1,3) = 0$. Then methods 1 and 3 are indifferent and method 2 which is obtained from 3 by reducing the quantity of labour is preferred to both of them.

$$\text{Q.E.D.}$$

16

The argument also shows that preference is reducible to an economy of labour between methods, and we obtain the well-known result :

Preference criterion : For a feasible profit rate, the preferred technique minimizes all prices in terms of the wage.

Proof : If method 2 is preferred to method 1, method 3 considered above is indifferent to method 1 with the same technical coefficients as 2, the difference between 2 and 3 turning solely on the quantity of labour : $l_2 < l_3$. Since prices in terms of the wage are given by $p = (\lambda I - A)^{-1} l$, a reduction of l implies that of prices.

Q.E.D.

In the generalization of these criteria to joint production, the condition $\Delta(1,2) < 0$ is to be replaced by "the sign of $\Delta(1,2)$ is opposite to that of $\det(\lambda B - A)$".

REFERENCES

[1]   Bharadwaj K., "On the Maximum Number of Switches Between Two Production Systems", Revue Suisse d'Economie Politique et de Statistique, 1970, vol. 106, pp. 409-428.

[2]   Debreu G., The Theory of Value, J. Wiley, New York, 1959.

[3]   Gale D., Nikaido H., "The Jacobian Matrix and global Univalence of Mappings", Math. Annalen, 1965, vol. 159, n°2.

[4]   von Neumann J., "A Model of General Equilibrium", Review of Economic Studies, 1945-46, vol. 13, n°1, pp. 1-9.

[5]   Nikaido H., Convex Structures and Economic Analysis, Academic Press, New York, 1968.

[6]   Salvadori N., "Existence of Cost-Minimizing Systems within the Sraffa Framework", Zeitschrift für Nationalökonomie, 1982, vol. 42, pp. 281-298.

[7]   Schefold B., "On Counting Equations", Zeitschrift für Nationalökonomie, 1978, vol. 38, pp. 253-285.

[8]   Sraffa P., Production of Commodities by Means of Commodities, Cambridge University Press, Cambridge, 1960.

[10]

SOME PROBLEMS CONCERNING THE NOTION OF COST-MINIMIZING SYSTEMS IN THE FRAMEWORK OF JOINT PRODUCTION*

by
REINER FRANKE†
University of Bremen

INTRODUCTION

The present paper is concerned with the issue of production prices and the underlying notion of equilibrium in linear joint production systems when the non-substitution theorem no longer applies. One could, of course, consider a given quadratic system of production processes and derive necessary conditions on the structure of demand such that it can be satisfied by an appropriate combination of these processes. Or, in other words, one could just postulate it to be contained in the net output cone. But this approach, on the one hand, leaves aside the question why it is just this system that has come into existence and, on the other hand, leaves unresolved how it is that demand is determined in such a way as to comply with the desired properties. To treat this issue in detail, the problem of the choice of techniques has to be discussed explicitly and the demand side has to be brought in right from the beginning. This leads to a certain notion of equilibrium which, following Salvadori (1982), we shall call a cost-minimizing system.

As a basis, input and output matrices A and $B \in \mathbb{R}_+^{n \times m}$ represent the production of n products in m processes ($m \neq n$ is admitted). Labour is supposed to be homogeneous and $l \in \mathbb{R}_+^m$ is the corresponding vector of direct labour inputs. Activity levels are denoted by column vectors $\times \in \mathbb{R}_+^m$, prices by row vectors $p \in \mathbb{R}^n$ (prices are not necessarily non-negative). As for distribution, a rate of profit $r \geq 0$ is considered as given. Wages are paid *post*

*Manuscript received 4.9.84; final version received 4.4.85.

†For helpful remarks I wish to thank U. Krause, N. Salvadori and I. Steedman, as well as an anonymous referee.

factum. We restrict our interest to situations in which they are positive and thus the nominal wage rate can be set equal to unity, i.e., all prices are in terms of labour commanded. The demand side, finally, will be represented by a function $d = d(p, x)$, $d \in \mathbb{R}^n$, of "requirements for use", to employ Sraffa's wording (*cf.* Sraffa, 1960, p. 43n). It is to be thought of as net of reproduction.

With respect to these data a *cost-minimizing system* is defined as a position in which all operated production processes earn the given rate of profit r, no non-operated process would yield surplus profits, and the resulting demand can be fulfilled. Formally, it is a pair $(p, x) \in \mathbb{R}^n \times \mathbb{R}^m_+$ such that

$$pB \leq (1+r)\, pA + l \qquad \qquad \text{......(1)}$$
$$pBx = (1+r)\, pAx + lx \qquad \qquad \text{......(2)}$$
$$Bx = Ax + d(p, x) \qquad \qquad \text{......(3)}$$

(This definition is a bit different from that of Salvadori, 1982 who, in addition, takes into account compatible price systems.)

In order for this notion to be meaningful, the first question at issue relates to existence. As the definition appears quite natural one might expect that the conditions on technology and demand by which existence is guaranteed are not unreasonable. The first section of this paper is devoted to a discussion of this issue. Whereas the approach introduced there seeks a high level of generality, the subsequent sections deal with more specific questions. Section II is concerned with an interpretation of negative prices and the role of costly disposal. Section III discusses a special phenomenon, namely the possibility of a cost-minimizing system without capital, in the usual sense. In the final section the notion of a cost-minimizing system is applied to the issue of a wage-profit frontier. We give a simple example of an economy generating a frontier that exhibits a peculiarity of a new type.

I

It is trivial that even if the technology (B, A) can produce a positive net output, for some function $d(.\,,\,.)$ a cost-minimizing system will not exist: just suppose that the net output cone does not contain the whole positive orthant and that $d(p, x)$ is always to be found in the complementary region. But there are other counter-examples which are less obvious (*cf.* Salvadori, 1982, p. 287). The unpleasant phenomenon of non-existence may also occur for the following most elementary function

$$d(p, x) = g\, Ax + c \qquad \qquad \text{......(4)}$$

where g is a given growth rate, $0 \leqslant g \leqslant r$, and the consumption vector $c \in \mathbb{R}^n_+$ can in fact be produced by some combination of processes of (B, A). This is due to the possibility that if c is contained in the g-net output cone of a, say quadratic, technique (by which we mean a set of production processes), then (with $g \neq r$), the corresponding vector of production prices cannot prevent some processes outside this technique from being more profitable. And the other way round, any technique supported by a price vector that rules out surplus profits is incapable of producing c as a g-net output. A concrete example of this was provided in Salvadori (1985).

So the problem is to find conditions on (B, A, l) and $d(. , .)$ which are able to bring into accord these two different sides. Since this question is of central importance we shall devote some space to it (and in order to be self-contained we take the risk of some repetition from Franke, 1984).

Salvadori himself has pointed out two possibilities. According to him a cost-minimizing system does exist

1. with respect to the function (4) if free disposal is admitted for all commodities, i.e., if all prices are non-negative and if (3) is relaxed to admit "$\geqslant$", where, in exchange, $pBx = pAx + pd(p, x)$ is required (see Salvadori, 1980, Theorem 4.2., p. 59);

2. or if there exists a commodity $u \in \mathbb{R}^n$ that has certain properties with respect to $d(. , .)$ and certain sets of prices and activity levels (here $d(. , .)$ need not be restricted to functions of the type (4)). Important cases for which existence can be proved in this way are $g=r$, on the one hand, and a sufficiently amenable kind of joint production like r-all-productive, r-all-engaging or r-s-partially-all-productive systems, on the other (see Salvadori, 1982).

Aiming at a higher level of generality, in Franke (1984) a different approach for solving the existence problem was set out. Its most significant feature is the assumption that the function $d(. , .)$, over its whole domain, obeys "Walras's Law", i.e., the identity

$$pBx = pAx + pd(p, x);$$

if, with respect to a time-discrete period model, p are the prices of the present production period and Bx is the vector of last period's gross output, this gives rise to a gross income pBx, out of which this period's demand $Ax + d(p, x)$ is to be defrayed.

A second point to be made is that for some selected commodities free disposal may be admitted (if their price turns out to be zero) or that, in another more stringent version, we wish a positive price to be associated with them. These commodities may be composite ones and they may even vary with the activity vector x. As for technology, it is postulated that the whole positive orthant is contained in the r-net output cone of (B, A) — which, by the way, holds true for single production systems whose maximal rate of profit exceeds r. In addition, all processes are costly in the sense that they require a positive amount of labour.

In detail, the assumptions are as follows. In a preparatory step, fix a given level of employment $L > 0$ and define

$$X := \{x \in \mathbb{R}_+^m : lx = L\}.$$

Furthermore, let J be a set of indices and, for each $j \in J$, $c^j(.)$ be a function from X to $\mathbb{R}_+^n$.

Assumption 1

The set J is non-void and finite, $1 \in J$, and $c^1(x) = c^1 =$ constant. All functions $c^j(.): X \longrightarrow \mathbb{R}_+^n$ are semi-positive and continuous.

The assumption is, in the first place, adopted for mathematical reasons of proof (it allows us to utilize an extended version of the Gale-Nikaido-Debreu Lemma; this hint also explains that all functions involved are assumed to be continuous). On the other hand, it will exclude the strange event that in a cost-minimizing system all prices happen to be negative, which, in the light of the positive wage rate $w = 1$, would lead to difficulties in interpretation (*cf.* Section II below).

Assumption 2

(i) $l_k > 0, \qquad k = 1, \ldots, m.$

(ii) For all $c \in \mathbb{R}_+^n$ there exists an $x \in \mathbb{R}_+^m$ such that $(B - (1 + r)A)x = c$.

(iii) There exists a neighbourhood V of c^1 such that for all $c' \in V$ an $x' \in \mathbb{R}_+^m$ can be found with $(B - (1 + r)A)x' = c'$.

Assumption 2(iii) is a bit stronger than 2(ii) in that it requires us to allow a negative component i in the vector $c' \in V$ if $c_i^1 = 0$. In other words, c^1 is supposed to be contained in the interior of the r-net output cone, whereas the other commodities $c^j(x)$ need not be.

As for the assumptions on $d(.\,,.)$, two cases are distinguished, according as to whether free disposal is admitted for all commodities $c^j(x)$ in J or whether we want it to be excluded for a subset J' of J. Define the sets

$$D := \{(p, x) \in \mathbb{R}^n \times X: (p, x) \text{ satisfies (1) and (2)}, pc^j(x) \geqslant 0 \text{ for all } j \in J\},$$

and, with respect to the subset J',

$$D' := \{(p, x) \in D: pc^j(x) > 0 \text{ for all } j \in J'\}.$$

Assumption 3.1

$d(.\,,.)$ is a continuous function $D \longrightarrow \mathbb{R}^n$ for which $pBx = pAx + pd(p, x)$ holds identically on D.

In contrast, Assumption 3.2 postulates that if for $j \in J'$ the price of a commodity $c^j(x)$ is sufficiently low, then so much (of this commodity or of another) is demanded that it cannot be produced with the given level of employment L. More specifically:

Assumption 3.2

There is a non-void subset $J' \subset J$ such that with respect to the correspondingly defined D' the following holds:

(i) $d(.\,,\,.)$ is a continuous function $D' \longrightarrow \mathbb{R}^n$ which is bounded from below;

(ii) $pBx = pAx + pd(p, x)$ for all $(p, x) \in D'$;

(iii) there exists an $\epsilon > 0$ with the property:

$(p, x) \in D'$ and $pc^j(x) < \epsilon$ for some $j \in J'$ implies the existence of some i such that

$$(Bx)_i + \epsilon < (Ax)_i + d_i(p, x).$$

A function of the rigid type (4) could be incorporated in this framework by defining

$$d(p, x) = g\,Ax + \left[\frac{p(B - (1 + g)A)x}{pc}\right]c \qquad \text{......(4')}$$

Assumption 3.2 is fulfilled if c is present in Assumption 1 and in the definition of D', say $c^1 = c$ and $1 \in J'$, and if on D' $p(B - (1+g)A)x$ is positively bounded away from zero. Because of $p(B - (1+g)A)x = p(B - (1+r)A)x + (r-g) pAx = lx + (r-g)\,pAx$, this will hold true in the following cases:

$g=r$ or g sufficiently close to r;

$c^j(x) = Ax$ for some $j \in J$;

all commodities can be freely disposed of, i.e., in formal terms, if $J = \{1, \ldots, n+1\}$, all functions c^j are constant, $c^1=c$, $c^{j+1} = j$-th unit vector for $j=1, \ldots, n$, $J' = \{1\}$, so that the domain of $d(.\,,\,.)$ becomes

$$D' = \{(p, x) \in \mathbb{R}^n \times X : (p, x) \text{ satisfies (1) and (2)}, p \geqslant 0,\, pc > 0\}.$$

Theorem

(i) Suppose that Assumptions 1, 2, and 3.1 hold. Then there exists a pair $(p, x) \in D$ such that

$$Bx = Ax + d(p, x) + c^* \qquad \text{......(5)}$$

where $c^* = \sum_{j \in J} \lambda_j\, c^j(x)$ for some $\lambda_j \geqslant 0$, and $\lambda_j > 0$ implies $pc^j(x) = 0$.

(ii) Suppose that Assumptions 1, 2, and 3.2 hold. Then there exists a pair $(p, x) \in D'$ bringing about (5) and $\lambda_j = 0$ for all $j \in J'$.

In particular, if $J' = J$ and Assumption 3.2 applies, then all λ_j vanish and, in fact, (3) is satisfied.

In summary, the approach put forward could be termed one of general equilibrium. Though general equilibrium theory is often considered to be the hallmark of neoclassical economics, this does not necessarily signify that our model and its assumptions are inconsistent with a classical mode of thought (as for the "visions" underlying classical and neoclassical modelling we confine ourselves to referencing A. J. and J. S. Cohen, 1983, pp. 194-200).

In particular, consumption demand need not be the only relevant component of the function $d(.\,,\,.)$. Moreover, since prices as well as activity levels enter as arguments, it provides a black box in which a variety of demand concepts could find their place (and they may be rather distinct from that of utility maximizing individuals).

II

The definition of a cost-minimizing system does not require all prices to be non-negative. Apart from the commodities $c^j(x)$, the existence theorem does not say anything more specific about this, either. However, some economists seem to think along the lines that, in the long run, only production processes which bring about non-negative prices will survive (or else the uniformity of the wage rate or the rate of profit can no longer be maintained). There need not necessarily be a contradiction here (neither has the postulate of uniformity to be given up). We shall argue that it suffices to modify the equations for the prices of production (in the activated processes) appropriately.

The starting point is to make disposal activities explicit: to get rid of a thing one has to make use of a production process and put it in there, as an input. This may be a special process that produces no output at all, but any other "normal" process will do (whether it is tolerated by the law need not matter). Thus, a negative price p_i makes sense if $-p_i$ is interpreted as the payment for a service, namely the service of disposing of one unit of product i in a production process k which entails some costs, in particular for the labour input $l_k > 0$. A corresponding redefinition of negatively priced products would make all negative prices disappear from the economy.

In writing down the production price equations, however, care has to be taken of the dating: the waste is delivered at the beginning of the period and it is already at this point of time that the service of its subsequent disposal has to be paid for. So, let I^+ and I^- denote the sets of indices of positive and negative prices, respectively. Then the production price equation of the k-th process can be rearranged to read

$$(1+r) \sum_{i \in I^+} p_i a_{ik} + \sum_{i \in I^-} |p_i| b_{ik} + l_k = \sum_{i \in I^+} p_i b_{ik} + (1+r) \sum_{i \in I^-} |p_i| a_{ik},$$

with costs, with respect to the end of the period, on the left and revenues on the right.

Note that whether the price of a certain product i turns out to be positive or negative in equilibrium, i.e., whether it turns out to be a good or a bad, is not only a matter of the structure of demand, but also depends upon distribution. A variation of the rate of profit will change p_i and it is perfectly possible that this has an impact on its sign as well.

If one follows this rationale for negative prices, then the idea that a certain commodity or service c is a consumption good will surely not be consistent with a situation $pc < 0$. This has been an economic reason for introducing Assumption 1 and the definition of the sets D and D'. A stronger version of the idea of an *a priori* consumption good can be grasped by Assumption 3.2(iii).

As regards the problem of disposal, even if free disposal is considered to be a hardly defensible supposition (and there are good reasons for this opinion), it may be acceptable to permit it for some few selected products, as they are specified in the goods $c^j(x)$ of Assumption 1. Part (ii) of the Theorem shows that by employing Assumption 3.2(iii) for all commodities $c^j(x)$, free disposal can be made completely absent in a cost-minimizing system—a sufficient reason being that there is no need for it. It might seem, at first sight, that this assumption also excludes any need for disposal in general. Observe, however, that besides the "normal" components of demand, demand for consumption and demand for means of production, the function $d(.\,,\,.)$ may equally include a "demand for bad i", to which, more meaningfully, corresponds the supply of the service of disposing of product i. Accordingly, on the left-hand side of (3) we may have the supply of a bad i, to which corresponds the demand for this service: for the sake of some other advantages, product i has been produced in the preceding period (as a by-product of a positively priced commodity), and in an equilibrium position now, at the beginning of the present period, by definition there has to be someone who is willing to take it. However, the actual disposal is subsequent and no longer an explicit part of the model.

III

The main idea behind the definition of a cost-minimizing system is, of course, to model some basic features of a capitalistic economy. Now, if $(pA)_k \leqslant 0$ for some production process k in such a system, the question arises as to what has become of the notion of capital in that process. Two points of view seem possible. Suppose

$$K_1 := \sum_{i \in I^+} p_i a_{ik} > 0, \; K_2 := \sum_{i \in I^-} |p_i| a_{ik} > 0, \; K_1 - K_2 < 0,$$

I^+ and I^- still being the sets of indices of positive and negative prices, respectively. According to the first point of view, an operator of process k, on the whole, receives a positive sum of money $K_2 - K_1$, at the beginning of the period and invests it in some other processes that earn a rate of profit r. At the end of the period he thus has a (gross) revenue $(pB)_k + (1+r)(K_2-K_1)$, and this is just sufficient to cover the wage bill, l_k.

On the other hand, he himself may advance the sum K_1, investing elsewhere all the payments K_2 received for his disposal services. Then his

net revenue amounts to $(pB)_k + (1+r)K_2 - l_k = (1+r)K_1$. Here K_1 could
be regarded as capital, whereas in the first case it has to be looked for elsewhere. However, the point to be made is that in both cases a positive profit
has to be realized outside k. This might not be too serious, but what of the
notion of (total) capital and profits if, economy-wide, $pAx \leqslant 0$ happens to
come about?

In fact, in the absence of more detailed information it cannot be excluded
that a system fulfilling equations (1)-(3) is incompatible with the classical
view of a capitalistic economy. Just consider the extreme case that $(pA)_k = 0$
for all operated processes, and $(pA)_k > 0$ for all processes that are not
operated (because of $(pB)_k < (1+r) (pA)_k + l_k$). Since in the classical
tradition the ultimate reason for a positive rate of interest is to be found in
the sphere of production, namely in the need of some production processes
to finance their positively priced inputs, r cannot be interpreted as a rate of
interest or as being in a certain relationship to it. By the same token, it
makes no sense to speak of profits and a rate of profit. On the contrary,
apparently the sole task of the number r is to prevent activation of the
processes with $(pA)_k > 0$.

We may conclude that, as a minimum, it is desirable that $pAx > 0$ in a
cost-minimizing system. This could be guaranteed by imposing Assumption
3.2(iii) not only on some consumption goods, but also on $c^j(x) = Ax$. The
justification for the former is that, at prices rendering pc sufficiently small,
the good c itself is demanded in such an amount that it cannot be produced
with the given level of employment. As for $c^j(x) = Ax$, the argument turns
on the structure of demand, rather than on scale. It entails that for small
pAx there is always one component i such that the demand $(Ax)_i + d_i(p, x)$
exceeds the existing quantity $(Bx)_i$ of this product. Which one does not
matter. It is quite possible that this i changes as p and x vary in the set,
say, $\{(p, x) \in D: pAx = \epsilon\}$ for some small $\epsilon > 0$. This assumption, however,
requires a certain flexibility of the function $d(. , .)$, especially if the negatively
priced products are not pure consumption goods.

IV

The existence theorem of Section I does not make any statement on
the uniqueness of a cost-minimizing system, not even in a local sense.
Likewise, one does not learn anything about the number of activated
processes, e.g., whether it is equal to the number of commodities actually
produced and traded, in which case it may be called a "Sraffian" system.
Now, examples of multiple or non-quadratic equilibria can be readily
constructed. But such an event is more than just a matter of pure accident
or of aesthetics, as will be seen when applying the notion of a cost-minimizing
system to the issue of a wage-profit frontier.

If a wage-frontier is considered at all in the framework of joint production *and* choice of techniques, it is often limited to a special case of requirements for use, namely the function $d(.\,,\,.)$ of (4) where free disposal and $g=r$ are both assumed. On the other side, the analysis uses the instrument of linear programming, and this already enters into the very definition of the frontier. If $g < r$ is admitted, however, it seems more natural to start from the notion of a cost-minimizing system and assign to each rate of profit r the real wage rates of all systems existing with respect to that r. The wage-profit frontier can, then, be defined as the locus of the maximal wage rates.

Let us apply this procedure to the following example of two commodities and two production processes,

$$B = \begin{bmatrix} 5 & 7 \\ 7 & 5 \end{bmatrix}, A = \begin{bmatrix} 1 & 2 \\ 2 & 1 \end{bmatrix}, l = (1, 1), c = \begin{bmatrix} 10 \\ 11 \end{bmatrix}, g = 0.$$

A cost-minimizing system exists for r contained in the interval $[0, 4)$. Fixing $L=7$, on the interval $[0, 3)$ one system is given by $x_1(r) = 5$, $x_2(r) = 2$,

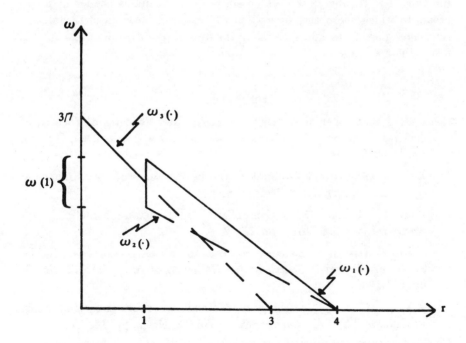

Fig. 1.

Some Problems Concerning the Notion of Cost-Minimizing Systems, etc.   307

and $p_1(r) = p_2(r) = 1/3(3-r)$. On $[0, 1)$ this is the only one. At $r=1$, a continuum of prices corresponds to it, namely the set $\{(p_1, p_2) \geqslant 0 : p_1 + p_2 = 1/3\}$. Maintaining the assumption of free disposal, for $1 \leqslant r < 4$ two additional systems appear, one in which exclusively process 1 is operated, with $p_1(r) = 1/(4-r)$, $p_2(r) = 0$; and, symmetrically, another in which only process 2 is operated, with $p_1(r) = 0$, $p_2(r) = 1/(4-r)$.

The real wage rate is given by $\omega = \omega(r) = 1/p(r)c$. Define $\omega_3(r) :=$ $(3-r)/7$, $\omega_1(r) := (4-r)/10$, $\omega_2(r) := (4-r)/11$, i.e., the real wage rate at r if both processes, process 1, and process 2, respectively, are activated. All possible wage rates are registered by the set-valued mapping $\omega = \omega(r)$ defined by

$$\omega(r) := \begin{cases} \omega_3(r) & \text{for } 0 \leqslant r < 1 \\ [\omega_2(1), \omega_1(1)] & \text{for } r = 1 \\ \{\omega_1(r), \omega_2(r), \omega_3(r)\} & 1 < r < 3 \\ \{\omega_1(r), \omega_2(r)\} & 3 \leqslant r < 4 \end{cases}$$

which is illustrated in Fig. 1. In particular,

$$\omega_2(1) < \omega_3(1) < \omega_1(1).$$

To sum up, each separate wage curve $\omega_k(.)$, $k = 1, 2, 3$, is a falling real function of r. However, at $r=1$ possibly a discontinuous change of prices occurs to which there may or may not correspond a switch of techniques. As a consequence, a slight increase in the rate of profit can induce a sudden rise in the real wage rate.

REFERENCES

Cohen, A. J. and Cohen, J. S. (1983). "Classical and Neoclassical Theories of General Equilibrium", *Australian Economic Papers*, Vol. 22, No. 40, pp. 180-200.

Franke, R. (1984). "Joint Production and the Existence of Cost-Minimizing Systems", University of Bremen, mimeo.

Salvadori, N. (1980). "On a Generalized von Neumann Model", *Metroeconomica*, Vol. 32, No. 1, pp. 51-62.

——————— (1982). "Existence of Cost-Minimizing Systems within the Sraffa Framework", *Zeitschrift für Nationalökonomie*, Vol. 42, No. 3, pp. 281-298.

——————— (1985). "Switching in Methods of Production and Joint Production", *The Manchester School*, Vol. 53, No. 2, pp. 156-178.

Sraffa, P. (1960). *Production of Commodities by Means of Commodities*, Cambridge, Cambridge University Press.

Part IV
Fixed Capital

[11]

Fixed Capital as a Joint Product

Fixes Kapital als Kuppelprodukt

Von Bertram Schefold, Frankfurt/Main

1. Introduction

Since the Reswitching Debate the point has become familiar that the means of production in a capitalist society represent different 'quantities of capital' depending on the prevailing rate of profit. But because these discussions were about a critique of the neoclassical theory of value and distribution and not about a new comprehensive theory of capital, they have been conducted either in terms of circulating capital without machines or in terms of production by means of one machine at different ages (cf. Hicks [1970], Nuti [1970]). Although von Neumann and Sraffa revived the 'old classical idea' (Sraffa) of treating what is left at the end of the year's process of production as an economically different good from the one which entered the process, very few[1]) have tried to construct

---

[1]) A remarkable exception is Mirrlees (1969) who obtains some of the results contained in this paper by starting from different assumptions including the rather mysterious assumption of 'R-efficiency' which is necessary (see his theorem 4) to ensure that the economy is capable of balanced growth and, consequently, of yielding positive prices at a positive rate of interest. The short and elegant paper of Stiglitz (1970) also ought to be mentioned. He proves a nonsubstitution theorem for a fixed capital model where, as in our paper below, machines may exhibit any depreciation pattern and where machines cannot be shifted from the production of one finished good to that of another. Our paper differs from those of Mirrlees and Stiglitz firstly in that a number of properties of a fixed capital model (such as the definition and characteristics of a basic fixed capital system, the functional dependence of prices of new and old machines on the rate of profit, truncation, and switching of techniques) are either discussed for the first time or in greater detail than in previous papers. The second, and perhaps most important difference is the following: it is shown here that the only fundamental assumption which has to be adopted to make the model work is that the system be productive, i.e. capable of static reproduction with a surplus. The existence of a maximum rate of profit, of balanced growth up to the same maximum, then follows. 'R-efficiency' can thus be derived. The important fact that positive prices at a rate of profit greater than the maximum will not exist in a fixed capital system with limited production alternatives (substitution possibilities) is not mentioned in Stiglitz' paper. In a technology such as that discussed below, Stiglitz' theorem 4 is true only if his rate of interest is smaller than the maximum.

The existence of a maximum rate of profit which is a striking feature of Sraffa's model

416   BERTRAM SCHEFOLD

models with several fixed capital goods which are explicitly distinguished
from other kinds of joint products.

It is true that the common approach of dealing with the problem of
fixed capital in special one-machine models and of dealing with the interaction between industries in special circulating capital models seems to
correspond to economic intuition. While joint production of the mutton-
wool kind creates a multitude of difficult problems, it is indeed the peculiarity of fixed capital as a joint product that it has properties similar to those
of circulating capital in as far as interindustry relations are concerned,
while some of the problems of the evaluation of machines can be discussed
in models with one consumption good produced by means of one machine.
But there are essential problems of the choice of technique in the presence
of machines that can only be understood in a more comprehensive and
more complex model.

This will be shown by means of a discussion of the more formal properties of fixed capital, and in particular of the relationship between interindustry relations and the efficiency pattern of individual machines. The
model is built on Sraffa [1960]. Switching of techniques and truncation
are discussed in this generalized framework.

It turns out (contrary to what might have been expected on the basis
of Nuti [1973]) that the same truncation may return at different levels of
the rate of profit, if more than one machine is involved.

2. Machines

Single product systems have a number of simple properties which do
not obtain in general joint production systems, but hold within fixed capital
systems. Commodities are e.g. separately producible in single product
systems with constant returns to scale, i.e. it is possible to produce a net
output consisting of only one commodity, using positive activity levels,
and in basic single product systems (with an indecomposable input matrix)
all processes will be indispensable, i.e. nothing can be produced without
activating all processes. The comparative ease with which fixed capital
systems as we shall define them are handled is due to the fact that new
machines are separately producible within them and that the prices of old
machines appear as derived from those of the new ones once their prices
are known. If the system is indecomposable, i.e. if the input and the output
matrix are not simultaneously decomposable, this will be reflected in the
fact that only processes using old machines will not be indispensable.

In order to define what we mean by a pure fixed capital system, we
distinguish between finished goods (circulating capital and new machi-

---

looks natural to those brought up in the classical tradition, but it once came as a surprise
to neoclassical theorists since neoclassical theory traditionally assumed limited substitution possibilities such that the rate of profit tends to infinity as the wage drops to
zero.

Fixed Capital as a Joint Product 417

nes) and intermediate goods (old machines of various ages). In order to isolate our problem from that of joint production in general, we assume that each process produces one and only one finished good (no super-imposed joint production). The processes engaged in the production of a finished good taken together will be said to form a group. We assume not only that no transfer of intermediate goods between groups takes place, but also that within each group only one machine at various ages is used. (The latter assumption is fairly easily relaxed, the former only under additional restrictions — see Schefold [1971]). There is always one primary process which uses exclusively finished goods as inputs, among them the new machine. After the end of the year the new machine leaves the process as a one year old machine together with the output of the finished good and enters the first intermediate process by which it is used and also reproduced as a two year old machine. The latter enters a second inter-mediate process etc. until the machine is worn out.

Our preliminary assumptions of admitting only one ageing machine in each group allows that the same kind of new machine may enter different groups. But as a consequence, each new machine will gradually turn into a different set of intermediate goods. They are characterized by the group in which they are used since no trade of old machines between groups takes place. The point is that the efficiency of the machines will vary to different degrees with age in that the amounts of finished goods produced, of raw materials, spare parts etc. used up, and of labour employed, will vary with the age of the machine. The efficiency may be falling, e.g. because an increasing number of spare parts has to be used to keep the output of the finished good constant. Efficiency may rise because a machine works more smoothly after it has been run in. More importantly: the model does not exclude the possibility that the processes representing the construction of a machine which (like a tanker) takes several years to be built are combin-ed to form one group with the processes using the completed machine to produce a finished good (oil transportation). In the processes representing the construction of the tanker no finished good would be produced, only the intermediate good 'tanker under construction'. Such a combination in one group of the processes for a machine under construction with the processes using it looks formally like the group representing a machine which is initially inefficient in the extreme because it produces nothing (in fact it is itself being produced), and suddenly its efficiency is positive when it starts to operate (i.e. when the output coefficients showing the amount of oil transported become positive). Constant efficiency is not ruled out either, but of lesser interest in so far as it excludes a meaningful treatment of the most characteristic problem of fixed capital, i.e. the problem of determining the economic lifetime of a machine as distinct from its maximum physical lifetime. If the efficiency of a machine consisting of many parts is constant, there is no reason why it should not last forever, if it is properly maintained, viz. if those parts which are of fairly constant efficiency but finite duration are replaced periodically (valves, light bulbs, etc.). We shall

not discuss everlasting machines explicitly, however, although they can be
included in the framework of our analysis without great difficulty. We are
mainly interested in machines the efficiency of which varies because not all
their parts are capable of periodic replacement for economic and/or technical reasons.

It will be seen that machines of falling efficiency may yield formal
solutions where old machines receive negative prices. In the last and most
important section of the paper we shall prove that it is always possible to
truncate old machines with negative prices from a given system without
affecting the net output of finished goods, provided only the system is
productive. Despite its importance, we do not turn to the problem of
truncation at once because the formal consideration of negative prices
which is unavoidable from a mathematical point of view can be given an
instructive economic meaning which will be discussed below.

We now turn to the formal definition: there is a total number of n
commodities in the system of which, say, the first f are finished, the rest
intermediate goods. If the machine involved in the production of finished
good i has a maximum physical lifetime of T_i years, the group of processes
producing good i may be written as follows:

$$(1 + r) [a_i (t) p_1 + m_i (t - 1) p_2] + w \, l_i (t) = b_i (t) p_1 + m_i (t) p_2; \ t = 1, 2, ..., T_i;$$

where p_1 is the f-vector of relative prices of finished goods, p_2 the $(n - f)$-
vector of prices of intermediate goods. $l_i (t)$ is the input of labour, $a_i (t)$,
$b_i (t)$ are f-vectors for inputs and outputs of finished goods, $m_i (t - 1)$
and $m_i (t)$ are $(n - f)$-vectors for input and output of intermediate goods,
all to the t-th of T_i processes for the production of good i. The wage-rate w
and the rate of profit r are assumed to be uniform as is customary in Sraffa-
type models.

Clearly, $b_i^j (t) = 0, i \neq j$. Since the total output of each commodity equals
one, we have

$$\sum_{t=1}^{T_i} b_i^i (t) = 1, \ i = 1, ..., f.$$

Processes with $b_i^i (T_i) = 0$ are economically not viable and will be truncated (see section 5), but $b_i^i (t) = 0$ for t smaller than T_i is not ruled out
(machine under construction, see above). Our main assumption is that the
system is productive, i.e.

$$\sum_{i, t} a_j^j (t) \leqslant 1, \ j = 1, ..., f.$$

The first process uses finished goods exclusively, i.e. $m_i (0) = 0, i = 1,$
..., f, and all primary processes use some finished goods as inputs, hence
$a_i (1) \geq 0; i = 1, ..., f$. Since the machine is used up after the last process,
$m_i (T_i) = 0$. If no machine is involved in the production of good i so
that the process uses circulating capital only, put formally $T_i = 1, m_i (0)$
$= m_i (1) = 0$. Finally, since each machine is both a different good at a

Fixed Capital as a Joint Product 419

different age and characterised by the process in which it is used (no trade between groups), the $(T_1 - 1) + \cdots + (T_f - 1) = n - f$ vectors m_i (t), $i = 1, .., f; t = 1, \ldots, T_1 - 1$; are all different unit vectors. All equations taken together can be written in matrix form as

$$(1 + r) \, A \, p + w \, l = B \, p$$

where

$$A = \begin{bmatrix} a_1\ (1),\ m_1\ (0) \\ a_1\ (2),\ m_1\ (1) \\ \cdots\cdots\cdots\cdots \\ a_f\ (T_f),\ m_f\ (T_f - 1) \end{bmatrix}, \ B = \begin{bmatrix} b_1\ (1),\ m_1\ (1) \\ b_1\ (2),\ m_1\ (2) \\ \cdots\cdots\cdots \\ b_f\ (T_f),\ m_f\ (T_f) \end{bmatrix}, \ l = \begin{bmatrix} l_1\ (1) \\ l_1\ (2) \\ \cdots \\ l_f\ (T_f) \end{bmatrix}, \ p = \begin{bmatrix} p_1 \\ p_2 \end{bmatrix}.$$

By a familiar procedure[2]) the intermediate goods can be eliminated from the system: one combines the equations of each group i by multiplying the t-th equation by a factor $(1 + r)^{T_1-t}$ and summing over t for each group i to get the reduced system

$$(1 + r) \, \tilde{A} \, (r) \, p_1 + w \tilde{l}(r) = \tilde{B} \, (r) \, p_1$$

where

$$\tilde{A} \, (r) = \begin{bmatrix} \tilde{a}_1\ (r) \\ : \\ \tilde{a}_f\ (r) \end{bmatrix}, \ \tilde{B} \, (r) = \begin{bmatrix} \tilde{b}_1\ (r) \\ : \\ \tilde{b}_f\ (r) \end{bmatrix}, \ \tilde{l}(r) = \begin{bmatrix} \tilde{l}_1\ (r) \\ : \\ \tilde{l}_f\ (r) \end{bmatrix},$$

$$\tilde{a}_i\ (r) = \sum_{t=1}^{T_i} (1 + r)^{T_1-t}\ a_i\ (t),$$

$$\tilde{b}_i\ (r) = \sum_{t=1}^{T_i} (1 + r)^{T_1-t}\ b_i\ (t),$$

$$\tilde{l}_i\ (r) = \sum_{t=1}^{T_i} (1 + r)^{T_1-t}\ l_i\ (t).$$

This system will be called the **integrated system** because of the following intuitive interpretation: instead of thinking of the T_1 processes of group i as of T_1 separate activities running side by side at the same time, imagine an entrepreneur producing finished good i in T_1 successive years. At the beginning of the first period he will have to buy a bundle a_i (1) of finished goods (including his new machine), at the end of the period he obtains b_i (1) as an output to be sold. He will have to buy a_i (2) to start production with the one year old machine and produce during the second period etc. till his machine is worn out at the end of the T_1-th period. Hence T_1 is the total turnover period of group i. Considering it as a whole, the entrepreneur may strike the balance by multiplying each input and output by that power of $(1 + r)$ which indicates the number of full periods that have passed by since it has been bought or sold. The resulting equation is

---

[2]) See S r a f f a (1960), p. 65.

the integrated process. As one should expect, it is identical with the
equation for group i in the integrated system which we obtained above by
mathematical elimination of the intermediate goods.

Before we consider its mathematical properties, let us discuss the integrated system in greater detail from an economic point of view.

If activity levels were such that at some time all integrated processes
with turnover periods $T_1, \ldots, T_t$ could start simultaneously, they would
all simultaneously end again after a time equal to the smallest common
multiple of $T_1, \ldots, T_t$ which we denote by T. Obviously, if the rate of
profit was calculated on the basis of T periods, we should then be confronted with a single product system since no net output of intermediate
goods would appear explicitly in the equations. Since the way in which
the rate of profit is calculated does not affect the technical characteristics
of the system, it is therefore intuitively plausible that finished goods are
separately producible and have positive values which are equal to those
obtained in the original system. When the rate of profit is zero, it does not
matter at which time the products appear. But if the rate of profit is positive,
the subdivision of the 'long period' T into the unit period of production
matters. To disregard the dating of inputs and outputs within the 'long
period' T would mean to add up all inputs used during the 'long period'
and to treat them as if they had to be available at its beginning and similarly
to add all outputs and to treat them as if they were to be available only at
its end.

By so doing one would obtain a system equal to the integrated system
at $r = 0$. The construction of the integrated system at $r = 0$ amounts
simply to adding up the equations for each group so that intermediate goods
cancel out. The integrated system at $r = 0$ provides therefore an approximation for prices at low rates of profit.

The quality of the approximation depends on the evenness of the distribution of inputs and outputs during the 'long period', i.e. on the efficiency pattern of inputs and outputs to integrated processes. Looking at it
this way one should make the following guesses: Prices of finished goods
are positive at least at low rates of profit. If all inputs and outputs are
evenly distributed over the 'long period', i.e. if all machines are of 'constant
physical efficiency', the system should essentially behave like a single
product system: prices in terms of the wage rate are positive and monotonically rising up to some maximum rate of profit. But if the distribution
of inputs is uneven, i.e. if the machines are of variable efficiency, the situation may get more complicated. E.g. if most of the output of an integrated
process is produced at its beginning, this may be of no effect at low rates
of profit, while high rates of profit may cause the value of the product to
fall, even relative to wages.

The possibility of a fall of prices of finished goods in terms of the wage-
rate leads to the possibility of a perverse relationship between the rate of
profit and the wage-rate and is, as we shall see, related to the occurrence of
negative prices of old machines as possible formal solutions of a productive

Fixed Capital as a Joint Product 421

fixed capital system. We do not exclude such negative prices at once as we could do by restricting our attention to the appropriate truncations of a given fixed capital system, because it is on the one hand instructive to discuss the relationship between various efficiency patterns of ageing machines and the positivity of their prices, on the other because negative prices of old machines are economically not inconceivable although they violate conditions of optimality. For we may imagine an economy in which only finished goods are traded in an actual market according to the prices corresponding to the integrated system while old machines always stay with the entrepreneur who first bought them when they were new. The prices of old machines are then nothing but book values which the entrepreneur may fail to ascertain (a negative book value implies that the entrepreneur misses the optimal truncation). It will eventually be proved that price competition in the actual market for finished goods alone leads even in this case to the choice of the superior truncation, but the process of competition may well pass through stages at which the rate of profit is reasonably uniform in the integrated system with prices of finished goods being positive and at which the prices of some old machines (being, according to this special assumption, book values not calculated by any entrepreneur) are negative. It may appear somewhat artificial to assume that prices of finished goods are established on the basis of a proper calculation according to the integrated system approach while book values of old machines are totally neglected, but the hypothesis is not entirely fanciful and it yields some valuable insights. The reader who does not wish to stretch his imagination to this point may, however, regard our consideration of negative prices as a purely mathematical exercise; it will be seen that the more natural assumption of competition with trading of both finished and of intermediate goods in actual markets at positive prices leads eventually to the same superior truncation as that via the trade of finished goods alone.

3. Integrated Systems and Finished Goods

The following two theorems summarize statements which are economically rather obvious from the point of view of the 'long period' (proofs given in the Appendix):

Theorem 3.1:

a) $\tilde{B}(0)$ is equal to the identity matrix.

b) $\det(\tilde{B}(0) - \tilde{A}(0)) \neq 0$, $\sum_{i=1}^{f} (\tilde{b}_i(0) - \tilde{a}_i(0)) \geq 0$.

c) If A, B form an indecomposable system, $\tilde{A}(r)$ is an indecomposable matrix for $r \geq 0$.

d) If all primary processes are indispensable, A, B form an indecomposable system.

e) $(\tilde{B}(0) - \tilde{A}(0))^{-1} > 0$, if A, B form an indecomposable system.

Theorem 3.2:

a) Finished goods are separately producible.
b) All primary processes (except possibly those producing spare parts) are indispensable.
c) Relative prices of finished goods are positive for all r, $0 \leq r \leq R$, where R is the 'maximum rate of profit'. R is positive.
d) There is a unique row vector
   $q > 0$ such that

$$q \, (B - (1 + R) \, A) = 0,$$

i.e. the fixed capital system has a positive 'standard commodity'; $q \, (B - A)$, the 'standard net product', is positive.

Spare parts are defined as finished goods which are used as inputs to secondary processes only. They play a special role because their production may not be necessary if the system as a whole remains productive when secondary processes using them are discontinued or "truncated"; hence the exceptions in theorem 3.2.b.

It is quite puzzling that it has been possible to state two important theorems about the fixed capital system without taking prices of inter-mediate goods explicitly into account. Already at this point we can show moreover that the 'rate of surplus value' is positive and uniform if the wage is a historically given subsistence wage. For it is then consistent to regard the labour force as homogeneous in its consumption pattern. Since the wage-rate is uniform, the workers in every industry will buy a fraction of the total wage $d = (d^1, \ldots, d^n)$ proportional to their number or (what amounts to the same thing) proportional to the labour time necessary in that industry so that the matrix $D = ld$ represents the real wage consumed by the workers in each industry. (This definition depends on the existence of a uniform wage-rate, but not on that of a uniform rate of profit! In this sense the rate of surplus value is 'prior' to, or can be defined independently of, the existence of a uniform rate of profit.) $l_w = Du$, $u = (B - A)^{-1}l$, is then the labour time the workers spend in each industry to earn their living. We assume that the wage consists of finished goods only. Since the labour values of finished goods are positive, and since clearly $d \leq e \, (B - A)$, *it* follows from

$$l_w = (l \, d) \, u = l \, (d \, u) = \alpha \, l$$

$$\alpha = d \, u < e \, (B - A) \, (B - A)^{-1} \, l = e \, l = 1$$

that the labour time the workers have to work for themselves (the 'neces-sary labour time') is a positive fraction of the time they spend working for the capitalists. That is to say, Marx's 'rate of surplus value' $\varepsilon = (1 - \alpha)/\alpha$ is uniform and positive, irrespective of whether the rates of profit are uniform in different industries. (The ratios of profit to wages are different in different industries, of course, if they are measured in price terms at a uniform rate of profit.) Conversely, if the rate of surplus value is positive, and if the rate of profit is known to exist and to be uniform, it must be positive also[3]).

Mr. Sraffa's straight line relationship between wages expressed in terms of the standard commodity $q\,(B-A)$ and a uniform rate of profit r can also be derived without prior knowledge about the behaviour of prices of intermediate goods. If prices are expressed in terms of the standard commodity, i.e. if $q\,(B-A)\,p = 1, 0 \le r \le R$, with q normalized so that $q\mathit{l} = 1$, we have

$$1 = q\,(B-A)\,p = r\,q\,A\,p + w\,q\,\mathit{l} = r\left(\frac{1}{R}\,q\,(B-A)\right)p + w = \frac{r}{R} + w.$$

Therefore, if the rate of profit is given, the 'value' of the wage in terms of the standard commodity equals $w = 1 - r/R$, whatever the goods of which the real wage consists.

The generality of these two results is not as great as might seem at first sight, however; whether there is an unambiguous tradeoff between profits and real wages depends on whether prices of wage goods rise monotonically in terms of the wage-rate as the rate of profit rises. Conditions which will ensure that this fundamental relationship of the theory of distribution holds will be derived presently. They are based on an analysis of prices of intermediate goods.

4. Prices of Intermediate Goods (Old Machines)

To calculate relative prices of intermediate goods is easy because the integrated system determines relative prices of finished goods. The T_i processes of group i

$$(1+r)\,(a_i\,(t)\,p(\,(r) + m_i\,(t-1)\,p_2\,(r)) + w\,\mathit{l}_i\,(t) = b_i\,(t)\,p_1\,(r) + m_i\,(t)\,p_2\,(r),$$

$$t = 1, \ldots, T_i,$$

can be transformed into the recursive relation

$$p_{i,t-1}\,(r) = \frac{1}{1+r}\,(Y_{i,t}\,(r) + p_{i,t}\,(r)), \ t = 1, \ldots, T_i - 1$$

$$p_{i,\,T_i-1}\,(r) = \frac{1}{1+r}\,Y_{i,T_i}\,(r)$$

where the following abbreviations have been used:

$$Y_{i,t}\,(r) = (b_i\,(t) - (1+r)\,a_i\,(t))\,p_1\,(r) - w\,\mathit{l}_i, \ t = 2, \ldots, T_i$$

$$p_{i,t}\,(r) = m_i\,(t)\,p_2\,(r), \ t = 1, \ldots, T_i - 1$$

and where a special notation has to be introduced for $t = 1$: $a_i\,(1)$ denotes the inputs of finished goods to the first process of group i including the

---

[3]) Cf. Morishima (1973).

new machine. Let $\dot{a}_i$ (1) denote the same inputs without the new machine, define

$$Y_{1,1} (r) = (b_i (1) - (1 + r) \dot{a}_i (1)) p_1 - w \, l_i (1)$$

and write $p_{i,0}$ for the price of the new machine (we assume in this section for the sake of simplicity that we can always point to one finished good entering the primary process as being the machine). $p_{i,t} (r)$ is the price of the machine employed by group i in process (or at age) t at rate of profit r. $Y_{i,t} (r)$ equals output produced by the machine employed by group t minus the value of the machine which leaves the process and minus "costs" of wages, profits and circulating capital. It represents the net return gene- rated by the machine at age $t - 1$ and at rate of profit r. The recursive relation means therefore that the price of the $t - 1$ years old machine is equal to that of its discounted output in the current year including the price of the remaining t years old machine. Or, as one could also put it, $Y_{i,t} (r)$ equals the difference between the price (including profits) of the machine entering the process and that of the machine leaving it.

From the recursive formulas one obtains by induction the discounting formula

$$p_{i,t} (r) = \sum_{\tau=1}^{T_i-t} \frac{Y_{i,t+\tau} (r)}{(1 + r)^\tau} \, , \; t = 0, 1, ..., T_i - 1,$$

for the formula holds for $t = T_i - 1$, and supposing that it holds for t, we get (omitting index i):

$$p_{t-1} = \frac{1}{1 + r} (Y_t + p_t) = \frac{1}{1 + r} \left(Y_t + \sum_{\tau=1}^{T_i-t} \frac{Y_{t+\tau}}{(1 + r)^\tau} \right)$$

$$= \frac{Y_t}{1 + r} + \sum_{\tau=1}^{T_i-t} \frac{Y_{t+\tau}}{(1 + r)^{\tau+1}} = \sum_{\tau=0}^{T_i-t} \frac{Y_{t+\tau}}{(1 + r)^{\tau+1}}$$

$$= \sum_{\tau=1}^{T_i-(t-1)} \frac{Y_{t-1+\tau}}{(1 + r)^\tau}$$

The discounting formula for $p_{i,t}$ expresses again that the value of a machine is equal to its discounted future earnings; now, all of them are shown. In the case of the new machine we get

$$p_{i,0} (r) = \frac{Y_{1,1}}{1 + r} + \frac{Y_{1,2}}{(1 + r)^2} + \cdots + \frac{Y_{1,T_i}}{(1 + r)^{T_i}} \, .$$

The price of a new machine is that of a finished good. Both in the original joint production system and in the derived integrated system this price appeared to be determined from the side of 'cost of production', here it seems determined by the sum of 'discounted expected returns'. The

Fixed Capital as a Joint Product 425

equality between 'costs of production' of a machine and its 'expected future earnings' has thus been deduced[4]).

The equality is usually presented as a 'fundamental equilibrium condition' linking the 'past' with the 'future'. However, in a joint production system in a selfreplacing state, it appears not as an assumption but as a consequence of the calculation of prices on the basis of a uniform rate of profit, given the prices of the produced means of production. The 'link between the past and the future' is automatically provided if the rate of profit is uniform for any one period. In a world where competition is so perfect that the prices of old machines are always known, competition will ensure a tendency for the rate of profit to equalize from period to period as in the case of circulating capital.

Although the formula for the equality of the price of a machine with its discounted future earnings should be considered as a consequence of the tendency of rates of profit to equalize rather than as its precondition — at least as long as prices of old machines are known — the formula provides a useful tool in our model, for it allows us to integrate the analysis of the prices of old machines with the known results about the prices of finished goods. First of all, we obviously have:

Theorem 4.1: If net returns are positive at all ages of machine i (if $Y_{1,t}(r) > 0$, $1 \leq t \leq T_1$) at rate of profit r, the machine has positive prices at all ages ($p_{1,t}(r) > 0$, $0 \leq t \leq T_1 - 1$) at rate of profit r.

The result is trivial: if a machine generates a positive income at all ages, its price will be positive.

We shall now define that a machine i is of (initially) rising efficiency in price terms at rate of profit r from age zero up to age θ, if we have

$$Y_{1,1}(r) \leq Y_{1,2}(r) \leq \cdots \leq Y_{1,\theta+1}; \quad 0 \leq \theta \leq T_1 - 1.$$

It is of (eventually) falling efficiency from age θ onwards, if

$$Y_{1,\theta+1} \geq Y_{1,\theta+2} \geq \cdots \geq Y_{1,T1}; \quad 0 \leq \theta \leq T_1 - 1.$$

Efficiency in price terms according to this notion depends on the rate of profit. A machine may be of rising efficiency in price terms throughout its life time at one rate of profit and of falling at another. But the notion does not depend on the chosen standard of prices.

Theorem 4.2: a) If a machine i generates negative returns from age zero to age θ, i.e. if $Y_{1,1} < 0, \ldots, Y_{1,\theta+1} < 0$, prices are positive and rising up to age θ.

---

[4]) The expressions 'cost of production' and 'expected returns' have been put into inverted commas because they may be as misleading as 'supply' and 'demand' in the context of the determination of the price of a basic in a single product Sraffa system (see Sraffa (1960), p. 9), if it is forgotten that 'cost of production' and 'expected returns' are interdependent like 'demand and supply'.

b) If a machine i is of rising efficiency up to age $T_i - 1$ all prices are positive.

Proof: a) By induction, using the recursive formula and the fact that $p_{i,0} > 0$.

b) Use "a" up to the age where $Y_{i,t}$ turns positive, and the discounting formula for $p_{i,t}$ afterwards.

Theorem 4.3: a) If machine i generates negative returns from age θ onwards up to age $T_i - 1$, prices turn negative no later than at age θ.

b) If a machine is of falling efficiency from age θ onwards with net return in the last year still being positive ($Y_{i,T_i} > 0$), prices are falling from age θ onwards.

Proof: a) Using the recursive formula and $p_{i,T_i-1} = \dfrac{Y_{i,T_i-1}}{1+r}$.

b) By induction using the formula:

$$p_{i,t} - p_{i,t-1} = \frac{Y_{i,t+1} - Y_{i,t}}{1+r} + \frac{Y_{i,t+2} - Y_{i,t+1}}{(1+r)^2} + \cdots + \frac{Y_{i,T_i} - Y_{i,T_i-1}}{(1+r)^{T_i-t}} - \frac{Y_{i,T_i}}{(1+r)^{T_i-t+1}}$$

where all terms on the right hand side are negative.

Why are the results about rising and falling efficiency so asymmetrical? Falling efficiency is easy to understand. Prices may turn negative (the machine may reach economic death before it is physically worn out) because the processes using old machines are in fact not indispensable and prices indicate that they have to be eliminated no later than the returns of the machine have turned negative, i.e. no later than the processes have turned unprofitable. A car, for instance, works only at the expense of excessive repairs after some years. (We shall return to this point below.) But machines of rising efficiency may have positive value in real life even before they produce a current positive return if there is sufficient confidence in their future productivity as in the case of a machine under construction. In our model the price is then assured to be positive because we have assumed that the system as a whole is both productive (i.e. capable of producing a surplus) and indecomposable so that each group is indispensable in the system (except possibly spare parts). What the theorem then says is that as long as the processes have not yet begun to yield a return, the machine can not have a negative price.

Although one can easily construct examples which confirm that a machine may be of rising efficiency at one rate of profit and of falling at another, it is to be noted that efficiency can nevertheless be independent of the rate of profit in very special circumstances. Machine i may be said to be of rising physical efficiency, if

Fixed Capital as a Joint Product 427

$$b_1 (1) \leqslant b_1 (2) \leqslant \cdots \leqslant b_1 (T_1), \ a_1 (1) \geqslant a_1 (2) \geqslant \cdots \geqslant a_1 (T_1),$$

$$l_1 (1) \geqslant l_1 (2) \geqslant \cdots \geqslant l_1 (T_1),$$

i.e. if physical output does not fall with age while physical inputs do not rise. Conversely for falling efficiency; the meaning of constant physical efficiency is obvious.

Since prices of finished goods are positive, it follows immediately that rising physical efficiency entails rising efficiency in price terms for all rates of profit. But situations such that rising or falling physical efficiency is unambiguously defined are a priori hardly more likely to occur than are situations in circulating capital systems such that the value of capital can be defined independently of the rate of profit. The Hicksian attempt (Hicks [1970]) to separate 'interindustry relations' (i.e. the analysis of prices in a single product system) from the 'time structure' of fixed capital (i.e. the analysis of the depreciation and the economic lifetime of a machine considering all other prices as given) is therefore apt to be misleading.

The separation of 'interindustry relations' from the 'time structure' of fixed capital is reminiscent of old attempts to reconcile partial and general equilibrium whose aim was to prove that what is true for the individual firms is true for their aggregate as well. E.g. the discounting formula is still often analysed under the assumption that the returns $Y_{1,t}$ are independent of variations of the rate of profit as seems correct from the microeconomic point of view. But this approach leads to conclusions which are the opposite of what holds for the 'macro' system. If $Y_{1,t}$ were constant, the price of a new machine would fall with a rise in the rate of profit. Some neoclassical text-books take this phenomenon which follows at once from microeconomic discounting as a proof for the negative interest elasticity of investment as a whole. But if prices are measured in terms of the wage-rate, the price of the new machine rises, as we shall see (after the appropriate truncation), because at least some of the $Y_{1,t}$ rise more strongly than $(1 + r)^t$. That economists should conclude from the assumption of invariable returns in the recursive formula that the price of a new machine is the less the higher the rate of profit indicates that it is just as dangerous and misleading to teach price theory exclusively from the point of view of the firm as it is false to teach that since a firm may protect itself in the face of a crisis by cutting wages and investment the same must be true for society as a whole.

5. Truncation Theorems

The reduction to integrated processes seems to allow to deal with the question of switching at a given rate of profit in a very simple manner. By means of a slight extension of any of the conventional methods one can prove (using statement "b" of the lemma for the proof of Theorem 3.2 in the Appendix):

Theorem 5.1: If two (or several) alternative integrated processes are given for the production of one finished good and if they are such that each resulting integrated system is productive, indecomposable and has a maximum rate of profit greater than a given rate of profit r, one of these techniques will yield prices in terms of the wage rate at r that are lower than or equal to those of the other technique (s).

The theorem suggests that the choice of techniques in a fixed capital system is determined by relations between finished goods alone. But this can be true only if intermediate goods yielding negative prices can be eliminated from the systems. And the wage-curves of each technique must be shown to be falling monotonically for it could otherwise be possible to increase both the wage and the rate of profit without changing the technique.

Since the wage-goods can reasonably be assumed to consist of finished goods only, the following theorem shows that a falling wage-curve is ensured if negative prices can be ruled out (proof in the Appendix):

Theorem[5]) 5.2: All prices of finished goods in terms of the wage rate $\hat{p}_1 (r) = \frac{p_1}{w}$ rise monotonically with the rate of profit r in a neighbourhood of $r = r_0$, $0 < r_0 < R$, if all prices of intermediate goods are nonnegative at r. More generally we obtain the following relationship for prices $\hat{p}_1$ of finished goods in terms of the wage rate

$$\hat{p}_1 (r_2) > \hat{p}_1 (r_1) \text{ for } r_2 > r_1, \text{ if } p_2 (r_2) > 0, 0 \leqslant r_1 < r_2 \leqslant R.$$

Next we have (proof in the Appendix):

Theorem 5.3: In a stationary state with a given composition of the surplus the ratio P/W of profits P divided by wages W, i.e. the rate of exploitation measured in price terms, rises monotonically with the rate of profit in those ranges of r where all prices are positive.

The main difficulty is now to show that the processes yielding negative prices can actually be eliminated from the system.

If some prices of intermediate goods are negative, some processes obviously have to be replaced or eliminated. It is a most remarkable result that the assumptions of indecomposability and productiveness of the system as a whole are in themselves sufficient to ensure that no new processes have to be brought in: it is possible to scrap or to 'truncate' some machines at any given rate of profit before they are worn out physically and to discontinue the corresponding intermediate processes in such a way that the remaining system is not only again a productive and indecomposable fixed capital system, but in addition yields positive prices.

More specifically: an admissible truncation consists in deleting some intermediate goods from the system together with the processes in which they are used in such a way that (1) if a machine of age t in group i is

---

[5]) For historical references about truncation theorems see Nuti (1973).

scrapped, all machines of ages $t, t+1, \ldots, T_1-1$ and all processes $t+1, t+2, \ldots, T_1$ in group i are eliminated from the system, (2) the resulting system is productive for approriate activity levels. The truncated system is therefore a fixed capital system. For each admissible truncation and for the original system we now draw the wage-curve w (r) where w (r) is the real wage measured in the number of baskets of finished goods that can be bought by one unit of labour at rate of profit r. The truncation is feasible at r if it yields positive prices at r. The truncation which yields the highest real wage at r is called superior at r.

If the superior technique is to be introduced through competition at a given rate of profit, two results have to be shown: Firstly, since finished goods are always traded against money in an actual market, their prices in terms of the wage-rate have to be lowest for the superior technique. (That, at least, is the reason usually put forward to argue why the superior of two alternative techniques in a circulating capital system comes into use. It implies that the superiority of the superior technique does not depend on the standard of the real wage provided it consists of finished goods, and it implies also that the adoption of the superior technique entails surplus profits for those capitalists who are the first to make the transition when the prices corresponding to the old technique are still ruling.) The fact that the composition of the real wage does not affect the ranking of the truncations as to their superiority at a given rate of profit means that the composition of output of finished goods does not affect the choice of truncations, or, to express it in neoclassical terms: a non-substitution theorem holds as far as demand for finished goods is concerned.

Secondly: Intermediate goods need not to be traded in an actual market, their prices may represent pure book-values. However, since the superior technique does not necessarily entail lower prices in terms of the wage-rate for intermediate goods, something else should indicate when truncation is advantageous in a competitive system where intermediate goods are traded to some extent within groups. In fact, we shall prove: the real wage can be raised at some rate of profit in a fixed capital system by truncation, if and only if the prices of some intermediate goods are negative in the untruncated system. And that explains the economic function of the occurrence of negative prices in our model.

The following theorem summarizes the assertions made at some length (proof in the Appendix):

Theorem[6]) 5.4:

1. If and only if some intermediate goods have negative prices at r, $0 \leq r \leq R$, there is a feasible truncation (i.e. with p (r) $\geq$ 0) yielding a higher rate of profit r' at the same real wage per unit of labour.

---

[6]) To each of these results about the rate of profit and the price system there corresponds a dual result about the rate of growth and the quantity system in a theory of steady growth under constant returns to scale.

2. If and only if some intermediate goods have negative prices at $\bar{r}$, $0 \leq \bar{r} \leq R$, there is a feasible truncation at $\bar{r}$ yielding a higher real wage per unit of labour.

3. The truncated system has lower prices of finished goods in terms of the wage-rate at r, if some prices in the original system are negative. Conversely, if prices are not negative in both, prices of finished goods in terms of the wage-rate are lower or equal in the original system.

4. The envelope of the wage-curves corresponding to the fixed capital system and its truncations falls monotonically between $r = 0$ and some greatest 'maximum' rate of profit $\bar{R} \geq R$. The corresponding prices of finished goods in terms of the wage-rate rise monotonically. The technique (original fixed capital system or truncation) appearing on the envelope at a rate of profit r, $0 \leq r \leq \bar{R}$, is feasible (is a productive fixed capital system with nonnegative prices at r and having a maximum rate of profit greater than r).

5. Its vector of prices of finished goods in terms of the wage rate is smaller at r than that of any other technique.

6. If $w\,(r_1) < w\,(r_2)$, $r_2 > r_1$, for a fixed capital system, there exist truncations which are superior at least between $r = r_1$ and the first $r_3 > r_2$ for which $w\,(r_3) \leq w\,(r_1)$.

The theorem exhibits an asymmetry which seems puzzling at first sight. Whenever a truncation is advantageous at a given rate of profit, negative prices of machines will indicate it. But the converse is not true. If a truncated system is given, it may have positive prices, and positive prices then mean that it would be advantageous to reverse the truncation provided the untruncated system also has positive prices.

The apparent paradox is resolved if we think of the truncated system as of an independent fixed capital system on its own. The processes which could be added to it ('grafted' onto it) appear to lie 'without' from this point of view so that the grafted system looks like an alternative technique. The advantage of grafting is therefore only revealed through the possibility of lowering the prices of finished goods in terms of the wage rate. Processes which are candidates for truncation, on the other hand, always lie within the system, so that the advantage of truncation is directly signalled by negative prices of intermediate goods, and is, in addition, but less directly, revealed through the possibility of lowering prices of finished goods in terms of the wage rate.

The pattern of feasible truncations may nevertheless be quite complicated even at one rate of profit; and it changes in an erratical manner if the rate of profit changes. The optimal lifetimes of machines fluctuate accordingly. In consequence, it may easily happen that the truncation chosen at the ruling rate of profit is inefficient when the Golden Rule condition is violated and the rate of growth and the rate of profit diverge. There is then a simple meaning to negative prices. If the rate of profit is 'normal' and the

Fixed Capital as a Joint Product 431

rate of growth is low, say near zero, the technique chosen at the ruling rate of profit may have positive prices and yet be compatible with negative labour values of old machines. The negative labour values clearly indicate that the same net product could be produced with less labour if the old machines having negative values were scrapped. A truncation which is appropriate at the given rate of profit may thus imply a waste of social labour. This solves the 'paradox of negative labour values' and provides a satisfactory explanation for the inefficiency of old machines.

The complicated pattern of truncations finds its most drastic expression in the fact that the return of the same truncation at different intervals of the rate of profit is — contrary to what Nuti [1973], p. 489, 494, emphatically asserts — possible and analogous to reswitching. In the following example involving two finished goods and one intermediate good the truncation is

corn (K)	new machine (M_0)	old machine (M_1)	labour	(K)	(M_0)	(M_1)
1/16	0	0	1/10	0	1	0
1/16	1	0	43/40	1	0	1
1/4	0	1	1	1	0	0

superior between $r = 1/3$ and $r = 1/2$ while the original system is superior between $0 \leq r \leq 1/3$ and $1/2 \leq r \leq R$ (where $3 < R < 4$). Accordingly the price of M_1 is negative between $r = 1/3$ and $r = 1/2$ and positive for $0 \leq r < 1/3$ and $1/2 < r \leq R$. The return of the same truncation is thus possible.

Now it is true that a return of the same truncation cannot occur if a machine is engaged in the production of a finished good i (with price p_i) without using any finished goods as inputs in the last process (which is to be truncated). For if a return of the same truncation were possible in such a case, we should have two intervals $r_1 \leq r \leq r_2$, $r_3 \leq r \leq r_4$, with $0 \leq r_1 < r_2 < r_3 < r_4 \leq R$ such that without loss of generality either the price p_{T-1} of the last machine is positive in the two intervals and negative in between (where it is truncated), or vice versa p_{T-1} is positive in between and negative in the two intervals. In the former case the untruncated system returns, in the latter the truncated system returns.

At any rate we should have $p_{T-1}(r_2) = p_{T-1}(r_3) = 0$ at the switch points r_2, r_3. Since the process T using the machine at age $T-1$ does not require any finished goods as inputs, the equation using the machine at age $T-1$ is

$$(1 + r) p_{T-1} + w \, l(T) = b_i^t(T) p_i.$$

Since at the switch points $p_{T-1}(r) = 0$, we get $p_i(r_3) = p_i(r_2)$, Hw (r_3) $= w(r_2)$. But this is impossible because the switch points are on the envelope. $p_i(r)$ is therefore monotonically rising between r_3 and r_4. A return of truncation cannot occur.

This conclusion does not hold, if process T uses some finished goods as inputs. The absence of the return of the same truncation is therefore most characteristic for one machine systems where a new machine is produced by means of itself and labour in the primary process, and in the secondary process by means of the old machines at various ages and labour alone. The absence of a return of the same truncation is thus analogous to the absence of reswitching in one commodity circulating capital systems.

Nuti and his predecessors were mislead because their analysis is based on one-machine systems. That is capital theory made too easy. Capital theory begins with the recognition that there are several finished goods. The often supposed inverse relationship between the rate of interest and the optimum lifetime of machines does not exist.

Appendix: Proofs of the Mathematical Theorems:

Proof of Theorem 3.1: "a" and "b" are trivial consequences of the corresponding assumptions about A and B, and "e" follows from "a", "b" and "c". To prove "c", suppose, $\tilde{A}$ was decomposable having s rows of zeros in columns $s + 1, s + 2, \ldots, f$ above the diagonal. A and B would then each have zeros in $T_1 + \cdots + T_s$ rows in $f - s$ columns $s + 1, \ldots, f$; i.e. there would be no inputs of finished goods $s + 1, \ldots, f$ to any of the first s groups. On the same rows only $(T_1 - 1) + \cdots + (T_s - 1) = T_1 + \cdots + T_s - s$ intermediate goods would be used or produced, hence $n - f - (T_1 + \cdots + T_s) + s$ columns of intermediate goods would have zeros on these rows, or, taken together, there would be $n - f - (T_1 + \cdots + T_s) + s + f - s = n - (T_1 + \cdots + T_s)$ columns with zeros on the $T_1 + \cdots + T_s$ rows which proves that A, B would form a decomposable system.

To prove "d": if the system was decomposable, there would be a sub-system of s, say, processes and goods such that

$$A = \begin{bmatrix} A_1^1 & 0 \\ A_2^1 & A_2^2 \end{bmatrix}, B = \begin{bmatrix} B_1^1 & 0 \\ B_2^1 & B_2^2 \end{bmatrix}$$

where A_1^1, B_1^1 are quadratic matrices of the same order. Suppose the output of the i-th finished good in the t-th process appeared (after the permutations) in B_1^1. The i-th machine at age $t - 1$ would then have to appear in A_1^1, the i-th machine at age t in B_1^1. In a like way the positive outputs and inputs of the entire i-th group would be found in A_1^1, B_1^1, hence if the i-th process of group i appears in either (A_1^1, B_1^1) or (A_2, B_2), the entire group appears in either (A_1^1, B_1^1) or (A_2, B_2). Therefore there are neither finished nor intermediate groups produced in $B_2^1, B_2^1 = 0$, and it follows that e $(B_1^1 - A_1^1) \geq 0$ where $e = (1, \ldots, 1)$ in contradiction to the assumption.

It is assumed that A, B form a productive, indecomposable system, hence $\tilde{A}(0)$ is an indecomposable matrix.

The following lemma is crucial for the proof of Theorem 3.2:

Fixed Capital as a Joint Product 433

Lemma: There is a root $R > 0$ of the equation $\det(\tilde{B}(r) - (1 + r)\tilde{A}(r)) = 0$ such that

a) $\det(\tilde{B}(r) - (1 + r)\tilde{A}(r)) \neq 0$, $\quad 0 \leq r < R$,
b) $(\tilde{B}(r) - (1 + r)\tilde{A}(r))^{-1} > 0$, $\quad 0 \leq r < R$,
c) the 'eigenvector' $\tilde{q}$ with

$$\tilde{q}(\tilde{B}(R) - (1 + R)\tilde{A}(R)) = 0$$

is positive and unique.

Proof: a) $\tilde{B}(r)$ is a diagonal matrix with positive elements for all non-negative r. The matrix $\hat{A}(r) = (\tilde{B}(r))^{-1}\tilde{A}(r)$ is a semipositive indecomposable matrix for any given r. There is therefore for each given $r > 0$ a unique $\lambda(r) > 0$ and $x(r) > 0$ with

$$\lambda(r) x(r) = (1 + r)\hat{A}(r) x(r)$$

and $\sum_{i=1}^{f} x_i(r) = 1$. By virtue of the preceding theorem

$$\lambda(0) = \lambda(0)\sum_{i=1}^{f} x_i(0) = \sum_{i=1}^{f}\sum_{j=1}^{f} \hat{a}_i^j(0) x_j(0) = \sum_{j=1}^{f}\sum_{i=1}^{f} \tilde{a}_i^j(0) x_j(0) < \sum_{j=1}^{f} x_j(0) = 1.$$

On the other hand $\lambda(r)$ tends to infinity for $r \to \infty$. To prove this, consider

$$\lambda(r) = \lambda(r)\sum_{i=1}^{f} x_i(r) = \sum_{i=1}^{f}(1 + r)\sum_{j=1}^{f} \hat{a}_i^j(r) x_j(r)$$

$$= (1 + r)\sum_{j=1}^{f}\sum_{i=1}^{f} \frac{\sum_{t=1}^{T_i}(1 + r)^{T_i-t} a_i^j(t)}{\sum_{t=1}^{T_i}(1 + r)^{T_i-t} b_i^j(t)} x_j(r).$$

Clearly, the sum should diverge as required if $\sum_{i=1}^{f} a_i^j(1)$ were positive for all j. Unfortunately, all $a_i^j(1)$ may be zero for all i, given j, if commodity j has the character of a "spare part"; i.e. if j is a finished good that is only used as an input in conjunction with old machines. But we have assumed that $a_i(1) \neq 0$ for all i. After suitable rearrangement the first s rows and columns of the (f, f)-matrix $(a_i^j(1))$ will form an indecomposable matrix. We change the normalisation of $x(r)$ to $\sum_{i=1}^{s} x_i(r) = 1$ and get

$$\lambda(r) = \lambda(r)\sum_{i=1}^{s} x_i(r) = (1 + r)\sum_{i=1}^{s}\sum_{j=1}^{f} \hat{a}_i^j(r) x_j(r) \geq (1 + r)\sum_{j=1}^{s}\sum_{i=1}^{s} \hat{a}_i^j(r) x_j(r).$$

Since each column of the matrix $(a_i^j(1))$, $i, j = 1, \ldots, s$, has at least one positive element, there is for each j at least one i such that $(1 + r)\hat{a}_i^j(r)$

is a rational function which tends to infinity as r rises. Hence one can conclude that $\lim_{r \to \infty} \lambda(r) = \infty$, while $\lambda(0) < 1$.

Since all elements of $\hat{A}(r)$ are continuous functions of r and since the dominant root of an indecomposable semipositive matrix is a continuous function of the elements of the matrix, there is a definite smallest positive R such that $\lambda(R) = 1$.

It follows that $\det((\tilde{B}(r) - (1 + r)\tilde{A}(r)) \neq 0$ for $0 \leq r < R$.

b) R is the smallest value for which the dominant root of the indecomposable positive matrix $(1 + r)\hat{A}(r)$ equals one. Hence dom $((1 + r)\hat{A}(r)) < 1$, $(I - (1 + r)\hat{A}(r))^{-1} > 0$ and $(\tilde{B}(r) - (1 + r)\tilde{A}(r))^{-1} = (I - (1 + r)\hat{A}(r))^{-1}(\tilde{B}(r))^{-1} > 0$, $0 \leq r < R$.

c) $\frac{1}{1+R}$ is the dominant root of the matrix $\hat{A}(R)$. R is therefore a simple root of the equation $\det(I - (1 + r)\hat{A}(R)) = 0$ and also of the equation $\det(\tilde{B}(R) - (1 + r)\tilde{A}(R)) = 0$. Consequently, the row vector q solving

$$\tilde{q}(\tilde{B}(R) - (1 + R)\tilde{A}(R)) = 0$$

is unique. By arguments similar to those already used, $\tilde{A}(R)(\tilde{B}(R) - \tilde{A}(R))^{-1}$ exists and is positive. Hence $\tilde{q} > 0$.

Proof of Theorem 3.2: a) Define the row vectors

$$\tilde{q}_i = e_i(\tilde{B}(0) - \tilde{A}(0))^{-1}$$

and the row vectors

$$q_i = (\underbrace{\tilde{q}_i^1, ..., \tilde{q}_i^1}_{T_1}, \underbrace{\tilde{q}_i^2, ..., \tilde{q}_i^2}_{T_2}, ..., \underbrace{\tilde{q}_i^f, ..., \tilde{q}_i^f}_{T_f}); \quad i = 1, ..., f.$$

Clearly, $q_i > 0$, where q_i is the vector of activity levels appropriate for the production of one unit of the i-th finished good.

b) The t-th of the T_i processes in group i cannot be activated without activating processes $1, 2, ..., t - 1$, too, if the net output of intermediate goods is not to contain negative elements. Therefore, if a positive output can be obtained while k primary processes are not activated, the corresponding k groups are not activated and the finished goods to be produced by them are not produced at all. But $\tilde{A}(0)$ is indecomposable. Hence every finished good is an input to some processes, and if a primary process is not activated, it belongs to a group producing a spare part.

c) Follows from the lemma and $\tilde{l}(r) > 0$, $0 \leq r < R$; $r = R$ is obvious.

d) There is a unique $\tilde{q} = (\tilde{q}^1, ..., \tilde{q}^f) > 0$ with $\tilde{q}(\tilde{B}(R) - (1 + R)\tilde{A}(R)) = 0$. It is easily checked that $q(B - (1 + R)A) = 0$ where

$$q = (\tilde{q}^1(1 + R)^{T_1-1}, \tilde{q}^1(1 + R)^{T_1-2}, ..., \tilde{q}^1, \tilde{q}^2(1 + R)^{T_2-1}, ..., \tilde{q}^f).$$

Fixed Capital as a Joint Product 435

To prove that q is unique, note that the rank of the matrix $B - (1 + R) A$ is equal to that of the triangular matrix

$$
F = \left.
\begin{array}{|c|c|}
\hline
\tilde{B}(R) - (1 + R)\,\tilde{A}(R) & \begin{array}{c} 0, \ldots, 0 \\[4pt] 0, \ldots, 0 \end{array} \\
\hline
\begin{array}{l}
b_1(2) - (1 + R)\,a_1(2) \\
\ldots \\
b_1(T_1) - (1 + R)\,a_1(T_1) \\
\ldots \\
b_f(2) - (1 + R)\,a_f(2) \\
\ldots \\
b_f(T_f) - (1 + R)\,a_f(T_f)
\end{array} &
\begin{array}{l}
m_1(2) - (1 + R)\,m_1(1) \\
\ldots \\
- (1 + R)\,m_1(T_1 - 1) \\
\ldots \\
m_f(2) - (1 + R)\,m_f(1) \\
\ldots \\
- (1 + R)\,m_f(T_f - 1)
\end{array} \\
\hline
\end{array}
\right\}
\begin{array}{c} f \\[40pt] n - f \end{array}
= \begin{bmatrix} F_1^1 & 0 \\ F_2^1 & F_2^2 \end{bmatrix}.
$$

$$\underbrace{}_{f} \qquad \underbrace{}_{n-f}$$

The matrix $F_1^1 = \tilde{B}(R) - (1 + R)\,\tilde{A}(R)$ has rank $f - 1$ since $\tilde{q}$ in the preceding lemma was unique. It is easy to see that the rank of the matrix F_2^2 is $n - f$, hence the rank of F is $n - 1$.

Proof of Theorem 5.2: By differentiation of

$$B\,\tilde{p}(r) = (1 + r)\,A\,\tilde{p}(r) + l$$

with respect to r, we get

$$(B - (1 + r)\,A)\frac{d}{dr}\,\tilde{p}(r) = A\,\tilde{p}(r).$$

The system obtained by multiplying each equation by $(1 + r)^{T_1 - t}$ and summing up for each group

$$\sum_{t=1}^{T_i} (1 + r)^{T_1 - t}\left\{ (b_i(t) - (1 + r)\,a_i(t))\frac{d}{dr}\,\hat{p}_1 + (m_i(t) - (1 + r)\,m_i(t - 1))\frac{d}{dr}\,\hat{p}_2 \right\}$$

$$= \sum_{t=1}^{T_i} (1 + r)^{T_1 - t}\,(a_i(t)\,p_1 + m_i(t - 1)\,\hat{p}_2);\ i = 1, \ldots, f;$$

is on the left hand side equal to

$$(\tilde{B} - (1 + r)\,\tilde{A})\frac{d}{dr}\,\hat{p}_1$$

since

$$\sum_{t=1}^{T_i} [m_i(t) - (1 + r)\,m_i(t - 1)]\,(1 + r)^{T_1 - t} = 0.$$

The right hand side is positive if $\hat{p}_2 \geq 0$.

The first assertion then follows from $(\tilde{B} - (1 + r)\,\tilde{A})^{-1} > 0,\ 0 \leq r < R$. The generalization follows by considering the first difference equation $(B - (1 + r_1)\,A)\,(\hat{p}(r_2) - \hat{p}(r_1)) = (r_2 - r_1)\,A\,\hat{p}(r_2)$ instead of the differential equation.

Proof of Theorem 5.3: If the total labour is numerically equal to unity, the sum of wages is numerically equal to the wage rate and

$$\frac{P}{W} = e\,(B - A)\,\frac{P}{w} - 1$$

where $e = (1, \ldots, 1)$. Now $e\,(B^2 - A^2) = 0$, since there is no net output of intermediate goods in the stationary state, therefore

$$\frac{P}{W} = e\,(B^1 - A^1)\,\hat{p}^1 - 1,$$

where $\tilde{p}_1$ rises monotonically with r if $\hat{p} > 0$.

Proof of Theorem 5.4: a) We start by proving (2) for $0 \leq \bar{r} < R$. Let the n-rowvector $d = (d_1, \ldots, d_f, 0, \ldots, 0)$ denote the basket of finished goods of which the total real wage at $r = \bar{r}$ consists. Of course, $0 \leq d \leq e\,(B - A)$.

The system

$$\left(A + \frac{1}{1 + \bar{r}}\,l\,d,\ B,\ l\right)$$

fulfills the formal requirements for a fixed capital system. It has a maximum rate of profit which must be equal to $\bar{r}$ since $\det\,(B - (1 + \bar{r})\,A - l\,d) = 0$ and $\det\,(B - (1 + r)\,A - l\,d) \neq 0$, $0 \leq r < \bar{r}$: Hence there are unique vectors $q > 0$ and $p = p\,(\bar{r})$ such that

$$q\,(B - (1 + \bar{r})\,A) = d,$$
$$(B - (1 + \bar{r})\,A)\,p = l.$$

Consider

$$\text{Max. } dx!\ \text{s.t. } (B - (1 + \bar{r})\,A,\ x \leq l,\ x \geqslant 0,$$
$$\text{Min. } y\,l!\ \text{s.t.} y\,(B - (1 + \bar{r})\,A) \geqq d,\ y \geqslant 0.$$

In this linear programme (it would also be possible to use the von Neumann model) any sufficiently small positive vector is feasible in the primal because $l > 0$ while q is feasible in the dual. The programme has therefore semi-positive solutions $\bar{x}, \bar{y}$. If $\bar{y} > 0$, there are equalities everywhere in the primal, hence $\bar{x} = p$ which is impossible since $p = p\,(\bar{r})$ is not semi-positive by assumption. Hence $\bar{y}$ is not positive. Delete all processes with activity levels which are not positive in $\bar{y}$. If an activity, say the t-th process in the i-th group, is deleted, the intermediate product produced by it (the i-th machine at age t) disappears from the system. Because $\bar{y}\,(b^j - (1 + r)\,a^j) \geq 0$, if j denotes an intermediate product, processes $t + 1, t + 2, \ldots,$ T_i in group i disappear as well. On the other hand $\bar{y}\,(B - A) \geq 0$. Hence no primary processes are deleted, primary processes being indispensable if no spare parts exist. (We assume this for brevity as we also assumed for brevity that A, B form an indecomposable system.)

If truncation occurs in group i, it involves deleting processes $t, t + 1,$ $\ldots, T_i$ where $t \geq 2$, while the machine of age $t - 1$ appears overproduced

Fixed Capital as a Joint Product 437

and fetches a zero price by virtue of the balancing theorem. Deleting the unutilized processes together with the intermediate goods used and produced by them from matrices A and B leads thus to a truncated system $\bar{A}, \bar{B}$ where $\bar{A}, \bar{B}$ are square matrices. Deleting the corresponding elements in $\bar{y}, \bar{x}, l$ leads to vectors $\bar{q} > 0$, $\bar{p} \geq 0$, $\bar{l}$ where

$$\bar{p} = (\bar{B} - (1 + \bar{r}) \bar{A})^{-1} \bar{l}$$

because $\bar{q} > 0$. $\bar{A}, \bar{B}$ have the same structure as a fixed capital system, and they are indecomposable because of the indispensability of the primary processes.

We now show that $\bar{A}, \bar{B}$ form a productive fixed capital system with a maximum rate of profit greater than $\bar{r}$. Let $C(r)$, $D(r)$ denote the integrated system of $\bar{A}, \bar{B}$, and $\hat{C}(r) = (D(r))^{-1} C(r)$. Denote the row vector consisting of the first f components of p by $\bar{p}_1$. Because $(1 + \bar{r}) \hat{C}(\bar{r}) \bar{p}_1 \leq \bar{p}_1$; $\bar{p}_1 \geq 0$, the dominant root dom $((1 + \bar{r}) \hat{C}(\bar{r}))$ of the indecomposable semipositive matrix $(1 + \bar{r}) \hat{C}(\bar{r})$ is smaller than one. Suppose dom $((1 + r) \hat{C}(\bar{r})) = 1$ for $r = \bar{r}$. We know from part (c) of the proof of the lemma and from (d) of the proof of the subsequent theorem that we should then have a row-vector $q > 0$ such that

$$(1 + \hat{r}) \hat{q} \bar{A} = \hat{q} \bar{B}.$$

But since

$$(1 + \bar{r}) \bar{A} \bar{p} \leqslant \bar{B} \bar{p}$$

$$(1 + \bar{r}) \hat{q} \bar{A} \bar{p} < \hat{q} \bar{B} \bar{p} = (1 + \hat{r}) \hat{q} \bar{A} \bar{p}$$

it follows that $\hat{r} > \bar{r}$. This establishes at the same time that the 'maximum' rate of profit of the system $\bar{A}, \bar{B}$ is greater than $\bar{r}$ and that it is a productive system since dom $(1 + r) \hat{C}(r)$ is continuous hence smaller than one, $0 \leq r < \bar{r}$. Thus, $\bar{A}, \bar{B}, \bar{l}$ are a feasible truncation. We have $(d_1, \ldots, d_f)$ $(\bar{p}_1, \ldots, \bar{p}_f) = \bar{q} \bar{l} < q l = d p$ so that the real wage per unit of labour has risen. This proves the first part of (2).

Conversely (using the same notation): if a truncation is possible which increases the real wage, we have $\bar{y} \geq 0$, where $\bar{y}$ is not positive, and

$$\bar{y} (B - (1 + \bar{r}) A) \geqslant d.$$

Suppose $p = (B - (1 + \bar{r}) A)^{-1} l \geq 0$. We get

$$\bar{y} (B - (1 + \bar{r}) A) p \geqslant dp.$$

The left hand side equals $\bar{y} l$, the right hand side $q l$, hence $\bar{y} l \geq q l$ and $\bar{y}$ is not optimal which is a contradiction.

b) Only techniques with nonnegative prices appear on the envelope of the wage-curves for all truncations and given d because of (2). This is clear for $0 \leq r < \bar{R}$, but it must also be true for $r = \bar{R}$, for if the technique appearing at $\bar{R}$ had a negative price, this would also be the case in contradiction to (2) at $r = \bar{R} - \varepsilon$ for some $\varepsilon > 0$ sufficiently small that the technique on the envelope was unchanged. This proves (4) by virtue of the preceding theorem.

(1) is then easily derived from (2) and (4); it could also be proved in a similar way as (2) was proved under (a) using the extremality properties of the von Neumann system instead of linear programming.

c) We shall now vary the composition of the real wage to prove (3). Suppose the wage-curve for a feasible technique I was higher than that of an admissible technique II at $r = \bar{r}$, and I was a truncation of II. Since technique II must then have some negative prices for intermediate goods at $\bar{r}$, it has to remain inferior whatever finished goods enter the real wage. Prices do not depend on the composition of the wage. Hence prices of finished goods in terms of the wage rate are lower for technique I, i.e. $\hat{p}_1^I < \hat{p}_1^{II}$. Conversely: if I is a feasible technique and is a truncation of a feasible technique II, the real wage of II must be at least as high as that of I, whatever its composition, hence $\hat{p}_1^I \geq \hat{p}_1^{II}$.

d) Now suppose there are two feasible techniques at $\bar{r}$ such that neither is superior to the other, i.e. such that neither $\hat{p}_1^I \leq \hat{p}_1^{II}$ nor $\hat{p}_1^{II} \leq \hat{p}_1^I$. We have to show that if no technique, III, with either $\hat{p}_1^{III} \leq \hat{p}_1^I$ or $\hat{p}_1^{III} \leq \hat{p}_1^{II}$ or both exists, a contradiction follows.

Since $\hat{p}_1^I > 0$, $\hat{p}_1^{II} > 0$, $f \geq 2$ ($f = 1$ is trivial), one can choose a d $= (d_1, \ldots, d_f, 0, \ldots, 0)$ such that $(d_1, \ldots, d_f) \hat{p}_1^I = (d_1, \ldots, d_f) \hat{p}_1^{II}$. Let p_1 be the price vector of finished goods of the original system, and $\delta = d\,\hat{p}_1$. The vector $(1/\delta)$ d can then be taken as the real wage which appears in the linear programme in (a). Under the assumptions stated, both techniques I and II yield solutions to this programme. Vectors of activity levels y^I and y^{II}, and of prices, x^I and x^{II}, correspond to these solutions. The vectors $\frac{1}{2} x^I + \frac{1}{2} x^{II}, \frac{1}{2} y^I + \frac{1}{2} y^{II}$, are then solutions, too. They define a feasible technique, III, of which I and II are both truncations since an activity level in III is positive if it is positive in either I or II. III is feasible at $\bar{r}$. But then $\hat{p}_1^{III} \leq \hat{p}_1^I$, $\hat{p}_1^{III} \leq \hat{p}_1^{II}$ by virtue of (3) in contradiction to the assumption. (6) follows from theorems 5.2 and 5.4, (2), for p_2 (r) can not be positive at any $r > r_1$ where $w(r) > w(r_1)$.

References

P. Garegnani (1970), Heterogeneous Capital, the Production Function and the Theory of Distribution; Review of Economic Studies, XXXVII, pp. 407–436.

J. Hicks (1970), A Neo-Austrian Growth Theory; Economic Journal, LXXX, pp. 257–281.

Fixed Capital as a Joint Product 439

J. Mirrlees (1969), The Dynamic Nonsubstitution Theorem; Review of Economic Studies, XXXVI, pp. 67—76.

M. Morishima (1973), Marx's Economics; Cambridge: University Press.

D. M. Nuti (1970), Capitalism, Socialism and Steady Growth; Economic Journal LXXX, pp. 32—57.

D. M. Nuti (1973), On the Truncation of Production Flows; Kyklos, XXVI, pp. 485—494.

B. Schefold (1971), Theorie der Kuppelproduktion, Basel (private print).

B. Schefold (1976, a), Nachworte; in P. Sraffa (1976); pp. 129—226.

B. Schefold (1976, b), Relative Prices as a Function of the Rate of Profit; Zeitschrift für Nationalökonomie. XXXVI, pp. 21—48.

B. Schefold (1976, c), Different Forms of Technical Progress; Economic Journal, LXXXVI, pp. 806—819.

B. Schefold (1977, a), Reduction to Dated Quantities of Labour, Roundabout Processes and Switches of Technique in Fixed Capital Systems; to appear in Metroeconomica.

B. Schefold (1977, b), Multiple Product Techniques with Properties of Single Product Systems; to appear in Zeitschrift für Nationalökonomie.

P. Sraffa (1960), Production of Commodities by Means of Commodities; Cambridge: University Press.

P. Sraffa (1976), Warenproduktion mittels Waren; Frankfurt: Suhrkamp Verlag (German translation of the above).

J. E. Stiglitz (1970), Non-Substitution Theorems with Durable Capital Goods; Review of Economic Studies, XXXVII, pp. 543—553.

Summary

In this multisector model where fixed capital is the only kind of joint product the interaction between 'interindustry relations' and the 'time structure of capital' is shown to be such that the latter is economically inseparable from the former (e.g. return of the same truncation analogous to reswitching is possible if there are several machines). In a productive fixed capital system prices of consumption goods, raw materials and machines are (after the appropriate truncation) positive, independent of demand, and rising in terms of the wage rate while those of old machines may fluctuate.

Zusammenfassung

In diesem Multisektorenmodell erscheint fixes Kapital als das einzige Kuppelprodukt. Es wird gezeigt, daß die Beziehungen zwischen verschiedenen Industrien und die zeitliche Struktur des Kapitals sich nicht voneinander trennen lassen (was z.B. bedeutet, daß eine Wiederkehr derselben Prozeßdauer in Analogie zur Wiederkehr derselben Technik in Einzelproduktsystemen möglich ist). In einem produktiven System mit fixem Kapital sind die Preise von Konsumgütern, Rohmaterialien und Maschinen nach Bestimmung der korrekten Prozeßdauer positiv und unabhängig von der Nachfrage. Ausgedrückt in der Lohnrate steigen sie monoton, während diejenigen alter Maschinen fluktuieren können.

Prof. Dr. Bertram Schefold, Institut für Markt und Plan der J. W. Goethe-Universität, Schumannstr. 60, 6000 Frankfurt am Main

[12]

Vol. 48 (1988), No. 1, pp. 1—17

Journal of Economics
Zeitschrift für Nationalökonomie
© by Springer-Verlag 1988

Fixed Capital Within the Sraffa Framework

By

Neri Salvadori, Naples, Italy*

(Received September 22, 1987)

1. Introduction

Von Neumann (1936) and Sraffa (1960) have both revised the "old classical idea" of treating old machines left at the end of each period as an economically different good from the machines which entered the production at the beginning of the period. But whereas the literature on von Neumann models never tried — as far as I know — to construct models with fixed capital as explicitly distinguished from other kinds of joint products, Baldone (1980), Schefold (1976, 1978, 1980b) and Varri (1980) did this within the Sraffa framework. However, these authors have dealt only with the even more special case of the existence of no more than one machine for each process of production.[1] This paper is devoted to

---

* This paper was financed by C. N. R. (the Italian National Research Council) with Contract No. CT 82.0067.10. A complete draft was written while I was Visiting Professor at the University of Paris X at Nanterre. I would like to thank the C. N. R. and the Univerity of Paris X for financial support and for providing a very stimulating research climate. Thanks are also given to Ch. Bidard (University of Paris X) for very useful comments to a previous version. Usual caveats apply.

[1] The few remarks dealing with jointly used machines contained in Baldone (1980), Schefold (1977, 1980b), Varri (1980) are false, as will be clear from examples presented in Section 5. Schefold (1976) is more accurate and avoids dealing with this issue. However, these remarks could be taken as correct if they refer to the special case in which several "new machines" are assembled to constitute a "plant", which is then treated as a single entity, so that, in this sense, a unique "used machine" is produced and utilized (see Salvadori, 1987).

2   N. Salvadori:

analyze jointly utilized machines. Some novel results emerge. Among these, the fact that the growth rate can play a role in determining the cost minimizing technique and, therefore, the prices in the long run. Nevertheless, the requirements for consumption do not matter in determining prices or operated processes.

From a formal point of view, the paper provides some axiomatic definitions of fixed capital technologies and some theorems exploring these concepts within the Sraffa framework. Definitions are introduced by assuming the possibility of partitioning the set of commodities and the set of processes in order to satisfy certain properties. If this is obtainable, then the subsets defined by these properties can be interpreted as "used machine set" and "final good set". This procedure allows us to avoid, in defining fixed capital models, the use of not previously defined words like "machine", which might transform the definition into a dubious one.

Several sets of assumptions are investigated. The first is formalizing only the non-transferability of used machines among sectors with no joint production of final goods. Some theorems show that in this quite general case prices are independent from consumption habits even if they may not be independent from the growth rate and do not need to be unique (but they do if the profit rate equals the growth rate).

Another set of assumptions formalizes the already studied situation when only a single used machine is allowed in each process and these machines can be ordered in the sense that each has an unambiguous age. The usual non-substitution results (prices are independent both from consumption habits and from the growth rate, and are uniquely determined) are, in this case, easily obtained both for the sake of completeness and as an introduction to some numerical examples which show the limits of validity, not always clearly stated and sometimes confused, of the usual results.

Two other sets of assumptions extend the previous models to introduce the possibility of fully utilized scrap. The previous results are restated in these cases.

2. Fixed Capital Technology

It is assumed throughout the paper that there exist m perfectly divisible processes and n perfectly divisible commodities. Each process of production i ($i = 1, 2, \ldots, m$) is defined by the triplet

Fixed Capital Within the Sraffa Framework   3

(a^i, b^i, l_i) where $a^i = (a_{i1}, a_{i2}, \ldots, a_{in})^T$ is the nonnegative[2] material input vector, $b^i = (b_{i1}, b_{i2}, \ldots, b_{in})^T$ is the nonnegative output vector, and l_i, a scalar, is the nonnegative labour input. Thus, the whole technology is defined by the triplet (A, B, l), where

$$A = (a^1, a^2, \ldots, a^m)^T$$
$$B = (b^1, b^2, \ldots, b^m)^T$$
$$l = (l_1, l_2, \ldots, l_m)^T.$$

The following assumptions are usually assumed to hold:

Assumption 1: It is not possible to produce something without using capital, i.e.,

$$e_j^T A \geq 0 \qquad j = 1, 2, \ldots, m.$$

Assumption 2: All commodities are producible, i.e.,

$$B e_j \geq 0 \qquad j = 1, 2, \ldots, n.$$

Assumption 3: Labour is indispensable for the reproduction of commodities, i.e.,

$$(x \geq 0, x^T(B - A) \gneq 0) \to x^T l > 0.$$

Up to now we have not introduced the assumptions regarding technology which will be explored in this paper. The *non-transferable fixed capital* assumption holds if

Assumption 4: There exist two subsets, S and T, of the set of commodities N such that:

(A.4.1) $S \cap T = \varnothing$, $S \cup T = N$;

(A.4.2)   Commodities in T are never consumed;

(A.4.3)   Each process produces one and only one commodity in S;

(A.4.4)   If commodity $i \in T$ is produced by process j producing commodity $h \in S$, then there exists no process producing a commodity $k \in S$, $k \neq h$, such that either it produces i or it utilizes i as an input;

(A.4.5)   For each process producing commodity $j \in T$ there

---

[2] The following conventions for vector inequalities are used: $x \geq y$ if $(\forall i)\ x^T e_i \geq y^T e_i$, $x \gneq y$ if $x \geq y$ and $x \neq y$, and $x > y$ if $(\forall i)\ x^T e_i > y^T e_i$, where e_i is the i-th unit vector. If $x \geq 0$ $(x \gneq 0, x > 0)$, x will be said to be *nonnegative (semipositive, positive)*.

4   N. Salvadori:

exists a process with the same inputs and the same
outputs except that commodity j is not produced.

For the sake of simplicity we can refer to the commodities in T
as "used machines" and the commodities in S as "final goods". If
this is done, the rationale of Axiom (A.4.1) is that a commodity is
either a used machine or a final good, but never both; the rationale
of Axiom (A.4.2) is that used machines are never consumed; the
rationale of Axiom (A.4.3) is that no joint production is super-
imposed; the rationale of Axiom (A.4.4) is that used machines
cannot be transferred among sectors; Axiom (A.4.5) states that
used machines can be eliminated with no cost and no scrap.

If Assumption 4 holds, then we reorder commodities and
processes in the following way: the first s commodities are in S,
then t_1 commodities are in T and are produced jointly with
Commodity 1, then t_2 commodities are in T and are produced
jointly with Commodity 2, ..., then t_s commodities are in T and are
produced jointly with Commodity s, some t_i may be equal to zero,
$t_1 + t_2 + ... + t_s = t$, $s + t = n$; the first m_1 processes produce
Commodity 1, then m_2 processes produce Commodity 2, ..., then
m_s processes produce Commodity s, $m_1 + m_2 + ... + m_s = m$. In
order to simplify notation, let us also introduce $t_0 = 0$ and $m_0 = 0$.
Therefore, if $j \in S$, $b_{ij} > 0$ if and only if $\sum_{k=0}^{j-1} m_k < i \le \sum_{k=0}^{j} m_k$; and if
$j \in S$ and $s + \sum_{k=0}^{j-1} t_k < h \le s + \sum_{k=0}^{j} t_k$, then $b_{ih} > 0$ or $a_{ih} > 0$ only if
$\sum_{k=0}^{j-1} m_k < i \le \sum_{k=0}^{j} m_k$.

The *one non-transferable machine* assumption holds if

Assumption 5: Assumption 4 holds and:

(A.5.1)   Each process produces no more than one commodity in
            T;

(A.5.2)   Each process utilizes no more than one commodity in T
            as an input;

(A.5.3)   There exists a natural number z such that the set of
            used machines T can be partitioned in z subsets T_1, T_2,
            ..., T_z in such a way that used machines in T_1 are
            produced without utilizing used machines, and each
            used machine in T_i ($i = 2, 3, ..., z$) is produced utilizing
            a used machine in T_{i-1}, with $T_i \cap T_j = \emptyset$ ($i \ne j$), and
            $\bigcup_{i=1}^{z} T_i = T$.

Fixed Capital Within the Sraffa Framework 5

For the sake of simplicity the commodities in T_i can be called *i year old machines*.

The following examples are to clarify the power of the definitions adopted.

Example 1: There exist two commodities whose production patterns are represented by Table 1 (+ is for a positive number); only Commodity 1 is consumed.

Table 1. *Input-Output Patterns of Example 1*

Processes	Commodity inputs (1)	(2)	Labour input		Commodity outputs (1)	(2)
(1)	+	+	+	→	+	+
(2)	+	+	+	→	+	+

It is easily recognized that Assumption 4 holds. Commodity 1 is a final good and Commodity 2 is a used machine. If both commodities were consumed, then technology would be a wool-meat type joint production one.

Example 2: There exist four commodities whose production patterns are represented by Table 2; only Commodity 3 is consumed.

Table 2. *Input-Output Patterns of Example 2*

Processes	Commodity inputs (1)	(2)	(3)	(4)	Labour input		Commodity output (1)	(2)	(3)	(4)
(1)	+	+	0	y_1	+	→	+	0	0	y_3
(2)	+	+	0	y_2	+	→	0	+	0	y_4
(3)	+	0	0	z_1	+	→	0	0	+	+
(4)	0	+	0	z_2	+	→	0	0	+	+
(5)	0	0	0	+	+	→	0	0	+	z_3

It is easily recognized that if $y_i = z_j = 0$, each i, each j, then Assumption 5 holds. Commodities 1, 2 and 3 are final goods and Commodity 4 is a one year old used machine. Nevertheless, it is unclear if there is a *new* machine: in Assumption 5 there is, in fact, no need for the concept of *new machine*. If $y_i = 0$, each i, and $z_j > 0$, some j, then Assumption 4 holds, but Assumption 5 does not. If $y_i > 0$, some i, then Assumption 4 does not hold.

6   N. Salvadori:

3. Sraffa Framework

A system of production is defined as a set of n processes of production — n being the number of commodities involved — that satisfy requirements for use, i.e., as a triplet $(\hat{A}, \hat{B}, \hat{l})$ such that $\hat{A} = (a^{i_1}, a^{i_2}, \ldots, a^{i_n})^T$, $\hat{B} = (b^{i_1}, b^{i_2}, \ldots, b^{i_n})^T$, $\hat{l} = (l_{i_1}, l_{i_2}, \ldots, l_{i_n})^T$, and there exists a nonnegative vector x such that

$$x^T(\hat{B} - \hat{A}) = d^T \tag{1}$$

where d are the requirements for use; d does not need to be constant and can be a function of process intensities, prices, wage rate and profit rate, matrices $\hat{A}$ and $\hat{B}$ and vector $\hat{l}$.

The price vector p and wage rate w of system of production (A, B, l) are defined, for a given rate of profit r, by equations

$$\hat{B}p = (1+r)\hat{A}p + w\hat{l} \tag{2}$$

$$e^T p = 1. \tag{3}$$

A *cost-minimizing system of production* is a system whose prices are such that no existing process is able to pay extra profits, i.e., $(\hat{A}, \hat{B}, \hat{l})$ is a cost-minimizing system at the rate of profit r if

$$Bp \leq (1+r)Ap + wl \tag{4}$$

where p and w satisfy equations (2) and (3) and B, A, l are as defined in Section 2.

Sraffa (1960, p. 43f.) mentions the "requirements for use", but they are not introduced by him in the formal analysis. This is so (Salvadori, 1982, 1985) because whereas the requirements for use are relevant for the choice of technique when joint production is involved this is a problem not really analyzed by Sraffa (see Sraffa, 1960, pp. 80—87; and Salvadori, 1985, pp. 163—164). It will be shown in this paper that if fixed capital with no superimposed joint production is introduced, then the growth rate (i.e., the requirements for investment) may play a role, but the requirements for consumption cannot (except for the axiom that used machines are not consumed). Moreover, the introduction of requirements for consumption as a function of incomes and prices involve further hypotheses which are never mentioned by Sraffa. Thus, it will be assumed throughout the paper that the requirements for consumption are represented as a given vector. The generalization to the more realistic cases in which consumption is a function of prices and incomes can be easily obtained following

Fixed Capital Within the Sraffa Framework   7

a procedure utilized in another paper (Salvadori, 1986). Hence d in equation (1) is defined as

$$d^T = gx^T A + c^T \tag{5}$$

where g is the growth rate and c is a given vector whose first s entries are nonnegative and the last t entries equal zero because of Axiom (A.4.2).

4. Main Results

Before going to state conditions for the existence and uniqueness of a cost-minimizing technique some Lemmata will be introduced.

Lemma 1: If the following Assumption 6 holds, and if $g \leq r$, then the following system of equations and inequalities has a solution:

$$[B - (1+r)A]y \leq l$$
$$q^T[B - (1+g)A] \geq a^T$$
$$q^T[B - (1+r)A]y = q^T l \tag{6}$$
$$q^T[B - (1+g)A]y = a^T y$$
$$q \geq 0, \quad y \geq 0$$

where a is a given semipositive vector.

Assumption 6: There exists an m-vector z such that

$$z \geq 0, \quad z^T[B - (1+r)A] > 0.$$

A constructive proof to Lemma 1 can be found in Salvadori (1980, Theorem 4.2).

Lemma 2: Let Assumptions 1—4 and 6 hold, let $g \leq r$, and let (q^*, y^*) be a solution to system (6) for $a = \hat{a}$, where $\hat{a}$ is a vector with each of the first s elements being equal to 1, each of the others being equal to 0. Then, there exists a vector q^{**} such that (q^{**}, y^*) is a solution to system (6) for $a = c$ $(c_1, c_2, \ldots, c_s, 0, 0, \ldots, 0)^T$, where $c_i \geq 0$ $(i \in \{1, 2, \ldots s\})$ and $\sum_{i=1}^{s} c_i > 0$.

Proof: Let $Q = [q_{hk}]$ be an $s \times m$ matrix such that

$$q_{hk} = \begin{cases} e_h^T q^* & \text{if } \sum_{i=0}^{k-1} m_i < h \leq \sum_{i=0}^{k} m_i \\ 0 & \text{elsewhere} \end{cases}$$

8   N. Salvadori:

Let us define the matrices D_0, C_0, D_1, C_1, obtained by the following partition of matrices QA and QB: $(D_0, D_1) = QB$, $(C_0, C_1) = QA$, C_0 and D_0 being square. Since Assumption 4 holds and since the first s entries of $\hat{a}$ are positive, all the others being equal to zero,

D_0, C_0, D_1, C_1 are nonnegative, D_0 is diagonal, diag $D_0 > 0$;   (7)

$$[D_0 - (1+r) C_0] y_s^* + [D_1 - (1+r) C_1] y_t^* = Ql;$$ (8)

$$[D_1 - (1+g) C_1] \geq 0, \quad [D_1 - (1+g) C_1] y_t^* = 0;$$ (9)

$$e^T [D_0 - (1+g) C_0] \geq e^T;$$ (10)

where $(y_s^{*T}, y_t^{*T}) = y^{*T}$. It is immediately recognized, because of (9), that if there exists a nonnegative solution v^* to the equation

$$v^T [D_0 - (1+g) C_0] = \bar{c}^T,$$

where $\bar{c}^T = (c_1, c_2, \ldots, c_s)$, then $q^{**} = Q^T v^*$ satisfy the Lemma.

To prove that v^* exists it is enough to apply the Theorem of Perron-Frobenius on nonnegative matrices to the square matrix $C_0 D_0^{-1}$ to obtain, because of inequality (10) and since $e > 0$, that matrix $[D_0 - (1+g) C_0]$ is invertible and

$$[D_0 - (1+g) C_0]^{-1} \geq 0$$ (11)

Q. E. D.

Lemma 3: Let Assumptions 1—4 and 6 hold and let $y^* = (y_s^{*T}, y_t^{*T})^T$ be defined as in Lemma 2, then $y_s^* > 0$ and the weak inequality (10) is satisfied as an equation.

Proof: Let (q_i^{**}, y^*) be a solution to system (6) for $a = e_i$, $i \in \{1, 2, \ldots, s\}$. Thus,

$$q_i^{**T} [B - (1+g) A] y^* = e_i^T y^*$$

$$q_i^{**T} [B - (1+r) A] y^* = q_i^{**T} l$$

i.e.,

$$e_i^T y^* = q_i^{**T} l + (r-g) q_i^{**T} A y^*.$$

Then, the first part of the Lemma is obtained since $(r-g) \geq 0$ and $q_i^{**T} l > 0$ because of Assumption 3. The second part of the Lemma is an immediate consequence of the first part.   Q. E. D.

Lemma 4: Let Assumptions 1—4 and 6 hold, and let $g \leq r$; then the following system has a solution:

$$[B - (1+r) A] y \leq l;$$ (12.1)

$$q^T [B - (1+g) A] = c^T;$$ (12.2)

Fixed Capital Within the Sraffa Framework   9

$$q^T [B - (1+r)A] y = q^T l;$$ (12.3)

$$q \geqq 0, \quad y \geqq 0.$$ (12.4)

Proof: It is a direct consequence of Lemma 2 and Axiom (A.4.5).

Q. E. D.

Lemma 5: Let (q^*, y^*) be a solution to system (12) with as less positive entries of vector q^* as possible. Then the number of operated processes is less than or equal to n.

Proof: It is sufficient to prove that the rows of matrix $[B - (1+g)A]$ correspondent to positive entries of q^* are linearly independent. Let $[\bar{B} - (1+g)\bar{A}]$ be a matrix arranged with these rows and assume that there exist $\bar{z} \neq 0$ such that

$$\bar{z}^T [\bar{B} - (1+g)\bar{A}] = 0.$$

Then $(q^* + \lambda z, y^*)$ is still a solution to system (12) for $\lambda \neq 0$ but close enough to zero, where z is an m-vector obtained by augmenting $\bar{z}$ with zeros. As a consequence it is possible to find λ^* such that $q^* + \lambda^* z$ is still semipositive, but has a zero entry more than q^*. Hence a contradiction.

Lemma 6: In the assumptions of Lemma 4, there exists a solution (q^*, y^{**}) to system (12) such that the number of weak inequalities which are satisfied as equations in (12.1) is larger or equal to n.

Proof: Let

$$[B^0 - (1+r)A^0] y^{**} = l^0$$

be such equations. Hence, it is enough to prove that if the rank of matrix $[B^0 - (1+r)A^0]$ is less than n, then the number of weak inequalities which are satisfied as equations in (12.1) can be increased by a change of y^{**}, q^* being unchanged. Then, assume that there exists a vector $v \neq 0$ such that

$$[B^0(1+r)A^0] v = 0.$$

Since Axiom (A.4.5) holds, if $e_i^T y^{**} = 0$, then $e_i^T v = 0$. As a consequence, $(q^*, y^{**} + \lambda v)$ is still a solution to system (12) for $\lambda \neq 0$ and close enough to zero. Hence, it is possible to find λ^{**} such that $y^{**} + \lambda^{**} v$ is still semipositive and such that either (i) it has a zero entry more than y^{**}, or (ii) a further weak inequality in (12.1) is satisfied as an equation. To prove the Lemma we just need to remark that statement (i) is a special case of (ii) because of Axiom (A.4.5) and Lemma 3.   Q. E. D.

10   N. Salvadori:

Theorem 1: If Assumptions 1—4 hold, then Assumption 6 is sufficient for the existence of a cost-minimizing system. The choice of
cost-minimizing systems is independent from the other properties
of vector $c [c^T = (c_s^T, c_t^T): c_s \geqslant 0, c_t = 0]$.

Proof: Since Lemmas 4, 5 and 6 hold, we can pick up n processes
in order to make up the system of production $(\hat{A}, \hat{B}, \hat{I})$ such that
equations (1), (2), (3), (5) and inequality (4) are satisfied.   Q. E. D.

Lemma 7: In the assumptions of Lemma 2, if $g = r$ and u is any
vector such that

$$u \geq 0, \quad [B - (1 + r)A]u \leq l.$$

Then $u_s \leq y_s^*$, where $(u_s^T, u_t^T)^T = u$ and $(y_s^{*T}, y_t^{*T})^T = y^*$.

Proof: Since

$$[D_0 - (1 + r) C_0] u_s + [D_1 - (1 + r) C_1] u_t \leq Ql$$

holds, we obtain, also because of inequality (9), that

$$[D_0 - (1 + r) C_0] u_s \leq Ql.$$

Then the Lemma is proved because equations (8), (9), and inequality (11) hold.

Theorem 2: In the assumptions of Theorem 1, if $g = r$, the prices in
terms of the wage rate of final goods actually produced are
uniquely determined, even if more than one cost-minimizing
system exists.

Proof: We will prove the Theorem under the assumption that all
final goods are produced. The generalization is trivial. Let us
assume that there exist two pairs of vectors (y^*, q^*) and $(\bar{y}^*, \bar{q}^*)$
satisfying system (6) for $g = r$ and $a = \hat{a}$, where $\hat{a}$ is as defined in
Lemma 2, then we obtain from Lemma 7 that

$$y_s^* \leq \bar{y}_s^* \leq y_s^*.$$

                                                    Q. E. D.

Lemma 8: If $g = r$, the vector y^*, as defined in Lemma 2, is a
solution to the programme

$$\text{Max } c^T y$$
$$\text{s. to } [B (1 + r) A]y \leq l \qquad\qquad (13)$$
$$y \geq 0$$

Fixed Capital Within the Sraffa Framework   11

where c is any non-zero vector whose first s entries are nonnegative, the others being equal to zero.

Proof: The system (6) with $r = g$ and $a = c$ is equivalent to programme (13).   Q. E. D.

Theorem[3] 3: In the assumptions of Theorem 1, if $g = r$, then the prices of final goods in terms of the wage rate are increasing functions of $r = g$.

Proof: It is a direct consequence of Lemma 8.   Q. E. D.

Theorem 4: In the assumptions of Theorem 1, if Assumption 5 also holds, then

(a) choice of cost-minimizing systems is independent of the growth rate;
(b) prices of actually produced final goods in terms of the wage rate are increasing functions of the profit rate and are uniquely determined even if more than one cost-minimizing system exists.

Proof: Statement (b) is an immediate consequence of statement (a) because of Theorems 2 and 3. To prove (a), let q^{**} and y^* be basic solutions of the following Linear Programming Problem and of its dual respectively:

$$\text{Min } q^T l$$
$$\text{s. to } q^T[B - (1+r)A] \geq \hat{a}^T$$
$$q \geq 0$$

where $\hat{a}$ is as defined in Lemma 2. Let F and G be transformation matrices such that GBF and GAF are obtained from B and A by dropping columns related to old machines which are not utilized in production and rows related to processes which are not operated. Then, Assumption 5 ensures that vector $G[B - (1+g)A] Fe_j (j > s)$ has one positive element and one negative element, all others being equal to zero; as a consequence there exists a vector $q^* \geq 0$ with positive elements only in correspondence with positive elements of q^{**} and such that

$$q^{*T}[B - (1+g)A]F = \hat{a}^T F.$$

Hence (q^*, y^*) is a solution to system (6) with $a = \hat{a}$.   Q. E. D.

---

[3] I am indebted to Ch. Bidard for this Theorem and relative Proof.

N. Salvadori:

5. Examples

This section is devoted to show that if Assumption 4 holds and Assumption 5 does not, then

(a) Assumption 6 is not necessary to the existence of a cost minimizing system;
(b) the choice of cost-minimizing systems may be dependent on the growth rate;
(c) if more than one cost-minimizing system exists, then
  (i) if $g < r$, uniqueness of prices, in terms of wage rate, of both final goods and used machines may not occur,
  (ii) uniqueness of prices, in terms of wage rate, of used machines may not occur even if $g = r$;
(d) if $g > r$, a price in terms of wage rate may be a decreasing function of the profit rate.

Example 3: There exist five commodities whose production patterns are represented by Table 3; only Commodity 1 is consumed.

Table 3. *Input-Output Patterns of Example 3*

Processes	Commodity inputs					Labour input	Commodity outputs				
	(1)	(2)	(3)	(4)	(5)		(1)	(2)	(3)	(4)	(5)
(1)	1	0	0	0	0	1	0	1	0	0	0
(2)	2	0	0	0	0	1	0	0	1	0	0
(3)	0	1	1	0	0	2	5	0	0	1	1
(4)	0	0	2	1	0	0	5	0	0	0	2
(5)	0	1	0	0	1	2	5	0	0	1	0
(6)	0	1	1	0	0	2	5	0	0	0	1
(7)	0	1	1	0	0	2	5	0	0	1	0
(8)	0	1	1	0	0	2	5	0	0	0	0
(9)	0	0	2	1	0	0	5	0	0	0	0
(10)	0	1	0	0	1	2	5	0	0	0	0

It is easily recognized that Assumptions 1—4 hold. Commodities 1, 2, and 3 are final goods; Commodities 4 and 5 are used machines. It is easily checked that

(b) if $0 \leq r \leq \alpha$, where α is the positive real solution of the equation

$$15 - 17 r - 36 r^2 - 16 r^3 - 2 r^4 = 0,$$

then, if $0 \leq g \leq (\sqrt{2} - 1)$, the system of production made up by

Fixed Capital Within the Sraffa Framework   13

processes (1, 2, 4, 5, 10) is cost-minimizing; whereas, if $(\sqrt{2} - 1) \leq g \leq \beta$, where β is the positive real solution of the equation

$$12 - 7\,r - 28\,r^2 - 17\,r^3 - 3\,r^4 = 0,$$

then the system of production made up by processes (1, 2, 3, 4, 5) is cost-minimizing;

(c) if $g = (\sqrt{2} - 1)\,(< \alpha)$ and $0 \leq r \leq \alpha$, then the previously mentioned two systems of production are both cost-minimizing, and

  (i) if $(\sqrt{2} - 1) < r < \alpha$, the prices of all commodities are different;

  (ii) if $r = (\sqrt{2} - 1)$, the prices of final goods are the same in both systems, but the prices of used machines are not.

Example 4: There exist two commodities whose production patterns are represented by Table 4; only Commodity 1 is consumed.

Table 4. *Input-Output Patterns of Example 4*

Processes	Commodity inputs		Labour input	Commodity outputs	
	(1)	(2)		(1)	(2)
(1)	25	10	1	125	25
(2)	1	1	1	40	1
(3)	1	0	20	5	1
(4)	25	10	1	125	0
(5)	1	1	1	40	0
(6)	1	0	20	5	0

It is easily recognized that Assumptions 1—4 hold. Commodity 1 is a final good; Commodity 2 is a used machine. It is easily checked that:

(a) Assumption 6 holds only if $r < \alpha$, where α is the positive real solution of the equation

$$r^2 - 3\,r - 39 = 0$$

whereas the system of production made up by processes (2, 5) is cost-minimizing if $g = 0$ and $(61/24) \leq r \leq 39$;

(b) if $0 \leq r \leq \beta$, where β is the positive real solution of the equation

$$309\,r^2 + 6073\,r - 11701 = 0$$

14   N. Salvadori:

then, if $0 \le g \le 1.5$, ihe system of production made up by processes (1, 4) is cost-minimizing; whereas, if $1.5 \le g \le 4$, the system of production made up by processes (1, 3) is cost-minimizing;

(c) (i) if $0 \le g \le 1.5$ and $\beta \le r \le (61/24)$ the systems made up by processes (1, 2), (1, 4), (2, 3) respectively are all cost-minimizing with three different price vectors;

(d) if the system made up by processes (1, 2) is adopted, the price of Commodity 1 in terms of wage is a decreasing function of the profit rate.

6. The Problem of Scrap

Up to now free disposal has been assumed. An interesting variant could be the introduction of a different assumption asserting that scrapped machines are fully utilized, directly or indirectly, for the reproduction of the final goods they are produced with. This variant will be formalized in this section.

Assumption 7: It is possible to mark outputs in such a way that two subsets, S and T, of the set of commodities N can be distinguished so that:

(A.7.1) $S \cap T = \emptyset, \quad S \cup T = N$;

(A.7.2)   Commodities in T are never consumed;

(A.7.3)   Commodities in T are never produced as marked outputs;

(A.7.4)   Each process produces one and only one commodity in S as a marked output;

(A.7.5)   If commodity $i \in T$ is produced by process j producing commodity $h \in S$ as a marked output, then there exists no process producing a commodity $k \in S$ as a marked output, $k \ne h$, such that either it produces i or it utilizes i as an input;

(A.7.6)   For each process producing commodity $j \in T$ there exists a process with the same inputs and the same outputs except that commodity j is not produced and some other commodities in S are produced as non-marked outputs;

Fixed Capital Within the Sraffa Framework   15

(A.7.7)   Commodities in S which are produced as non-marked outputs are fully utilized, directly or indirectly, in the reproduction of the marked outputs they are produced with, i.e., let B_1, B_2, and B_3 ($B_1 + B_2 + B_3 = B$) be $m \times n$ nonnegative matrices such that the positive entries of B_1 are the marked outputs, the positive entries of B_2 are the non marked outputs of commodities in S, the positive entries in B_3 are the outputs of commodities in T, then

$$(x \geq 0, \ x^T(B - A) \geq 0) \rightarrow x^T(B_2 - A) \leq 0.$$

For the sake of simplicity we can refer to the commodities in T as *used machines*, the commodities in S as *final goods*, the non-marked outputs of final goods as scrapped machines.

Assumption 8: Assumption 7 and axioms A.5.1, A.5.2, and A.5.3 hold.

Theorem 5: In Theorems 1, 2, 3 Assumption 4 can be substituted with Assumption 7; in Theorem 4 Assumption 5 can be substituted with Assumption 8.

Proof: To prove the Theorem we just need the following Lemma 9.

Q. E. D.

Lemma 9: Let A, C, D be square matrices of the same dimension such that

(i) D is diagonal and diag $D > 0$,

(ii) $(x \geq 0, \ x^T(D + C - A) \geq 0) \rightarrow x^T(C - A) \leq 0$,

(iii) $\exists q : q \geq 0, \ q^T(D + C - A) > 0$.

Then the matrix $(D + C - A)$ is non singular and $(D + C - A)^{-1} \geq 0$.

Proof: It is sufficient to remark that

$$(x \geq 0, \ x^T(D + C - A) > 0) \rightarrow x > 0;$$

then the proof follows as Arrow's (1951) proof of Non-Substitution Theorem, and it will be omitted.   Q. E. D.

7. Concluding Remarks

In this paper Sraffa's idea of dealing Fixed Capital as a "species" of the "genus" Joint Production has been formalized.

16   N. Salvadori:

This has been done by introducing some special assumptions on the input and output matrices relative to the linear description of technology. Suitable interpretations of these assumptions as referring to models of Fixed Capital (allowing just one machine or several jointly used machines, with or without production of scrap) with no joint production superimposed have been provided. This formal apparatus has been utilized to investigate the existence and the uniqueness of cost-minimizing systems within the Sraffa Framework. Sraffa's idea of dealing with joint production by analyzing square systems of production in order to find the cost-minimizing one (see Sraffa, 1960; Schefold, 1980a; Salvadori, 1986) emerges as a valid one. It has been shown that demand for consumption does not matter in determining the cost-minimizing systems, but demand for investment (i.e., the growth rate) does. The paper is completed with some numerical examples showing that some desirable properties do not hold in general.

References

Arrow, K. J. (1951): "Alternative Proof of the Substitution Theorem for Leontief Models in the General Case." In *Activity Analysis of Production and Allocation,* edited by T. C. Koopmans. New York: John Wiley.
Baldone, S. (1980): "Fixed Capital in Sraffa's Theoretical Scheme." In *Essays on the Theory of Joint Production,* edited by L. L. Pasinetti. New York: Columbia University Press.
Salvadori, N. (1980): "On a Generalized von Neumann Model." *Metroeconomica* 32: 51—62.
— (1982): "Existence of Cost-Minimizing Systems within the Sraffa Framework." *Zeitschrift für Nationalökonomie* 42: 281—298.
— (1985): "Switching in Methods of Production and Joint Production." *The Manchester School* 53: 156—178.
— (1986): "Fixed Capital within the von Neumann-Morishima Model of Growth and Distribution." Mimeo. Catania.
— (1987): "Il Capitale Fisso come 'specie' del 'genere' Produzione Congiunta: Ulteriori precisazioni ed una risposta." *Economia Politica* 4: 265—275.
Schefold, B. (1976): "Reduction to Dated Quantities of Labour, Roundabout Processes and Switches of Technique in Fixed Capital Systems." *Metroeconomica* 28: 1—15.
— (1978): "Fixed Capital as a Joint Product." *Jahrbücher für Nationalökonomie und Statistik* 191: 415—439.
— (1980a): "Von Neumann and Sraffa: Mathematical Equivalence and Conceptual Difference." *Economic Journal* 90: 140—156.

— (1980b): "Fixed Capital as a Joint Product and the Analysis of Accumulation with Different Forms of Technical Progress." In *Essays of the Theory of Joint Production,* edited by L. L. Pasinetti. New York: Columbia University Press.

Sraffa, P. (1960). *Production of Commodities by Means of Production.* Cambridge: Cambridge University Press.

Varri, P. (1980): "Prices, Rate of Profit and Life of Machines in Sraffa's Fixed Capital Model." In *Essays on the Theory of Joint Production,* edited by L. L. Pasinetti. New York: Columbia University Press.

von Neumann, J. (1936): "Über ein ökonomisches Gleichungssystem und eine Verallgemeinerung des Brouwerschen Fixpunktsatzes." *Ergebnisse eines mathematischen Kolloquiums* 8: 73—83. (English translation: "A Model of General Economic Equilibrium." *Review of Economic Studies* 13 [1945/46]: 1—9.)

Address of author: Neri Salvadori, Professor of Economics, Istituto di Studi Economici, I. U. N., Via Acton 38, I-80133, Naples, Italy.

Name Index